Mountain Movers

Mountain Movers

George M. Ella

Go *publications*

Go Publications
The Cairn, Hill Top, Eggleston, Co. Durham, DL12 0AU, ENGLAND

© Go Publications 1999
First Published 1999

British Library Cataloguing in Publication Data available

ISBN 0 9527 074 4 6

Cover Pictures: Views of the Matterhorn, Switzerland
Courtesy of Switzerland Tourism

Printed and bound in Great Britain by
Creative Print & Design Group (Wales), Ebbw Vale

This book is dedicated to:

Frank and Lavinia Thirkell

in appreciation of their warm fellowship
and prayerful support.

Table of Contents

		Page
Foreword		9
1.	The Compassing Cloud of Witnesses	13
2.	John Jewel (1522-1571): Reformer of the English Church	45
3.	John Whitgift (1530-1604): Puritan Archbishop	57
4.	William Whitaker (1547-1595): Author of the Lambeth Articles	67
5.	John Davenant (1572-1641): The Jewel of the Church	77
6.	Joseph Hall (1574-1656): Man of Peace	99
7.	James Usher (1580-1656): The Light of Ireland	111
8.	Daniel Featley (1582-1645): Contender for the Faith	123
9.	Richard Mather (1596-1669): Pioneer of American Congregationalism	143
10.	Herman Witsius (1636-1708): Man of the Covenant	155
11.	Tobias Crisp (1600-1643): Exalter of Christ Alone	161
12.	John Janeway (1633-1657): The Saint Who Lived in Heaven On Earth	173
13.	Increase Mather (1639-1723): Relator of God's Illustrious Providences	183
14.	Ralf Erskine (1685-1752): Revealer of Christ's Beauties	199
15.	Cotton Mather (1663-1728): New England Pietist	205
16.	John Gill (1697-1771): Pastor-Scholar	221
17.	Philip Doddridge (1702-1751): Teacher of the Rise and Progress of Religion in the Soul	229
18.	William Grimshaw (1708-1763): Apostle of the North	235
19.	James Hervey (1713-1758): The Prose Poet	247
20.	William Romaine (1714-1795): Evangelical Pillar	255
21.	David Brainerd (1718-1747): God's Hiawatha	261
22.	Risdon Darracott (1717-1759): The Poor Man's Preacher	267
23.	John Collet Ryland (1723-1792): Evangelical Educator	275
24.	John Gano (1727-1804): Preacher in the Spirit of the Gospel	281

Page

25. William Cowper (1731-1800): Christian Campaigner — 291
26. Augustus Montague Toplady (1740-1778): A Debtor to Mercy Alone — 307
27. William Huntington (1745-1813): Pastor of Providence — 319
28. Hannah More (1745-1833): The Woman who Stopped a Revolution — 341
29. Robert Hawker (1753-1827): Zion's Warrior — 347
30. Hans Nielsen Hauge (1771 -1824): God's Tramp — 363
31. Henry Martyn (1781-1812): Pioneer Missionary — 371
32. Isaac McCoy (1784-1846): Apostle of the Western Trail — 379

Bibliography — 395
Indices — 425

Foreword

Dr Ella has performed a number of useful services by writing this book. First he has put in manageable form the lives of many good men who have made a great contribution, under God, to the religious life of this nation and further afield. Many of these lives are only found in larger books which are now out of print and inaccessible to most people. So here is a chance for a new generation to become familiar with the lives of great reformers and puritans.

Secondly, he has done much to rehabilitate the reformers and puritans of the Church of England for which I, as an episcopalian, am grateful. Since the revival of interest in the puritans some fifty years ago, the emphasis has been largely on those of a Nonconformist persuasion. Here, Dr Ella shows what an eminent contribution was made by those of the Established Church. These men brought about not merely an outward reformation of forms and practices in the Church of England, but a doctrinal reformation that found expression in the Thirty-Nine Articles, the Lambeth Articles and the Synod of Dort. Augustus Toplady showed in his *Historic Proof of Doctrinal Calvinism in the Church of England* how a Calvinistic consensus was held and maintained in the national church right up to the time of Charles I.

Following that time, however, although the official teaching of the Articles remained unchanged, Arminianism gained ground both in the Church of England and in Nonconformity. A book which had semi-official standing appeared in 1657 entitled *The Whole Duty of Man*. It set out a doctrine of mitigated human obedience. The work of Christ, it maintained, was to enable us to do what God requires. He takes off the hardness of the law given to Adam, and requires of us 'only honest and hearty endeavour' and where we fail God will accept sincere repentance. The effect of this was to turn Christ into an enabler, but not a Redeemer and Saviour. This Neonomianism became the new orthodoxy, so that those who continued to preach the doctrines of grace were regarded as extremists, hyper-Calvinists and antinomians. It was these circumstances that caused Romaine to lament that he knew of so few real evangelicals, and Huntington to declare that he had never heard of the Thirty-Nine Articles until he was twenty-five years of age, and that were they to be read, 'they would be a candle to the congregation, and a flash of lightning in the face of the blind guide who was reading them.' When he came to an experimental knowledge of their teaching he threw out *The Whole Duty of Man*.

This brings me to the third thing I wish to say about this book, which is that it illustrates the truth that there is a true apostolic succession of doctrine in the church. It is not to be found in any one denomination, but it is seen in those who adhere to the doctrines of free grace, those who are often called hyper-Calvinists, who in fact are the true Calvinists, but because the Scriptural doctrines of grace are so foreign to the average church minister and member, they are considered to be extreme. The line of true apostolic succession is to be found amongst those of whom Dr Ella writes in this book and of course amongst many, many more. But what is interesting is that this view of apostolic succession fits in perfectly with the modest claims of the English Reformers.

'Succession', said Bishop Jewel in answer to Rome, 'is the chief way for any Christian man to avoid Antichrist, I grant you, if you mean the succession of doctrine.'

I trust Dr Ella's book will do much to encourage interest in the truths for which these great men stood.

Dr David N. Samuel

Mountain Movers

If
ye have faith
as a grain
of mustard seed,
ye
shall say
unto this mountain,
Remove hence
to yonder place;
and
it shall remove;
and nothing
shall be
impossible
unto
you.

Matthew 17:20

Though known as the King and Queen of the Lapps, Anders and Regina Danielson were two gracious Christians who lived in a humble bark and turf hut. They sang their favourite hymn each dawn. It was about the angels' joy in heaven over converted sinners. Now they are joining in the angels' praise in glory themselves, surrounded by all those whom they have led to Christ or blessed in their lives.

1. The Compassing Clouds of Witnesses

One of the first passages of Scripture to attract my attention, long before I became a Christian, was Hebrews 12:1, 'Wherefore seeing we also are compassed about with so great a cloud of witnesses, let us lay aside every weight, and the sin which doth so easily beset us, and let us run with patience the race that is set before us.' There was much in this text to interest me. I was a keen track athlete and the idea of running a race with patience puzzled me as I believed a race ought to be a mad rush from beginning to end. Then I realised that a race must be planned patiently, working out how to start well, how to build up speed, how to maintain the pace and how to make a good finish. In a way, each race is a life in miniature from birth to death, from start to finish. So many races are run with competitors dropping out along the way, not qualifying for the final heat, not reaching their best time and never receiving a prize.

Life is so like this. The difference is, of course, that each sporting event may be repeated but we have one life to live and only one way of reaching the goal. Another difference is that in light athletics only the best man wins but all of us who have been chosen to compete in Christ's team with the Son of God as our Manager are sure of a prize. In the Christian life, the real life, there is a team prize, dependent on the victory of our team Captain-Manager. This is because Christ has run the whole race before us and gained the absolute victory, an all time record, for Himself and His own team-Church. Now He runs with every member of His team, making sure they are in the right form to reach the same goal by His sure and certain methods. There is another difference, however. Athletes have but one trainer, at the most two. Each Christian who runs with Christ is qualified by His Captain to coach and train others.

Here the mixed metaphors of Hebrews 12:1 again come to our help. Each of those whom Christ chooses for His team has a huge cloud of trainers who themselves have been taught by Christ. This picture used to puzzle me much as a child and I actually thought there was a misprint in my Bible. I felt it should read 'compassed about with so great a *crowd* of witnesses.' Then I found out that the word really meant a *cloud* and began to imagine thousands of faces of by-gone Christians in Heaven forming an immense cloud in the skies all looking down at me, watching and guiding my every step. In my early teens, that feeling often made me most uncomfortable indeed. When I began to learn Science and Greek, I found out that a cloud is indeed composed of millions of particles and that the Greek word used for cloud in Hebrews is absolutely scientifically accurate describing a thronging around of countless and limitless particles, inanimate and animate, be they droplets of water, a crowd cheering a leader, a mighty army at war or Christ's ministers on earth. I learnt that these countless millions of men and women who, to return to the Bible account, had 'obtained a good report through faith', were now my trainers, or as my Swedish Bible tells me, and it was in Sweden that the Lord revealed Himself to me as my Saviour, my *teachers* and *leaders* (Hebrews 13:7).

This book is a book of thanks to God my Heavenly Father through Christ my Captain and Saviour for the many faithful witnesses and trainers He has provided me with in my heavenwards race. I have therefore only included men and women who have been a personal blessing to me, though I know they were also a great blessing to many others. Other Christians will have other trainers but all Christ's team train according to the same rules and, God willing, my readers might discover that those who have trained me so faithfully and conscientiously have also a handbook of tips for them, too. As I have been greatly influenced by trainers from the entire European Continent besides from Britain and the USA, perhaps I may introduce some English speaking Christians to good trainers of whom they have never heard. But first I must tell you about how I personally came to run in this heavenly race and be chosen for Christ's team.

I started school in 1942 which was the third year of World War Two. It was a terrible time when the whole grown-up world was playing at being silly, spoilt children and doing their best to scratch out one another's eyes. My earliest memories are of being evacuated here and there, moving home umpteen times because of the dangers of living in a large industrial town and the bombs which had dropped in the streets where I lived. Another early memory is standing one night with my parents and sister high up on the cliff side of Bradford's Peel Park and seeing buildings down by the town centre aflame. From the same place, I remember seeing the magnificent display of fireworks, including a large picture of the king and the playing of the National Anthem when peace was declared.

During this period our school was an absolute chaos. There were few teachers as all the clever and strong had been called up for war service. Our teachers were the old, the sick and those who were thought too silly or too immoral to be soldiers. I shall never forget the big broad Headmistress with her thick black stick which she did not hesitate to use, nor the long tall male teacher who loved to tell tiny children to touch their toes and then he would give them a brutal kick in the pants. Then there was the perverse lady teacher who loved to take down the boys' trousers and spank their bottoms to the embarrassment but often delight of the girls. I remember the nightmare struggle I had with her, buttoning up one side of my braces as that female monster unbuttoned the other until she gave up by brutally pushing me aside, but I had kept my integrity before the class by the grace of God. Then there was the highly nervous and bad-tempered lady who would come from ARP night work in her uniform to part teach, part shout and part sleep for the day. Perhaps the worst teacher was the lady who beat us with wooden spoons until they burst into smithereens. I well remember her holding my tiny hand and beating it until the spoon split down the middle. Those were certainly not the good old days for Bradford's children and those teachers had certainly not been trained aright.

All the mums had to work with the dads in the factories so all the children from three years of age were put in day school or boarding school and crowded into enormous classes with an age difference of five years amongst the pupils. My dear father, who was the most peaceful man on earth and really a coal-miner, was forced by the government to make bombs. I was placed in a class of far bigger boys and girls who had more muscle than brain and more cunning than intelligence. Because I could read well at three and read very well at five, the teacher used me as a junior assistant to teach the big boys and girls how to read. They were quiet in class, mainly because of the weapons the teachers carried in the form of canes, boots and wooden spoons. My! How those big boys and girls bullied me in break time and after school. The beatings I had!

Life was not all fear and unhappiness at school, though there was very much of those elements present. My parents were too poor to buy books but I was supplied freely with them by the school and my six-year old sister took me to two public libraries. I remember the elderly librarian in Wapping refusing me membership at three years of age because the rules said you had to have completed six years. After reading aloud from a book he gave me at random to prove that I was under reading age, I remember the old man looking at me with fond amazement and writing out for me a membership form without another second's hesitation. How I praise God for those books I read. They were all good books and priceless treasures.

My older sister Mavis also took me to my second joy when I was still three years of age. It was to a Sunday School at a place called Bradford Home Mission, Heap Lane where I hardly missed a Sunday's attendance for the next twelve years. I loved the place. The amazing things I learnt there have remained with me still. They tell me now that it was a Church of the Nazarene and an Arminian place but I knew nothing of that, indeed I have no memories at all of ever hearing un-Biblical teaching there. It was Solomon the Wise who once said, 'Train up a child in the way he should go: and when he is old, he will not depart from it.' Believe me; he knew what he was talking about. Those Sunday School teachers, the Hemsleys, the Clarks, the Keighleys, Mr Lee, Miss Keating and Mr John Hicks certainly had been well-trained.

I was first put into the infants' class under the sound and skilful leadership of Miss Keating. That dear lady is still alive and about ninety-five years of age. She taught me the meaning of sin through the verse, 'Be sure your sins will find you out.' I shall never forget her story to illustrate the verse. Mummy had just baked a lovely apple pie and, before she went shopping, she told little Jenny not to eat any of the pie because Auntie Janie was coming to tea. As soon as Mummy was gone, little Jenny began to think that the pie looked ever so delicious. Instead of going into the garden to play and so ridding herself of the temptation, she gazed longingly at the pie which grew more and more tasty in her covetous imagination. 'Nobody will mind if I just break off a bit of the crust,' she thought. Just as stolen apples always seem to taste best until the farmer catches you out, little Jenny thought she had never tasted anything so good. She had another nibble, just to make sure it was really so tasty and then did not realise that she was eating up the entire pie. Soon the pie had gone and all that was left was a sticky plate and a dirty spoon. Before you could say Jack Robinson, Mum was standing in the kitchen gazing at the empty plate. Quick as a flash Jenny's fallen nature got the upper hand. 'Oh yes,' cried Jenny, 'it was Pussy, that beastly cat. I could not stop her.' Mummy looked sadly at her naughty daughter and a tear came to her eye. 'Jenny,' she said, 'Pussy does not eat with a spoon. Be sure your sins will find you out.'

At the Sunday School I also learnt that God was ever ready to care for those who came to Him. The second verse I learnt there was also written by King Solomon, 'Trust in the Lord with all your heart and lean not unto your own understanding. In all your ways, acknowledge Him and He will direct your paths.' I soon realised that this meant that if we allow ourselves to be guided by God and not always think we know best, then we will always be on the right track and do the right things.

This helped me enormously in my young life but I still had problems about how to talk to God. Then God helped me. High up at the front right hand side of the Sunday evening meeting hall above the doorway, there hung a hand-painted sign. It said 'Prayer Changes Things.' Now somehow, though everybody said I was a brilliant reader and whenever we had a special pupils' Sunday I had to do most of the reading, it took me ages to read that sign. I understood the 'prayer' bit all right and the 'things' but somehow could not get my tongue around the word 'changes'. I had a secret suspicion it meant 'Chinese' and began to think that prayer was something for wee Chinese children and nothing for me. How stupid I was!

Then I learnt my third text off by heart, 'Take your problems to the Lord and He will help you.' I then worked out that this meant that God would change my situation if I asked Him to. My trouble would go and my life would be different and better. But how? I then thought of the sign which I had never understood. I went to look at it again and found that it said, 'Prayer CHANGES things.' Now I realised that when I was in trouble, the Lord invited me to go to Him IN PRAYER and He would change things for me. At last my heavenly Father had got into my thick skull and made me understand what I ought to have understood years before. You see, I was now seven years old and the greatest truth in the world had escaped me because I was still blind to the fact that prayer changes things. My advice to all young readers of this book is work hard at learning to read, write and study. Even if grown-ups tell you that you are brilliant and the best reader for miles around. Do not give up learning hard. There is some little word, somewhere, to which you are still blind and it is preventing you from going ahead with your education and spiritual growth. Never think you know everything, not even if you live to be a hundred and ninety-nine! Pray every day, 'Lord teach me more that I might understand Thee better.'

Now to go back to my school Barker End in the town of Bradford, and the county of Yorkshire and the bullies, or rather one particular fiend, years older than myself, who used to boast of his origin with the words:

> Bradford born and Yorkshire bred.
> Strong in t'arm and weak in t'head.

This large boy, whom we must pity, used to wait until the lessons were over and I was on my way home or walking in the playground when he would suddenly dive on my back and fell me to the cobbled-stone ground with all his weight. This happened day after day, week after week, month for month. My body was bruised, my clothes were torn but he showed no mercy. My fellow pupils did, however, and a number always shouted when the bully looked as if he were going to pounce on me. This all happened when I was learning to pray at Sunday School but had not learnt to try it out.

One day, I remember it well, I was sad and weary. The bully had told me he would 'get me' after school and I was terrified. As I left the class-room for the break (American school-children call it recess-time), I saw the look of pity on many of my classmates' faces but knew they could do nothing to help. Then, I thought of the words, 'Take your troubles to the Lord, and He will help you,' and 'Prayer changes things.' I found a deserted spot in the play-ground which we called the cellar-head. It was a small landing where the stairs went down to the basement. I knelt down there, as I had seen grown-ups kneel and, for the first time in my life, I poured out my heart to God. I remember my prayer vividly. It had nothing directly to do with the bully, it had everything to do with Christ coming into my life and managing not just the bully but all of my future. The words of a Sunday School chorus came onto my lips, 'Come into my heart, Lord Jesus. Come in today. Come in to stay. Come into my heart, Lord Jesus.'

I stood up, feeling somehow refreshed and walked calmly across the play-ground. Suddenly the cry that I now least expected rose up. 'Watch it, George. Watch it. He's coming!' I had no need to ask, 'Who?' but I thought in panic, 'How can this be? I have prayed for Jesus to come into my life and help me.'

I felt the presence of the human monster coming up speedily behind me. I felt him jump—and as he was jumping, I turned round in absolute panic, throwing my arms up in the air and crying out in a scream of agony. The next thing I saw, the bully was lying on the floor, bleeding profusely from the nose. Then he got up quickly and ran howling into the school. A great cheer went up and all the children started applauding me but I still did not know what had happened. I realised only slowly. I had turned round so suddenly, a thing that I had never done before, and my panic-stricken hand, propelled by fear, had caught the bully hard under his well-proportioned nose. He was knocked down flat.

The bell went and we all rushed into the next lesson. The big bully, who sat at the back, groaned and sniffed and wept because the spoilt child had never experienced pain like this before. He had only tortured others for fun. Suddenly the teacher cried out, 'What is the matter with you boy? You are always disturbing the lessons with your talk and now you are sniffing and wailing as if Captain Marvel had swept the floor with you.' Then a voice in the class said, 'Please Sir, Ella (we used surnames only through my school time) has beaten him up and it serves him jolly well right.' The teacher looked at me in amazement and I could think of nothing to say. There was a terrible silence in the class, like the calm before a storm. We all expected that soon the teacher's cane would be dusting my pants.

Our teacher, God bless her, was speechless, too. She continued to stare at me, obviously greatly puzzled. Suddenly the clouds of fear were blown away. The teacher began to smile, bright as the sun. In embarrassment, she gripped her book and hid her face behind it and the lesson continued. After the lesson, the bully approached me defiantly, fists clenched, but it was his last bluff. On reaching me, he could not look me in the eye for one second but meekly turned round and walked away. He never bothered me again. Nor did he seem to realise that it was not my strength that knocked him off his pedestal but God's strength made perfect in my weakness.

Back at my Sunday School, the Lord continued to instruct me through brave old Mr Hicks, the Superintendent after Maurice Helmsley, who was my spiritual mentor and companion for many years into adulthood. He was a tiny man who walked in stiff nervous jerks but was a mighty man of valour in gospel matters. One day, years after leaving the Sunday School, when I had been running the race set before me for a number of years, I visited my old mentor who told me a marvellous story. We were sharing testimonies and I commented on the fact that, though nigh eighty years of age, he still could run after a bus and jump on the landing stage whilst it was speeding along. 'It was not always so,' he replied. 'Before the Lord came into my life, things were very much different.' Wondering what jumping on a bus had to do with a work of the Lord, I asked my old friend to tell me his story. It was what we might call unbelievably true. Mr Hicks was born paralysed from the waist down. When other children stopped crawling and began to toddle and eventually walk and run, my friend had to keep crawling along. His hard-worked but loving mother found young Hicks a great burden as he had to be carried upstairs and down and never left for a moment because he could not relieve himself of natural waste as other children and was always in danger of falling down the steep stone staircase leading up to his room.

When my Sunday School teacher was five years of age, his mother took him to a Salvation Army meeting where there was what is unwisely termed 'the altar call'. Child Hicks, with tears in his eyes told his mother that he wanted to be carried to the front as he so wished to have Jesus as his Saviour. Mrs Hicks, who would have done anything for her child, did as she was asked and her small invalid child dedicated his own life to the Saviour's service that evening.

Next morning, whilst his mother was preparing breakfast below, young Hicks called downstairs, 'Mummy, do you believe that God can make me walk like other children?' 'Yes, of course He can,' answered his mother, hardly knowing what she was saying. Back came the astonishing reply, 'Good, then you have no need to come up and fetch me, mother, for I am coming down to breakfast myself.' Imagine how little Hicks' mother praised the Lord when she saw her small child walking towards her with his little shrunk jerky legs.

You will agree that this was a miracle but you might be wondering why God did not go the whole way and remove the jerkiness from young Hicks' legs. Do you know, Mr Hicks' was very thankful for that jerkiness because it did not hinder him at all but was a daily reminder of the goodness of God which he never forgot. This was obviously why God healed him in that particular way.

Soon after my experience with the school bully, I began to attend the adult Sunday evening meetings. I always sat on the front bench to the left near Mr Lee the organist. It was because Mr Lee was my Sunday School teacher at the time but also because he would often give me a silver sixpence. It was then that I came under the ministry of Mr David Moyes who made abundant use of the Scriptures in preaching, spiced by many illustrations from his experiences with Christ. Pastor Moyes shepherded his flock part time, his other occupation being foreman at a woollen mill. My early remembrances of him, however, are limited to the awe I displayed when he took out his pot eye and then placed it back again. When I grew older, Mr Moyes introduced me to Spurgeon and many other contenders for the faith. His theology was pure Bibline and I grew to love him dearly. We had no caretaker at the mission for a while and our two storied building was getting rather grubby. We all took turns to tidy the place up. Imagine my surprise when I reported for duty at the chapel and found almost blind Mr Moyes, now over eighty years of age, perched at the top of a very long shaky ladder with a bucket of water in one hand and a cloth in the other, cleaning the upper storey windows!

Years later, long after Mr Moyes' death, I was looking through some books in Kirkgate Market when I saw a complete set of Matthew Henry's commentaries. I had always wanted them but they were too expensive. These volumes cost next to nothing so I gladly bought them. My delight and praises were great when, on returning home, I found that the volumes had belonged to Mr Moyes and were signed by him and contained notes in the handwriting that was so well-known to me.

Coming back to my teens and Mr Hicks' careful concern for my spiritual welfare, I am reminded of the New Testament he gave me around 1954. On opening it now, I read once again the loving greetings in Mr Hicks' beautiful tiny hand-writing upon a blank page to me, his thankful pupil, 'With Christian love and fervent prayer to God for his spiritual welfare,' with which he started me out on my deeper search for peace with God. The first verse in Mr Hicks' spiritual *vade-mecum* was 2 Timothy 2:15:

> Study to show thyself approved unto God, a worthy workman that needeth not to be ashamed, rightly dividing the word of truth.

Then he goes on to quote 2 Timothy 3:14-17:

> But continue thou in the things which thou hast learned and hast been assured of, knowing of whom thou hast learned them; And that from a child thou hast known the holy scriptures, which are able to make thee wise unto salvation through faith which is in Christ Jesus. All scripture is given by inspiration of God, and is profitable for doctrine, for reproof, for correction, for instruction in righteousness: That the man of God may be perfect, throughly furnished unto all good works.

I can scarcely imagine that Timothy could have been more grateful to Paul for giving him this wise advice than I am to John Hicks and I am sure Timothy drew his strength and inspiration from those words continually in his life as I have done. I am also sure that Timothy saw through Paul to his Master, Christ, and, dearly as he must have loved Paul, he realised that even Paul was counselling him by the grace of God. So as to make it quite plain in whose authority Mr Hicks was writing, my dear friend and mentor closed with those sober words to both counsellor and the counselled:

> Knowing this first, that no prophecy of the scripture is of any private interpretation. For the prophecy came not in old time by the will of man: but holy men of God spake as they were moved by the Holy Ghost.

These words were in my head and, I believed, in my heart as I was compelled to leave my Bradford Sunday School at the age of 15. I had been a pupil at Hanson Grammar School for four years and had progressed from a C form to an A form, receiving the annual school prize for outstanding progress. I was now looking forward to taking my General Certificate of Education and eventually studying to become a forester. Outdoor life and Natural History had always been a passion of mine and besides being an active Boy Scout, I was already the youngest member of the local Natural History, Geological and Archaeological Societies. My family, however, were very poor and my parents told me the sad news that I would have to leave school without any academic qualifications and start working manually as my parents could no longer afford to keep me. Through the kind intervention of Mr Jackson, Curator of the Cartwright Memorial Museum, whom I occasionally assisted, I was introduced to the forester of the North East Conservancy division of the Forestry Commission in York and was promptly accepted as an apprentice skilled worker.

Though I quickly joined a local church and Scout Group, it seemed impossible to find another mentor like Mr Hicks and I missed the security of being with the Lord's people of his calibre very much. I was most conscious of my sin, which I felt had not really been dealt with and I had a true longing for an assurance of salvation and for signs from the Lord that He was my own personal Saviour. This led me to attend confirmation classes at St Clement's church but I felt I was not progressing correctly and pestered the Vicar to give me more tuition. He kindly offered up two evenings a week to help me and his friend the Bishop prayed for me that the Holy Spirit would fill me and transform me for Christ. I saw no change in my life and gradually began to go the proverbial way of my fellow-apprentices so appropriately pictured by Hogarth. On hearing that a Billy Graham film was to be shown by the Christian Alliance in Bradford, I went to see it. I saw and heard the word being preached and actors pretending to be repentant sinners going through what they thought was a portrayal of a conversion experience but they did not move me and, indeed, I came to hate that form of mock evangelism which uses the make-believe in an attempt to persuade people to turn to Christ. I sought Christian counsel and found a true man of God, called interestingly enough Mr Bradford, who tried his level best to lead me to a deeper, saving knowledge of Christ but I could not experience what he was talking about. I was trying to understand everything instead of simply trusting. I would rather trust in the Lord anytime now than lean on my own understanding but I just could not do so then. A number of years later, after the Lord had revealed Himself to my heart, I was able to contact Mr Bradford and tell him that his labour had not been in vain in the Lord.

After this intensive search, I despaired of ever finding the assurance I wanted so earnestly and decided to drop the matter and get on with living without God. Indeed, I determined to get as far away as possible from Christian witness. As this was impossible in Yorkshire where Christian witness was thick around me, I decided to go abroad where I could be free from the claims of God who obviously, I thought, did not back up His claims with the proof I wanted. I was offered through the Boy Scouts Association a free trip to Australia, a country that had already drawn off many of my relations, so first planned to go there. I discovered, however, that though forest-workers were in high demand, the wages paid to an apprentice were not sufficient to keep a boy alive without parental support. As my parents were terribly poor, I had to turn down the offer. Eventually, however, I became desperate to be off and gone and, though it was in the middle of winter and I had only enough money for the boat ticket, I decided to travel to northern Scandinavia where I would be able to hide myself in the woods and nobody would bother me about religion. A previous visit to Sweden had convinced me that the Swedes were a very free-living race. This helped my decision. I had also been teaching myself Swedish for some time, so I knew I would be able to make myself understandable to the people. So, with a tiny rucksack on my back, a gift of a scouting friend, and with an old pair of trousers in it for work and hardly anything else, I boarded the Svea line for Gothenburg, intending to hitch-hike up to the northern forests and the land of the midnight sun. I was now sixteen years of age and thought I was very grown-up.

I began to enjoy life at once. The coast of Sweden was covered in thick ice and the ice-breaker in front of us thumped its way through with our ship starting and stopping continually behind it. This caused the ship to move forward in jerks and almost everybody was sea-sick. Imagine my pleasure when I went down to meals and found I was alone at a table spread with the choicest of food which, because of our extreme poverty, I had never even dreamt about. How ignorant I was of the tummy pains and green faces of my fellow passengers as I polished off the portions which were meant for them. I was in Cloud Cuckoo Land.

Gothenburg lay covered in ice and snow and it was getting dark, although it was early in the afternoon. I was almost tempted to pray but remembered my vow to have nothing to do with religion. Suddenly the finest cars imaginable were lowered by a crane from the boat and a group of elegant looking Englishmen gathered on the pier. I heard them saying that they were to test Ford prototypes in Lapland and their interpreter had gone missing. What were they to do? I was able to answer their question at once. I introduced myself as a person who was coincidentally going the same way and would be pleased to interpret for them. The nicely dressed gentlemen looked on the shabby teenager in surprise but soon hands were shaken all round and I was employed as the Ford Motor Company's official translator in Sweden.

'Now it is time to eat,' said the leader of the group and we entered Sweden's most famous restaurant where the waiters stood one behind each chair. I who had never been in a restaurant in my life had my chair pulled away by a waiter in a dress suit and pushed under my sit-upon so that I might be seated in style. Then came the courses, one after the other, with chains of light-footed waiters almost dancing backwards and forwards reminding me of a ballet I had once seen at school. Again, I felt that running away from Christian influence was the most sensible thing I had ever done.

We travelled all through the night and I was able to order food, organise petrol and oil, find toilets, deal with the authorities, all in a country that seemed to be populated by people who worked round the clock. The next evening we reached Örebro and the gentlemen booked in at their posh hotel. They were quite willing to pay for a room for me but none was available. Then I remembered Rolf Gård. He had been a friend of mine in the Bradford Scouts and, before returning to Sweden, after taking military courses in England, he had given me his address. I looked at the address in my notebook and found that Rolf actually lived in Örebro, the very town we were now in. I thus told my new friends that I would visit my scouting friend and come and collect them in the morning for the journey to Lapland. I found my friend's house very quickly and timidly rang the bell. The door opened and there stood a lady with the kindest, motherly face I had ever seen, but she looked quite different to my picture of Swedes. She had raven black hair. Behind her stood a tubby man with such a jolly face that I just knew I was amongst friends and would be able to spend the night there. I gave my name and explained my connection with Rolf but he was not at home. Nevertheless, the couple whisked me into the kitchen in no time and just as quickly set a plate of delicious things, none of which I recognised, in front of me and I was told to eat and eat and eat. Believe you me, I was not disobedient!

The Gårds not only insisted that I should stay the night but insisted that I should stay as long as I liked and that I should tell the Englishmen on the following morning that I had found a new home and work. Then Rolf came. Rolf was a friend in a million, though a few years older than I was, he never made a point of reminding me and we were truly one heart and one soul as we spoke of escapades we had got up to together.

Then I received the shock of my life. The Gårds began to pray. They talked to the Lord as if they knew Him personally, and indeed, they did. I was dumbfounded and amazed. I felt such things only happened in England and that is why I left that country. Then Mr Gård told me that he was not only a believing child of God but a Methodist pastor to boot and he and his wife and an elderly lady who joined us gave me such a wonderful testimony of the grace of God in their lives that again, I found I wanted to be like them.

To cut a long story short, the Gårds found out about my plans to continue my apprenticeship in Sweden and helped me to obtain a post in the Swedish Forestry Commission. It was not easy as I had apparently emigrated illegally and, as a minor without parental accompaniment, I could not sign any employment contract. The Gårds, however, were good at praying and I trusted in them fully and had no doubt all would go well and so it did.

My next shock, however, was the work in the forest where it was 35 degrees minus centigrade. A good 25 degrees colder than I had ever experienced. The cold was not the shock, however. Perhaps you may guess what it was. I was secretly pleased to be on my own again and outside gospel influence and as I was felling a large area on piece work, with nobody anywhere near me to bother me, I felt quite safe. Then I met my new boss. Seconds after the initial greeting, he was witnessing to me about Christ. He was a convinced Christian and his aim was to have all his staff come to a saving knowledge of the Lord. And so it went on for almost a year. Wherever I turned, whether backwards or forwards, there was a man of God blocking my way. I began to realise the deep divine truth of Psalm 139:7-13:

> Whither shall I go from thy spirit? or whither shall I flee from thy presence? If I ascend up into heaven, thou art there: if I make my bed in hell, behold, thou art there. If I take the wings of the morning, and dwell in the uttermost parts of the sea; Even there shall thy hand lead me, and thy right hand shall hold me. If I say, Surely the darkness shall cover me; even the night shall be light about me. Yea, the darkness hideth not from thee; but the night shineth as the day: the darkness and the light are both alike to thee. For thou hast possessed my reins: thou hast covered me in my mother's womb.

Now the verse that I had learnt at Sunday School came continually to my mind. 'Trust in the Lord with all thine heart ... and He shall direct thy path.' I began to wonder whether or not God was guiding my path as it seemed the more I tried to go my own way, the more I went in the very opposite direction to what I intended. I wanted to leave Christianity behind but wherever I turned, professing Christians not only blocked my path but provided me with so much generosity and kindness that it made me ashamed. I thus decided to move on. There were two reasons. First, my inner conviction that I must be free to go my own way and that way was as far away from a Christian testimony as possible. The second reason was that I had left school with no qualifications whatsoever due to the financial situation of my family which could not allow for me to go on to take university entrance exams. I now began to feel that I ought to go on to study and my school reports encouraged me to feel that the attempt might be worthwhile. I thus determined to hitch-hike down to Germany and France to find work there and learn the languages and then through private study strive to take either the Swedish 'Studenten' exam or the English General Certificate of Education in order to matriculate.

I need not tell you that what I had experienced in Sweden was repeated every step of the way. Two incidents must suffice as examples here. I must confess that I had begun to pray again for the first time in about two years.

On arriving in Germany, I obtained a job in a dairy to learn German and worked there for around five weeks before going on to France. It was now Christmas day and I was standing in the freezing snow on the roadside in Luxembourg just across the border from Germany before entering France. I wore, starting from the bottom, a pair of summer shoes with holes in their soles and my legs were covered in thin black jeans, the only pair of jeans I have ever had. I had worked a month in the dairy without a change of outer clothing and my jeans were so covered in cheese and butter stains that, when I took them off, they could literally stand up on their own. A shirt covered the top of my body under a cheap imitation leather jacket which did not even cover my hips. The zip had broken and the jacket was held together at the front by an old, bent safety pin. I had no hat or overcoat or scarf and I had left my gloves in a car the day before in Trier, Germany.

Car after car drove by for several hours but not one stopped. I need not tell you how I was feeling, but you can be sure that my heart, in the process of being worked on by the Lord was praying for some kind of deliverance and Mr Hicks' verse was continually in my mind. As I was opening my thoughts to God in this way, a large car came towards me at great speed and suddenly braked. Out jumped the man in whose car I had left my gloves the day before. 'Thank God I have found you,' he cried, 'I have been looking for you throughout Luxembourg for hours and they told me at the Youth Hostel that you were making for France.' The man took hold of me firmly but kindly and bundled me into his car. It was such a relief to flee from the cold wind that I could not utter a word of protest. After a short while, I asked the man where he was taking me. He smiled and told me that I must wait and see. I then protested as he was travelling back towards Germany so I asked him to stop and let me out of the car. The man turned round to me, one hand on the wheel and the other brandishing a revolver. 'Be quiet,' he said, 'I am your friend and I mean well. You must trust me and see what happens.' Quickly we sped over the border and entered the ancient Roman city of Trier with its great old merchant houses and castle ruins. We drove into a wide, dark lane flanked by great villas on either side and pulled up outside of one of the largest. There was no street lighting but the door of the house opened and such a cascade of light and warmth poured out so that all my fears disappeared and I felt full of peace and joy. 'Come with me into the house,' said my armed but friendly companion. I followed him through the open door and heard happy children's voices singing. I knew that where children are happy and content peace must reign and drew closer. I was led into a very large living room centred by a huge round table. A gigantic decorated Christmas tree stood by a great fireplace which was full of burning Yuletide logs. Around the table sat the most jolly crowd of well-dressed people you ever did see, three generations of them, all with huge friendly smiles on their faces. There were two empty places at the table. 'Take one,' said my 'kidnapper', pointing to a chair, and he took the other. A plate was then set before me and again piled up with delicacies that I had never seen before in real life but often dreamed about in my childhood and youth of great poverty. My tears began to flow. 'Why are you doing this?' I asked. 'It is Christmas,' back came the reply. 'It is the season of good will to mankind to celebrate the coming of our Lord Jesus Christ. I just had to look for you and fetch you home.' And truly, I felt very much at home with these people who, I found out, did many such good deeds of faith in all seasons. I trust I did not neglect to thank God for their wonderful kindness.

After the meal, the gentleman apologised for threatening me with a gun. He said that he was frightened that I would jump out. Though a German, he worked for the British occupying forces and was in charge of some top security work which explained the weapon. The man gave me some money and when I protested, out came the gun again. Then his family, especially his jovial old mother, heaped food presents upon me. I told the family of my urge to get to France to learn the language so that I could take university entrance examinations. On hearing this, the man packed me into his car again, took me to the rail station, bought me a ticket to France, said farewell and drove off.

When I arrived in Amiens, France, I wondered what to do and how I could better the French that I had learnt for four years at school. On my first visit to Sweden, I had visited a school in Gothenburg and spoken to the headmaster who had asked me to give a few lessons and introduced me to a boy who took me to his home. I decided to try the same method in France. So I entered the first school, a Grammar School, I found and asked to see the headmaster. He was a most academic, severe-looking gentleman and, as my clothing was still streaked with cheese from the German dairy, I was pleasantly surprised that the gentleman bothered to talk to me at all. He turned out to be a most polite and sympathetic man indeed and told me he had a very trustworthy pupil who would only be too pleased to take me home with him. He then called over the intercom for the boy who happened to be just my own age. How different from me, however, was his appearance. He looked as though he had an IQ double that of mine, as I had no doubt he had, and was dressed in a way I thought was reserved for the very rich. The boy had a double portion of that friendliness and courtesy I have found in almost every French person I have ever met and we were soon good friends. I discovered that Continental people knew nothing of that class snobbery which I had encountered head on so often in England. My new friend was even too polite to tell me that I smelt like gorgonzola gone bad! He took me to visit his beautiful, kindly-faced mother and his lawyer father who looked like the ideal Scoutmaster, i.e. my ideal of how a man should look. He had a little old-fashioned twelve-year-old sister who was a delight to talk to.

Now you will not be surprised to find out what happened next. At table, the lawyer bowed his head and thanked the Lord for the food. After that his wife told me that the school was a Roman Catholic school with only one Protestant pupil in it whose parents were in the French Reformed church and committed Christians. The wise headmaster, guided by the wiser Lord of my life, had introduced me to that one boy, fully knowing that the pupil would receive me in Christian kindness. In no time the family was witnessing to me, feeding me and treating me as their own son. Wondering how I could repay them, I noticed that their windows were a little grubby and soon found a bucket and cloths and was able to delight my new friends with sparkling windows on all the floors of their mansion-like house. These people were very rich but had learnt to live knowing that all their wealth, just like their hearts, belonged to the Lord. The lawyer translated my English and Swedish testimonials and eventually found me a job on a farm as a milker.

I do not want you to think that only those who are rich are generous. Whilst in France, I was invited to spend the night at the home of the poorest of the poor. The father had picked me up in his tumble-down lorry and taken me home to an area bombed in the war and which, ten years later, was still in ruins. There was no furniture whatsoever in the house and Father, Mother, the six children and myself slept covered by a big blanket on the floor. For supper, we had broken bread soaked in milk coffee and for breakfast we had the same. I am sure that dinner and tea was of the same ingredients for them as there was nothing else in the house. The love that family showed me was quite equal to that showed by the man who was a lawyer and judge in the human courts. The Judge of all the world in the Courts of Heaven has His dear ones in all walks of life and society.

You will believe that by now I was repeating Proverbs 3:5 to myself all the time and believing it, and you will be right. I still, however, could not identify myself as a Christian. Some people say that mules are stubborn. Believe me, there is no mule on this earth as stubborn as a sinner who will not see God though His works are displayed daily. It was time to move on again as I had to return to Sweden to claim some holiday pay which was only paid out at the end of the year. I needed that money badly as I was now stony-broke again.

How I got from France to Sweden on board an oil tanker is another story. Suffice it to say that after travelling from Stockholm back to my former place of work and sleeping out two nights in temperatures of over 30 degrees below zero, I eventually reached my old apprentice quarters. As I approached the outside door, I heard a heated conversation going on inside. A group of forestry workers were angrily running the gospel down and making fun of the ways of God with man. I entered the room, took off my rucksack, sat down, and, hardly knowing what I was doing, began to tell my fellow youngsters of the way of salvation and of what Christ had done in my life and for my soul. Then I stopped in my tracks, realising what I was doing. Then I saw that I was the Lord's after all and told the startled group that I believed every single word of what I was saying and once believed as they did but now knew that Christ was my Lord and Master and that though I had not trusted in Him, He had directed my path until now, and at this very moment, I really did trust Him. The heated debate ended with the youngsters giving me a free hand and I discerned by their faces that their inmost desire was also to find Christ and His salvation.

There is a sequel to this story. Two years later, I was putting the final touches to preparations for matriculation so that I could enter the London Bible College. I had had to leave my forestry work a few weeks earlier so that I could study hard. My money had, however, run out too soon and I had nothing to eat. I knelt before the Lord and asked Him if this meant that I had to give up all hope of ever studying theology, which I felt called to do, or must I go back to work in the woods to earn money. That very day a gigantic parcel arrived, though I had told no one of my predicament. I unpacked tinned meat, preserves, tins of fruit, smoked sausage and a host of other foodstuffs and goodies which would last me all through the examinations. My shoes were badly in need of repair but the parcel even included shoe-mending equipment and rubber heels. Truly the Lord knows our every need and does not suffer the least of His own to perish or fall. I looked at the address of the sender on the parcel. It was from the same family in Trier who had brightened up my Christmas and my life. I do not know to this day how they had obtained my address. The parcel was God's miracle of timing by which He showers love on His own and governs His world.

Please do not be like I was and be guided by God like a grandmother taking the ear of an unwilling child and dragging him to the sink to have his neck washed. Take God at His Word. Commit your ways entirely to Him and He will direct your path.

After my conversion, I found out the wonderful thing about this earthly race from birth to death which I outlined at the beginning of my story. It was not that I had to run it under my own power and energy, it was not that winning or losing depended on me at all! Christ Jesus, my Manager had run the race before me, indeed, without me, and had gained the prize and that prize included my prize. As a result of Christ's active fulfilling of all the rules of the competition, I could share that prize with Him. It was in effect a team prize in which the best man of the best team could win the best prize for all. Jesus had succeeded! Now life began to be for me, not a mad, hell-bent rush as it had been but a patient enjoying the prize of the high calling in Christ that He had won for me and living a life in service to the Beloved Saviour who had worked this all out for me.

I have spoken of Miss Keating, Mr Moyes and Mr Hicks who helped me towards faith, now my thoughts go back to those of my mentors who helped me from faith to grow in grace and a knowledge of my Saviour. I must relate something of their influence on my life before going on to tell of the people of the far past who have been of equal value to my soul.

One of my great mentors was Franz-Oskar Lindé of Gäddede, North Sweden. He was a miracle and giant of a man, who, hardly recognised by the world or even his own church, walked and waded daily 15 to 20 kilometres through midge-infested bogs to bring the gospel of life to the Lapps of North Sweden and Norway. He said to me when we first met in 1960, 'I am a wanderer, my home is not here. I am marching towards the City of Gold.' It was my privilege to wander with Franz-Oskar on many occasions and witness to the dear Same people. This is their true name as the name 'Lap', meaning a rag, is a derogatory name given to them by the Swedes and Norwegians. I was not ashamed to call that man openly my hero. He was my first major trainer after my conversion and a better Master in Israel I could not have had. Frans-Oskar was greatly plagued by the evil one. Hardly a night passed by without him having terrible nightmares. I have laid at his side in the turf and birch-bark dwelling of the Lapps and been scared out of my wits by his intensive screams in the night. He told me that during the day, he felt the presence of the Lord as no other but his nights were spent under a strong conviction that he was lost and the devil was pulling him away to hell. He actually experienced the physical tugging at his body. Hearing that man preach to and pray for his Lapp friends, I know who won the tug of war for his soul. I remember attending a meeting of the Board of the Inner Mission responsible for sending out Frans-Oskar. They spoke of him as if he were the village idiot. He had no education and all he was good for was preaching to the Lapps, their chairman said. Could we not save money by scratching this liability from our lists? How these arrogant, racist, professing Christians looked at me when I told them they were slandering the greatest soul-winner on their staff and a man of God whose like they would perhaps never see again, nor did they deserve to.

Franz-Oskar was a chip off the old block, so I must tell you about his father, too. Though over ninety years old, he still preached regularly. This time he was preaching on Elijah in Rönnefors. He had reached that marvellous passage where Elijah was called home. Frans-Oskar's father then stretched out his hands towards Heaven and cried in a loud voice, 'Behold, the chariots of Israel and the horsemen thereof,' and immediately took that chariot himself because he fell down dead at that very moment. Blessed are they who die in the Lord!

In the same vast county, Jämtland, there lived two others whom the Lord used to help establish my faith and put spiritual strength in my limbs. This was a couple called Alvar and Mirjam Olson. Alvar means 'serious' but Alvar and his Finnish wife were as happy as the day was long. I remember skiing with them through the night almost two thousand metres up on the border between Norway and Sweden. Materially speaking, we

Franz-Oskar Lindé, missionary to the Lapps and evangelist at-large.
Frans-Oskar was truly 'an Israelite indeed in whom there is no guile'.

only had the stars and our compass to go by but, my, how we felt the guidance of the Lord! Thought it was well over 40 degrees minus centigrade, we did not notice the cold at all but swished along, discussing the ways of God with man and sharing such sweet fellowship. Alvar had also a story to tell of the Lord's goodness. He was brought up at a time when the nearest doctor was over a hundred miles away and far too expensive for the common man to visit him and pay for him. I have witnessed myself the most primitive medical conditions in Lapland. One day the Lapps all came out of their kåtas and sat in a row on the grass, holding fast to clumps of weeds. A helicopter arrived from Norway and a man got out with a huge pair of pliers. He was the only dentist for hundreds of miles. He went up to the row of Lapps and began pulling teeth with no anaesthetic. There was not a shout of pain or groan from any of the Lapps. The task done, the Lapps had a cup of coffee with the dentist and then got on with their work.

But I am wandering from Alvar. He was born with a huge number of allergies. You name it, he had it. His worst, because he was a farmer's son, was hay fever and asthma. He could hardly breathe when hay-making and his Christian parents prayed and prayed for healing. Children were the only work force on a farm in those days and if Dad and Mum were not assisted by the children, there would be no harvest. But Alvar could not work. Then Alvar heard that you could be inoculated against hay fever and there were cures for asthma. He knew that such treatment was out of the question for poor hand-to-mouth farmers but he had heard from an old man how you could inoculate yourself. One evening, Alvar stole into the barn, wheezing and sneezing and buried himself in the hay up to his neck, breathing in deeply. His parents found him unconscious. When he came round, young Alvar was completely healed and never suffered again. When I first met him, he was as strong as an ox and as swift as an eagle in flight. He looked the very picture of health and he gave God the glory for it.

I must mention Alvar's Labrador dog here. Are not animals also God's creation and used for His purpose and are often better 'Christians' than men? How often have animals shown me love when humans have withdrawn it! One thing I hated, however, was a dog in my bedroom—worse still, a dog in my bed! I was out with Alvar and we had to spend the night in quarters hardly warmer than the freezing cold outside. My feet were numb and my legs stiff and frozen. I felt the cold creep up my body as if I were turning into a block of ice. How I prayed for sleep and warmth! Then, as a perfect answer to prayer, Alvar's big dog came as if from nowhere and laid himself over my legs. The ice-cold disappeared and where coldness had crept, now warmth spread. I slept deeply enveloped in the cosy company of a large, sweaty, smelly dog. Thank God for Alvar's hound!

Then I must tell you of Mr Henry Oakley my Greek teacher at the London Bible College. He had almost sightless eyes but every time I looked into them I saw that City of Gold in all its glory. What treasures I have gained from him! He could take a humdrum Greek word of no interest whatsoever and change it into a message direct from God. No magician has ever been able to do that! I found Greek an impossible task for the first year and when we took the mock exam for the Prelims, I found I could not understand a single word. I turned to Mr Oakley in almost blind panic, doubting my calling and more than doubting myself. Mr Oakley had me calm in seconds and explained what I was doing wrong in minutes. He then gave me extra tasks to do, accompanied by extra hints. A few weeks later, I took the prelims and found only one word in the whole paper which I did not know and that was merely a temporary lapse. My Manager had given me the very best trainer in Mr Oakley, God's special witness to me!

How clearly I remember Christmas with Mr Oakley. The LBC year was always ended with a party and a variety show. After two hours or so of acting the goat, when the mickey was taken out of the lecturers, jokes were told and funny songs sung, it came to Mr Oakley's turn. He stood up, looking up to heaven as he always did as he saw more there than in front of him. With no notes but with his open Bible he then gave us the real Spirit of Christmas. The variety show had seemed like a farewell party from college life back into the silly world outside, but Mr Oakley's talk made us long to come back to Bible School and learn more of the Lord. When I left the LBC, I missed Mr Oakley so much that I once travelled all the way to his St Albans home, hoping that I would at least gain a sight of him to do my soul good. I gained not only a sight but was invited to have a meal with the old saint, a cup of coffee afterwards and, praise be to God, a long, long chat. He is the only person whom I have ever known who could look at others and in merely looking at them, solve their problems and take away their cares. Mr Oakley was truly a father in the faith. How I thank God that I was privileged to know him!

I cannot forget Leslie Barnard, a poet, prophet and teacher all in one. He was considered 'dangerous' by the College authorities and for a time we were banned from hearing Mr Barnard's gospel-tones. Freshers at London Bible College were always told by older students that if they wanted doctrine, they must go to hear the 'Doctor', i.e. Dr Martyn-Lloyd Jones of Westminster Chapel, but if they wanted the delicious taste of heaven to be ever present on their lips, they should have fellowship in Mr Barnard's Sunday afternoon Young Peoples' Class. You can be sure I took their advice—and passed it on to others. I learnt at the Abbey Road Baptist Church that there were sowers, reapers and pruners. I spoke with Mr

Barnard once on this subject as many were being converted but then left Abbey Road for what we called 'the preaching shop' at Westminster Chapel to be pruned into doctrinal shape. I attended some meetings and Bible studies there for about four years and was immensely blessed by the ministry but Westminster Chapel never really seemed like a church. It was always refreshing to return home to the Abbey Road services which happily were often at different times to the Westminster ones. The Wednesday evening Bible Studies gave us real practical fellowship as the Word was discussed together and testimonies given. The business meetings, however were a torture. There was a gigantic ugly stained-glass window behind the Lord's Table depicting a man, purported to be Christ, with outstretched massive hands which were completely out of proportion. Most of the older people could talk for hours about how we could preserve this marvellous work of art, cost what it will. We youngsters thought that if the horrible image were not there, business meetings could be conducted speedily, efficiently and more to the glory of the real Christ.

Perhaps I was still going through having my faith sown or was still in the process of being reaped at Abbey Road. Whatever the case might be, I was certainly surprised to find so much prejudice amongst the more high ranking teaching staff at the 'milk' which Mr Barnard allegedly provided. I personally found it all strong meat, so strong that I have been chewing at it ever since and still obtain good nourishment from it. For over thirty years, I do not think a day passed without my thanking God for Mr Barnard. His sermons rang clearly in my ears. Now, when my memory is feeble, I often forget Mr Barnard and what he said, then suddenly memories come thick and fast and I experience a period of true spiritual bliss.

Then there was Professor James Atkinson of Hull University. Bible college people had warned me for years about studying theology at university and the worldliness of the professors. I went up to Hull fearing the worst. Canon Atkinson of Durham Cathedral was to hold the opening lecture of the new academic year. The *audi max* was full with not only students but all 'the dons on the dais serene' with the Lord Mayor and other public dignitaries to boot. Instead of the usual start of term *laudatio* in praise of the university, Prof. Atkinson praised Christ before the masses and presented the students, faculties and guests with His achievements.

I shall never forget my first theology lecture under that gracious man of God. He faced a class full of post-graduate students, many of whom felt that they had nothing more to learn and made this quite clear. The dear, humble Canon told them that he realised that a good number probably thought theology described the method of standing above the Word of God and making judgement upon it. He explained that he trusted that throughout the year's course, we would learn to stand under the Word of God and let it judge us. Though faced at times with immense opposition from Liberals and Roman Catholics, the latter non-students turning up especially to taunt him, it was never opposition for long. Prof. never lost his childlike faith and mature serenity and, before long, he knit his class together into a Christ-praising church and led many a Papist to Christ. When the Second Vatican Council proclaimed that fresh winds were blowing in that dark institution, Canon Atkinson's prayers were that it might be so. Sadly, he has been criticised recently by over-zealous English and American Presbyterians who have no sympathy for the old Reformed Church of England and blame Canon Atkinson for his past hope. This was, after all, but a reflection of every true Christian's heart, namely that God will draw His elect from all corners of the earth through their coming to acknowledge His Son and His grace alone in salvation. Modern English Presbyterians who have discovered the doctrines of grace in recent years must realise that it is by grace that they have done so and that for well over two hundred years, whilst many Anglicans maintained their place in that faithful cloud of witnesses, the Presbyterian churches in England were nowhere to be seen. Surely the doctrines of grace must take preference over denominational and political bickering about Anglican functions and Presbyterian offices (which are really of the same Biblical order), about white cassocks and the black gowns of philosophers. One of my most treasured possessions is a sweet, tender, pastoral letter from Prof. Atkinson from America where he taught for a time. Those precious blessings reaped during Prof. Atkinson's lectures have ever remained with me and have been of major service in moulding my faith which holds the *Lambeth Articles*, the *Thirty Nine Articles* and the *Canons of Dort* dear.

I confess that I cannot understand the usual complaint amongst evangelical Christians against the universities. I must defend university life here in some way as I have met up with so many Christian witnesses in academic gowns. My studies and later career have associated me intimately with Hull, Uppsala, Hamburg, Duisburg and Essen Universities, yet only one professor amongst very many has ever asked me how I could be so naive as to believe in God. When I asked him, in turn, how he could be so naive as not to believe in God, he saw the point and was most amiable ever afterwards. Even in science subjects, one often finds professors who seek to live a Christian life and have a testimony to give of God's saving grace. Even those who have no such experience themselves.

Returning to the topic of that blessed time at Hull, it was usual there to lecture to the freshers about the birds and the bees and warn the co-ed group of the dangers of fraternising too closely between the sexes.

This was given at Hull by the biology professor. He did not appear to be a converted man but told his students to mark the lives of Christians and watch their ways. There were a few giggles at this but the professor went on to say that it seemed that no one but Christians could really live clean lives. Whilst at Hull, I worshipped regularly at the Swedish Seamen's Church run by the Svenska Kyrkan. There by the grace of God, I found an ad in a church magazine for a teacher to go out to Lapland and teach in Hållands Folkhögskola and Änge Nomadskola.

Whilst studying at Uppsala, I was privileged to have a majority of professors and lecturers who professed Christ. My Greek tutor, Professor Riesenfeld from Darlarna was never too proud to fellowship and pray with his students and even to take us with him on his preaching engagements and catechetical work outside of the University. He had a marvellous nose for finding out where there was spiritual and material need and he would then invite certain students to help him look after the needy ones. I shall always treasure his expositional lectures on the Lord's Prayer in Greek which showed us how to combine academic thought with devotional and experimental living. Bishop Sundkler, who I had for Ecumenical Studies and Missionary Evangelism, was such a bright and shining light that his lectures were all spiritual sunshine. Though a Lutheran himself, his favourite missionary was William Carey and I remember as if it were yesterday how he had Carey's famous *Enquiry* copied and presented to each member of his class. Since then, Carey has been my favourite missionary. Bishop Sundkler thought Carey had no equal and viewed him for the sake of his own testimony and works alone. In England and North America, Carey always tends to be viewed under the shadow of his friends in England who had far less clear insight into the work of the gospel. This has damaged his testimony as he is identified with people who were his spiritual, theological and academic inferiors. The Swedish brethren, I believe, view Carey more objectively and thus in a far better light.

Dear Professor Sundkler. His mind was all in Heaven and he never really knew what was happening on earth. He was invited to speak on television about his former work in Africa. During the live broadcast, he told viewers that he could explain things better if he had a map. He then said spontaneously, 'Oh I saw a map of Africa somewhere in the studio, wait here and I will go and get it.' Then he marched off to look for the map leaving all the cameramen to follow after him, if they could. He then returned with a large globe, oblivious to the panic he had caused, thanked the viewers for waiting and carried on with the talk. He used to turn up at meetings and ask what was on the agenda. When told, he would apologise and leave the room, saying he was to attend a meeting on another theme so must have chosen the wrong venue. We had then to run after him and tell him that he had chosen the right place but prepared the wrong topic but this did not matter at all as we loved to hear him. He would then talk to us off the cuff, quite oblivious to what had happened and thrill our hearts. His oral examinations were a God-send in more ways than one. Nobody could put a nervous student more at ease and he could entice information out of the candidates that they never imagined had been there. One left his exams full of refreshing blessings. Students nearly always did well in Bishop Sundkler's examinations; not because they were particularly easy but because no one wished to disappoint such a fine man. When I think of Benkt Sundkler, I cannot help saying, 'Bless the Lord, O, My Soul!'

Once, however, our dear professor had a deep, deep disappointment. There was a young man in the class who was an evangelical of the evangelicals. His one aim in life was to become a missionary to the underprivileged in South Africa, then ruled by apartheid. How he was going to transform the lives and conditions of those native Africans! Bishop Sundkler arranged for him to be sent out by the Svenska Kyrkan.[1] He warned our friend to win over both whites and blacks by love and the gospel and not get mixed up in extreme politics. The young idealist, however, maintained stoutly that he would strive to break the back of apartheid. The student set off to fulfil his ambitions and six months went by. Meanwhile, Bishop Sundkler received an invitation to South Africa himself and arranged to visit his anti-apartheid protege on an inspection visit. Bishop Sunkler was to fly to the out-station and our one-time friend gathered his Sunday School children at the side of the airstrip to greet the beloved guest. Bishop Sundkler stepped down from the small aircraft and immediately saw all the tiny children and his heart went out to them. Quick as a flash he rushed over to them and started to shake each by the hand and give each an encouraging word. His greetings were almost drowned by an angry shout. 'Professor Sundkler!' the words screamed out, "How can you possibly give the Blacks your hand. How dare you disgrace me in this way. Why, you are actually hugging the Negroes!" The hysterical voice came from our once ardent lover of the African natives. In his short stay in South Africa, he had become an equally ardent apartheidist. Let him who thinketh he standeth, take head lest he fall.

My Hebrew tutor Professor Ringren was rather different. A man of acute and precise knowledge and always very much the gentleman but too reserved to reveal his Christian feelings. Many wanted to make him a bishop but he refused, saying he was a teacher and nothing else. Though we never really could enjoy fellowship with him, his teaching was illus-

---

[1] The Swedish state Lutheran church.

trated, even decorated, with evangelical maxims of the purest kind. His rules for grammar and punctuation and vocalisation were all taken from basic Christian teaching. For instance, in Hebrew there is the letter 'shin' which originally was the sign for a tooth with its three roots on the top side. If a dot is placed above the root on the right side, it is pronounced 'shin'. If the dot is placed on the left root, it is pronounced 'sin'. 'It is easy to remember,' said Professor Ringren. 'All you must know is that "sin is not right". If you learn that at university, you learn well.'

My student days in Germany and my many years there as a Senior Civil Servant with duties in schools, colleges and universities did not bring me into contact with evangelicals as in London, Hull and Uppsala where many other interesting events occurred which must be left for another testimony. Whilst doing what was called 'a candidate year' at Hamburg, however, I experienced a unique longing for the Word of God amongst the students but there were few evangelicals to be had. My Hebrew tutor, a Baptist Minister, whose name I shall not repeat as I can say nothing good about his teaching, taught us absolute trash and could not find anything sensible or positive to say about the Word of God. Then I heard that Helmut Thielicke had begun to preach the gospel, inspired by his love for doctrines which he had found in his work on Spurgeon. Soon the word spread like wildfire throughout the university campus. A hundred went to his lectures instead of the usual handful, then two hundred and more. Then students attending Thielicke's lectures were numbered in the thousands and the gigantic audi max burst its seams. One day I arrived at the gigantic lecture room to find a notice saying, 'Hall too small, gone to St Pauli.' This was at first taken as a joke as St Pauli was the Hamburg centre of vice on the notorious Reeperbahn. But there stands the largest Protestant church building in the country which holds thousands. When I arrived punctually, there was squeezing room only. Students sat on the pews, sat on the floor and sat on the window sills and even on the Lord's Table. There was nowhere else to sit or stand and I found myself crawling between gaps left by legs. They told me that the church was filled with five thousand students who had come to hear an ordinary university lecture. The word spoken was clear and very well received. It was not quite the message that I had been indulged with in England and Scandinavia but it was soaked in like dry sand soaks up the first drops of rain. It was the beginning of a new movement of the Spirit in Germany which is now growing in momentum. The clouds of witnesses are thickening in this home of Luther's which has been unoccupied for so many years.

Coming nearer the present, I must tell you about my good friend Werner Goßlau, Doctor of Music. I had the privilege of assisting him for several years in the United Church of North-Rhine Westphalia (Lutheran and Reformed). When he preached the church, which had seating for six hundred, was full. When his highly liberal and ignorant co-pastor, who had been foisted on the church by some political intrigue, preached, the church was empty. Werner was called up before the Second World War broke out and, to his dismay, when the Nazis came to power, he was forced to remain a soldier. The forces were drilled not only in warfare but in a new religion called 'German Christianity'. The only thing that was Christian about the movement was part of the name. It was not even 'German' as the sentiments came from Walhalla rather than Berlin. Werner was a professing, born-again believer and all eyes were on him. But Werner kept a good testimony. Squealers were placed in Werner's dormitory and things were done to tempt him to give cause for complaint. His personal possessions began to disappear. Careful of his wording, Werner asked his comrades who had organised his things. He carefully chose the word 'organise' because this is polite soldier slang for having things disappear, borrowed, picked up or stolen. The last interpretation was jumped on at once. Werner Goßlau had insulted the Führer's armed forces by saying they were thieves. He was speedily ordered to be shot. Happily, the senior judge in the area was Werner's uncle and he set all his powers into motion to have Werner severely reprimanded and imprisoned rather than executed. Werner's life was spared to become one of Germany's most successful preachers of the gospel. But why am I telling this story? Because our modern generation tends to think that all those Germans who lived and worked and served in the armed forces were evil men and women. It was not like that as God had His cloud of witnesses at work in Germany as elsewhere. But as I said, the modern generation does not realise this. Just before Werner retired, when he was old and physically weak, he was preaching Christ in a filled church when the doors were rudely burst open and the co-pastor marched into the church followed by a crowd of young, noisy hooligans who never went to church. The co-pastor came to the pulpit stairs and pointed to Werner and said, 'Where were you in the days of Adolf Hitler and why did you do nothing to stop him.' Then the whole crowd of pagans began to jeer and cry 'Nazi, Nazi'. Werner managed to end the service in a manner befitting a Christian and took no disciplinary measures against his wayward colleague. After all, he had not known that during the war, his colleague had been sitting in a cell, waiting to be shot. On the day of Werner's retirement, after serving the church for over thirty years, the co-pastor marched up to the manse door, thumped on it loudly and ordered Werner and his ailing wife out of the house and had their furniture brought out into the garden in the pouring rain so that he could take over the house himself. At the thanksgiving dinner given by Werner's friends, this worldly co-pastor marched up to the microphone and announced in a large boasting, childish voice, 'Now *I* am the senior pastor in this church. I can do things as *I* like.' He was as good as his word and in no time had preached his extreme left-wing social gospel so enthusiastically that his congregation shrunk, many going to the Roman Catholic church nearby. I went to preach there a year later at very short notice and was surprised to find only 49 believers at the service. I mentioned the difference to Werner's days to the organist who told me that usually far fewer came to hear the pastor who often never turned up himself and attendance at my preaching was the highest for some time and would have been higher had it not happened at short notice. Then some friends invited Werner to preach at the church on his seventy-fifth birthday. It was like old times. How Werner's successor must have felt ashamed! The church was so full that extra seats had to be brought in and soon the aisles, gallery and porch were full. I had the privilege of assisting Werner with the service and with the Lord's Supper. It was the first communion service for many for years and we seemed to be celebrating for hours, so large were the numbers. Werner preached Christ as if he were a young man in full powers, though the signs of physical death were on him. Soon after, he was called to glory. Dear friends, do not give up praying for Germany so that the clouds of witnesses will descend and lead a very hungry people to God.

Leaving the present, I would like to testify to the great blessings, comfort and teaching that I have received from a number of great men of the past. It is here that I have my difficulty as my readers will obviously not have the same tastes and needs as myself and may look for other things in God's witnesses for their edification. I do believe, however, that the people of whom I write have a firm testimony for everyone who has been chosen to follow Jesus and this is one of my reasons for choosing them.

I must emphasise, however, a major weakness in much of the negative criticism I have experienced in the past. Nowadays, we are far more party or denomination-conscious than our fathers and I know a number of brethren have taken offence because I refuse to denounce men of God because of the church in which they were members. Invariably these criticisms were from churches who considered themselves more reformed, more Biblical or even more sacramental than others. It is the old story of the beam and the mote. I have received several complaints from readers who appear to always identify a writer fully with his subject. If he writes positively about a soldier, he must be a war-like man himself. If he writes favourably of a Baptist, he must be such himself, if he delights in the writings of the old pre-Laudian Church of England, then he is proclaimed a lover of Catholicism and a supporter of a church with a ministry of mere governmental Civil Servants. I have been accused of preaching Arianism because I quoted a missionary poem by Whittier, commenting favourably on it because of the poet's description of Henry Martyn's closeness to the Lord, which no man could doubt. I have been accused of wishy-washy theology because I wrote on the life of Phillip Doddridge, whom I believe was mightily used of God in his day. I have been accused of membership in all sorts of strange organisations because I have quoted people who belonged to those organisations. I have been called an Antinomian, a Hyper-Calvinist, a Hypo-Calvinist, an Arminian, a Calminian, a Paedobaptist, an Adult Baptiser and many other titles because I have mentioned God's witnesses whom my critics thought, often wrongly so, were of these categories. My membership of the local church I am part of depends on the fact that they are a people of God with whom I am in deep fellowship, whatever outward conventional signs separate them from the people of God in neighbouring churches. I believe that baptism should be within the Covenant of Promise and thus within the Church and that celebrating the Lord's Supper is equally a Church matter and should be closed to believers only but not solely for denominational members or even for local church members only. It is not a local organisational celebration but a celebration of the elect in union with their Lord preparatory to the Marriage Supper of the Lamb. I believe sincerely and passionately in the doctrines of grace but it is these doctrines which give me the call to work with all lovers of those doctrines in the gathering in of the elect, no matter whether they are Episcopalian, Presbyterian, Dissenter, Baptist or whatever. There are many jewels in the Lord's crown, not just diamonds and pearls and I have felt free to pick out precious gems, whatever their setting. Nor are my spiritual mentors placed in any order of preference as I love them all. I have sought, however, to place them in a rough chronological order so that readers will gain more insight into the work of the Holy Spirit in history.

The people I am about to present to my readers are all Christian stalwarts who were burdened with their bodies of sin and were only perfect in the righteousness which they had from Christ which was certainly none of their own. I thus ask the reader to be discerning in what they read. A case in point is the liberty which we all seek to exercise in Christ. The early American Congregationalists, for instance, often came from very live churches in England, which they had left without shepherds for new experiences of liberty in the New World. Whilst there, however, they did not wish to share this liberty with others of different church persuasions and thus became even more enemies of true liberty than the people they had left behind. Thus John Cotton and Richard Mather, good men as they were, were moved to ban Roger Williams from their fellowship and from their colony because he had argued as they had done in England. However, when Williams became settled in Rhode Island, he thought it right to deny Samuel Gorton much the same rights that he was carving out for himself. Such behaviour has marred most, if not all, of our denominations and so-called non-denominational or inter-denominational institutions bringing shame on the true Church of Christ. I do not defend action of this kind at all but still see something of our liberty in Christ reflected in all these people who exercised various ideas of liberty. We shall always see through a glass darkly until we are face to face with the Lord.

Many of the enclosed biographies started out as articles in the *Banner of Truth Magazine*, the *Evangelical Times*, the *Baptist Standard Bearer*, *Focus*, *New Focus*, the *Bible League Quarterly*, the *Baptist Quarterly*, *The Banner of Sovereign Grace Truth* and several other smaller US., Canadian, Swedish and British periodicals, denominational and church magazines whose names I have forgotten. Perhaps my readers will find these brief testimonies to the lives of my mentors a very mixed bag. This is inevitable as some have been of more importance than others and I know some better than others. I have studied William Cowper and the Mathers for many years and have read all of Cowper and very much of the Mathers as well as literally hundreds of books and articles composing secondary literature. Though highly blessed by Risdon Darracott, I have found only snippets here and there about his life. John Janeway's testimony has attracted me for years but I have only discovered three brief biographies and a number of brief references in general works on church history. I have had a similar embarrassment with my Bibliography appended within this book. I originally intended to provide a bibliography under the names of each character described. This would have caused too much overlapping and repetition as I have used many collections of biographies and works such as those on the Reformed Church of England stalwarts where several of my subjects were contemporaries and friends and are therefore mentioned in the same biographies. I have thus listed all books merely alphabetically according to authors' names. This method, impractical as it is, seemed to be the best solution. I have, however, distinguished between biographical works, general or background material and magazine articles. I have not listed all the various works of my subjects, nor even all those that I have read. As my subjects were mostly prolific writers, the mere bibliographical details of their works would run into at least five volumes. Anyone who has seen catalogues of the Mathers' books will know what I mean.

JOHN JEWEL (1522-1571)

2. John Jewel (1522-1571): Reformer of the English Church

A jewel in Christ's crown

One of the largest jewels in Christ's crown during the British Reformation actually bore the name of Jewel himself. This was John Jewel who was born May 22, 1522 in Buden, Devonshire and died on September 23, 1571 in Monkton Farleigh in the diocese of Salisbury over which he had been the Bishop since January 1560. It is no longer customary to call Jewel a British Reformer but this is a mistake of history. Jewel pioneered the break with Rome in an England overshadowed by Bloody Mary and he was one of the first Englishmen to bring the cup back into celebrations of the Lord's Supper. Jewel's works fully deserve to be counted as Reformation literature. Spurgeon rightly classified Jewel with the Reformers in his *Commenting and Commentaries* and Dr Michael W. Dewar in his *They Subdued Kingdoms* says, 'No Scottish or Swiss Calvinist could be more strongly "Reformed" in his doctrine of the Lord's Supper.' The Continentals looked upon Jewel's works as the epitome of the Reformation and they were translated into many languages. The editor of the standard 1837 edition of Neal's *History of the Puritans* says of Jewel's *Apology for the Church of England*, 'It promoted the Reformation from Popery more than any other publication of that period.'[1]

John was born into a very large family which quite impoverished his father who had started his adult life fairly well-to-do. From his earliest years, young John showed a great talent for learning. So swift was his academic progress that he was judged mature enough as a scholar to enter Merton College whilst scarcely thirteen years of age. Immediately, he came under the supervision of men with sound doctrines such as John Parkhurst,

---

[1] Op. cit. vol. i, p. 183.

who became Bishop of Norwich, under whose guidance John received a deep affection for the Word of God then already translated into English by Coverdale and Tyndale.

Jewel studied diligently, rising up at four each morning to do so, paying special attention to the Greek language. So ardent were his early morning labours in his badly heated draughty rooms that he soon developed rheumatism which grew so serious that whilst still at university, he became a cripple for life. Jewel was thankful to escape with his life as many of his fellow-students at the time had died of the plague which spread through the student body. In 1539, Jewel transferred to Corpus Christi College from where he took his B.A. in the following year. By this time Jewel's friends were becoming anxious for his life as he was working almost non-stop from four in the morning until ten at night and often forgetting to eat. Various university posts were now offered to Jewel and for the next seven years he lectured in Humanities and Rhetoric, taking his M.A. in 1544.

Mary the Bloody

Peter Martyr Vermigli (1500-1562),[1] the Italian Reformer was at Oxford from 1547 to the accession of Queen Mary, called 'The Bloody',invited there by Thomas Cranmer (1489-1556). Vermigli became very popular with the Protestant school in the university, chiefly through his lectures on Corinthians and Romans, besides assisting the Church with the Reformed Liturgy. Jewel was highly influenced by Vermigli and took his side when the Marian Papists began to protest at Vermigli's influence at Oxford, writing his defence. In 1552, Jewel took his B.D. and became vicar of a small church outside of the town, always walking to and from Oxford to his flock in spite of his lameness. Jewel could have taken any number of wealthy livings at this time but preferred to be poor amongst the poor.

As soon as Mary came to the throne in 1553, Jewel was expelled from Oxford by the fellows for refusing to take the Roman mass which they had introduced. Jewel's farewell lecture to his students is extant and depicts the great sorrow in which he took leave of the calling that had become so dear to his heart. Ironically enough, the university still asked Jewel, because they had no better orator, to convey the universities congratulations on Mary's accession. Naively believing that Mary would keep her promise not to alter the Church of England and threatened by death unless he signed a document accepting Mary and her doctrines, Jewel complied, but still his enemies wished for his death, chiefly because

---

[1] Usually called Peter Martyr by English-speaking people.

of his support of Peter Martyr. Jewel escaped being murdered by them one day, as, warned of their intention, he fled on foot, eventually receiving assistance from Sir Nicholas Throgmorton to flee to Germany. John Parkhurst, as soon as he heard that Mary intended to break her word and restore the Popish mass, fled too, with many others.

Reformers in exile

At Frankfurt Jewel met up with a large group of British refugees, several of whom had been his close associates at Oxford. They urged Jewel to renounce any allegiance to Mary and her Popish ways and retract his written assent. So on the first Sunday after reaching Frankfurt, Jewel announced from the pulpit of the English Church, 'It was my abject and cowardly mind, and faint heart, that made my weak hand to commit this wickedness.'[1] Jewel showed such a genuine distress at the way Britain had been deceived and repentance for his own action that Erasmus Middleton tells us the whole auditorium felt more drawn to Jewel than if he had never pledged allegiance to Mary and her Popish ways. Middleton also adds that it is easy for those who were never tried to criticise Jewel but we can only be guided by the Word of God in this that tells such critics, 'Let him who thinketh he standeth, take heed lest he fall.'

Vermigli, who had also made his escape from Britain after the sad loss of his wife, settled at Straßburg and now invited Jewel to join him. Meanwhile the Papists worked off their frustration at Vermigli's escape by opening his wife's grave, exhuming her body and re-burying it under a dung heap. Once in Straßburg, Jewel found that many men who had been leading British churchmen under Henry VIII and Edward VI were there and shared deep fellowship with such as Edward Grindal, later to become Archbishop of York. Soon, however, Vermigli was appointed Professor of Hebrew at Zürich university and took Jewel as his assistant with him. There both men soon discovered another group of British refugees and plans were laid for restoring the Church of England after Mary. When the Papist Queen's henchman, Bishop Stephen Gardiner heard of this, he strove to root out and punish all those still in Britain who were supporting their exiled brethren, boasting that he would make the exiles eat their own finger-ends for hunger before he was finished with them.

Back home to a hero's welcome

Comforting himself with the thought, 'These things will not last an age,'

---

[1] Neal's remark in his otherwise first-class mini-biography of Jewel in his *History of the Puritans* that Jewel had not the courage of a martyr is fully out of place when taking the full situation into account. See vol. i, p. 183.

Jewel continued his studies throughout the four years of his exile and helped Martyr prepare his works for the press. On November 17, 1558, an anniversary which should be celebrated as a National Holiday in Britain, Mary the Bloody, mercifully for her people, went to meet her Judge. The mass exodus from the Continent back to England was great and Queen Elizabeth gave most of the exiles a hero's welcome. One of the first church reforms Elizabeth put into action, aided by those whom Mary had persecuted, was to put the Church of England service and the epistles and gospels used in worship into the English language. The elevation of the sacrament was now abolished and the prison doors opened to the thousands who had been cast there by Mary's Popish vassals. Jewel was now appointed as a commissioner to travel the country, examining the churches to try and estimate the degree of corruption they had undergone throughout Mary's reign. After making his report, Jewel was made Bishop of Salisbury and his friend Parkhurst Bishop of Norwich. Jewel soon found, however, that his Popish predecessor, John Capon, had embezzled church funds and even sold off the livings attached to the diocese for his own enrichment and the bishopric was financially bankrupt. Jewel also found much Romanism still in his diocese and challenged the papists openly to come forward with any evidence from Scripture or even the early church to back up their superstitious claims for the papacy and he would grant them the freedom of undisturbed public debate. A Mr Harding took up the challenge, both sides publishing a number of works on the topics raised.

The Church of England versus the Papacy
Jewel's greatest work against the Papacy, written in 1562 in Latin was his *Apologia pro Ecclesia Anglicana*, which gained the personal backing of the Queen and the entire church hierarchy. In it, Jewel shows that the criteria for what is heresy or not does not rest in church history or church traditions but solely in the acceptance or non-acceptance of the Word of God. Similarly, church authority has nothing to with ideas of succession as such but on whether a church is built on the Word of God and lives by it. He thus says in his *Introduction* to his great work:

> But seeing they (the papists) can produce nothing out of the Scriptures against us, it is very injurious and cruel to call us heretics, who have not revolted from Christ nor from the apostles, nor from the prophets. By the sword of Scripture Christ overcame the devil when he was tempted by him; with these *weapons every high thing that exalteth itself against God* is to be brought down

and dispersed; 'for all Scripture', saith St. Paul: (2 Tim. 3:16), 'is given by inspiration of God, and is profitable for doctrine, for reproof, for correction, for instruction, that the man of God may be perfect, and thoroughly furnished unto all good works;' and accordingly, the holy fathers have never fought against heretics with any other arms than what the Scriptures have afforded them. St. Augustine, when he disputed against Petilianus, a Donatist heretic, useth these words: 'Let not (saith he) these words be heard, I say, or Thou sayest, but rather let Thus saith the Lord; let us seek the church there, let us judge of our cause by that.' And St. Jerome saith, 'Let whatever is pretended to be delivered by the Apostles, and cannot be proved by the testimony of the written word, be struck with the sword of God.' And St. Ambrose to the emperor Gratian, 'Let the Scriptures (saith he), let the apostles, let the prophets, let Christ be interrogated.' The Catholic fathers and bishops of those times did not doubt but our religion might be sufficiently proved by Scripture; nor durst they esteem any man an heretic, whose error they could not perspicuously and clearly prove such by Scripture. And as to us, we may truly reply with St. Paul, Acts, 24:14 'After the way which they call heresy, so worship I the God of my fathers, believing all things which are in the written law and the prophets;' or the writings of the apostles.

Jewel's *Apologia* was seen in England as primarily a defence of the Anglican Church, but the Continental Reformed churches also saw it as a defence of Protestantism and the Reformed Faith par excellence. This alone puts to flight the odd idea propagated by the Presbyterians that Jewel was really one of them but merely lacked the courage to come out. Jewel was an Anglican through and through. In this work, Jewel refutes the fond idea of the pope that Trent was a general church council representing all the churches, therefore its findings were to be accepted by the Church of England. Peter Martyr Vermigli, still at Zürich was delighted to receive a copy of Jewel's work and promoted the book in Europe during the closing months of his life. His letter of thanks to Jewel is still extant and shows how respected amongst the Continental Protestant churches was not only Jewel but the Church of England at large. Vermigli writes:

By the favour of the bishop of London, most worthy prelate and my very good lord, there was brought me one of your Apologies for the Church of England; which neither I nor any others hereabouts before had seen: It is true in your last letter you rather intimated that it might come out, than signified that it should; but however it came not hither till about the middle of July. And from hence your lordship may consider how much we suffer from the distance of places. It hath not only given me an entire satisfaction, who approve and am strangely pleased with all you do; but to Bullinger and his sons, and sons in law: And it seems so very wise, admirable and elegant to Gualter (Zwingli's son in law) and Wolfius, that they can put no end to their commendations of it, as not thinking there hath been any thing printed in these times of so great a perfection. I do infinitely congratulate this great felicity of your parts, this excellent edification of the church, and the honour you have done your country; and I do most earnestly beseech you to go on in the same way; for though we have a good cause, yet the defenders of it are few in comparison of its enemies; and they now seem so awakened, that they have of late won much upon the ignorant multitude, by the goodness of their style, and the subtlety of their sophistry. I speak this of Staphylus and Hosius, and some other writers of that party, who are now the stout champions of the papal errors. But now you have, by this your most elegant and learned Apology, raised such an hope in the minds of all good and learned men, that they generally promise themselves, that whilst you live, the Reformed religion shall never want an advocate against its enemies. And truly I am extremely glad, that I am so happy as to live to see that day which made you the father of so illustrious and eloquent a production. May the GOD of heaven of his goodness grant that you may be blessed in time with many more such.

                                          Zurick, Aug. 24, 1562.

This was one of the last letters written by Vermigli. He had lived to see a great work written by his former pupil which would rally Reformed believers throughout Europe around the cause of the Reformation in their battle against the corrupt machinations of Rome. Peter Martyr Vermigli died on November 12, 1562.

The work of Reformation

The Church of England at this time, with men like Jewel at her head, was seen internationally as the very spearhead of the Reformed movement with Presbyterian churches willingly allowing her the lead. Vermigli himself was one of the greatest of Reformers and most radical in stripping church officers of any vestiges of popish power. Bullinger (1504-1575), Zwingli's successor, is famous for his co-work with Luther, Calvin and Zwingli in which church offices were hardly considered of any importance in the work of Reformation. Bullinger drew up the Second Helvitic Confession which was adopted in Switzerland and in several other German-speaking states such as Bohemia and also by the Reformed Church in Hungary. This confession was also very influential in Elizabethan England and Bullinger was highly respected by the Church of England. Bullinger's hundred or so works are hardly known amongst present day Reformed people and a number of books on justification by grace and the authority of Scripture and various expository works are still awaiting the attention of translators. Several editions of his sermons were printed in English.

Given these facts, it is no surprise to learn that when the British delegates from the Reformed Church of England arrived at the Council of Dort in 1618, they were greeted as representing the furthest extent which the Reformed faith had developed in Europe. Bishop George Carleton, the High Calvinist official leader, was assured that this was because of their church discipline and order which reflected their doctrines. Thomas Fuller in his famous *Church History*, shows how the Reformed Church of England always looked upon Switzerland as the nursery of the Reformed faith and when Jewel's contemporary Archbishop Whitgift heard that Geneva was in danger of slipping back into papist hands as it had declared itself bankrupt, he organised a national collection to help pay the city's debts. Whitgift, too, was responsible for issuing the *Lambeth Articles* of which Presbyterian Princeton scholar Samuel Miller says:

> The famous Lambeth Articles, drawn up in 1595, during the reign of Queen Elizabeth, are acknowledged by all who ever read them, to be among the most strongly marked Calvinistical compositions that ever were penned.[1]

Oxford University now awarded Jewel the degree of Doctor of Divinity. As the papist Council of Trent was sitting at the time (1545-1563), Jewel's book on doctrine and church order was discussed there and two men, an Italian and a Spaniard, were authorised to answer it. Meanwhile it was translated into some fifteen languages, English being one of the last as it had sold well enough in its Latin edition. One of Jewel's major intentions had been to have the book circulated in churches still under Rome's

---

[1] Introduction to Thomas Scott's translation of *The Canons of Dort*, 1841.

influence. The *Apology In Defence of the Church of England* had, indeed, an enormous influence on the continental churches as well as the British. Perhaps this is why the two Roman Catholics who were supposed to answer the work never really took on the task. However, Queen Elizabeth associated herself staunchly with the work, which angered the pope no end. He thus decided to condemn Jewel's defence and the Queen's approbation of it by pompously using his empty powers to excommunicate the Queen. Jewel immediately wrote a defence of the Queen entitled *A View of the Seditious Bull Sent into England by Pius V.* and appended a treatise on the Word of God to it for the pope's pontifical edification.[1]

Preaching the Word

Now Jewel began to publish profusely, most of his works being of an expositional kind. Here, Martyn Lloyd-Jones, who mistakenly views all Puritans as being Presbyterian and Separatist, shows a most inaccurate view of the Anglican church of this time and her attitude to preaching, arguing:

> On the whole, the Anglican method was to take a subject, sometimes a theological subject or an ethical subject, or some general theme, and then to preach a disquisition on this particular subject.[2]

He then explains how true Puritan preachers always took a text, then explained its meaning, after which they drew out the doctrine in the text and applied it to the needs of his people. Here again, the evidence Lloyd-Jones produces, quite contradicts his theory. Thomas Cartwright, the Archbishop's ward, whom Lloyd-Jones regards as the Proto-Puritan, great expositor as he was, often used the method Lloyd-Jones disparages. Some indication of this is found in Spurgeon's *Commenting and Commentaries* on the Pastoral Epistles where he praises the depth, accuracy and discursiveness of Bishop Davenant and the liveliness of Bishop Jewel, but though he praises Cartwright's rich spirituality, he says of his commentary on Colossians, 'This is but a small affair, consisting of scanty and second rate "notes" by a hearer.'[3] No other comments on Cartwright's works such as his expositions of Proverbs and Ecclesiastes and his *Har-*

---

[1] Edward Hinson has included this fine work on the Scriptures in his book *Introduction to Puritan Theology*, Foreword by James I. Packer, Guardian Press.

[2] See the chapter on Preaching in Lloyd-Jones' *The Puritans*

[3] P.165.

mony of the Gospels are made.[1] Of Bishop Hall's *Contemplations*, however, Spurgeon says, 'If its price were raised in proportion to its real value, it would become one of the most costly books extant.'[2] This is not so much depreciating Cartwright's preaching skills as affirming that the Reformed Church of England produced expositors of Scripture who ought to be given their rightful place amongst the very best.[3]

In all fairness to Cartwright, it must be added that there is a further point where Cartwright failed to meet Lloyd-Jones' criteria for a Puritan at no discredit to himself. He certainly was not a Separatist. Nor did William Perkins, whom Lloyd-Jones sees as a great Puritan preacher, fulfil Lloyd-Jones' criteria in any way apart from his preaching. He never complained of his status in the Church of England hierarchy, he emphasised the catholicity (the word that raises Lloyd-Jones' blood-pressure) of his Reformed faith and he was praised by bishops and archbishops and loved by Arminians as well as High Calvinists. He lived and died a minister of the Church of England and there is no sign of his ever expressing Separatist views. I am not arguing that Perkins was not a Puritan, he most certainly was! I am arguing that Perkins was an Anglican Puritan of Puritans and that Lloyd-Jones theory that Anglicans were at best what he calls 'part Puritans' is denounced in all its fullness by not only Perkins but also by Jewel, Whitaker, Whitgift, Hall, Abbot, Davenant and Ward and a host of other Anglicans from this period.

Like Perkins, Jewel was an excellent expository preacher. So great was his love of this calling that he always said, 'A bishop should die preaching,' and the words continually impressed on his mind were, 'Happy art thou, my servant, if, when I come, I find thee so doing.' Anyone who feels the Church of England never produced fine preachers should read Jewel's exposition of 2 Thessalonians 2:13 reprinted in Middleton's *Biographia Evangelica*, 'But we are bound to give thanks always to God for you brethren beloved of the Lord because God hath from the beginning chosen you to salvation through sanctification of the Spirit and belief of the truth.' Expounding this text, Jewel says:

> GOD hath chosen you from the beginning His election is sure
> for ever. The Lord knoweth who are his. You shall not be deceived

---

[1] Even though Spurgeon has a special chapter for Gospel Harmonies and records far lesser known authors under all three headings..

[2] P. 40.

[3] A most sympathetic biography of Cartwright was written by Anglican Erasmus Middleton in vol. ii of his *Biographia Evangelica*.

with the power and subtlety of antichrist. You shall not fall from grace. You shall not perish. This is the comfort which abideth with the faithful, they behold the fall of the wicked; when they see them forsake the truth and delight in fables; when they see them return to their vomit, and wallow again in the mire. When we see these things in others, we must say, alas! they are examples for me, and lamentable examples. Let him that standeth take heed that he fall not. But God hath loved *me*, and hath chosen *me*, to salvation. His mercy shall go before me, and his mercy shall follow in me. His mercy shall guide my feet, and stay me from falling. If I stay by myself, I stay by nothing; I must needs come to ground.— He hath loved me; he hath chosen me; he will keep me. Neither the example nor the company of others, nor the enticing of the devil, nor my own sensual imaginations, nor sword, nor fire, is able to separate me from the love of God which is in Christ Jesus our Lord. This is the comfort of the faithful.—Whatever falleth upon others, though others fall and perish, although they forsake Christ and follow after antichrist, yet God hath loved you and given his Son for you. He hath chosen you, and prepared you unto Salvation, and hath written your name in the book of life. But how may we *know* that God hath *chosen* us? how may we *see* this ELECTION? or how may we *feel* it? The apostle saith, through *sanctification*, and the *faith* of truth. These are *tokens* of God's *election.*—This (viz. the Holy Spirit) comforteth us in all temptations; and beareth witness with our Spirit that we be the children of God; that God hath chosen us; and doth love us, and hath prepared us to salvation; that we are the heirs of his glory; that God will keep us as the apple of his eye; that he will defend us; and we shall not perish.[1]

Anyone doubting Jewel's Calvinism would also profit from such a reading. Jewel also keeps to the Reformed tradition of going through a whole book verse by verse rather than preaching on isolated passages. He believed that this gave his hearers a better conception of the entire gospel. It was this commentary which caused Spurgeon to see in it the work of a

---

[1] The full commentary is found reprinted in *The Fathers of the English Church*, vol. vii, pp. 125-415. The above quote is on pp. 385 ff. Middleton has omitted parts for reasons of space but I have quoted from him as his works are more available than Jewel's commentaries themselves.

true Reformer with the positive exception that Jewel was more 'lively' than most others.[1]

Lord Jesus, come quickly

Jewel became very ill shortly before his fiftieth birthday and he knew the Lord was calling him home. His almost super-human labours of preaching, writing, caring for others and walking on foot to his various engagements, though extremely feeble in body and very lame, made him an old man before the usual time. Jewel then made his will, giving all his estate to his servants, the poor and to needy scholars. His last sermon was preached to his own household and was on the Lord's Prayer. On closing, he told his hearers that the time had come for him to leave them. One of them protested, saying that the Lord could restore him. Jewel answered, 'A crown of righteousness is laid up for me. Christ is my righteousness. Father let thy will be done: Thy will I say, and not mine, which is imperfect and depraved. This day, quickly, let me see the Lord Jesus.' Then the Lord Jesus came quickly and took his servant John Jewel home on the very same day.[2]

---

[1] *Commenting and Commentaries*, p. 166.

[2] The 767 pages of *Fathers of the English Church*, vol. vii are all devoted to Jewel's life and works, including the *Apologia* in English.

JOHN WHITGIFT (1530-1604)

3. John Whitgift (1530-1604): Puritan Archbishop

Discovering that the Scriptures provide no foundation for Romanism
Called the undaunted champion of the Reformed Church of England, John
Whitgift was born in 1530 in Grimsby, Lincolnshire, the son of Henry
Whitgift, merchant and Anne Dynewell, both of leading Lincolnshire fami-
lies, though John's father is thought to be a descendent of the West
Riding Whitgifts. John was named after his uncle John Whitgift who was
Abbot of Wellow Monastery in Lincolnshire and took care of his nephew's education. John Whitgift Sen., though a papist, told his pupil that the
Church of Rome could not last as he had read the Scriptures from beginning to end and knew that they provided no foundation for Rome's beliefs
and what is not built on Scripture cannot last. Thus it was a Roman Catholic monk who put young Whitgift on the Reformed path. On his uncle's
advice, John was sent to St Antony's School in London and was boarded
out at an aunt's in St Paul's Churchyard where her husband was verger to
the Cathedral. John's aunt strove to send him to mass and had the Cathedral canons help her in her efforts to Romanise her nephew. He withstood
their efforts as his heart was already set on Reformed truths. Finally, John's
aunt gave up the struggle and refused to house him saying that when she
first met him, she thought he was a saint but now she knew he was a devil.

Not ashamed of the gospel
Once more under the care of his uncle who was gradually allowing the
Reformation's light to penetrate his soul, John was trained for matriculation and entered Cambridge when about 18 years of age. After a brief time
at Queen's, he entered Pembroke College under the supervision of Gregory
Garth, taking his B.A. in 1553. Here John was taught by such heroes of the
faith as John Bradford and Nicolas Ridley, the martyrs and Edmund Grindal

who escaped martyrdom by the skin of his teeth. Two years later, Whitgift received a fellowship at Peter House and received his M.A. in 1557. When Cardinal Pole came to inspect the university to drive out men of the Reformation, the Vice-Chancellor Dr Perne hid Whitgift so that he escaped persecution. By 1560, however, the popish queen was dead and Whitgift was ordained for the ministry, preaching his first sermon on Romans 1:16, 'I am not ashamed of the gospel of Christ.' In the same year, he was given the rectorship of Teversham and went on to take his B.D. in 1563 and became Margaret Professor the same year. Now Whitgift was known nationally as a hero of the Reformation and the Queen appointed him her chaplain confessing that his sermons edified her. Whitgift, however, wrote to the chancellor, William Cecil, asking him to use his influence to stop a new ruling concerning the wearing of surplices in the university. When this came to the ear of the Queen, Whitgift fell out of her good books but became even more popular at the University which was rapidly becoming reformed. Whitgift's salary was raised to £20 a year and in token of his great popularity as a preacher, he received a licence to preach anywhere, without let or hindrance throughout the entire country.

For the Church of England against the Anti-Christ
Now Whitgift was befriended by Edmund Grindal, always on the look-out for good Reformed men. His popularity in the university grew and he was quickly appointed Master of Pembroke Hall and Regius Professor of Divinity but held the posts only for a few months as he was appointed to the Mastership of Trinity College on the sudden death of Dr Beauchamp. All these preferments had robbed him of leisure to study but now he finished off his thesis for his Doctor of Divinity on the topic *Papa est ille antichristus*, which, being interpreted, means *The Pope is the Anti-Christ*. This theme must be born in mind when analysing Whitgift's attitude to his Dissenting brethren who wished to remain within the Church of England but be given special privileges. When they did not receive the very special and privileged treatment they required, the cry went up that the Church of England was still popish. Thus, if one reads through the pages of such writers as Daniel Neal who strove to promote the Presbyterian image, Whitgift is portrayed as being an enemy of Puritanism, other writers going even further and portraying him as a friend of the papists. This is a totally false picture of Whitgift who pleaded for unity in his church and believed that this could only be obtained by preventing all revolutionary, anti-Episcopalian and doctrinally unorthodox men from receiving influential posts in the church via the many back doors that the English socio-political structure had allowed. Thus men who would not take the vow of alle-

giance, would not even accept the episcopacy as an alternative practical means of church government and who refused to subscribe to the *Thirty Nine Articles* were being given churches, lectureships and professorships by non-ecclesiastical patrons who had inherited or bought certain 'rights' to certain 'livings' or other ecclesiastical posts. Whitgift saw this as being tantamount to entrusting one's sheep to hirelings. In order to counteract this tendency, Whitgift, now Vice-Chancellor, gave his full support to Archbishop Parker (1504-1575), England's first Reformed Archbishop after Mary's death. Parker's reforms were being handicapped at the time by Queen Elizabeth who strongly resented Parker's refusing to introduce the crucifix and celibacy. After finding that the church dignitaries and universities were with him, Parker ordered all ministers in the Reformed Church of England to subscribe to the *Thirty Nine Articles* or give up their claim to be members of that church. Parker commissioned Whitgift to publish a defence of this measure to which Whitgift appended letters from Calvin, Beza, Bullinger, Gualter, Bucer, Zwingli and Peter Martyr listing the pros and cons of both the Episcopacy and Presbyterianism but coming down securely and firmly on the side of the Episcopacy.

The Anglican Puritans and Thomas Cartwright: An exercise in tolerance

Here, too, must be mentioned Whitgift's treatment of Thomas Cartwright whose case is usually put forward to brand the Anglican Puritans as persecutors of Non-Conformists. As Spain was now preparing to invade Britain with her Great Armada in the name of the pope, one can understand the sensitivity of the English at any display of disrespect for her establishments. Yet, Cartwright in his younger years refused to acknowledge either the powers of the Queen or the ministry, discipline and doctrines of the church in which he wished to hold influential and lucrative offices. His stance at the time was doubly tantamount to treason as he not only denied the rights of the Queen but was suspected of turning the clock of the Reformation back to the doctrinal days of the papists. This indeed was the opinion of Dr William Whitaker, author of the *Lambeth Articles*, whose Calvinism and allegiance to the Reformation has never been doubted. Whitaker remained a friend of Cartwright's, though disagreeing with him on many issues, where he felt Cartwright was still too near Rome. Perhaps Whitaker's fears in relation to Cartwright were based on the alternative church hierarchy with which Cartwright wished to replace the rather simpler and more practical Anglican system. In fact, this matter was the one great weakness of the Presbyterian/Separatist opposition. They could not agree in any practical way on the matter of church offices although they all thought that bishops should go. Cartwright and his fellow Presbyterians, however, put the brake on any further concessions which the Anglicans might have allowed them by arguing that their bread-givers were heretics and that heretics, even after repenting and returning to the true faith must be put to death. This gave the Anglicans some foretaste of what would probably happen if Presbyterianism, which they viewed as an entirely political force, should one day oust the Anglicans. This fear made some Anglicans less tolerant.[1]

Nevertheless, if one examines how Cartwright was treated by the Anglican Puritans in relation to the way his fellow Presbyterians and Separatists criticised his writings and his doctrines, it is no wonder that Cartwright confessed his closer allegiance to the former and not the latter. The Reformed Anglicans had suffered religious persecution themselves under Mary and had had enough of it. Indeed, if we compare Cartwright's case with that of the ejected clergy, when Cartwright's earlier politics and views of the ministry were eventually supported by Parliament, Cartwright was treated in a most brotherly, exemplary way. The Anglican Calvinists fared much worse under the Anti-Episcopalians of the Revolution. Moreover, though Whitgift is quite unjustly branded as the one who persecuted Cartwright, he was actually the one who protected and even befriended him. The evidence of this is too overwhelming to be brushed aside by the naive party-policy of saying Anglicanism is bad, Presbyterianism is good. In 1591 when Cartwright refused to take the Oath of Allegiance, Whitgift intervened on his behalf and at the risk of being thought unpatriotic himself used his influence to gain Cartwright's release from the Fleet prison where he had been awaiting trial. The Queen was furious at Whitgift's intervention and even the Presbyterian Puritans hypocritically attacked Whitgift on the grounds that he was openly challenging the Queen's powers – powers which they, themselves, were continually questioning, though usually in a more clandestine way.[2]

---

[1] See Robert L. Ottley's book *Lancelot Andrewes* for an excellent, balanced account of the differences between the Anglican and Presbyterian Puritans. This author greatly respects the life and work of Lancelot Andrewes, a key figure in the development of the Reformed Church of England. Andrewes just missed being included in this work because of his 'churchiness' which this author does not share but does not condemn.

[2] See Dudley Fenner's *Counter-poyson*. It is interesting to note that Fenner complains that the Anglicans are so stubborn in defending 'a few trifling ceremonies' yet he is equally guilty of such apparent stubborness. Why was he prepared to split the church on matters which he considered mere trifles? See Neal, *History of the Puritans*, vol.i, pp. 316-317 and McGinn's *John Penry and the Marprelate Controversy*, p. 41 ff.

Using coals of fire as coals of grace

Whitgift made sure that Cartwright received a teaching post and financial security, the two men exchanged visits and letters until Cartwright, overcome with a sense of Whitgift's kindness, confessed that he had been treated far better than he could have expected, was sorry for the schism which he had instigated and ought to have conformed.[1] This is one of the many beautiful features of Cartwright's honest character; he was able to confess when he was in the wrong.[2] When Cartwright wrote this confession just one of his several posts as hospital chaplain was bringing him in £100 per annum and both Thomas Fuller and Isaak Walton tell us that he had grown rich. Indeed, towards the end of his life, we find Cartwright urging conformity to the Church of England and submission to its episcopacy on the grounds that otherwise the Dissenter will be separating himself from the Church of Christ.[3] All this is a further example of Sir Henry Wotton's summing up of Whitgift as one who 'by lowliness of spirit did flourish in highest examples of Virtue.'[4] Seen practically and tactically, Whitgift was master of the art of using 'coals of fire' which his friends called his 'coals of grace'. Perhaps the best epitaph given Cartwright was that of Thomas Fuller who wrote:

> No English Champion in that Age, did with more Valour or Successe, charge and rout the Romish Enemy in matters of Doctrine. But when that Adversary sometimes was not in the field, then his active spirit fell foul in point of Discipline, with those which otherwise were of his own Religion.[5]

Whitgift's reforms and how they were received

Notwithstanding the Queen's occasional signs of displeasure at Whitgift's Reformed views, he received a number of ecclesiastical and university appointments in swift succession and was ordained as Bishop of Worcester in April, 1577. Indeed, the Queen made her opinion known that Whitgift should take over the Archbishopric of Canterbury as the present occu-

---

[1] Original sources and quotes are given in *Bibliographia Evangelica*, vol.ii. See entries for Whitgift and Whitaker.

[2] See Erasmus Middleton's lovely biography of Cartwright in his *Bibliographia Evangelica*.

[3] See above, also Donald J. McGinn, *John Penry and the Marprelate Controversy*, pp. 29-33.

[4] See *Life of Mr. Richard Hooker* in Isaak Walton's *Lives* where Whitgift and Cartwright are discussed.

[5] *The Church History of Britain*, XVII. Cent. IX. Book, p. 943 (or 3 of instalment).

pant, Edmund Grindal had asked to be relieved of his post due to failing health. Whitgift, however, refused to consider the post as long as his friend was alive. After Grindal's death in 1583, Whitgift succeeded him. One of the first things he did on becoming Archbishop was to call various conferences with those Puritans who were campaigning for fundamental changes in the structure, discipline and doctrines of the church. Middleton tells us that this gesture of tolerance even brought with it threats on his life from the opposition. Whitgift's next move was to see that the many bishops' seats which had been left vacant after the ejection of the papists were filled by Reformed men. Whitgift strove to see that tithes were given to the people for whom they were designed i.e. to help support ministers, rather than find their way into patrons' pockets. He also campaigned for the abolishment of the royal practice of forcing clergymen to supply arms in time of warfare. He also saw to it that fees charged in ecclesiastical courts should be lowered and that the proposed bill for having 12 laymen decide over the suitability of ministers should be stopped. Whitgift also campaigned for more care for the sick and the poor and had the largest hospitals ever known in Britain built. Whitgift, who was now a member of the Privy Council, went on to deal with the cathedral churches in the land which had been the most Romanist in their principles and practice and had them conform to the doctrines and discipline of the Reformation.

Whitgift's less popular interventions were concerning the freedom of the press as he was for some form of state and ecclesiastical censure. This move caused protests because the Archbishop was not strict enough and protests that he was too strict. One bill that Whitgift asked the Queen to oppose has left history wondering what he was thinking at the time. This was the bill that ministers should be allowed to marry at whatever time of the year they wanted. Whitgift also lost some popularity on the Non-Conformist side by condemning those who had put Mary Queen of Scots to death without the consent of the Sovereign. A further matter which angered the Non-Conformist party was that Whitgift allowed certain popish books to be imported for reasons of research and so that Romanism might be refuted more knowledgeably. The Presbyterians made a great mountain out of this molehill but when Dr Reynolds (who never could make up his mind whether he was a Presbyterian or an Episcopalian and died a bishop) complained to the King concerning such imports, his Majesty told him, 'There is no such licentious divulging of those books, and none have Liberty, by Authority, to buy them, except such as Dr Reynolds, who was supposed would confute them.'[1]

---

[1] See text of Hampton Court Conference 1603-4 in Fuller's *Church History of Britain*, XVII. Cent. X. Book.

Foreign ecclesiastical interference in Britain

Whitgift was not only criticised by Arminians and Non-Conformists from within his fellowship but also from a few Continental Presbyterians who had developed their ideas of church government beyond Calvin. Theodore Beza (1519-1605), Calvin's successor at Geneva, with whom Whitgift had been on most amiable terms and had shown him many gestures of kindness, now began to interfere in English church matters, urging Anglicans to abandon their bishops and deacons and appoint elders in their place. Indeed, the idea of 'forraigne Presbytery' was seen by many in England as a political threat which strove to dismantle its independence from foreign powers, i.e. Rome, so newly won. As Geneva itself was threatened with being overrun by the popish powers at the time, it was taken for granted by many that Presbyterianism led back to popery. Now Whitgift, Richard Bancroft (1544-1610), Adrian Saravia (1531-1613) and others took up their pens to protest at this foreign interference. Saravia, a refugee both from Continental Roman Catholicism and a too rigid, High Church Presbyterianism, told Beza that he shared fellowship with the Reformed Church of England as it was free of foreign tyranny and had its Episcopalian roots deep in Scripture.

The Martin Marprelate controversy

A different cry, however was raised by the notorious Martin Marprelate Tracts. These claimed that the devil and all his works were attached to the name of 'bishop' thus the Anglicans must rid themselves quickly of all 'that depend upon that ungodly and tyrannous hierachie of Lord Byshops, together with their government.'[1] Martin Marprelate, whoever he was, made it clear that his Presbyterians wanted their own way of worshipping. He also made it very clear that he did not mean to give different minded people the same rights. The relative tolerance of the Episcopalians was to be countered by absolute dogmatic intolerance. Whitgift's policy was quite different. He strove very hard to live at peace with all sections of the Reformation. This was his *via media*, which was certainly not, as wrongly represented by modern hard-shell Presbyterians, a mixture of Calvinism and Arminianism. When he heard, for instance, that Beza's Geneva was in financial trouble, and was in danger of being absorbed into the surrounding papist states, being full of thankfulness to God for all that the city had stood for during the Reformation, Whitgift determined that its testimony should remain. He therefore took a large sum of money out of his own purse and moved his church to donate equally substantial sums of money

---

[1] McGinn, p. 168.

for the upkeep of the Reformed stronghold which was now threatened for theological, political and financial reasons with losing its identity. Thus Episcopalian tolerance and brotherly care helped to save Geneva as a Presbyterian stronghold.

Anglican discipline and Anglican doctrine

To counteract the short-sighted bickering in the churches which seemed to revolve around anything but strong Reformed doctrine, Whitgift commissioned Bancroft to write his *Survey of Discipline* (1592) and Whitaker to draw up the *Lambeth Articles* (1595). Thus it was plain to all but the most fanatic marprelates that a church could be ministered by bishops and yet shun the world the flesh and the devil and believe in doctrines that both Peter and Paul were proud of. For a time, criticism of Whitgift's doctrines seemed to wane but those who have a will to criticise will always find a way. Whitgift had been instrumental in performing so many charitable works for the sick and the poor that evil tongues proclaimed that he must be rolling in money as he was able to afford all this. Niggardly as they were themselves, they reasoned that Whitgift would only have given a fraction of his money to charity, keeping the rest for his own pleasure. This caused Whitgift to produce a financial statement of his entire income, purchases and charities since becoming a bishop years earlier.

The death of the Queen and the Archbishop

The Queen had always thought highly of Whitgift and seemed to secretly admire him for being one of the few men in her kingdom who could stand up to her. She thus looked to the Archbishop for spiritual comfort in her last illness during which Whitgift helped her to meet her Maker. Whitgift's own home-call was, however, not far away. The last official duty he performed was to sit at the Hampton Court Conference held from January 14-16,[1] 1603-4 (O.S.), though in bad health. This conference brought a few minor changes to the forms of worship including a passage forbidding baptism by the laity[2] and the word 'examination' being added to the passage on confirmation. Historians are completely divided as to who called the conference, some saying it was the Archbishop, some the King, some the Dean of Chester and others the lower political powers. Its main finding, however, and the crowning act of Whitgift's term of office was the plan conceived to have the Bible translated into an Authorised Version.

---

[1] Fuller gives January as the month but Middleton July.

[2] Here Whitgift took the side of the Puritans which seemed too 'high church' for many Anglicans.

Whitgift, now seventy-three and obviously at eternity's door, determined to die in harness, travelling up and down the Thames in a barge, meeting with various bishops and churchmen in preparation for the coming Parliament. Rumours were already rife, suggesting it would be a Parliament in which King, country and church would be severely tested by revolutionary ideas. It is obvious that Whitgift dreaded what that parliament might bring but the severe cold he caught from his winter river journeys, turned into his final illness and he never lived to see Parliament reopen. Whilst meeting with the King and the bishops, he became paralysed down his right side and lost his powers of speech. The King told Whitgift that he was praying for him and if God spared his life it would be the greatest blessing to the kingdom. The Archbishop strove to speak but the only words which could be understood were *'pro ecclesia Dei'* (for the church of God). He then tried to write down his last words to the King but could not grasp the pen. The next day, February 4, 1604, John Whitgift whom Thomas Fuller described as 'one of the worthiest men that ever the English Hierarchy did enjoy', went to be with his God.

LAMBETH PALACE

4. William Whitaker (1547-1595): Author of the *Lambeth Articles*

Great intellectual abilities soon demonstrated

William Whitaker was born in 1547 in Holme, Bournley, Lancaster, in the family's ancestral home. He spent his early school years at Bournley but moved to London at the age of thirteen to enter St Paul's School and board at his Uncle Alex's home at the Deanery of St Paul's Cathedral. William matriculated at Trinity College, Cambridge at the age of eighteen and was put under the tutorship of a Mr West. Here, his favourite reading included the works of Bishop Jewel which he translated into Latin to gain a more practical knowledge of that language. William speedily took his B.A. and M.A. degrees and though still very young was appointed Professor of Philosophy because of the outstanding academic reputation he had already gained.

Now William left studying Plato and Aristotle in the original language, becoming more and more interested in New Testament Greek. He read his Bible diligently and studied the works of sound theologians until well into the night. He quickly gained his B.D. and began to publish highly evangelical Reformed works and catechetical material for the students. At this time, he formed a close friendship with Anglican Puritan John Whitgift, then Regius Professor of Divinity. Whitaker was speedily recognised as a man whose academic abilities measured up to his strong personal and experimental faith and was thus of immense value to the Reformed and Protestant testimony of the university. Whenever theological and doctrinal topics were aired in university debates, Whitaker was the man chosen to represent his college. When Dr Chaderton resigned from his post as Professor of Divinity and President of Queen's College after becoming a bishop, Whitaker was chosen before all the older candidates as the man to replace him. Those who thought that Whitaker was far too young for the post soon confessed that the best man had indeed been chosen.

The new President of Queen's College now began a series of expository lectures on Luke, proceeding to Galatians and then on to the Pastoral Epistles. This must be emphasised as modern critics of the Anglican Puritans stress that they revered the Old Testament more than the New. Whitaker did not neglect the Old but used it, as in his series on The Song of Solomon to present the New Testament story as the fulfilment of the Old.

Whitaker soon recognised as a pillar of the Reformation

During the 1580s, Whitaker had to leave much of his expositional research to dispute with the papists, in particular the Jesuits, who were striving to undermine the doctrines of the 'Old Religion' and the 'Old Paths' which had been brought back into right focus. So successful was Whitaker that he was declared one of the pillars of the Reformation and Rome's most distinguished opponent. Whitaker was made a Doctor of Divinity in 1582 and from that year on into the 90s, he published works against such papists as Edmund Campian and Nicholas Saunders. This prepared Whitaker for his great debate with Robert François Romulus Bellarmine (1542-1621), nephew of Pope Marcellus II. who claimed absolute spiritual and temporal powers for the papacy. Indeed, Bellarmine's novel ideas revealed in his *Disputationes de Controversius Christianæ Fidei* (1581-93) show how modern Rome has her roots in Bellarmine's theories rather than the 'Old Religion' that grew from Biblical roots. Whitaker dealt with Bellarmine's innovations one by one showing the political and sectarian nature of an institution which called itself 'the true visible church' though it lacked true visible Christianity. The story goes that when the Jesuits last century collected Bellarmine's papers in their efforts to find evidence to promote his beatification, they came across his autobiography printed in 1761 which revealed such an un-saintly character that they strove to destroy all copies so as not to spoil the picture of the 'saint' which they wished to place before the pope.

It is interesting to note that Whitaker had criticised the immorality of the Roman clergy and their warped views of matrimony. Those papists who wrote against Whitaker countered his criticisms my denouncing Whitaker as an immoral minister of the gospel because he was married! It seems that Rome always comforts her moral conscience with the idea that an unwed fornicator who calls himself 'priest' is more acceptable than a morally chaste married clergyman.

A summary of the reformed faith

In 1595 John Whitgift, now Archbishop of Canterbury, called Whitaker to his assistance along with the Bishop of London, Richard Bancroft, the Bishop of Bangor, Richard Vaughan and the Bishop of Ely, Humphrey Tindal. These and various other university men and Queen Elizabeth's own spiritual advisors, drew up a summary of the faith taught by the Reformed Church of England which was to be used as a standard in the university for judging the eligibility of candidates for the preaching and teaching ministries. Thomas Fuller reproduces this list in his *The Church History of Britain* also quoting a letter from the Archbishop declaring that the Articles recorded below represented the faith of the Church of England which was also established by law:

1. God, from eternity, hath predestined certain men unto life: certain men he hath reprobated unto death.
2. The moving or efficient cause of predestination unto life is not the foresight of faith, or of perseverance, or of good works, or of any thing that is in the persons predestinated: but only the good will and pleasure of God.
3. There is pre-determined a certain number of the predestinated, which can neither be augmented, nor diminished.
4. Those who are not predestinated to salvation shall necessarily be damned for their sins.
5. A true, living, and justifying faith, and the Spirit of God justifying, is not extinguished, falleth not away, vanisheth not away, in the elect, either finally or totally.
6. A man truly faithful, that is, such a man who is endued with justifying faith, is certain, with the full assurance of faith of the remission of his sins, and of his everlasting salvation by Christ.
7. Saving grace is not given, is not communicated, is not granted to all men, by which they may be saved if they will.
8. No man can come unto Christ, except it shall be given unto him, and unless the Father shall draw him: and all men are not drawn by the Father, that they may come to the Son.
9. It is not in the will or power of every one to be saved.[1]

After these tenets were drawn up by the Archbishop of Canterbury, his colleague Matthew Hutton, Archbishop of York, 'did also fully and freely in his judgement Concurr with these Divines' as witnessed by the Latin letter Fuller gives as evidence.

---

[1] XVI. Cent. IX Book.

The significance of these doctrines
The drawing up of this summary of Christian doctrine is of great historical and doctrinal relevance as:

a. It proves that the Reformed Church of England during the reign of Elizabeth was indeed Reformed in its ministry, administration and teaching and second to none as a true gospel church.

b. It served to clarify the true meaning of the *Thirty-Nine Articles* when a few vociferous High Church critics from both the Anglo-Catholic and Presbyterian/Separatist sides were each striving to find Roman teaching in such gloriously Reformed Articles as Articles X, XI and XVII.

c. It demonstrated that the Reformation in England was now at its peak. Members of all ranks and callings had come together to set out their faith without any let or hindrance from the secular arm, indeed, without the secular powers having anything to do with the church's decisions. Both the Synod of Dort and the Westminster Assembly were called at the instigation of the secular powers-that-be, but this conference was purely church-organised and church centred. Sadly, however, this was the last time that a national church in England was to possess and exercise that freedom.

d. No other national church or major denomination in England was to make a statement of faith on its own initiative which was so fundamentally Reformed in the sense known as High Calvinism. The Irish following Usher's leadership produced a fine statement of faith in 1615 which was in use up to the papist and Presbyterian revolution and a number of British Baptist churches were to produce local association declarations of faith of a similar strong Calvinist nature but these sadly never became generally applicable in the denomination.

William Whitaker was attributed with being the spirit and the brain behind these *Nine Articles* which became known as the *Lambeth Articles* because, as Erasmus Middleton says, 'Dr Whitaker drew them up at the palace of Lambeth.' Middleton adds, 'they contain the undoubted sense of our most orthodox church, respecting those important doctrines of predestination, election, perseverance, free-will, assurance, saving faith, efficacious grace, &c..'[1] It is thus no wonder than the *Schaff-Herzog Encyclopaedia of Religious Knowledge*, a work usually most severe in its criticism of Reformed Anglican divines,[2] yet says of Whitaker, 'He was a man of great learning, very staunch in his Protestantism and Calvinism.' It is sad to relate that such is the ignorance of the bulk of the Anglican clergy today that many of their ministers are as completely ignorant of the *Lam-*

---

[1] *Bibliographia Evangelica*, vol. ii, p. 286.

[2] See how the work seeks to destroy Whitegift's testimony heedless of the historical evidence.

beth Articles as they are of Archbishop Usher's fine *Irish Articles* that breathe the same evangelical and Reformed spirit.

Whitaker most assuredly a Puritan

In more modern years, it has become common in Dissenting circles to deny that Whitaker was a Puritan. Martyn-Lloyd Jones' work *The Puritans* does not even mention him.[1] Benjamin Brook, in his famous *Lives of the Puritans* protests strongly against such thinking. In his excellent sketch of Whitaker's life, he writes:

> Some of our historians affirm, that this celebrated divine was
> not a puritan; for which, indeed, they produce very little evidence,
> or rather no substantial evidence whatever. That which is com-
> monly pleaded for evidence in this case, is Dr. Whitaker's letter to
> Dr. Whitgift, in which be gives his sentiments with great freedom,
> concerning Mr.Cartwright and his opinions, as follows:- 'I have
> read,' saith he, 'a great part of that book (Cartwright's second
> *Reply*) which Mr. Cartwright lately published. I pray God I live
> not, if ever I saw anything more loosely and almost more child-
> ishly written. It is true that for words, he hath great store, and
> those both fine and new: but for matter, as far as I can judge, he is
> altogether barren. Moreover, he doth not only think perversely of
> the authority of princes, in causes ecclesiastical, but also flieth
> into the holds of the papists, from whom he would be thought to
> dissent with a mortal hatred. But in this point he is not to be
> endured: and in other parts also he borroweth his arguments from
> the papists. He playeth with words, and is lame in his sentences,
> and is altogether unworthy to be confuted by any man of learn-
> ing.' Our author adds that Dr. Whitaker wrote this letter about the
> time that he began to write against Campian. And what does the
> whole of it prove? It is designed to reproach Mr. Cartwright, his
> book, and his sentiments, and to prove Dr. Whitaker to have been
> no puritan, of which it certainly contains no substantial evidence.
> For, admitting the letter to be genuine, it only contains Dr.
> Whitaker's opinion of Mr. Cartwright and his publication, and no
> evidence either for or against the puritanism of the writer. But
> there is some reason to suspect that the letter is a forgery, and
> devised only to blacken the memory of the puritans. It rests upon
> the sole authority of Dr. Bancroft, one of the bitterest and most

---

[1] *The Puritans*, pp. 255-266.

violent of all their enemies; and is said to have been written near
the time when Dr. Whitaker united with other learned divines in
soliciting Mr. Cartwright to undertake an answer to the Rhemist
translation, in which, among other commendations, they addressed him as follows: 'It is not for every one rashly to be thrust
forth into the Lord's battles; but such captains are to be chosen
from amongst David's worthies, one of which we acknowledge
you to be, by the *former battles undergone for the walls of our
city, the church.* We doubt not, if you will enter this war, but that
you, fighting for conscience and country, will be able to tread
under foot the forces of the Jebusites, which set themselves to
assault the tower of David.'

The former battles which Mr. Cartwright is here said to have
undergone for the walls or discipline of the church, and for which
he received so high a commendation from Dr. Whitaker and his
brethren, were the controversies he had with Dr. Whitgift but
when the same controversies are described by the unworthy pen
of Dr. Bancroft, Dr. Whitaker is made to speak the language of
keen reproach, both of Mr. Cartwright and of his former battles.
How can the two things be reconciled? Shall we conclude that
Whitaker was guilty of such palpable inconsistency? This was
no trait in his character. Did he then completely change his opinion of Cartwright and his controversy, during the short interval of
joining in the address to this divine, and writing the foregoing
letter to Whitgift? This would be contrary to numerous facts, as
will presently appear. Did he address Whitgift, now Archbishop
of Canterbury, merely to flatter him, and procure his favour? He
never lost his favour, and no one was ever less guilty of flattery.[1]

Bancroft's apparent severity did not indicate cruelty

Bancroft (1544-1610) has gained few friends from writers on the Puritans,
whether they refer to the Episcopalian or Presbyterian kind. Thomas Fuller[2]
in his *Church History of Britain*, tells us that Bancroft was seen as a
greater statesman than a divine and a better divine than a preacher. In
Bancroft's defence, however, Fuller says:

> I finde two faults charged on his memory, *Cruelty*, and *Covet-
> ousness, Un-Episcopaliall* qualities, seeing a *Bishop* ought to be

---

[1] *Lives of the Puritans*, vol. ii, p. 78

[2] See Coxon's *Christian Worthies*, vol. ii, p. 238 ff. for a most sympathetic introduction to the life and works of this excellent minister of the gospel and church historian.

godly and *hospitable*. To the first, it is confessed he was most stiffe and stern to presse *Conformity*. And what more usuall than the Offenders to *nick-name* necessary severity to be cruelty? Now though he was a most stout *Champion* to assert *Church Discipline*, let me passe this story to posterity from the mouth of a person therein concerned. An honest and able *Minister* privately protested unto him, That it went against his conscience to conform, being then ready to be deprived: *Which way*, saith the Archbishop, *will you live if put out of your Benefice?* The other answered, *He had no way but to go a begging, and to put himself on Divine Providence. Not that* (saith the Archbishop) *you shall not need to doe; but come to me, and I will take order for your maintanance.* What impression this made on the Minister's judgment, I am not able to report.[1]

Fuller goes on to do away with the other complaints against Bancroft so that one hardly gains the impression that Bancroft was of such a low character as to forge the letter. Such an opinion of Cartwright was expressed by many good men, including Archbishop Whitgift himself.[2] Furthermore, when the Presbyterians came to power they out-bancrofted Bancroft in their severe views on conformity, especially regarding church order and the ordinances.

Life or death equally welcome to the true believer

Whitaker was more used to study than travelling and the journey to London in the middle of winter and the days and nights spent in hard study in large, chilly rooms at the capital left him weak and ill. He returned to Cambridge a dying man but was heard to pray, 'O Lord my God, though thou killest me, yet, I am sure, with these eyes I shall see thee; for in thee do I hope.' On being told that the marks of death were upon him, Whitaker answered, 'Life or death is equally welcome to me, which God pleaseth: But death will be my gain. I desire not to live, but only so far as I may promote the honour of God, and do his church service.' At eight o'clock on Thursday morning, December 4, 1595, Whitaker, aged forty-eight, gained death and eternal glory. Seldom has there been a man of God on this earth who was so well fitted out with intellectual and academic attainments yet lived so humbly and served God so dutifully.

---

[1] X. Book, pp. 996-997 under entry for 1610.

[2] See previous chapter on Whitgift's attitude to Cartwright.

Twenty-one year old Joseph Hall, bishop to come, composed *Hermae*,[1] his first published poem of seventeen stanzas, in memory of William Whitaker of whom he said, 'Never man saw him without reverence, nor heard him without wonder.' Stanza 15 of Hall's tribute to Whitaker reads:

> *Open ye golden gates of Paradise,*
> *Open ye wide vnto a welcome Ghost:*
> *Enter, O Soule, into thy Boure of Blisse,*
> *Through all the throne of Heauens hoast:*
> *Which shall with Triumph gard thee as thou gos't*
> *With Psalmes of Conquest and with crownes of cost.*

Whitaker died a poor man but his College insisted on giving him a state funeral with public dignitaries delivering funeral orations. It would have all been most embarrassing to the deceased but he had been greatly loved by the Church of God, the academic world and the common people. The only thing of value he left behind were his books and manuscripts which Queen Elizabeth and Whitgift purchased for their own libraries. Whitaker's earthly remains were interred in the chapel of St John's College and an ornate plaque set up with the following inscription:

> This Monument is erected
> to the memory of DOCTOR WHITAKER,
> formerly the royal interpreter of Scripture
> His interpretations were adorned with elegance of lan-
> guage; his judgment was acute,
> his method beautiful,
> his memory strong,
> his labours and perseverance invincible,
> and his life most holy.
> With these very rare endowments of mind,
> his candour, virtue, and humility,
> shone with the greatest splendour.
> He was a prudent Master of this College
> more than eight years,
> being a firm defender of all that was right,
> and an avenger of whatever was wrong.

---

[1] A four-cornered pillar. See the *Collected Poems of Joseph Hall*, ed. A. Davenport, Liverpool, 1949, p. 4.

.

JOHN DAVENANT (1572-1641)

5. Bishop John Davenant (1572-1641): The Jewel of the Church

The faded reputation of the greatest theologian since Augustine
In this chapter, I would like to deal briefly with the life and works of Bishop John Davenant once widely called the Jewel of the Reformed Churches for his sound preaching, teaching and doctrinal works. Archbishop Usher, no mean theologian himself and a close friend of Davenant's, voiced the opinion that he was the greatest theologian since Augustine. Sadly, Davenant's reputation has faded due to the present negative historical reassessment of the English Reformers and the Canons of Dort taking place in nominal Reformed churches. Davenant played a major part in establishing the Biblical doctrines of grace as the fundamental belief of the Established Church. This fact needs to be stressed today as amongst Presbyterians especially, there is a dire lack of knowledge concerning the Reformed Church of England before the introduction of Arminianism by William Laud who was executed for high treason in 1644. This lack of knowledge is sadly shared by the Post-Restoration Church of England who has seemingly little time for Davenant's doctrines. Instead, they mistakenly apply his emphasis on Calvinism before Calvin, and his tracing of doctrines back through Augustine to Biblical times, to their views of High Church hierarchical ecumenical succession on the weak grounds that Davenant was fully convinced of the original nature and utility of Anglican orders in governing the church. One must ask what the one has to do with the other. Davenant was an ecumenist as nearly all the delegates at Dort were, but this was an ecumenism based on the unity of the churches around the Bible, the *Belgic Confession*, the *Heidelberger Catechism*, the *Lambeth Articles*, the *Thirty-Nine Articles* and the canons they worked out at Dort. Davenant's teaching has blessed my own soul more than any

other works bar Cowper's, Gill's and Hervey's and I find in it not only the clearly defined Five Points of Calvinism but the entire orthodox teaching reflected in the churches since the days of the apostles. This is highly refreshing today when one could easily gain the impression from reading many modern Reformed writings that Christianity can only be traced back to the Reformation before which there had been no orthodox witness since New Testament times.

One who behaved well in controversy

Davenant, too, is an example to me of one who behaved well in controversy. I certainly am not of the High Church opinions of Davenant's biographer Morris Fuller, though I would sympathise with him in wishing to retain the term Catholic to define true Christian orthodoxy, as used by John Gill and many non-Anglican divines, but his description of Davenant is entirely just:

> Few men appear to have been more honoured and venerated by all parties than Bishop Davenant. In all the works of friends and opponents, there is not to be found a single sentence approaching even to disrespect, much less anything that can tend to cast the slightest reflection upon his deportment in any measure of his public and private life. His profound learning, acuteness of intellect, Catholic spirit, active benevolence, and meekness, are constantly adverted to; and the phrases, 'the good Bishop Davenant', 'the excellent Bishop Davenant', 'the learned Bishop Davenant', &c., are the usual appendages to his name, even in the writings of those who took up the pen in express hostility to certain of their theological views.[1]

One who was sound in his exposition

Charles Haddon Spurgeon had always an eye for a good, sound Biblical expositor and he says of Davenant's *Exposition of Colossians*, apparently quoting Charles Bridges, 'I know no exposition upon a detached portion of Scripture (with the single exception of Owen on the Hebrews) that will compare with it in all points. Leighton is superior in sweetness, but far inferior in depth, accuracy, and discursiveness.' Needless to say, Spurgeon thus gave Davenant the maximum number of stars in his method of grading the usefulness of commentaries.[2]

---

[1] *Life and Writings of Davenant*, p. 5.

[2] *Commentating and Commentaries*, p. 165.

Feeding on the doctrines of grace with his mother's milk

John Davenant was born in Watling Street, London on May 20, 1572 into a family proud of their ancient lineage and achievements but careful to give God all the glory for such privileges. John's father of the same name was a prosperous City of London merchant and a man of great learning, renowned for his mathematical skills and fluency in the Greek and Latin languages. He was said to start each day between four and five in the morning, studying until seven before going about his occupational business. Our subject's mother, Joan Davenant, daughter of John Tryer of Clare in Suffolk, gave birth to him after only seven months' pregnancy. The Davenants had three elder sons, Edward, William and James and two daughters, Judith and Margaret. It is said that John sucked in the doctrines of grace with his mother's milk and from that time 'lived moved and had his being' in them.

Davenant's education

John learned mathematics and the classical languages from his father and attended Merchant Taylors School as a day scholar in accordance with family tradition. On July 4, 1587, he entered Queen Margaret's College, Cambridge (usually called merely Queen's),[1] as a pensioner,[2] little knowing that he would eventually take over the chair formerly held by Erasmus.[3] The President of the college at that time was Humphrey Tyndall and there were around 230 scholars, including tutors, making the college one of the largest at Cambridge. Fuller, the church historian and Davenant's nephew estimated the total number of students at around 300. Davenant enjoyed excellent tuition by godly men in Classical and Biblical languages, Logic, Ethics, Rhetoric, History, Mathematics, Science, Law, Politics and Divinity. He completed this seven years' Liberal Arts course in three and a half years and after subscribing to the *Thirty-Nine Articles*, took his B.A. degree with the highest credits in Lent 1590 when still only eighteen years of age. From then onwards, Davenant's progress both in church and academic life was swift. He received his M.A. in 1594 and became a Fellow of Queen's College in 1598. Actually, he had been offered this position some eight years before but had not accepted it because of his sturdy financial

---

[1] Margaret of Anjou, wife of Henry VI. Although Margaret started the building, it was Elizabeth, wife of Edward IV who had it completed.

[2] One who is not on a scholarship but pays his own way.

[3] Erasmus' biographer Ephraim Emerton questions this traditional view, suggesting that Erasmus never actually filled this chair. See his *Desiderius Erasmus of Rotterdam*, G. P. Putnam's Sons, 1899.

circumstances at the time. His father insisted that such fellowships ought to go to scholars who could not afford to pay their own way so Davenant refrained from accepting the fellowship out of respect for his father until his funds reached a much lower ebb. Davenant was ordained a minister of the Church of England in 1597 and between then and 1601 received the posts of Examinator, Lector Gaecus and Decanus Sacelli at the university. He became Rector of Leake in Nottinghamshire around 1601 but soon gave up the living for an ordinary vicarship. In 1609 he took his Doctor of Divinity and in the same year became Lady Margaret Professor of Divinity.[1] He was made President of Queen's College in 1614. During his Professorship, Davenant gained international reputation through his commentaries, works on righteousness, justification and God's eternal decrees.

James I's part in the setting up of the Synod of Dort

In 1618, Davenant, three other Anglicans and a representative of the Church of Scotland were selected by King James I to represent the British churches at the Synod of Dort. The calling of such a synod to discuss the doctrinal problems of the day, prompted by the international threat of Arminianism had long been the wish of the King who had read his fill of Vorstius one of the Continent's Arch-Arminians. Supported by Archbishop Abbot, he begged the European universities not to accept such people into their professorships and contacted the European nobility and church dignitaries of the Continental Protestant churches, pressing for an ecumenical action which would define once and for all the Reformed Christian faith. James even threatened to break fellowship with the Dutch should they introduce Arminianism into their universities and told them he would not only prevent the British from studying at such infected places as Leyden but consult all the Reformed churches, encouraging them to stay firm against Arminianism. James looked on askance at the States General who, in an effort to appear tolerant of Arminianism, were even persecuting those of the Reformed faith.

James found a co-operative ally in Maurice, Prince of Orange, Head of the United Provinces, and soon steps were taken by the States General to call a National Synod of the Belgic churches only but this idea was soon dropped in favour of an international synod of all Reformed churches, chiefly through pressure put on them by King James backed by Prince Maurice. Eventually, delegates from the Belgic churches, Great Britain, the Palatine (Pfalz), Brandenburg, Hessen, Zürich, Berne, Schaffhausen, Geneva, Bremen and Emden were invited. The French Reformed Church pre-

---

[1] Founded 1502 by Lady Margaret mother of Henry VII.

pared to send a delegation but were stopped by their Roman Catholic king. This was an act of grace on God's part as the French Protestant churches were greatly split on the Amyraldian issue at the time which might have led them to urge for compromise with the Arminians.

The British Episcopalians at Dort highly respected

The British delegates were George Carleton, Bishop of Llandaff; Joseph Hall, Dean of Worcester; John Davenant, Margaret Professor of Divinity; Samuel Ward, Archdeacon of Taunton and also Professor at Cambridge; and Walter Balcanqual representing the Church of Scotland. Dr Hall became ill during the debates and had to return home. He was replaced by Dr Thomas Goad, Chaplain to Archbishop Abbot. Samuel Miller of Princeton, a Presbyterian, emphasises the strong Calvinistic doctrines of these Anglicans and expresses the opinion that the 1595 *Lambeth Articles* 'are acknowledged by all who ever read them, to be among the most strongly marked Calvinistical compositions that ever were penned.' These articles were designed as a summary of the *Thirty-Nine Articles* and *Homilies* of the Church of England and accepted by both Archbishop Whitgift of Canterbury and Archbishop Hunter of York as representing the teaching of their church. They certainly reflect the theology of the five British delegates to Dort. Miller argues that the presence of the British Episcopalian delegates was, 'a practical recognition, of the strongest kind, of the Presbyterian Church, as a true Church of Christ; and demonstrated that the great and learned and good men who directed the counsels of the Church of England at that time, never thought of denying, either in word or act, her just claim to this character.' [1] This judgement is perfectly true as the British delegates put belief in the doctrines of grace before external practices of church functionaries, order and dress. Thus more is the pity that when, heavily backed by a revolutionary military government, those British Presbyterians who had been treated so brotherly by their Episcopalian brethren, fought for a total dismantling of the Church of England, forcing their very brethren who put doctrine before fashion at Dort to be denounced, thrown out of their churches and even persecuted to the death.

We trust that Dr Miller was also aware that, at first, the British delegates were rather apprehensive of how they would be accepted on the Continent, fearing they might have to take a back-seat position because of their ancient stand concerning the function of the bishop. Happily, the European Reformed churches looked upon the British delegates as having

---

[1] See Miller's Introductory Essay to Thomas Scott's *The Articles of the Synod of Dort*, Sprinkle Publications, 1993 reprint.

carried the Reformation even farther than many Continental Reformers both in doctrine and discipline. Indeed, they looked upon the Church of England in envy because she had withstood the impacts of acute Arminianism under which they were suffering. It was explained to the British delegates that episcopacy was their aim but this had been denied them because of the political situation in their countries.[1] Indeed, throughout the synod, the modesty and moderation of the British delegates besides their high spirituality and vast learning gave them a moderating function and Davenant was asked to mediate between the various minor conflicts which cropped up during the synod and in the follow-up work. John Bogerman, who presided, was delighted to have Davenant advise him, especially on church history and law. The very fact that Davenant was termed 'the pillar of the Synod' speaks volumes for his importance during the synod and shows how weak-founded is the present day criticism from Presbyterian quarters that the British delegates played a very minor role in the Dortian debates.

British strategy at Dort
Archbishop Abbot, Davenant tells us, briefed the delegates on their appointment, advising them to brush up their Latin and practise it intensively as the debates would be held in that language. The five were also told to always discuss the proposed agenda before entering the debates and arrive at a conclusion which they could present unanimously. If any point should be raised in a debate which they had not expected, they should reserve judgement until they had time to discuss it privately with one another. They should also make sure that the findings should be put into a suitable language to be given from the pulpit. They were advised to introduce no novelties but keep to the old confessions and particularly not to put forward views contrary to the Anglican articles. The Archbishop, however, told them that there was no objection at all in their taking part in the worship of sister Reformed churches and conforming to their order and discipline. The delegates were then advised to seek for peaceful solutions, referee where necessary, seeking God's glory in all and conduct themselves as befitted their calling and station. The King then invited Davenant and Ward to discuss matters further with him and, after a two hour talk, dismissed them with the words, 'May God bless your endeavours.'

---

[1] See Morris Fuller's *Life and Writings of Davenant*, p. 88 and his quotes from Collier and Carleton. Also the statement to this effect signed by the British delegates and quoted in full by Fuller on pages 99-107.

The British delegates soon found that though the majority at the synod held to the Sublapsarian view of election, i.e. that God had saved some of those damned by their own sin and passed by others, there were a few Supralapsarians such as Gomarus who insisted that God had predestinated man to sin and often lost his temper with his Arminian opponents. George Carlton reminded Gomarus to speak with charity and moderation and defended Article Seventeen on Predestination and Election against Gomarus criticism. He no doubt would have told Gomarus, who was, by the way, most un-Calvinist[1] in his theology, that the parts of the Seventeenth Article to which he most objected were taken verbatim from Calvin's *Institutes*. Davenant had to resist a number of Dutchmen strongly on the *Second Head of Doctrine* concerning the death of Christ and redemption. In fact, if it were not for Davenant's intervention here, the Five Points of Calvinism might well have been reduced to Four.[2]

The Five Points of Calvinism

The outcome of the synod was that five 'heads of doctrine' were agreed upon which refuted the Five Points of Arminius respecting his darling heresies free will, conditional election, universal atonement, resistible grace and the uncertainty of a believer's salvation. These became known as the Five Points of Calvinism which were originally 1. Of Divine Predestination; 2. Of the Death of Christ and the Redemption of Men Thereby; 3-4. (taken up under one heading) Of the Corruption of man, His Conversion to God, and the Manner thereof; 5. Of the Perseverance of the Saints. These points have been traditionally summed up in the initials T.U.L.I.P, i.e. total depravity, unconditional election, limited atonement, irresistible grace and the perseverance of the saints. It is interesting to note that these doctrines have received the name of Calvinism, though John Calvin is nowhere mentioned in relation to them in the *Canons of Dort*. Indeed, although the Reformer undoubtedly believed them and re-emphasised them, the delegates of Dort were careful to show that they had been the belief of the orthodox church since the apostles taught them and the Canons of Scripture were drawn up. Thus, when William Cowper replied to his young relation, John Johnson who was about to study theology and had asked Cowper for advice, the poet said, after discussing his curriculum:

---

[1] Gomarus is viewed by history as a Hyper-Calvinist but this term is a misnomer as if any one is more hyper than Calvin, he obviously cannot be called a Calvinist.

[2] Personally, I hold Article 3 of the *Second Head* to be perfectly understandable when the synod's *Rejections 1-7* accompanying it are taken into account. Left on its own, however, which is invariably the case when attacked by anti-Calvinist critics, it is open to misinterpretation.

Life is too short to afford time even for serious trifles. Pursue
what you know to be attainable, make truth your object and your
studies will make you a wise man. Let your Divinity, if I may advise, be the Divinity of the glorious Reformation. I mean in contra-
distinction to Arminianism and all the isms that were ever broached
in this world of error and ignorance. The Divinity of the Reformation is called Calvinism but injuriously; it has been that of the
Church of Christ in all ages; it is the Divinity of St. Paul and of St.
Paul's Master who met him in his way to Damascus.[1]

The various versions of the Synod's findings
Immediately after the *Canons of Dort* were signed, Arminian opposition
published them in various fraudulent forms to make them as obnoxious as
possible. In Britain, such forgeries were legend, this being one of the major
reasons today why few of any side seem to know what they are taking
about when referring to them. The original forgeries have been traced to
Remonstrants Bishop Tomline, Bishop Womack and Dr Peter Heylin, but
anyone nowadays browsing through the Internet will find many very var-
ied and often very false representations of these canons.[2]

Davenant consecrated a bishop under trying circumstances
When Davenant returned to England after a seven months' absence, he
was raised to the bishopric of Salisbury which entailed leaving the university. Samuel Ward, his companion at Dort, took his place on Davenant's
recommendation. On saying good-bye to his old servant, humble Dr
Davenant asked that he would remember his former employer in his prayers
as he was about to enter a sphere of great temptation. Davenant's consecration occurred under two historically important developments in the
Church of England. The first was that the Archbishop of Canterbury, Dr
Abbot, was prevented from performing the ceremony by a commission of
bishops. Abbot had been asked by his friend Lord Zouch whom he was
visiting at the time to join him on a hunt in his grounds. The Archbishop
replied that he was not cut out for a hunter at all and could not even use a
crossbow but his friend insisted and took him to a field where a stag was
at bay, put a crossbow into his hands and told him to have a shot. The
Archbishop fired as best he could and was not surprised to see his arrow

---

[1] Letter written June 7, 1790.

[2] For my personal study I use Dr Thomas Scott's English translation. See also *The
Canons of Dort* reprinted in *The Psalter*, Eeerdmans, 1991 for a more modern rendering.

fail its mark. The surprise changed to horror, however, as the arrow sped on and buried itself in the breast of a keeper, killing him on the spot. Although this was a terrible accident, several bishops felt that a person with blood on his hands could no longer exercise the function of an Arch-bishop.

The second new development, directly relating to Dr Abbot's be-ing removed from office was the part William Laud played in the matter. He, too, was due for consecration to a bishopric and hated Abbot for his staunch Reformed theology. Indeed, Abbot had opposed Laud's election to high office all along on the grounds that he, as an obvious Arminian, was not a true son of the Church of England and the Reformation. Laud now saw his chance of getting even with Abbot, and, using the Archbish-op's plight for his own ends, he protested loudly that he could never be consecrated by a murderer. He became one of the major voices, though not yet a bishop himself, to have Abbot removed from his position by the commission of bishops. Thomas Fuller tells us that Davenant did not share this 'squeamish and nice-conscienced' point of view but Laud's view won the day. Thus one of the finest Reformed ministers of the Church of England was suspended from office and the ascent began of the very person who was to lead the Church of England away from its central doctrines and into the hands of the anti-Anglican Presbyterians and poli-ticians. Sad to say, the pro-Presbyterian ministers in the church, did not support Abbot for the sake of his doctrines and out of an understanding of his predicament but joined the tiny pro-Rome section in the church in wishing to oust him. In this way, they greatly increased opposition to the Reformed Church of England from within and opened the doors for Laud's Arminianising and Amyraldianising of the church.

Davenant's bishopric had been occupied by his brother-in-law Robert Townson, now deceased, who had held the See for less than a year. Townson and his wife Margaret, Davenant's sister, had fifteen children and the new bishop invited the children and their mother to live with him at his palace and promised to keep them under his care. This is perhaps why King James waived the usual fees due to him by a newly installed bishop and advised Davenant that he had better not marry and have a family himself as he already had enough mouths to feed.

Davenant opposed by Presbyterian obsession for details rather than doc-trine
Sadly, although Davenant took great strides to see that Reformation prin-ciples were put into practice and doctrines were taught that would appear

as High or even Hyper-Calvinism to many modern Reformed churches of the 'Modified Calvinism' type, it was the so-called Presbyterian Puritans, in spite of their claims to be Calvinists, who resisted Davenant the most. They protested at every little piece of church furniture and church discipline which they felt, often quite wrongly, was 'popish' instead of supporting their bishop in promoting the doctrines of grace and allowing niceties to be dealt with in their wake. Thus one 'Puritan', Henry Sherfield, took exception to the stained glass windows in Salisbury Cathedral, especially one depicting God creating the earth. He thus used his 'Christian liberty' to smash the window with his stick. When Davenant sent him a mild rebuke, rather than an attorney's order, the vandal threatened that he would not desist until all the cathedral windows were broken. Thus the empty rattle of hooliganism was set up against sound doctrine and church order. Here we see, of course, that the dark shadow of the coming revolution of the Long Parliament, the Fifth Monarchy Men and those who wished for a church government directly instigated by civil law and controlled by the civil magistrates was already falling. Happily for him, Davenant was called home before the shadow-bearer came to power. However, history shows us that God's reforming hands were on the Diocese of Salisbury as, besides Davenant who helped mould the Five Points of Calvinism, such great men of Reformed principles as Reformer John Jewel, Martyrologist John Foxe, hymn-writer George Herbert and church historian Thomas Fuller graced that place.

Combating the three major heresies of the day
Once settled in his new ministry, Davenant continued his writings against Pelagianism, Semi-Pelagianism and Arminianism, not desisting from even addressing the weaknesses he saw in the Reformers themselves. In these undertakings, he was greatly supported by his old friend, Samuel Ward. Writing to Ward on December 9, 1624, Davenant airs his criticism of George Spalatin of Eichstädt, chaplain to Frederick the Wise and one of Luther's closest allies:

> 'Salutem in Christo
> Good Mr Dr Ward,
>
> The opportunity of this bearer, hath made me salute you with these few lines. I have nothing to impart unto you worth the writing; but only to let you understand, that according to your motion I have run over part of the 11th chapter of Spaltensis his 7th

book, wherein he disputes of freewill, & the generality of grace. In my opinion he is as far gone in Pelagianism, as ever was Pelagius himself. In the reading of his discourse, I have set down some cursory animadversions upon such points as I took to be unsound. When God shall grant us our next meeting, we will have further conference upon these matters. In the meantime wishing you health & happiness, I commit you and your labours to the blessing of the Almighty, resting ever
Your assured loving friend
    Decemb. 9, 1624.
        Jo. Sarum'[1]

Spreading three pieces of good news
Almost a year later, we find Davenant corresponding with Ward on the topics of election, predestination and perseverance which had been brought to public note by a Dr Richard Montague who had not only criticised the doctrines of the Synod of Dort but also the British delegates' action there and even argued that Bishop Carleton and the others had undersigned documents that had condemned the discipline of the Church of England. Though Fuller calls him 'a moderate Calvinist', Davenant obviously thought Montague was quite unreformed as he writes:

> Your vindication of those that were at the Synod of Dort, from the rash & and false imputation laid on us by Mr Mountague was a laudable and necessary work I could wish for his own good that he had a more modest conceit of himself, and a less base opinion of all others – who jump not with him in his mongrel opinions. He mightily deceives himself in taking it for granted that Dr Overal,[2] or Bucer, or Luther were ever of his mind in the point of predestination, or falling from grace, the contrary may evidently be shewn out of their writings, but the truth is he never understood what Bucer or Luther mean, when they speak of extinguishing faith or loosing grace and as little does he understand that canon of our church, which he makes his main foundation, whether *reprobus* may be *vere justificatus, verum et vivium membrum sub Christo Capite, vere adoptatus*, I confess may out of Aug: & prosp: be

---

[1] *The Life, Letters and Writings of John Davenant, D. D.*, p. 162. I have modernised the spelling and some punctuation.

[2] Bishop of Norwich who added the gloss to Article XVII on predestination according to the wishes of the Puritans at the Hampton Court Conference and by royal authority.

probably held both ways but yet let all places which seem to imply contradiction about this matter be laid together, and such other as may serve for intrexation be also cast into the balance, and in my opinion it will be found that St. Augustine does more incline to the opinion that only the predestinate attain unto a true estate of justification, regeneration and adoption. But I am called off. I commit you to God and rest always

> Your very loving friend,
> Oct. 10th, 1625
> Jo. Sarum'[1]

In further correspondence, Davenant reveals that he is tackling these problems in his commentary on Colossians and is of the opinion that Luther and Bucer both believed in election and taught that the reprobate could not attain to justification, adoption and sanctification, arguing that Montague's mongrel Calvinism was a direct affront to the tenets of the Church of England. As he is having temporary eye-trouble, he says he is leaving his manuscript in the hands of Ward, for final editing and printing. James Hervey speaks of the finished work with words of great praise. After mentioning Bishops Beveridge, Hopkins and Reynolds as being pillars of sound Anglican doctrine, he says:

> To this illustrious triumvirate, let me join Bishop Davenant, who for his great abilities, and unquestionable integrity, was appointed one of our religious plenipotentiaries at the renowned Synod of Dort. In his very valuable exposition of the epistle to the Colossians,[2] he writes to the effect: 'Ye are complete in Christ. Ye are furnished, in that all-sufficient Redeemer, with whatever is requisite to everlasting salvation. With wisdom, since it is the consummation of this noble endowment, to know Christ, and him crucified. With righteousness; because he has perfectly satisfied the law, and thoroughly expiated our guilt. With sanctification; because his Spirit, dwelling in our hearts, mortifies our corrupt affections, and renews the soul after the image of its Creator.

In a footnote to the above, Hervey adds:

---

[1] *Life, Letters and Writings*, p. 164.

[2] *Exposititio Epistolæ D. Pauli ad Colossenses*, Cambridge, 1627, translated into English London 1831, 2 vols.

Let me beg leave to intimate, that this exposition of the epistle to the Colossians, for perspicuity of style, and accuracy of method, for judgement in discerning, and fidelity in representing the apostles meaning, for strength of argument in refuting errors, and felicity of invention in deducing practical doctrines, tending both to the establishment of faith, and the cultivation of holiness – is, I think, inferior to no writing of the kind; and richly deserves to be read, to be studied, to be imitated by our young divines.[1]

Davenant aids the Gallican Church against the teaching of John Cameron

Davenant's witness and learning had so impressed the Continental churches that he received many pleas for help and advice from a variety of churches. The French Reformed churches or the Gallican churches as history calls them, were prevented by the Roman Catholic Sun King from attending the Synod of Dort. As hinted earlier in this work, the gracious hand of God can be seen in this incident as the Gallican churches were going through a time of inner-controversy, with certain parties arguing staunchly against the very basis of the Reformed faith. These parties had been influenced by a Scotsman named John Cameron who had taught Divinity in Bordeaux and Saumur from around 1600 until his death in 1626 and had also become seriously involved in politics. He introduced a System of Universal Grace in which he sought to unite Calvinism with Arminianism, leaning heavily to the latter and thereby was of strong influence in leading his pupil Moses Amyraut into his Neonomian heresy of a new, less stringent, law for Christians. Cameron became notorious for using orthodox terminology to deceive those with whom he disagreed, only to give those words a completely different meaning when speaking to his followers. One French writer in a tract entitled *On the Controversy, among the French Divines of the Reformed Church, concerning the Gracious and Saving Will of God towards Sinful Men*, argued that the Cameronites were teaching that salvation was guaranteed to all, depending on the will of the sinner who must take the initiative in gaining his own salvation. He protested that he thought 'the opinion of Cameron and his disciples as pure Arminianism, a hydra of errors, opposed to the Synod of Dort, a subversion of the nature of the Divine law, of the Gospel, of the necessity of the Christian religion' and begged the 'opinion of the Divines of England, the most celebrated in the

---

[1] *Theron and Aspasio*, Letter III, *Hervey's Works*, 1837, pp. 329-330.

whole Christian world' on the matter so that peace might be restored to the French churches.

The Judgement of the Synod of Dort on Cameronism and Amyraldianism
It was decided by the leading British churchmen that an answer had to be drafted in terms of the Synod of Dort and that Davenant should be the one to draw it up. So what was initially called *The Judgement of Bishop Davenant* was really *The Judgement of the Synod of Dort*. On taking up the challenge, Davenant quotes Cameron as allegedly saying:

> The gracious and saving will of God towards sinners is to be considered as effectually applying to some persons, of His special mercy, the means of saving grace, according to that saying of the Apostle, He hath mercy on whom He will: or as appointing sufficiently for all. Of His common philanthropy, the means of saving grace, applicable to all for salvation, according to the tenor of the Covenant of grace as the Evangelist has said, *God so loved the world*, etc. Those whom the Divine Will, or good pleasure embraces under the first description, on them it always confers the means of saving grace in this life, and the end of grace, that is life eternal, or glory in the world to come (Rom. 8:28-29 and Eph. 1:3-5 etc.). Those whom the Divine Will embraces only under the latter description, on them it sometimes confers the means of saving grace, and sometimes does not: but it never confers the end of grace, that is, eternal life.

Concerning the first sentence, Davenant argues that Cameron's view is legitimate providing he means that God's sovereign action also determines the will of the sinner. If he does not mean that, he has fallen into Semi-Pelagianism. Concerning the second sentence, Davenant says it is totally confusing, full of ambiguities and a mixture of truths and falsehoods. This sentence, he argues, must be studied piece by piece.

a. The view that Christ died with some general intention for all men
Davenant argues that there are universal benefits of Christ's death according to the common order of Providence as long as man is in this world but it cannot be said that Christ died for each individual savingly and that none is excluded. If anyone rules out God's specific intention and special effectual will in saving His elect and leaves salvation to man's making good use of his own will, this is Semi-Pelagianism indeed. He quotes Aquinas to the extent that 'Whatever God simply wills, He performs.'

b. The view that God's universal grace grants salvation to all men according to their will

Quoting Augustine, Prosper and Fugentius against Pelagius, Davenant protests at the use of the term 'universal grace' and argues that any universal grace to the non-elect only exists in the sense of God's general philanthropy to the world at large and should not be confused with saving grace. It is thus an erroneous and even offensive term, again reflecting Semi-Pelagian thinking.

Davenant will not even accept Cameron's idea that 'God, through this universal grace, by an invitation suitable and sufficient in itself, calls all men to repentance,' arguing that the 'experience of time and the contrary event of things' refute this. 'For if he speaks of repentance, which remission of sins and eternal life follows, that invitation or calling is not apt or sufficient of itself for such repentance, which does not send the penitent to Christ.' Davenant is arguing that when God calls His elect to repentance, He gives them the wherewithal to repent by His sovereign will and that 'an invitation and calling apt and sufficient for saving repentance is not given to all men.' If it were, all men would be saved.

c. The fact that a man is not saved is because of the hardness of his heart

This is true, but it is universally true in that no man, because of the fall can do otherwise than exercise a hardness of heart against the gospel. Davenant, however, adds that there is no hardness in the human heart which God cannot soften if He will and He wills to soften the hearts of all His elect and does so. The bishop obviously interprets Cameron as believing that some men can soften their own hearts.

Davenant therefore concludes that the divines at Dort neither taught universal grace nor acknowledged that 'apt and sufficient means of salvation are granted to all men individually upon whom the Gospel hath not shone.' He allows that there is a general intention or appointment concerning salvation in Christ for those who believe which is in harmony with the fact that 'the absolute and not to be frustrated intention of God, concerning the gift of faith and eternal life to some persons, is special, and is limited to the elect alone.'

The sufficient extent of the Atonement

It was not only the Gallican churches who were threatened by Pelagianism and Amyraldianism but the two sectarian movements in the Anglican Church represented by Bishop Laud on one side and a number of Presbyterian-minded ministers on the other were clambering for new statements concerning the sufficiency and efficacy of the atonement, seeking to revise the *Thirty-Nine Articles* and the *Lambeth Articles* and even denounce the findings of Dort and bring in various forms of Universalism into the churches. Davenant felt called by God to defend the orthodox faith once committed to the saints.

In his *Dissertation on the Death of Christ* written around 1627,[1] Davenant starts by quoting John 6:39-40 'of all which he has given me, I should lose nothing,' and after denouncing Pelagianism, he takes up the idea which a number of his ministerial brethren were propagating 'that Christ died for all sufficiently, but for the elect effectually.' Davenant explains how in terms of salvation, the question is not whether a method is hypothetically sufficient or not but whether God actually accomplishes what He wills to do or not. In God's saving work, 'whatever God simply wills He performs.' Davenant illustrates this with an apt prison illustration:

> Suppose my brother were detained in prison for a debt of a thousand pounds. If I have in my possession so many pounds, I can truly affirm that this money is sufficient to pay the debt of my brother, and to free him from it. But while it is not offered for him, the mere sufficiency of the thing is understood, and estimated only from the value of it, the act of offering that ransom being wanting, without which the aforesaid sufficiency effects nothing. For the same reason, if many persons should be capitally condemned for the crime of high treason, and the king himself, against whom the crime was committed, should agree that he would be reconciled to all for whom his son should think fit to suffer death; now the death of the son, according to the agreement, is appointed to be a sufficient ransom for redeeming all those for whom it should be offered.

After reading this, no one could fairly accuse Davenant of teaching 'hypothetical universalism' as he clearly states,
a. Sufficiency is savingly linked to efficacy not the other way round.
b. All are redeemed for whom Christ thought fit to die and for whom His Sacrifice was sufficient.

God did not equally will the salvation of all men in Christ
In the above dissertation, Davenant takes the Pelagians to task for denying that 'this death of Christ infallibly brings eternal life to certain persons and does not bring it to others.' He continues:

---

[1] Published in Cambridge 1630. Other sources give 1650. One theory is that this work was based on Davenant's college lectures perhaps even pre-dating Dort.

They referred it to the human will as the primary cause of this difference, presuming that God equally willed the salvation of all men in Christ, not by a special decree of predestination, endued some persons with that faith and perseverance through which they should apply to themselves the death of Christ for salvation. On the contrary, Augustine with the orthodox contended that that persevering faith, by means of which the death of Christ brings salvation to individuals, is extended to the elect by a singular gift of mercy, and does not arise from the good use of free will in the one, rather than in the other. Here the controversy directly regards the grace of predestination and free-will, and obliquely touches upon the death of Christ, inasmuch as the orthodox, assigning a reason why it eventually brings salvation to some persons, always ascend to the divine predestination, the Pelagians descend to the human will.

It immediately becomes clear from such teaching that modern views, widely accepted as being Calvinistic, such as 'Hypothetical Universalism', and the so-called 'free offer' based on such universalism, were quite foreign to the findings of the Synod of Dort.

Christ not only pardons but justifies

Smeaton, in his *Atonement According to Christ and His Apostles*, explains how Cameron took over the heretical idea of Johannes Fischer (1546-1625), otherwise known as Piscator, who denied the sufficiency of Christ's active obedience in gaining our justification.[1] Christ's passive death is seen as securing the chance of salvation for all which must be supplemented by the sincere obedience of the believer. One need not read far in Davenant's works to find a total rejection of this error. In his *On the Death of Christ*, he says:

> when we speak of the *death of Christ,* we comprehend in it the whole obedience of Christ, active and passive, the completion of which and as it were the last act, was effected in His death; on which account Divines are accustomed by synecdoche to attribute to His death what relates to His entire obedience. Whatever therefore Christ did, and whatever He suffered, from the cradle to the cross, the whole of the meritorious and satisfactory work of the Redeemer we comprehend in our proposition to be allied to and

[1] Pp. 540-544.

connected with His death. Thus the Apostle in Rom. v. 19 makes *the obedience of Christ* universally considered, the cause of man's salvation. *By the obedience of one shall many be made righteous.* And in Phil. ii. 7, 8, when it is said, *That He humbled Himself and became obedient unto death, even the death of the Cross,* the Apostle does not exclude from His meritorious work any part of the antecedent obedience of Christ, but rather considers it included, and teaches that this meritorious obedience of Christ began at that time when He took the form of a servant, and was consummated when He offered Himself on the cross.

This is the theology that assigns to Christ His entire work, whereas Cameron and Amyraldus preached a work half done.

Davenant's bravery in witnessing to Charles I

Davenant, by the grace of God, was able to maintain his full Christian witness during the Stuart and Laudian persecutions. When Charles I, banned the doctrines of grace from Britain's pulpits, all the ministers connected with the Court and most in the country chose to remain silent or emigrate. Davenant refused to do either, believing that earthly powers must be ruled by God's Word. When called upon to preach before Charles, Davenant chose the topic *Eternall life is the gift of God, through Jesus Christ our Lord* and taught the King the doctrines of election and predestination, explaining what a comfort these doctrines are to one who is under God's saving grace and receives the crown of righteousness. Davenant's Arminian enemies were sure that Davenant's career and life were now at an end. The King sent men to the block for less 'insolence' and summoned Davenant before the Council Table. The Temporal Lords were very courteous to Davenant, begging the kneeling bishop to stand as he was only accused and not condemned. Nevertheless, Archbishop Harsenet of York made a lengthy speech pronouncing Davenant guilty before hearing his defence. Davenant simply explained that he believed all that the King had authorised to be preached according to the *Thirty-Nine Articles* of the Church of England the Seventeenth of which, on *Predestination and Election*, he had faithfully expounded according to the Royal Commission. Historians tell us that, for once in his life, the King's knave and official persecuting agent William Laud was speechless and merely paced angrily up and down as Davenant spoke. How could he condemn a man who believed in the Articles of the church whose minister he was and which the King as Defender of the Faith had authorised and pledged himself on oath to follow? The result was that Davenant's examiners, declared that he had done no wrong, thereupon Davenant requested leave to kiss the King's hand, was granted this and there the matter ended. Davenant dedicated his next book, *A Treatise on Justification* to the King.

Predestined to life and death

Davenant now thought it was high time to publish his views on preaching Predestination and though he normally wrote in Latin, these were issued in English for general circulation. In his *Animadversions* he thus states:

1. It (predestination) serveth to illustrate many of God's attributes, and exceedingly manifesteth those Divine properties which every Christian ought rightly to know and acknowledge, and which they who impugne this doctrine can never acknowledge as is meet.

2. The doctrine of Predestination doth serve to kindle in the hearts of the faithful a most ardent love towards God.

3. This doctrine is a great spurre and encouragement to the study of true godlinesse unto all those who are affected with a lively sense of their election.

4. The fourth use of this doctrine is this, that it is a speciall means to bear down the pride of man, and to beget in him true humility.

5. Fifthly, this orthodox doctrine of Predestination and Reprobation doth arm the faithfull against diffidence, and against all the temptations and assaults of Satan whereby he laboureth to throw them into despair.

6. Sixthly, The consideration of election doth stirre up the faithfull to constancie in prayer.

7. It is manifest when the doctrine of Predestination is rooted in our hearts, it doth exceedingly enable us patiently and meekly to sustein all adversitie.

God decrees absolute, not conditional, salvation

From time to time the old Amyraldian and Arminian claims that Davenant taught conditional salvation and therefore was one of them appear in Christian magazines. In the above work, Davenant answers such errors of judgement by saying:

The sublapsarian way (which Davenant held) of considering this high mystery of Predestination and negative Reprobation, is

the way which the Church of England taketh, as the more easy for
our understanding. And it so walketh in this way, that it maketh
Predestination *an absolute decree* of giving grace and glory unto
the predestinate, and not *a conditionate decree* foreseeing their
gracious actions, and thereupon predestinating them: and by this
it silently teaches what to think of negative Reprobation, which
cannot be severed from Election.

He also says,

If God from eternity absolutely elected some unto the infallible attainment of Grace and Glory, we cannot but grant that those
who are not comprised within the absolute decree are as absolutely passed by as the other are chosen.

and explains, as John Gill later,

... that all God's decrees concerning man's salvation are not
products of a time sequence as Arminius would have it but 'all
things with God abide with an equal infinity of eternity.

As in the case of Hervey, Toplady and Usher, Arminian enemies
rumoured that Davenant rejected his Calvinism during his last years. Hearing this rumour, Davenant made a public declaration that he abided by his
doctrines.

The blessings of afflictions that call a saved sinner home
John Davenant was called home to glory on April 20, 1641 at 71 years of
age, shortly before the notorious Long Parliament began to dismantle the
Church of England. His last months were troubled by asthma and consumption. Davenant had experienced no worries all his life, taking whatever happened patiently as from the hand of God. Even when threatened
with the death penalty he kept entirely serene. Unknown to his friends and
family, however, this fact had exercised him greatly as he had believed that
whom the Lord loves, He chastens, and had often wondered if his carefree
life meant that he was not a true child of God. When affliction eventually
came in the illness which was to end his life, Davenant was overjoyed,
receiving signs of God's deep love for him which he had never experienced
at this depth. Before his home-call, the dying bishop spent many minutes
in a prayer of ecstatic joy, praising God for giving him this last and final

blessing. Davenant's nephew Thomas Fuller, the church historian, was present and tells us that after praying aloud in this way, his uncle 'sweetly fell asleep in Christ, and so we softly draw the curtains about him.'

JOSEPH HALL (1574-1656)

6. Bishop Joseph Hall (1574-1656): Man of Peace

Early instruction in experimental religion and holiness

Joseph Hall was born on July 1, 1574 in Bristow Park, Ashby-de-la-Zouch in Leicestershire. His father was an officer in the service of Lord Huntingdon who had his seat in Hall's town of birth. Joseph's mother Winifride was of the House of Bambridge and he writes of her rare sanctity though she was very frail of body and suffered from deep depressions. Whilst Joseph was still a child, however, she began calmly to take all her sufferings as from God and was given grace to bear them to His honour. In this she was assisted by the ministry of Anthony Gilby who was able to lead her to the saving mercies of Christ. After this experience, she began to instruct her twelve children daily in the paths of experimental religion and Joseph said that it was difficult for anyone to leave his mother's presence without becoming holier. Speaking later in life of his mother's practical divinity, Joseph, now Bishop Hall, says, 'Never any lips have read to me such feeling lectures of piety; never have I known any soul, that more accurately practised them, than her own.'

Joseph's call to the ministry temporarily thwarted

Joseph felt called to become a minister from his childhood on but, after a successful time at the local Grammar School, it seemed that the calling was to be made impossible. His father decided not to send him to university but have him tutored a little longer at home by a local minister. After consultation with Nathaniel Gilby, a fellow of Emmanuel College, Cambridge, Joseph's elder brother pleaded with his father to allow Joseph to continue his education at Emmanuel. His father complained that this would be too expensive as he had fourteen mouths to feed. Joseph's brother bargained unselfishly with his father saying that he could sell off some of the land he was to inherit to pay for Joseph's education. Eventually, Hall Sen. relented and allowed his son to enter Emmanuel but caused Joseph much anxiety as he made it obvious that this was probably a temporary measure until he found a post for his son as master in a Grammar School. Joseph was actually withdrawn from Cambridge two years after matriculating but a friend of the family Edmund Sleigh of Darly pleaded with Joseph's father to send his son back to Emmanuel College, promising to bear half the expenses himself.

Early teaching experience and difficulties in the ministry

Hall gained his B.A. after three years' study. The B.A. was considered a mere preliminary in those days to an M.A. and a B.D. which were necessary to enter the ministry but lack of funds again seemed to close all doors. Hall was thought eligible for a fellowship but his county was already represented by Gilby. Lord Huntingdon now came to the rescue, appointing Gilby as his private chaplain on condition that he gave up his fellowship. Gilby agreed to do so and Hall received his fellowship and was able to complete his studies until 1596 when he took his M.A.. After staying on at college some six years as a lecturer, during which time he gained his B.D., Hall was offered the rectorship of Halsted in Suffolk, which he accepted. There he found a most neglected work and the rectory deserted and in ruins. At Halsted, Hall entered on forty-nine years of happily married life. Otherwise Hall's stay at Halsted was not very happy as the patron, probably angry at Hall's anti-popish sentiments, evangelical preaching and published *Meditations*, kept his purse shut and in 1606 refused to give Hall a penny, forcing him to leave the rectory he had rebuilt and the parish he had greatly edified.

Hall's anti-papist works misunderstood

Oddly enough, it is Hall's anti-Rome works which was one of three major reasons why Presbyterians and some Puritans became suspicious of him. First, in pointing out where Rome went wrong and separated herself from Biblical Christianity, Hall strove to emphasise the rightness of the Reformation. Others mistakenly took this as a sign that Hall was saying that Rome was basically sound. This misunderstanding arose from Hall's firm belief that there had always been a continuing universal church and the papists had sought to alter it, whereas many critics of Episcopacy demanded a total new beginning on the basis of a Presbyterian church order. A second reason was that Hall questioned the views of his critics regarding a 'true visible church', which was understood to be a 'pure church'. Hall argued that true visibility could go hand in hand with many a false belief[1] and it was the mystical union with Christ that saves souls, not outward conformity to a supposed 'pure' church. The third reason develops naturally from the second. Hall always preached to a mixed congregation whom he believed consisted of the saved and the unsaved. Many of his brethren addressed their congregations as if they were the true flock of Jesus Christ, without a goat in them. This is why Hall cautioned against Dissent where the full membership was regarded as a church-state. He was finding that the new birth was not preached in certain churches on the assumption that the hearers were all saved. Hall believed that the only true visible church which was pure would establish itself in Heaven. Sadly, Joseph Hall was to receive the greatest criticism from the Reformed churches for emphasising teaching which he felt was at the very heart of the Reformation and indicated the greatest breach with Rome who had identified their own visible presence as the Body of Christ. In other words, Hall looked on the Dissenters of his day as striving to lead the Church back to the ways of Rome which he abhorred.

Hall finds sponsors

Now Prince Henry stepped in to assist Hall as he had been much impressed by his preaching and writings. The Prince made Hall one of his chaplains, asking him to remain permanently at his court. Hall explained however, that he was called to the pastoral ministry of the common people and not to be a court preacher. Lord Denny then provided Hall with a new living in Waltham, Essex where he remained twenty-two years. In 1612, Hall gained his Doctor of Divinity and at the same time was made a Prebendary and in 1616 a Dean. The latter post seems to have been a way of rewarding Hall for his international engagements, especially in Belgium and France. In 1617 Hall was made personal advisor in spiritual matters to the King and accompanied him to Scotland as chaplain for discussions with the Scottish divines. Through the influence of Hall, the 1603 recognition of the Church of Scotland by the Anglican Convocation was openly ratified by the King. This meant that Anglicans and the Crown formally accepted churches with Presbyterian discipline as sister churches.[1]

---

[1] The Reformed Church of England Puritans distinguished carefully between 'heresy' and 'error.' They felt for instance that the Presbyterians were in error because of their separistic ideas and views of church discipline and order but could share fellowshipü with them as they adhered to the fundamental doctrines of the Christian faith.

Being at Dort like being in Heaven

In 1618, Hall was chosen by King James to represent the churches of his kingdom at the Synod of Dort. Hall had gained swift recognition as a man of balanced evangelical views and was greatly appreciated by the Continental delegates. He, in turn, was so charmed and uplifted by the work of the Synod that he confessed that it was like being in heaven there. Sadly, Hall's health failed and after a few months he had to leave for home, a very sick man. Before leaving, however, he preached a short Latin sermon (reproduced in Fuller) to all the members of the Synod who more than covered his expenses and presented him with a large gold medal for his services. Hall was replaced by Thomas Goad, Chaplain to George Abbot, Archbishop of Canterbury. Writing of this incident in his famous *Church History of Britain* thirty-three years later, Thomas Fuller mentions that Hall, in spite of his weakness and poor health, had outlived all the other British delegates.[1]

Hall's opponents, according to Davenant, wrangled rather than reasoned

Having already refused the bishopric of Gloucestor, Hall was pressed to accept the bishopric of Exeter in 1627. At that time, he was writing his famous (for some 'notorious') book against Rome with its gigantic title *'The Old Religion,' a Treatise wherein is laid down the true state of the difference betwixt the Reformed and Roman Church, and the blame of that schism cast upon the true authors. For the vindication of our innocence, for the settling of waverer's mindes, for a preservative against Popish insinuations, 1628.* Hall was shocked at the response from a number of Presbyterians and Separatists who had obviously hoped that he would have denounced episcopacy as also being popish. Hall, however, was judging Rome on the basis of Article XIX. Overlooking his condemnation of both the Papacy and Pelagianism in the work, Hall's critics pronounced it popish, too. Hall appealed to John Davenant, reminding him of his stance at Dort against the Papists and Arminians. Davenant told Hall in a very long reply that some of his definitions were ill-sounding to those who put a different sense on the words, but in Hall's sense of what a true church is, it is clear that he had shown, 'the Roman Church is no more a true Church in respect of Christ, or those due qualities and proper actions which Christ requires, than an arrant whore is a true and loyal wife unto her husband. I durst, upon mine oath, be one of your compurgators, that you never in-

---

[1] Cent. XVII, X Book, 1656 ff. p. 1020. (Numbered from first instalment, otherwise p. 20)

tended to adorn that strumpet with the title of a True Church in that meaning. But your own writings have so fully cleared you herein, that suspicion
itself cannot reasonably suspect you in this point.' Davenant comforted
Hall by concluding that his opponents were better at wrangling than reasoning.[1]

Hall seeks to balance the scales between too extreme parties

From now on, Hall found his steps followed closely by what can only be
called spies from popish Arminian and Presbyterian camps. Each faction
complained when Hall was thought to be too lenient to the other and could
not realise that Hall could tolerate any number of externals providing the
heart of the man was right with God and allowed his discipline to work in
harmony with his doctrine. High-Churchman Richard Montague claimed
that Bishops Morton, Davenant and Hall were 'violently bent against the
church of Rome' and were the major enemies of discussions between the
Church of England and the See of Rome.[2] Montague's faction objected to
the many lectureships Hall set up for Puritan preaching. The Arminians
claimed that Hall had given their Dutch allies a hard deal and even taken an
oath to damn the Remonstrants whatever their defence. Yet the Presbyterians complained of Hall's acceptance of what they felt were popish ceremonies. This, in spite of the fact that Hall went much further than they did
in denouncing the pope as Anti-Christ. Hall told Laud that he would be
quite prepared to desist in wearing the surplice if it would ease the slander-
ous superstitions of a number of his fellow-ministers. It appears that Hall
actually did discard his vestments for a time for the sake of the weaker
brethren and suddenly he was popular with those who preferred wearing
black gowns in church to white. When however, the Bishop of Orkney
renounced the function of a bishop around 1640, publicly apologising for
ever allowing himself to have committed such an 'offence', Hall took up
his pen to author his *Episcopacy by divine right asserted.* Edmund Calamy,
far more moderate on the Calvinist side than Hall, but a fierce disputant for
secondary matters, openly contested Hall's facts with a number of Separatist friends.

Political and sectarian intolerance gains the upper hand

This was the time of the fanatical Fifth Monarchy men, the hardly impartial
Long Parliament and the calling of the Westminster Assembly which led to

---

[1] See *Letters on 'The Old Religion,' The Life Letters and Writings of John Davenant
D.D.,* Fuller, 1897, pp.247-249.

[2] *Life of Archbishop Laud, by a Romish Recusant,* 1894, pp. 236-239.

the disbanding of the Reformed Church of England. It is interesting to note that whereas Hall argued from Biblical authority, Calamy and his friends argued on strongly Erastian principles.[1] During this debate, Hall, now Bishop of Norwich, was committed to the Tower along with ten other bishops on charges of high treason which, being interpreted, meant that Hall had defended the ecclesiastical rights of episcopacy, including their ancient right to sit in the House of Lords.

Before continuing with the story of Hall's sufferings at the hand of Parliament, a comparison must be made between the attitude of the majority of the Anglicans and their Presbyterian opponents concerning the episcopacy. The Anglicans of Elizabeth's and James' days were not at all rigid in their view of this order, or church function as they preferred to call it. They did not see anything sacramental in the calling of a bishop but did believe most strongly that it was of Biblical origin. They also believed that the Presbyterians' claim that the Church of England had been in error for over 1600 years had nothing to support it. Though showing a different understanding of 'divine right' than Anglicans such as Hall and Davenant, Mrs Macaulay in her three-volumed *History of England*, well sums up the Anglican point of view:

> The founders of the Anglican Church had retained episco-
> pacy as an ancient, a decent, and a convenient ecclesiastical
> polity, but had not declared that form of church government to
> be of divine institution. We have already seen how low an esti-
> mate Cranmer had formed of the office of a Bishop. In the reign of
> Elizabeth, Jewel, Cooper, Whitgift, and other eminent doctors
> defended prelacy as innocent, as useful, as what the state might
> lawfully establish, as what, when established by the state, was
> entitled to the respect of every citizen. But they never denied
> that a Christian community without a Bishop might be a pure
> Church. On the contrary, they regarded the Protestants of the
> Continent as of the same household of faith with themselves.
> Englishmen in England were indeed bound to acknowledge the
> authority of the Bishop, as they were bound to acknowledge the
> authority of the Sheriff and of the Coroner but the obligation was
> purely local. An English churchman, nay even an English prel-
> ate, if he went to Holland, conformed without scruple to the es-
> tablished religion of Holland. Abroad the ambassadors of Eliza-

---

[1] The bishops were excluded from Parliament at this time and Parliament set up the Westminster Assembly of which Calamy became a most vocal member.

beth and James went in state to the very worship which Elizabeth and James persecuted at home, and carefully abstained from decorating their private chapels after the Anglican fashion, lest scandal should he given to weaker brethren. In the year 1603, the Convocation of the province of Canterbury solemnly recognised the Church of Scotland, a Church in which episcopal control and episcopal ordination were then unknown, as a branch of the Holy Catholic Church of Christ. It was even held that Presbyterian ministers were entitled to place and voice in ecumenical councils. When the States General of the United Provinces convoked at Dort a synod of doctors not episcopally ordained, an English Bishop and an English Dean, commissioned by the head of the English Church, sate with those doctors, preached to them, and voted with them on the gravest questions of theology. Nay, many English benefices were held by divines who had been admitted to the ministry in the Calvinistic form used on the Continent; nor was reordination by a Bishop in such cases then thought necessary, or even lawful.

The Papacy and Presbyteriancy agree on their High Church view of clerical orders

However, two church factions developed who looked upon the order of the clergy as a sacramental and ritualistic necessity for the very being of the Church. Romanists protested with Presbyterians at the Anglican 'low' view of the priestly office. Indeed, as already reported, critics of Presbyterian High-Churchmanship such as John Milton saw the church which had split off from the Reformed Church of England as practising priestcraft writ large.[1]

In this matter, the British Presbyterians differed greatly from their Continental brethren, in particular those who had signed the *Canons of Dort* as witnessed by the testimony of Bishop George Carleton, called fondly 'The Northern Apostle'. Carleton, one of the English delegates to the Synod of Dort, explained to the Continental brethren gathered there that it was the Anglican episcopacy which had saved them from like inroads of Arminianism from which the Continental churches were suffering. If they had had bishops who made sure that their diocese were cor-

---

[1] Milton was referring to the fact that the English word 'priest' is a shortened form of 'presbyter'. See Chapter VIII in Neal's *History of the Puritans*, vol.ii, where he records the efforts of the High Presbyterians to have their view of the divine right of Presbyterianism established by law. Being Erastians to a man, they appealed to Caesar (Parliament) for verification but Caesar took little notice of them.

rectly run and disciplined, the doctrinal chaos which existed on the Continent would not be so pronounced. Carleton also countered the Presbyterian idea that all New Testament offices were of fully equal nature by showing how the Twelve were to be distinguished from the Seventy and that we gather from the New Testament that the office of *primus inter pares* was a Scriptural function. Carleton says their answer was:

> that they did much honour and reverence the good order and discipline of the church of England; and, with all their hearts, would be glad to have it established among them; but that could not be hoped for, in their state. Their hope was, that, seeing they could not do what they desired, God would be merciful to them, if they did what they could.[1]

The Anglicans saw the Continental acceptance of Presbyterian orders as a mere political expediency, brought about by the unstable nature of mainland Europe and the fact that the Reformation was not making such headway as it was in Britain. Lancelot Andrewes told French Presbyterian Peter du Moulin:

> Something is lacking, I said from your churches which is of divine right; but I said this was due not to any fault of yours, but to the misfortune of the times. Your country had not kings so well disposed in the reform of the Church as our Britain; when God gives you better days this also that is lacking will perhaps be supplied.[2]

It must be added that so respected was Carleton and his fellow-delegates at the Council of Dort that the Dutch Presbyterians invited them to assist in the new Dutch translation of the Bible and also prepare annotations to it. Carleton, Davenant, Hall and Ward all worked on this translation for a number of years. It was finally printed in 1637 and translated twenty years later into English under the title *The Dutch Annotations upon the whole Bible; together with the Translation, according to the direction of the Synod of Dort, 1618.*

---

[1] See *Biographia Evangelica*, vol. ii, p.455-459 for a wider discussion of Carleton's importance.

[2] Quoted by Ottley in his *Lancelot Andrewes*, p. 118.

Punished without being tried in either a church or legal court.
Hall and his brother bishops denied the preposterous indictment that their views of the episcopacy amounted to high treason but their trial, which they were convinced would vindicate them, never took place. Instead they were 'freed' after six months' imprisonment on payment of a £5,000 fine which had no legal basis. As this money was not immediately forthcoming, the bishops' seats, estates, homes and personal belongings were confiscated in lieu of the fine. The bishops were now rendered churchless, homeless and wageless. Hall took all this as the humble Christian he was, merely saying that he had never been worthy to become a bishop anyway. After his estates were seized, Parliament had the evil audacity to demand from Hall that he paid for their administration and upkeep but refused to allow him to be paid a penny from ecclesiastical funds for his pastoral work. A very small allowance was granted his wife, however, which was seen as a further public humiliation to Hall. Officers were even sent to confiscate all the bishop's clothing and were ordered also to take the very clothes the bishop stood in, but they could not bring themselves to strip the man. Happily for Hall, two rich friends bought up his house and personal possessions including two horses and a picture of his children and gave them back on loan to the bishop until he could raise the money himself, which they must have known was now an impossibility. To make Hall's humiliation complete, Parliament demanded that he should raise money for arms for their support and then even accused him of hiding arms for a sinister purpose. The troops who searched his house found no such weapons but took one of Hall's 'borrowed' horses for their trouble. Then the mobs, egged on by such as popular demagogue turncoat Cornelius Burgess, one time chaplain-in-ordinary to the King, stormed through Hall's house crying 'No bishops'. Just as in the days of Mary, the ejected Reformed pastors had to worship and preach in secret according to their Anglican practice. Hall even ordained sound ministers to carry on the Reformed Church of England's testimony should the Lord in His Providence allow her freedom once again. Hall, now very elderly, and his family were thrown out of their home and had to find rented quarters. Hall soon died and was buried without even a stone to mark his grave.

The value of Hall's testimony
One can imagine Arminian fanatics such as John Goodwin with his Fifth Monarchy backing, humiliating Hall and his fellow-bishops in this way. Hall had angered Goodwin by refuting his evil slander concerning the British commissioners at Dort and Goodwin and his ilk were only too keen

to take revenge. However, it is a sad reminder of the fickleness of man that the three British delegates to the Synod of Dort who were still alive at the fall of the monarchy, Hall, Ward and Balcanqual, were also persecuted by those who solemnly swore to uphold the very Five Points of Calvinism which were worked out at that Synod. These Presbyterian Separatists did not hesitate to join hands with Arminian Fifth Monarchy men to work the downfall of mighty men of God whose only thorn in Presbyterian eyes was their episcopacy. Worse still is it to know that one-time bishops who exchanged their vestments, titles and political allegiance at the upsurge of Presbyterianism, did not hesitate to take over the private property of expelled bishops such as Hall, yet nevertheless sat with a 'good conscience' as members of the Westminster Assembly bringing shame both on the now defunct Reformed Church of England and the many Presbyterian and Separatist churches which were to split off from it. May the tragic story of Joseph Hall teach us to avoid politics that destroy the true Christian heart and keep the doctrines of grace free from the corruption of filthy mammon.

JAMES USHER (1580-1656)

7. Archbishop James Usher (1580-1656): The Light of Ireland

James Usher came from an ancient lineage of Irish men and women who were renowned through their literary and political abilities. He transcended them all in fame because of his great piety, hard work as a shepherd of souls and high scholarship.

Taught by the physically blind to see spiritual truths
Our subject was born in St Nicholas Parish, Dublin on January 4, 1580, the son of Arnold Usher, clerk to the Irish chancery and Margaret, née Stanihurst, daughter of the Speaker of the Irish House of Commons. As a child, he came under the care of two maiden aunts who had been blind from infancy yet enlightened by the gospel. Through the care of these dear ladies, James, like the child Timothy, learnt the Scriptures which made him wise unto salvation. Amazingly, these two blind aunts also taught James to read by giving him a Bible, and coaching him through the verses which they knew off-by heart. By the time James was eight years of age, he knew the Scriptures almost as well as his aunts. After this initial instruction, James was placed under the care of James Hamilton and James Fullerton who had been appointed teachers in Dublin by another namesake of James Usher's, King James VI of Scotland. For the next five years, James studied hard and was always conscious of his spiritual needs, often retreating to a lonely place where he would confess his sins in prayer. At the age of ten, his heart was opened to the gospel message of Romans 12:1, 'I beseech you, therefore, brethren, by the mercies of God, that ye present your bodies a living sacrifice, holy, acceptable to God, which is your reasonable service.' Once converted, young James grew in grace by furthering his studies in the Scriptures, supplemented by reading the works of Augustine and William Perkins.

Usher rids himself of worldly snares

Though just turned thirteen, James was judged so advanced in learning that he was matriculated at Dublin College which had come into being through the energies in Parliament of his maternal grandfather and a paternal uncle. Out of respect to his father's wish, James first studied law but his father's death in 1598 left James free to study for the ministry. James Hamilton continued to supervise James' tuition as he became the new college's first professor. He was dismayed to find, however, that his young protege became very interested in card-playing. James soon discovered that his love for cards was suppressing his love for the Saviour, so he renounced the former and prepared to confess his faith in Confirmation and partaking of the Lord's Supper. James now became deeply interested in the study of church history, making detailed notes on his reading which were to become the basis of his earliest publications.

Young Usher debates with the papists

Now James studied both papist and Reformed authors diligently as his mother's relations put great pressure on him to turn to Rome. Chief amongst these was James' maternal uncle, Richard Stanihurst, who wrote extensively to propagate Roman beliefs. James did not flinch from his Reformed position and soon made a name for himself in debate against Rome's staunchest Irish supporters. When barely eighteen, James heard that Henry Fitz-Simmons, a learned Jesuit, had challenged anyone of the Reformed faith to openly debate with him on the principles of the Reformation. Great was the papist's surprise to find himself challenged by a mere boy. Nevertheless, Fitz-Simmons arranged with James to debate publicly with him once a week until the defeated party withdrew. Fitz-Simmons withstood the young whipper-snapper for two weeks and then retreated with the excuse that he refused to debate with a mere boy. Years afterwards, however, Fitz-Simmons confessed that his opponent had been 'the most learned of those who were not catholics'.

Early promotion and ordination

At the age of nineteen or twenty,[1] James Usher took his M.A. and was immediately asked to stay on at the college as proctor and catechetical lecturer. He turned the offer down, thinking himself too young for such a post. The university insisted on Usher's acceptance, telling him that they believed strongly that it was God's will for him. After over a year's prayer and soul-searching, Usher accepted the call. Immediately, he began to

---

[1] 1600. It is not certain whether Usher was born in 1581 or 1580.

expound systematic theology in the university, pointing out the follies of Rome and also giving his students a list of rules for Christian student behaviour. Feeling strongly called to the ministry, he was ordained by his uncle Dr Usher, then Archbishop of Armagh and took up work in conjunction with his university lectures as afternoon preacher at Christ Church in Dublin. His two aims in preaching, he declared from the pulpit, were to win souls daily for Christ and convince his hearers of the 'errors of the Romish church'.

Usher becomes established as a leading reformer

Always an avid reader, Usher, now twenty-three, assisted Sir Thomas Bodley in setting up the famous Bodleian Library in Oxford. On being given a grant of £1,800 for their work, Usher and university fellow Dr Luke Chaloner established a library in Dublin. Whilst Usher was away in London and Oxford, conferring with Sir Thomas, the Jesuits made an intensive effort to gain his mother for Rome, arguing that it was the ancient religion of her family. Mrs Usher succumbed to this pressure and now remained antagonistic to her son's beliefs all her remaining life. The papist claimed this as a great triumph. At twenty-seven, Usher gained his B.D. and became Divinity Professor and Chancellor of St Patrick's where he preached every Lord's Day. He still preached daily besides giving his university lectures and refused lucrative posts including the provostship of Dublin University so that he could continue this work. By 1612, Usher had gained his doctorate and had published his first book on the western church. This was a continuation of Bishop Jewel's great *Apology* proving that the Reformed tenets are those of the true Biblical Church and not those of Rome. Usher's publication took the history of the doctrines of the Church up to the thirteenth century and he prepared manuscripts of the continued history up to his times. The latter were sadly lost when the popish rioters stormed and plundered Usher's house and the Presbyterians confiscated Usher's library during their militant efforts to disestablish the Episcopalian churches. Archbishop Abbot, a staunch Puritan, presented a copy of Usher's work to King James and Usher became something of a favourite with the King. To crown his success, Usher now married Phoebe Chaloner, whose father had worked with him in founding Dublin College library. The couple enjoyed forty years of marriage until Phoebe died.

The *Irish Articles of Religion*

In 1615, Usher drew up the *Irish Articles of Religion* which reflect the strongly Puritan *Lambeth Articles* of 1595 and the *Canons of Dort* still to

come. The 104 Articles of this declaration of faith are perhaps the most
thorough-going of any Reformed creed. Like his Anglican friends John
Davenant and Samuel Ward, Usher did not fight shy of tackling the question of reprobation and writes *Of God's eternall decree, and Predestination*:

11. God from all eternitie did by his vnchangeable counsell ordaine
whatsoeuer in time should come to passe: yet so, as thereby no
violence is offred to the wills of the reasonable creatures, and
neither the libertie nor the contingencie of the second causes is
taken away, but established rather.

12. By the same eternall counsell God hath predestinated some
vnto life, and reprobated some vnto death: of both which there is
a certaine number, knowen only to God, which can neither be
increased nor diminished.

13. Predestination to life, is the euerlasting purpose of God,
whereby, before the foundations of the world were layed, he hath
constantly decreed in his secret counsell to deliuer from curse
and damnation, those whom he hath chosen in Christ out of
mankinde, and to bring them by Christ vnto euerlasting saluation,
as vessels made to honor.

14. The cause mouing God to predestinate vnto life, is not the
foreseeing of faith, or perseuerance, or good workes, or of anything which is in the person predestinated, but onely the good
pleasure of God himselfe. For all things being ordained for the
manifestation of his glory, and his glory being to appeare both in
the workes of his Mercy and of his Justice; it seemed good to his
heauenly wisedome to choose out a certaine number towardes
whome he would extend his vndeserued mercy, leauing the rest to
be spectacles of his iustice.

15. Such as are predestinated vnto life, be called according vnto
Gods purpose (his spirit working in due season) and through
grace they obey the calling, they bee iustified freely, they bee
made sonnes of God by adoption, they be made like the image of
his onely begotten Sonne Jesus Christ, they walke religiously in
good workes, and at length, by God's mercy they attaine to
euerlasting felicitie. But such as are not predestinated to saluation,
shall finally be condemned for their sinnes .

16. The godlike consideration of Predestination and our election
in Christ is full of sweete, pleasant, and vnspeakeable comfort to

godly persons, and such as feele in themselues the working of the spirit of Christ, mortifying the workes of the flesh, and their earthly members, and drawing vp their mindes to high and heauenly things: as well because it doth greatly confirme and establish their faith of eternall saluation to be enioyed through Christ, as because it doth feruently kindle their loue towardes God: and on the contrary side, for curious and carnall persons, lacking the spirit of Christ, to haue continually before their eies the sentence of Gods predestination, is very dangerous.

17. Wee must receiue Gods promises in such wise as they be generally set forth vnto vs in holy Scripture; and in our doings, that will of God is to be followed, which we haue expressely declared vnto vs in the word of God.

Usher gains recognition at the court of James and continues his reforming work

The Archbishop and Bishops of Ireland and representatives of the clergy convocated and ratified the articles which remained binding for the Irish church until the papist and Presbyterian revolutions put an end to them. Indeed, the latter now spread rumours that the *Irish Articles* had disgraced Usher before King James but the monarch had equally staunch Episcopalian Puritans such as Abbott and Hall as his advisors. Instead of rebuking Usher, the King discussed the articles with him, expressed his satisfaction, had Usher preach before the House of Commons and then had him appointed Bishop of Meath in 1620. Now Usher increased his preaching activities rather than diminished them and took to expounding the Word in public halls because the papists and Presbyterians would not attend his church. In this way many were called to leave Rome and a more Old Testament based theological system and enter into the joys of the doctrines of grace. This was a real break with tradition for Usher who paved new ways by ordaining good sound men from the working classes whom he found were called to the ministry irrespective of their lack of academic training. At least one of these former artisans became extremely successful in persuading Romanists to return to the true fold. Usher also made sure that those he ordained should speak the Irish of the common man and postponed ordination of those who were fluent in Latin but could not yet speak their mother tongue. This action proved sympathetic to the Presbyterians who, when they came to power, persecuted Usher far less than they did other Episcopalian Puritans and Synod of Dort men such as Hall, Ward and especially brave Balcanqual, who was hounded to death.

(George Carleton and John Davenant, the other Dortian delegates died before the Revolution). These men used to argue that it was wrong to make church order the touchstone of orthodoxy and not experimental faith and doctrine and pointed out that Arminius remained a Presbyterian in spite of his rejection of the orthodox faith. Though Richard Baxter was one of those Dissenters who could not accept Usher's strongly Reformed theology, he was greatly influenced by Usher's evangelical fervour and it is said that his *A Call to the Unconverted*, grew out of what he learned concerning evangelism from Bishop Usher.

Usher's Puritan works published by royal command

Because of his services to his God, King and country in winning many papists for the faith reflected in the *Irish Articles*, King James appointed Usher as a privy counsellor for Ireland. Meanwhile, Usher was busy producing works on church history and doctrine to show that the leading tenets of Rome were all late novelties brought into the Christian church by those who proved its enemies. The King was so impressed by Usher's preaching abilities that he had him preach before the court and had his sermons printed by royal command. The Cistercians, Franciscans and Jesuits, however, clubbed together against Usher chiefly because he had taken the oath of allegiance to his king which the papists maintained was unlawful.

Usher now threw his energies more and more into preaching and catechising, emphasising the responsibility of Christians to gather together in worship as a church. He also sought to reform the ecclesiastical courts so that the church would busy itself with church discipline leaving the secular politicians to perform the work of a magistrate. The Presbyterian Puritans objected to his catechising ministry and emphasised expositional lectures from Presbyters rather than meetings for common worship with priest and people taking part. They also allied with the papist in rejecting the oath of supremacy. The Presbyterians were also angered by Usher's teaching that the doctrines of grace are blessings to be lived out rather than scholastic dogmas which one must be formally forced to adhere to as if they were laws of the land. Usher could only warn against such legalism. He never could understand the Presbyterian's high church view of the 'divine right' of church dignitaries, believing that they made too much of their offices and that his calling as a bishop was a utility function in the family of the church.[1]

---

[1] See his *Origin of Bishops and Metropolitans*, 1641.

At James's bidding, Usher now wrote a further work showing how the gospel first came to Britain and how the Roman Catholic church had nothing to do with this historic event. He was the King's guest whilst doing research in England but broke off his visit to return to Ireland and debate in writing with the Jesuit William Malone who had challenged Usher to refute his claims that the Roman Catholic faith had always been the true faith of Christian Ireland. At the death of the Archbishop of Armagh, Usher accepted the call of the church and the approval of the Sovereign in taking over that church function. Usher now increased his daily preaching and became very ill because of his efforts to spread the gospel and combat heresy.

Usher defends the Reformed faith against Jesuit Beaumont

When Usher heard that Roman Catholic Lord Mordaunt of Drayton had challenged him to dispute on the points in controversy between Rome and the Reformed faith, he made the lengthy journey to Northamptonshire to enter into the disputation, though he was still very ill. Actually the request had come from Lady Mordaunt. Her husband wanted to win her for Rome and had told her that he would choose a debater for Rome and she should choose one for the Reformed faith. Lord Mordaunt was confident that Rome would win the day as the debater he chose was none other than the Jesuit Beaumont, alias Rockwood, who had a reputation of being invincible. The two combatants now lined up for the fray and decided that they would dispute for five hours each day until one of them surrendered. Beaumont bravely stood his post for three days but on the fourth day sent word to Usher with the honest confession that he had no arguments left. This statement was weakened by Beaumont's further claim that his weakness was because of his bad conscience at entering into a debate without the permission of his superiors. He confessed, however, that he had not reckoned with so learned an antagonist. After convincing Beaumont that he had no arguments, Usher turned to his Lordship who quickly gave up his allegiance to Rome and confessed Reformed doctrines. How much this confession displayed his heart is not known but his wife maintained a fine Christian witness. Lady Mordaunt remained also a close friend of Usher's and protected him in his declining years against his popish and Presbyterian persecutors. Meanwhile, Usher had returned to Ireland where he continued to preach diligently and train preachers and worked on such great books as his *Immanuel* (published 1638) on the Incarnation of Christ. He also published pre-Roman Irish Christian works from 592 to 1180. A brief perusal of Usher's works shows the fallacy of Rome's claims on the Emerald Isle. The country had a strong Celtic Church long before she became papist by submission to the conquering English allies of the Pope and not by free choice. Historians and churchmen alike tend to forget that Ireland first came under Rome's politico-religious yoke when in 1171 Henry II invaded Ireland with the Pope's Bull in his pocket and a large army at his back.

The end of one church, one faith, one baptism

When Usher revisited England in 1640, it was to learn that the rebels had plundered his property back home. It now appeared that because of the troubled political and religious nature of the times, he would never be able to take up his former work again. Usher was promised several sources of income by King Charles but whatever was offered to Usher, the Presbyterian controlled Parliament managed to take for themselves. Usher was now offered teaching posts in several foreign universities but he felt that he could not desert his own country and moved to Oxford where he maintained a preaching ministry. Possibly unknown to Usher, troops had been sent to various ports to stop him should he seek to flee from the country. In 1643 Usher was called by the Parliament sponsored Westminster Assembly to debate with them on their plans to oust the established churches and set up a new form of orthodoxy. Only one of the twenty or so Episcopalians invited actually attended the Assembly as it was so clearly held against the hitherto orthodox faith and the laws of the land which still had not been repealed. Furthermore, the condition forced upon Episcoplalians for their partaking in the Assembly was that they should take the so-called Negative Oath and denounce their former allegiances to church and King. This was papacy pure to the Anglican Puritans. Anglican, Daniel Featley, never one to dodge a good debate, did attend the initial meetings until he found that his invitation was a dishonest trap and he was accused of being a King's spy. It was said that he had informed outsiders of the Assembly's dealings. Actually, this was nonsense, as Featley told them, because he had merely discussed the Assembly in writing with Usher who had also been invited to the Assembly and was therefore an 'insider'. As the Westminster Assembly was called during the reign of Charles I and held on Crown property it was quite ridiculous to speak of Featley's being the King's spy. Rather, those acting unconstitutionally against the Sovereign could be called 'spies'. The second accusation against Featley was equally absurd. He was supposed to have acted against the Solemn League and Covenant which had not yet been enacted and therefore had no legal or ecclesiastical basis. Notwithstanding, Featley's property was confiscated and plundered. He was thrown into prison and died whilst a Presbyterian prisoner. It is interesting to note that before Cromwell's regime, numerous Westminster rebels had plotted in league with the Laudians and papists against the Anglican Puritans. Nor did they show any scruples in taking over the stolen houses and property of the English, Irish and Scottish ministers whom they had defrocked. Worse, when Charles II came to power and the Episcopalian church was re-established, a number of these Episcopalian persecutors were quick to renounce the 'Solemn League' and adorned themselves with Episcopalian robes.

Usher faces the rebels of church and state bravely

Knowing that he risked acute criminal persecution, James Usher told the Conference members straight that they had set up an illegal assembly. This was embarrassing indeed for the Presbyterians who had broadcast that they could win Usher over easily to their way of thinking. In revenge at this snub, the rebel Parliament issued an order to confiscate all Usher's property but as the papists had taken everything but Usher's books, the Presbyterians had to make do with them. Featley, not yet in prison, tried to save the books and have them kept in one library but most of Usher's correspondence and many unpublished manuscripts were lost. Usher, now penniless, was offered many lucrative bribes by Oliver Cromwell and the Presbyterians should he renounce his King and church allegiance. Cromwell himself intervened to protect Usher's person but refused to grant the Archbishop and his fellow Episcopalians freedom of worship. In this, Cromwell was less tolerant than King James who had allowed a fair degree of non-conformity, especially in northern England, Scotland and Ireland.

Usher's last prayer

From now on, Usher concentrated on preaching and writing but he became almost blind and deaf and during his final year of life he did not speak publicly. The Mordaunts took Usher into their care and he spent his last year writing at sunny windows, moving from one to the other as the sun moved so that he could see his books. Everyone was amazed at his composed nature, his deep trust in sovereign salvation and his ability to take all as from the Lord. His last days were sheer torture as burst veins and pleurisy gave him great pain and made breathing a torment. The last words of this saintly man, who had never ceased to shepherd the sheep and never avoided a known duty, were, 'O Lord forgive me especially my sins of omission.' It was March 21, 1655 and Usher was seventy-six years of age.

Plans had been made to bury Usher quietly in the Mordaunts' family vault at Rygate but Cromwell insisted on giving Usher a state funeral and a burial in Westminster Abbey. This fact has always been quoted in praise of Cromwell's generosity. Cromwell could well afford to be generous as he had compelled Usher's friends to carry all the costs of the state funeral, though no one, except Cromwell, wanted it. The Lord Protector did make one great concession, however, which was highly pleasing to those of the old orthodox faith, he allowed Usher to be buried according to the Anglican custom. Nicholas Bernard took the service and preached from 1 Samuel 25:1, 'And Samuel died, and all the Israelites were gathered together and lamented him, and buried him.'

If such an incessantly hard-working man as James Usher prayed that his sins of omission be forgiven, what ought we to pray who do not spend a fraction of the time he did in the service of the gospel?

DANIEL FEATLEY (1582-1645)

8. Daniel Featley (1582-1645): Contender for the Faith

A man of great natural skills and abilities gained by much study

As we are all made differently, obviously we are attracted to different people in different ways. Some people are able to attract most and some people none. There are also those who seem to have only devoted friends and absolute enemies and have no attraction whatsoever for those in between. The present writer has found that several of his subjects portrayed in this book fall into this latter category but perhaps no one more than Daniel Featley. In judging him as either black or white, the Baptists were an exception. These showed a mixture of the two extremes which can perhaps only be described as 'love-hate'. Instead of hounding Featley to death as did the Presbyterians, the Baptists faced him in free debate. When all the bad-mannered verbalisms of both sides are swept aside as but a sign of the turbulence of that age, we find that no Anglican ever spoke so highly of the Baptists after their departure from within the Anglican Church[1] as Featley did. On the other hand, no Baptists have ever allowed themselves to be so influenced in their creed-making by non-Baptists as they were by Featley in his arguments against their particular views. We must also note that the Baptists themselves, on the whole, have distanced

---

[1] The present author believes that the Baptists were tolerated within the broad structure of the Anglican Church, as still indicated in the rubric on Baptism, until the definite break in the 16th century. He thus allies himself with the Baptist Successionists to a certain extent. Tindal, for instance, was most tolerant of Baptist views as being within the Anglican framework but finally rejected them on the grounds that they were too sacramental and ritualistic. This is, however, a most debatable point and is stated here as being merely a 'by the way'.

themselves from the Anabaptist and Arian elements which Featley so ardently condemned in his contemporary Baptist scene. It is also noteworthy that few disputants against the papist were as successful as Featley and few were feared by them as he was, yet so acute was his learning and skill in debate that he was held in high repute by his antagonists and treated accordingly. Indeed, the two titles that stayed with Featley from his youth, namely *acutissimus* and *acerrimus*,[1] were given him by papists who were out-debated by him. The roots of these titles refer both to natural skills and those gained through study.

Featley's early life

The subject of this short biography was born into an ancient but lowly Lancashire family named Fairclough which was pronounced locally as Featley,[2] which our subject adopted as the correct spelling of his name. Featley was, however, born in Charlton-upon-Otmore, Oxfordshire on March 15, 1582 where his father, John Fairclough was cook to Lawrence Humphrey, then President of Magdalan College, Oxford. Of his mother, we know nothing. Because of his father's connections, Daniel was sent to the Grammar School which adjoined Magdalan College so that, though of humble origin, he was able to rub shoulders with his equals in learning though better-situated in society. Featley matriculated at Corpus Christi College in 1594, took his B.A. and became a probationary fellow of his college in 1602 and a fellow in 1604. It was then that he felt called to dedicate his life to the gospel and began to study theology, taking his M.A. in 1605. It is not known when Featley was ordained but it must have been before 1610 as he spent three years in France as Sir Thomas Edmondes' chaplain between 1610 and 1613 when Edmondes was made ambassador to France. It was in France that Featley made a name for himself as a debater with the French Jesuits and as a preacher. Featley's collected sermons, seventy in number, published in 1636 under the title *Clavis Mystica* contain twenty-one of his sermons preached in France. It was during this time that Featley received the two titles referred to above out of respect for his disputations.

---

[1] Keenly intelligent and shrewd.

[2] This explanation has been considered far-fetched but Lancashire speakers often interchange hard 'c' and 't'. This is because they use a glottal stop after a vowel and before a hard 'c' which is rendered 'k' or 't' accordingly. See 'bo"el', 'bokkel' and 'bottle' for the same word. This is known in linguistics as 'free variation'.

Debating, preaching and teaching the Reformed faith

Once back in England, Featley took his B. D. and, in 1613, was about to be appointed to a Cornish church as rector when the Puritan Archbishop George Abbot invited him to become his personal chaplain. Featley remained with Abbot for a number of years and served also as the rector of Lambeth in Surrey, taking his doctorate in 1617. Featley continued to debate publicly and soon many sought to capture some of Featley's importance by challenging him to debates themselves. This often proved embarrassing for the would-be disputants as fellow anti-Arminian John Prideaux[1] found on challenging Featley to a verbal dual. Being defeated by Featley was rather a let-down for the King's close advisor and a quarrel ensued with Featley which could only be settled by Archbishop Abbot's intervention. Thereafter, Featley did pastoral work in London and Middlesex, apparently still in the services of the Archbishop of Canterbury, before becoming provost of Chelsea College. During this time, Featley married and published numerous devotional works such as his *Ancilla Pietatis or The Handmaid to Private Devotion* (1626) which ran into eight editions and the *Practice of Extraordinary Devotion* which also became popular. These writings, however, made Featley unpopular with the new Archbishop of Canterbury, William Laud, as he wrote depreciatingly of the St George legends. It is said that Featley was forced to go down on his knees before Laud and cry '*peccavi*', though this appears to have as much historical basis as the story of George and the Dragon. From now on, up to the Long Parliament and the beginning of the Civil War, Featley attended to his pastoral duties and spent his time writing books and combating with the papists and occasionally with the Baptists. He also debated against the works of British opponents of the Reformation.

The 'protestants' seek to murder Featley

In spite of the fact that Featley was a known Calvinist, friend of the Reformation and held no high church function, he soon became a target for the Presbyterians and parliamentary army who called themselves 'protestants'. In 1642 soldiers stationed at Acton, searched for Featley in order to murder him. As the minister had received warning, the soldiers found empty rectory, stables and barns and wreaked their wrath on these, destroying all

---

[1]An anti-Arminian is not the same as a Calvinist as Dominicans and Jansenites were anti-Arminians. Fuller, however, classifies Prideaux with the 'Doctrinal Calvinists', *Life of Bishop Davenant*, p. 519, Hutton calls him a Puritan, *History of the English Church from the Accession of Charles I to the Death of Anne*, p. 95.

Featley's possessions. Not being satisfied with this, the 'protestants' heard that Featley was preaching at Lambeth that Sunday so they stormed his church with drawn swords and pistols, killing and wounding worshippers and declaring that they would, 'chop the doctor himself as small as herbs for the pot, for suffering the Common Prayer to be read in the church.' Again Featley was either not present or could make his escape. Erasmus Middleton, editor of the famous Gospel Magazine and himself persecuted because of his orthodox faith, commented on this 'protestant' action with the words, 'Excellent protestants, to vow destruction to one of the first protestant ministers of the age!'[1]

Presbyterians and rebel politicians meet at the Westminster Assembly
In 1643, the Westminster Assembly, composed of one hundred and twenty-one rebel English ministers, six Scottish Commissioners, and thirty lay members of both Houses was called by Parliament to 'reform' the church. In calling this assembly, parliament ignored the wishes of the established church and the King and went down in history as the first occasion when a purely political body in Britain established a church on Erastian principles.[2] Few Anglican puritans were asked to take part and all those who were invited, except Featley, refused the invitation, their reason being that the assembly was illegal as it had not been called under church authority and took place in direct opposition to normal constitutional political procedures. Featley was invited and attended in order to debate with the Assembly concerning their illegal, unprecedented course. The Assembly, however, did not wish to give any reasons for their conduct but were only interested in denouncing Featley on the most trumped up of charges imaginable. He was first accused of being a King's spy on the grounds that he had informed outsiders of the Assembly's dealings. Actually, this was nonsense as Featley told them, because he had merely discussed the Assembly in writing with Usher who had also been invited to the Assembly and was therefore an 'insider'. As the Westminster Assembly was called during the reign of Charles I and held on Crown property it was quite ridiculous to speak of Featley's being the King's spy. Rather, those acting unconstitutionally against the Sovereign could be called 'spies'. The second accusation against Featley was equally absurd. He was sup-

---

[1] *Biographia Evangelica*, vol. iii, p. 167.

[2] Called after Thomas Erastus (1524-1583), an anti-Calvinist who believed in state supremacy in ecclesiastical causes. Ironically enough, the religio-political system he helped to establish excommunicated him as a heretic.

posed to have acted against the Solemn League and Covenant which had not yet been enacted and therefore had no legal or ecclesiastical basis. Notwithstanding, Featley's property was again confiscated and plundered and he was imprisoned, though never brought to anything like a normal trial. The deed can only be called dastardly.

A prisoner of the Presbyterians asked to destroy Rome

The Religio-Political Parliament of Presbyterians and Separatists, however, were to add insult to injury showing how hypocritical their action was and how low true religion had sunk in the rebel churches. A certain papist had sent out a challenge to all protestants, boasting that he could refute all their claims to orthodoxy. The Presbyterians and Parliament looked high and low for a man amongst them who was capable of defending the faith - and found none. It seemed that rebels do not make good theologians and debaters. As a last resort, the challenged 'protestants' thought of Featley. None was as skilled in debate as he, though he was ill in the cold and damp of prison, robbed of all his books and papers. Thus, by order of Parliament, Featley was chosen to defend the protestant cause, though they had thrown him into prison for allegedly being a traitor to it. Now, one would think that Parliament would have freed Featley with gracious apologies if not compensation, fitted him out with the library they had stolen from him and put all their resources at his disposal. A Christian man would naturally think so, but this is not what happened. Parliament told Featley that he must stay in his cold, clammy prison but that he would be graciously allowed three books at a time with whose help he should defend Parliament's and the Presbyterians' protestantism - yet remain their prisoner. Thus Featley, placed under the most difficult conditions for a man who was to defeat popery single-handed, commenced his task and within a year had produced his great work *Roma Ruens*.[1]

Featley debates with the Baptists

In January, 1644, Featley published his *The Dipper Dipt*[2] in which he challenged the Baptists who had invited him to debate, on similar lines to his protests against Presbyterianism, i.e. he queried their authority in sepa-

---

[1] Destroying Rome.

[2] This is Featley's interpretation of his debate with four Baptists, for the Baptists equally coloured version see Goadby's book, *Bye-Paths in Baptist History*, Chapter VII, 'Public Disputations on Baptism'.

rating from the Church of England and establishing separatist churches.[1] Even Archbishop Laud had allowed that, according to Anglican teaching, men could be ordained and administer the sacraments *in casu necessitatis*, but Featley could find no such necessity in the contemporary situation. He saw no scriptural or historical need for either the Presbyterians or the Baptists to separate from their former church. The two parties had met two years before in Southwark but the debate had not been very profitable to either side. The strategy of the Baptists was to determine the course of debate as they had initiated it, whereas Featley wanted to see his opponents' ecclesiastical credentials first and sound them out on doctrine. He wanted to know by what or whose authority the Baptists had founded their churches and whether or not they identified themselves with Continental Anabaptists. He felt that it was necessary to clear up such matters before a debate on separatist particulars was possible. He especially wanted to know where the Baptists stood regarding the Trinity which would give some indication of the validity of their baptism. As many Anabaptists were Arian, the Church of England could not recognise their baptism, even when given for the first time as it could not possibly be given in the Triune Name. This had been the method used in the churches to test the validity of a possible heretical baptism since earliest times. It was still common church practice amongst Anglicans.[2] Featley was, however, debating with people who appeared either ignorant of traditional debating methods or who saw no advantage in following them. He thus strongly suspected he was dealing with the dreaded Arians.

The *Thirty-Nine Articles* mainly composed to counter Anabaptist heresies

Featley was a member of a church whose *Articles of Faith* were formulated when Rome was exiled from Britain in 1534 with the hope that she would return no more. However, Anabaptist extremes were threatening to take Rome's place as the major source of theological error in Britain. Heresies were now being propagated which even the Church of Rome, in keeping with the councils of Nicea, Constantinople, Ephesus and Chalcedon had condemned. These heresies, such as Sabellism, Socinianism, Arianism

---

[1] The venue of this debate was Southwark and the date was probably 1642.

[2] See 'Donatism: the third investigation: Synodal Letter of the Council of Arles to Silvester, Bishop of Rome, 1314-35', *Documents Illustrative of the History of the Church*, ed. B. J. Kidd, vol. i, p. 255.

and the teaching that Christ's human nature preceded His human birth were prevalent in the preaching of the Anabaptists, who stressed that those who joined their ranks must undergo a new form of baptism, whether they were already Baptists or not.

In 1536 ten basic articles of faith were agreed upon 'to stablyshe christen quietnes and unitie amongst us, and to avoyde contentious opinions.' These articles displayed more Medieval tradition than sound doctrine, so Reformers such as Cranmer and Hooper demanded 'an entire purification of the Church from the very foundation'. A letter is preserved from Hooper to Baucer (also anglicised as Bucer) dated June 25, 1549 in which the Reformer complains that the Anabaptists are flocking to his lectures denying the incarnation, affirming sinless perfection yet teaching that those who fall into sin after partaking of the Holy Ghost will be lost for ever. In the same letter Hooper complains that 'a great portion of the kingdom so adheres to the popish faction as altogether to set at naught God and the lawful authority of the magistrates'. [1]

The *Ten Articles* were quickly revised and added to until they had reached 42 in number by 1553, including those against the papists. The number was reduced to 39 in 1571 when most of the papists had separated themselves from the English Church as the result of a papal bull. Articles I, II and III were aimed at Anabaptist errors concerning the Trinity whereas Article IV defended the doctrines of the Incarnation and manhood of Christ. The main heretic in mind, here, was Casper Schwenckfeld (1489-1561) who, in 1528, contended that Christ's flesh was never that of a created human and, after the resurrection, Christ dropped all resemblance of humanity.[2] Article VI defends the canonical status of the Old Testament which was rejected by many Anabaptists. Articles VIII to X dealing with original sin, free will and grace were aimed at the Pelagian Anabaptist doctrine which taught that Adam's curse did not apply to his offspring and that man, of his own will, was able to co-operate with God in salvation. Article X attacks the Anabaptist teaching that man's sin was a fiat of God. Articles XV and XVI oppose the Anabaptist heresy that sins committed after baptism cannot be repented of and thus redeemed. Article XVIII is against the Anabaptist error that sincere followers of pagan religions will be saved even if they wilfully reject Christ. Article XXIII stresses that ministers of

---

[1] Charles Hardwick, *A History of the Articles of Religion*, Cambridge, 1859. p. 90.

[2] Schwenkenfeld's teaching is still looked upon as a ´continuation of the Reformation´ by certain British Baptists and Charismatics such as the Apostolic Church and is still very widespread amongst evangelicals on the Continent.

the Gospel must be called to preach through their church, thus attacking the Anabaptist doctrine that all believers are seen as exercising a teaching and pastoral function. This was one of the major points Featley wished to clear up in the Southwark debate but the Baptists were too much on the defensive and obviously were insulted at his questions which, because of the historical circumstances, were, nevertheless, highly valid. Article XX, one of the oldest post-Reformation articles, deals with God's Word as the sole authority in decreeing rites and ceremonies and the sole authority in controversies regarding faith. This was worded against any additions to what the Church of England believed was Scriptural, whether they came from the side of Rome or from the side of too radical protestants. Thus Featley firmly believed that 'it is not lawful for the Church to ordain anything that is contrary to God's word written, neither may it so expound one place of Scripture, that be repugnant to another' and, as the Baptists professed to repudiate this basic Article along with the other 38 Articles, they were to be treated as enemies of the Church.

The validity of John's baptism for Christians questioned

It was Anglican practice at this time to accept a baptism in the name of the Lord or in the name of the Trinity by immersion or sprinkling but not the baptism of John. The Baptists' claim that John's baptism was Christian baptism appeared to the Anglicans to be contrary to Scripture. Thus John Newton in his famous *Apology* gives the Baptists' acceptance of John's baptism as the pattern for Christian baptism as one of the reasons why he cannot join the Baptists whom he, nevertheless, greatly respected. That is, until they started accusing him of wrong motives in remaining an Anglican minister. This point is still a hot topic of debate not only between Baptists and non-Baptists but amongst the Baptists themselves. Article XXXVIII is a direct refutation of the view of many Anabaptists that Christians should have all their goods in common.

Featley was nearer Kiffin and his friends than they were to other Baptists

After the debate, Featley, whether rightly or wrongly, concluded that the Baptists were quite unaware of the origin, teaching and purpose of the *Thirty-Nine Articles*. Furthermore, as his opponents argued dogmatically that the Articles were against the Word of God, he could only conclude that the British Baptists were thus defending the very Anabaptist heresies against which the *Thirty-Nine Articles* were drawn up.

Actually, the doctrinal gap between the British Particular Baptists and the more radical Continental Anabaptists was far, far wider than that

between say William Kiffin,[1] who appeared to be the main Baptist Southwark debater, and Featley or the Particular Baptists and the *Thirty-Nine
Articles*. This distinction was not yet recognised in 1642 by the Anglicans
but nor was it recognised to any great extent amongst Baptists themselves
who were already splitting into numerous widely differing factions by this
time. Admitting there were exceptions, it is roughly true to say, with historical hindsight, that the nearer Baptists came to the Particular Baptists,
the nearer they came to the *Thirty-Nine Articles*, *Lambeth Articles* and the
Irish Articles, but the nearer Baptists came to the General Baptists, the
closer they were to Anabaptist positions. However, even Thomas Crosby
(c. 1685-1752), who was supposed to be a Particular Baptist, in his *History
of the Baptists* published in 1738, based on Benjamin Stinton's notes,
complains about the lines drawn between Generals and Particulars and not
only directly identifies the British Baptists with the Continental Anabaptists
but also criticises the strict way the Anglicans handled Arians.

John Gill more of one mind on the Anabaptists with the Anglicans
Baptist John Gill (1697-1771) in contrast to Crosby, made it quite clear in
his dealings with the Anglican Church that they would find no trace of
Anabaptist doctrines in him. Indeed, he protested against one Anglican
minister in Wales who was:

---

[1] See B. A. Ramsbottom's excellent, sympathetic biography of Kiffin, *Stranger than
Fiction*. Chapter 6 'The Grand Ringleader of that Seduced Sect' deals with Kiffin's
contacts with Featley. As Kiffin is Ramsbottom's biographical subject and not Featley,
he obviously defends Kiffin where he can. Sometimes this leads to speculative infer-
ences such as his statement, 'We have no account from the Baptist side but it appears
that the Baptists stood their ground courteously' (p. 28), whereas Featley is portrayed
as scurrilous and abusive and the fact that Featley spells Kiffin's name incorrectly
(although Ramsbottom himself allows for different spellings which would have led to
different pronunciations) leads Ramsbottom to think that Featly was 'contemptu-
ous'. Ramsbottom bases his findings on an understandably highly prejudiced view of
Featley's *Dipper Dipt*, perhaps forgetting that the book was a reaction against the
Baptists' statements and accusations at the Southwark debate which must have appeared suspect to an orthodox Anglican. It is odd that this debate was claimed as a
victory by Baptists from the day it took place, a victory which is still proclaimed,
figuratively speaking, from Baptist housetops, yet evidence of this victory was neither published, nor preserved. Which just goes to show that the Southwark debate is
still on and the last word still unspoken. Nowadays, the Baptists have most able
debaters such as Mr Ramsbottom but where are the Featleys amongst the Baptists'
brethren outside of their denomination? Who is able to reconcile these reconciled of
the Lord? When are the dipped and sprinkled going to live in peace?

not content highly to commend the church of England, as the purest church under heaven, but reflects greatly on dissenters, and particularly on such whom he calls rebaptisers; and repeats the old stale theory of the German Anabaptists and their errors, madnesses and distractions; and most maliciously insinuates, that the people who now go by this name are tinctured with erroneous principles; for he says, they spread their errors in adjacent countries, which are not fully extinguished to this day; whereas they are a people that scarce agree with us in any thing; neither in their civil nor in their religious principles, nor even in baptism itself; for they were for the repetition of adult baptism in some cases, which we are not, and used sprinkling in baptism, which we do not; the difference between them and us, is much greater than between the papists and the church of England.[1]

The *First London Particular Baptist Declaration of Faith*

It was to take another two years before the Particular Baptists produced the creed which Featley asked for in Southwark in 1642 and this creed came into being to a great extent because of that joint debacle. Thus the *First London Particular Baptist Declaration of Faith* begins with a clear statement that the seven churches who drew up the Declaration reject Anabaptist tenets and they profess that it is thus false to call London Particular Baptists by that name. In this way, Featley was of lasting value to the Baptist movement as the 1644 *Declaration of Faith* is still seen by today's Particular Baptists as the finest statement of Baptist faith ever produced. It is indeed a feast of good things and this present author feels it is a far stronger testimony to the particular doctrines of the Baptist faith than the 1689 *Second Declaration* which is mostly a re-statement of the Presbyterian *Westminster Confession*.

The Southwark debate was most unsatisfactory for both sides

The Southwark debate got off to a bad start as neither side really understood what the other was aiming at in the discussions. Both partners went into the offensive rather than listen and defend. Many red-herrings were thrown up and inessentials were hotly debated. The Baptists accused Featley of making an idol of his church and argued that bishops must be ungodly men as they persecuted Baptists. They also claimed that the

---

[1] *The Dissenter's Reasons for Separating from the Church of England*, London, 1763, pp. 18-19.

Thirty Nine Articles and other Anglican statements of faith and practice
were contrary to the Word of God. Featley kept up his accusations that the
Baptist had no sending, no calling and no imposition of hands, therefore
no church authority, laying his finger on points of difference and understanding, not only between Anglicans and Baptists but also amongst the
Baptists of his day, themselves. He also emphasised rather too much that
he was dealing with unlearned men who could not even stand up for their
faith when catechised.

Kiffin sought to discredit Episcopalianism by arguing that bishops
lived in known sin. Featley thought this was most unfair, especially as
there had been a recent scandalous case in the London Baptist churches.
He asked Kiffin if he never had cause to ask God's forgiveness for sin.
Kiffin replied that he had but that did not mean he approved of bishops
with known sin. Featley could not nail Kiffin down to names and places
here but told him of the bishops he knew who were of blameless lives,
including the one who had ordained him. Kiffin then doubled back from
his argument, stating that even if particular bishops were good men, God
did not give the power of ordaining to particular men but to his Church. To
this, Featley agreed, but pointed out that God appointed certain men in the
Church to exercise the power of ordination, otherwise no ordination would
take place. Ordination is always at the hand of a person or persons appointed by the Church.

It must have been clear to both parties by this time that the debate
would have been better for having never occurred.[1] Taking this fact into
consideration, Goadby's accusation that Featley's report of the Southwark debate was a 'savage attack' on the Baptists and that he was their
'bitter defamer' can hardly be called a balanced view of the debate. It
would also be difficult for a judicious reader to accept Cramp's extraordinary one-sided comment in alleging that Featley's defence of what he held
to be Scriptural teaching and the doctrines of his church 'are the words of
a defeated champion, venting his spite against his opponents.'[2] Actually,
both sides failed miserably to put their point across but the debate did
serve to make both parties think out their policies regarding each other
more carefully.

---

[1] For a wider discussion of Anglican-Baptist controversies, see my *John Gill and the
Cause of God and Truth*, pp. 110-131.

[2] *Baptist History*, p. 267.

The aftermath of the Southwark debate

After the publication of his *Dipper Dipt*, the Baptists were reported as accusing Featley of popish beliefs and one Baptist, Henry Denne, wrote in 1645 against the ailing Featley under the title *Antichrist Unmasked*. Denne, who became a Baptist at the disruption of the Church of England, was imprisoned for a short time with Featley but soon released and, though now a Baptist, was given an ejected Anglican's living which he held for a short time before becoming a professional soldier. Actually, Featley and Denne got on very well during their joint imprisonment so it must have been a shock for Featley to find that his fellow-sufferer thought he had been fellowshipping with 'Antichrist'. Following Baptist historian Crosby's colourful account of Featley, Neal mentions that 'it does not appear that the doctor ever replied'. He could not do so, as shortly after the publication of Denne's work, Featley was called home.

Goadby relates how Baptist Samuel Richardson felt that his fellow Baptists were very sorrowful to see Featley's blindness and hardness of heart. Such writing is as unworthy of Christian debate as the Southwark encounter and assumes that the Baptists were all clear-eyed and soft-hearted which neither Featley's nor Goadby's accounts suggest. Nor can it be said with any degree of objectivity that Featley's remarks against what he held to be Anabaptist views were more scathing than those of the opposition who did not hesitate to call him an Anti-Christ and spoke of him as if he were a dyed in the wool papist.

Actually, Featley did the Baptists a great service in accepting their challenge, in his complimentary remarks on them. In his analysis of several points that he believed smacked of faulty doctrine he was of strong influence on Baptist creed-makers who modified their statements to fit in with Featley's accurate criticism. Goadby does indeed credit Featley with saying accurate things of the *First London Particular Baptist Confession*. However, he begrudges Featley his most positive remarks by voicing the opinion that Featley made them 'abashed' and with 'manifest reluctance' and closes his patronising comments with the words, 'A valiant champion this, in good sooth, and one at which the Baptists must have smiled with pity.'[1] Featley was now dying of pleurisy and under-nourishment at the hands of his jailers and risked his neck further in complimenting the Baptists, which hardly suggests that his heart was not in what he said as it would have been far more comfortable for Featley not to have said it. Featley's words concerning the 1644 *London Declaration* were:

---

[1] Ibid, p. 117.

If we give credit to the Confession and the Preface thereof, those who among us are branded with that title (Anabaptists) are neither heretics, nor schismatics, but tender-hearted Christians, upon whom, through false suggestions, the hand of authority fell heavily, whilst the hierarchy stood; for they neither teach free will, nor falling from grace, with the Arminians; nor deny original sin, with the Pelagians; nor disclaim magistracy, with the Jesuits.

Indeed, Goadby's complaints are not so much a defence of the Baptist position as an all out attack on the Reformed Church of England of Featley's day, which is further evidence to prove that one must approach Featley's criticisms with a more balanced frame of mind. When one considers the antagonism from *within* the Baptist churches against the *1644 Particular Baptist Confession*, one will see that Featley defended in the Particular Baptists what other Baptists attacked. Thus Featley's remarks cannot be seen as anti-Baptist *as such*. The London General Baptists were quick to counteract their Baptist brethren's work with their *Fountains of Free Grace Opened* in 1645 in which they defended the doctrine of general atonement. Both Featley and Kiffin were in full agreement here against the General Baptists. Rather than smile with pity at Featley as Goadby recommends, Lumpkin relates in his famous *Baptist Confessions of Faith* that, 'In consequence of the attack by so famous a man as Featley',. . . 'it was decided to work over the Confession, changing as far as possible the language to which Featley objected, and to submit the resulting document to the House of Commons.'[1]

Further unjust accusations against Featley

Now Featley's enemies began to hit him where it hurt most. He had been chosen by Parliament to represent protestant England against papist Rome and now Britain, Europe and the New World colonies knew that Featley was as anti-Rome as ever anyone objectively could be. Yet these enemies, reputed to be Baptists, accused Featley, of being in the service of that bishop. We must remember that Featley was still imprisoned for defending the *Thirty-Nine Articles* which maintain that 'The Bishop of Rome hath no jurisdiction in this Realm of England.'[2] The threadbare reasons these critics gave showed the base moral, spiritual and intellectual level of their arguments. 'Did not Featley possess papist books?' was their cry, 'Therefore he must be a papist!' Now Featley's library had been taken from him

---

[1] Op. cit., p. 147.

[2] Article XXXVII.

by his Presbyterian enemies but Parliament had provided him with a few papist books so that he could debunk their arguments. Featley, now with asthma and dropsy added to his other deadly sufferings, published a manifesto, declaring his doctrinal allegiance and avowed opposition to the papist cause and challenged his accusers to a debate on the question of his Reformed orthodoxy.

Sadly, the debate between Featley and the Baptists is wrenched out of its historical background by many Baptist writers and seen merely as an example of Paedo-Baptist persecution of Believers' Baptists. Oddly enough in view of the circumstances in which Featley found himself, they see him as the main supporter of state interference in matters of religion.[1] It is interesting to note that Cramp mentions 1640 as the date when Baptist persecutions in England started to become intense. This was the first year of the Long Parliament whose attitude to Baptists was mild in comparison to how they treated Anglicans. Kiffin was not a victim of this persecution in any way,[2] though ministers of the Church of England, Ireland and Scotland such as Featley, Usher, Ward, Hall and Balcanqual certainly were. Indeed, the Baptists on the whole, and including Kiffin, espoused the cause of the Revolution whole-heartedly, thus joining the persecutors. Most Baptist writers make little of Featley's sufferings, Cramp ignores them completely and presents *Dipper Dipt* as if it represents the work of the persecuting authorities of the time. Yet when they come to Kiffin's story, his so-called sufferings after the Restitution are stretched out over pages. Yet considering the fact that the Baptists were chiefly instrumental in murdering Charles I and Baptist Major General John Harrison gave the order, after the Restitution, Kiffin was treated lightly by Charles II and James II, indeed, he was offered comparatively high local government offices. Furthermore, because of his enormous wealth, Kiffin was able to ward off trouble on numerous occasions, which was never directly concerned with his being a Baptist, by generous donations of money or payments of fines which he worked out with the leading lawyers of the nation. Other Baptists, less endowed, fared worse or, as in the case of further Baptist regicides, they fled the land and settled in Holland or the New World. Featley's one and a half year's imprisonment led to his martyr's

---

[1] See Whitley's *A History of British Baptists*. The author seems oblivious of Featley's sufferings and says that Featley was so proud of his *Dipper Dipt* 'that he published it again and again'. The only edition Featley had printed was the one dated 10 January, 1644. He did not live long enough to have it published 'again and again', Whitely himself says that Featley's book was re-issued around 1660 (p.107), fifteen years after his death, so the above sentiments must have been an emotional slip of the pen.

[2] Kiffin received a mild warning once from the Lord Mayor.

death.[1] Featley believed firmly that the Presbyterian revolt was putting the clock of the Reformation back a century and his maxim was certainly not, 'If you cannot beat them, join them.'

The Baptists' support of the Presbyterians presents a puzzle

That the Baptists should ally with the Presbyterians against the Anglicans is, to say the least, odd. The Anglicans, for instance, accepted the Baptism of newcomers to the faith by immersion, providing this did not lead to re-baptisms but the Presbyterians rejected baptism by immersion and established a sprinkling only rule. The Presbyterian doctrine of the church was also further from the Baptists than the Anglicans. The latter demanded a profession of a faith which displayed the new birth to be shown at departure from childhood at the earliest as anchored in Confirmation for children of families in covenant. They practised believer's baptism on expression of faith for pagan converts. On the other hand, the Presbyterians abolished Confirmation, yet they established a very High Church view of baptism.[2] The Anglican articles stressed that the Scriptures were the sole rule of faith and conduct but the original *Westminster Standards* emphasised Scripture plus the correct Presbyterian interpretation (i.e. tradition) rather than *sola scriptura*. Furthermore, except for a very short period under Bancroft and later Laud, no Anglican had objected to receiving those with Presbyterian ordination into the church, thus archbishops and bishops such as Abbot, Hall, Davenant, Ward, Carleton and Andrewes, shared the Lord's Table with Presbyterians and sat gladly under their preaching. Hall strove to have the Presbyterian orders recognised as equal to Episcopalian orders but those to whom he showed great generosity and understanding became his intolerant persecutors. The Presbyterians were far more High Church in their view of church offices than the Anglicans and had Parliamentary laws passed during 1640-42 to have all bishops defrocked with the excuse that 'episcopacy was against the wishes of the people,' but 'the people' had little or no say in the matter. Baptists, however, used the title of 'Bishop' and even 'Apostle' well into the eighteenth century. It is also interesting to note that few of the very few 'Baptists' whom earlier Anglicans were supposed

---

[1] Kiffin gave, on the whole, a clear and sound Christian testimony. He appears rather negative here as this is Featley's story and Baptist authors are unanimous in using Kiffin as a lever to oust Feately from his position as the sound, scholarly, spiritual and integral Christian he undoutably was. The picture thus must be adjusted in the way I have chosen here.

[2] See Article XXVII of the *Thirty-Nine Articles* and Article XXX of the *Westminster Confession.*

to have persecuted were indeed Baptists in the sense of the majority of Baptist churches of today. Featley, for instance, is heavily criticised for castigating a local 'Baptist Church' for heresy, which is often quoted to show that he had a persecuting spirit. Whitley, though accepting the group as 'Baptists', points out that they were weak on the deity of Christ and says, 'about 1916 it ended the indecision of nearly three centuries by deciding to rank itself with Unitarians.'[1] Indeed, few Baptist writers are as orthodox as John Gill in proclaiming what a Baptist ought to believe and, on the whole, classify 'Baptists' as being of any doctrinal persuasion whatsoever, providing they 'baptise on profession of faith'.[2]

A most unfair and dishonourable attack backed by theological error

One of the most unfair attacks on Featley came from the pen of Baptist Samuel Richardson who published his 18 paged *Some brief Considerations On Doctor Featley his Book, intitled, The Dipper Dipt, Wherein In some measure is discovered his many great and false accusations of divers persons, commonly called Anabaptists, with an Answer to them, and some brief Reasons of their Practice*, in February, 1645 as a reaction to Featley's 227 paged work on the Baptists. Richardson, knowing that Featley had written his *Dipper Dipt* from prison and was at the mercy of a Parliament who looked upon him as a traitor because of his allegiance to the King and the Church of England, opened his work with a highly polemical, political attack against Featley. Richardson's first heading thus reads: *I. Dr. Featley his secret and haynous accusing the honourable Parliament.* In this introduction, Richardson argues that it was not so much Featley's aim to attack the Anabaptists as Parliament itself. This extraordinary claim was made by Richardson on the grounds that Featley had complained in his book that his reply to the Baptists was made difficult by his imprisonment and the confiscation of his property, including his books. Richardson argues that in complaining most naturally as he did, Featley 'strikes the Parliament, and secretly wounds them with his malignant pen'. Richardson pretends to be surprised that Featley does not understand that the reason he is in prison is to heal him of this malignity. It is already quite evident here on whose side the malignancy abounds. This is made plainer still when, instead of dealing with Featley's theological points one by one,

---

[1] *History of British Baptists*, p. 47.

[2] See, for instance, Christian's *A History of Baptists*, vol. i, pp. 148-152 and passim. When Featley pointed out this lack of orthodoxy in the Anabaptists in *Dippers Dipt*, such Baptist historians as Armitage take this as 'proof' that Featley's book is 'ridiculous'. See his *History of the Baptists*, vol. 1, p. 471.

Richardson goes on to accuse Featley of quite unproven, grave anti-parliamentary activities which not even Parliament's lawyers had thought of bringing against the saint. The tactic is obvious. Richardson sought to destroy Featley's reputation by making him politically undesirable and so awake a prejudice in his readers which would give them a receptive ear for Richardson's theological arguments against Featley.

These theological arguments, however, are very slow in coming and when they do come, they are in the form of condemnations of Featley's faith, couched in most exaggerated terms which shows clearly that Richardson is an Anabaptist of the Anabaptists and that his own doctrines if not down-right heretical, are certainly highly erroneous at times. Indeed, where Kiffin and his friends plainly reject the title of Anabaptist, Richardson seems to accept it.[1] This is surprising as Richardson's name appears as one of the subscribers to the *1644 Declaration of Faith*. Richardson denounces the Episcopalian system of church government as anti-Christian and the Church of England as anti-Christian and idolatrous. He brings forward arguments against Featley reminiscent of Donatist hardliners in their quarrels with Bishop Caecilian, i.e. that it is wrong for Featley to argue that repentant sinners should be accepted back into the fold of the Church without re-baptism. Richardson shows Arian tendencies by accusing Featley of blasphemy because he teaches that Christ is the eternally begotten Son of God. Richardson's view was to plague the Baptists for many years to come. It is thanks to the Baptists' greatest theologians John Gill and J. C. Philpot that this erroneous doctrine was discarded for the orthodox teaching represented in the Scriptures and the Anglican Articles.

One weakness in Featley's arguments does show up clearly in Richardson's defence of his own doctrines. Featley had not differentiated between the varying and contradictory views held by the Anabaptists or Baptists and had tarred them all with the same brush. However, this is precisely the same argument that Richardson aims at Featley. Some Anglicans have lived contrary to Christian holiness, he maintains, so the whole

---

[1] Lumpkin says in his introduction to the 1644 *Baptist Confession of Faith*, 'In order to distinguish themselves from both the General Baptists and the Anabaptists, the Calvinistic Baptists of London determined to prepare and publish a statement of their views. The seven London churches, already informally associated together by 1644, evidently pushed aside their prejudice against the use of confessions and prepared their own statement for apologetic purposes.' *Baptist Confessions of Faith*, p. 145.

church must be in error. Featley, like Caecilian with the Donatists, is eager to seek out and emphasise what the two factions have in common.[1] Richardson, like the main-line Donatists, sees nothing of value whatsoever in the faith of his opponent.

Featley prepares to be ever free from his tormentors

Now, realising that Featley's earthly course was ending, his doctors begged parliament to remove the sixty-five year-old invalid from the squalid, deprived conditions in which he lived. His tormentors decided to allow Featley to return on bail to his home at Chelsea College for six weeks to recuperate but then he must go back to prison. Featley used this freedom to set his house in order and write his will which opens with the words:

> First, for my soul, I commend it to him, whose due it is by a
> three-fold right: My Creator, who infused it into me: My Redeemer,
> who freely ransomed it with his dearest blood: My Sanctifier, who
> assisteth me now in my greatest and latest assaults of temptation...

On August 17, 1645, the Parliamentarian Presbyterians made preparations to escort Featley back to prison as it was the last day of his six weeks' freedom. Whilst these preparations were being made, Featley called his friends to him to give them a last testimony of his faith and commit them to the Lord who He was now to meet face to face. After this, he fell peacefully asleep but was revived by his nephew who poured some drops of liquid refreshment onto his lips. On seeing the weeping relations and friends around him, Featley said in a firm voice, 'Ah cousin, the poor church of God is torn in pieces.'

As those who were much to blame for tearing the church into pieces entered Featley's chamber, they found their prisoner released from all his chains. The Lord had called His beloved child home before his tormentors could lay their hands on him. They were left with Featley's fine Christian testimony and their own bad consciences. One biographer (Anthony Wood) rightly says, 'He was esteemed by the generality, to be one of the most resolute and victorious champions of the reformed protestant religion in his time; a most smart scourge of the church of Rome, a compendium of the learned tongues, and of all the liberal arts and sciences.'

---

[1] See John Mee Fuller's excellent long essay on the subject under Donatism, *A Dictionary of Christian Biography*, vol. i, pp. 881.-896

RICHARD MATHER (1596-1669)

9. Richard Mather (1596-1669): Pioneer of American Congregationalism

Introduced to the Word of Life at an early age

Richard Mather[1] was born in 1596 of ancient yeoman stock, though reduced to poor circumstances, in the village of Lowton, near Liverpool, the son of Thomas and Margaret Mather. The young boy was sent to the grammar school at Winick four miles away to be educated, and because of the poor condition of the roads he was forced to become a boarder for the winter months. At Winick, Richard's education consisted in learning the classical languages at the expense of his mother tongue. Lasting benefits from this narrow education did, however, ensue. Richard was introduced to the Greek New Testament which became to him the Word of Life. He also came under the ministry of a local clergyman whose ministry was of a 'penetrating efficacy ... as was not in the common sort of preachers.' In spite of these privileges, all was not easy-going at the grammar school. Richard's teacher, Mr Horrocks, believed in deepening his pupils' knowledge by a fervent use of the rod which drove unhappy Richard to beg his father to remove him from the school. Cotton Mather, who heard tales of the mother country from his grandfather's knee, describes Horrocks as being harsh and fierce, saying he was the kind of teacher who believed in whipping boys when they were at fault but also whipping them when they were not at fault to be on the safe side.[2] Thomas Mather thus looked

---

[1] Mather's name is invariably pronounced to rhyme with 'wafer' by modern English speakers but Richard Mather pronounced his surname to rhyme with the northern English pronunciation of the word 'lather', i.e. with a short 'a' vowel. This pronunciation is preserved in parts of North America.

[2] *Magnalia Christi Americana*, vol. i, pp. 444-445.

around for an alternative to keeping Richard at school and finally arranged
to send his son to Wales to become apprentice to a Roman Catholic merchant. This was too much for Horrocks who implored Richard's father not
to leave his son to such a fate and, after a long interview between the two
men, Richard was able to continue his education, free from an all too
strenuous use of the rod and threats of being 'made the target of Popish
education', as Horrocks argued. By the year 1611 when Richard was still
only fifteen years of age, Horrocks felt that he could teach Richard no
more and was so impressed with his pupil's proficiency that he arranged
for him to become the founder tutor of a new grammar school at Toxteth
Park financed by the citizens. Ever thankful for Horrocks' intervention,
Mather nevertheless could not help writing one day when the thought of
his schooldays came upon him:

> But, O that all school-masters would learn wisdom, modera-
> tion, and equity, towards their scholars! and seek rather to win the
> hearts of children by righteous, loving and courteous usage, than
> to alienate their minds by partiality and undue severity; which
> had been my utter undoing, had not the good providence of God
> and the wisdom and authority of my father prevented.

Richard's life is radically altered
Whilst at Toxteth Park, three things helped to radically alter his life. Young
Mather lodged with the Aspinwal family whose piety thoroughly impressed
Richard and served as a fine Christian testimony, so different from his own
family life. Richard also attended a sound ministry at Hyton and learned
that 'Except a man be born again, he cannot enter the kingdom of heaven.'
The third major influence on Richard, now eighteen years of age, were
books by William Perkins (1558-1602) describing the lives of sinners saved.
Perkins' work was highly criticised by his less Reformed fellow-ministers
who were so shocked at his doctrine of the fall and consequent damnation
that they totally forgot to examine his great doctrine of salvation and
restitution. Bishop Robert Corbet, who had more wit than piety, on reading
Perkins' *A Survey or Table, declaring the Order of the Causes of Salvation and Damnation*,[1] the work which so influenced Mather, wrote a poem
about a mad puritan who had lost his senses on reading Perkins and
declared:

---

[1] Written in 1616.

> I observ'd in Perkins' tables
> The black line of damnation;
> Those crooked veins
> So stuck in my brains,
> That I fear'd my reprobation.[1]

Happily, Mather read of hopes of salvation in Perkins' writings. A hope which he was given grace to make his own.

All these factors joined to fill Richard with misery at his own sins and inability to master and tame them. But happily, to use the words of Mather's grandson, Cotton, they 'were the means whereby the God of heaven brought him into the state of a *new creature.*' His conversion came slowly, interspersed with times of doubt but also with periods in which assurance of salvation filled his heart.

Ramus influences young Richard

In 1618, Richard left his school to matriculate at Brasenose College, Oxford where he chiefly studied the works of Peter Ramus under the tutorship of Dr Woral. Petrus Ramus, or Pierre de la Ramée (1515-1572) became famous for his rejection of the Aristotelian logic and afterwards he became equally notorious amongst Roman Catholic powers for his acceptance of Reformed doctrines. Ramus was one of the thirty thousand victims of the evil St Bartholomew's Massacre in 1572. This was seen by perverted papists as the great bloody triumph of Rome when the Pope took Herod's slaughter of the Holy Innocents as his cue to murder the saints and struck a medal to remind him of his victory, with a scene of the slaughter on one side and his own wicked face on the other. This dastardly massacre was enough to make any decent-minded student interested in the works of those who were slain because of their faith alone. After only a year at university, Mather received and accepted a call to Toxteth Park Church, presumably influenced by Dr Morton, Bishop of Chester. At Toxteth, it is said, Mather preached to a 'vast assembly' of people. After the ordination ceremony, the Bishop asked to speak with Mather privately and the latter feared that his superior was going to warn him not to neglect the ceremonious side of Anglicanism. Not a bit! The Bishop knew what a man of prayer Mather had become and begged the newly ordained clergyman to remember him personally before the Throne of Grace.

---

[1] *The Distracted Puritan: Mad Song the Second* in The Percy Reliques. Corbet, successive Bishop of Oxford and Norwich, died in 1635 but the full poem was not published until 1648 in his *Poetica Stromata.*

Early leanings towards congregationalism

In spite of his friendship with Bishop Morton, Mather's sympathies were towards the Congregationalist scheme of church government rather than the Episcopalian and he was more than pleased to discover that his new church supported him strongly in this conviction. This soon became widely known and became something of a problem when Mather asked Edmund Holt of Bury, a stalwart churchman, for the hand of his daughter, Katherine, in marriage. All hindrances to the match were gradually overcome, especially as Katherine made it quite clear to her father that it was to be Richard Mather for her or none other, and Richard married his Katherine on September 29, 1624. Six sons were born to the couple, all of whom lived to adulthood and four of whom became ministers of the gospel. This was something of a double record, especially in days when child mortality was very high. The Mathers lived for fifteen years in deep harmony and fellowship with their church.

The tragic figure of William Laud

In 1630, the notorious Archbishop William Laud (1573-1644) came to power at Charles I's side. Laud was a most tragic figure. In his zeal to make of the Church of England a 'pure' church, he became a persecutor of those whom he thought were traitors, not only to his church, but to his King and country. In doing so he made so many errors of judgement that he was at last found guilty of the charge of being a traitor himself and was beheaded by the public executioner. It is a strange characteristic in the history of the Church of England that though she has always emphasised her comprehensive nature, she has, at times, done justice and mercy, and therefore the cause of God, a great disservice by persecuting those of her own ranks who disagreed with her about minor matters such as the wearing of a surplice or the reciting of a liturgical prayer.

During 1633, however, Laud's powers and freedom to persecute were at their highest and even Richard Mather, hidden away from the cares of the world in a tiny Lancastrian parish of souls who loved him, did not escape Laud's scrutiny. As a consequence, Mather was suspended from his office, most likely because of his Tuesday lectures in nearby Prescot which were apparently not conducted according to Anglican rites. Such lectures had been not only tolerated but encouraged by previous archbishops. This time, Corbet's *Distracted Puritan* describes Mather best as he stood condemned before Laud:

I appeared before the archbishop,
And all the commission;
I gave him no grace,
But told him to his face,
That he favour'd superstition.
Boldly I preach, hate a cross, hate a surplice,
Mitres, copes, and rochets:

Though Mather's influential friends, including his Bishop, managed to have Mather reinstated for a while, he was again suspended, this time through the intervention of the Archbishop of York, and told to conform. A story is related which, if true, shows that certain office-bearers in the Church of England had de-churched themselves before attempting to de-church Mather. Apparently, Mather was asked by the authorities how long he had been a minister, and they received the reply, 'Fifteen years.' He was then asked how many times he had worn his surplice and replied, 'Not once.' Thereupon, the church official proclaimed, interspersed with oaths, 'What! Preach fifteen years and never wear a surplice? It hath been better for him that he had gotten seven bastards.'

The New World calls
Now a private man, Mather heard of the greater freedom in religious matters in the new American colonies and, after corresponding with John Cotton and Thomas Hooker on the subject of emigration, Mather sailed with his wife and children from Bristol for Massachusetts Bay on the good ship James on May 23, 1635. Subsequent biographers and authors of school text books have greatly exaggerated and romanticised the reasons for these founder pilgrims journeying to the New World. Invariably they are portrayed as giants of humanity and men of iron who were convinced through eschatological speculation that the Old World was lost and they were the chosen ones to rekindle the light put out in Britain and Europe, on the shores of New England. Though undoubtedly many of the pioneers of the new colonies were men of God such as Cotton, Hooker and Mather, many were drawn to New England because of a feeling of nowhere else to go or because of a better chance to start a new life with their old aims, whether these aims were to the glory of God or purely material. In Mather's case, it seems that he merely wished to flee from temporary difficulties, in no way wishing to break permanently with the country of his birth. His first thoughts turned to Holland as a place of refuge and then to Barbados. In fact Massachusetts was one of his very last thoughts concerning a

place of freedom and this was only, through providence, because he had already made good friends in Boston and met like-minded brethren in London who had already planned to journey to America. Thus the Richard Mather who finally left Britain's shores did so as a sad outcast bound for a place of exile with a deep longing in his heart to worship and serve God in the fashion which he believed was God-honouring.

Mather sums up his reasons for leaving England
Though Mather's move obviously opened new doors of ministry for him, his church back home, who had been one mind with him on church issues and certainly one mind with him on doctrine, found themselves abandoned by the shepherd of their choice. Laud was executed in 1644 whilst Mather's church still corresponded with their pastor in an effort to persuade him to return. This has caused at least one balanced critic of Mather's desire to seek 'one's own preservation', to make the comment, 'Richard Mather's mood in this part of the argument was hardly exalted. Hope was gone, and he was looking for a way out.'[1] The 'way out' which sealed Mather's decision to leave England was expressed more honourably in his own words as:

I. A removal from a *corrupt* church to a *purer.*
II. A removal from a place where the truth and professors of it are *persecuted,* unto a place of more *quiet* and *safety.*
III. A removal from a place where all the *ordinances* of God cannot be enjoyed, unto a place where they may.
IV A removal from a church where the *discipline* of the Lord Jesus Christ is wanting, unto a church where it may be practised.
V. A removal from a place, where the ministers of God are unjustly inhibited from the execution of their functions, to a place where they may more freely execute the same.
VI. A removal from a place, where there are fearful signs of *desolation,* to a place where one may have well grounded hope of God's protection.

On the voyage out, a number of passengers died of scurvy. Mather and his family, however, had prepared themselves well against developing this deadly disease. They were thus able to supplement the ship's diet of salted fish and beef with bacon, buttered pease, steamed and boiled pud-

---

[1] Middlekauff's *The Mathers*, p. 21.

dings filled with dried fruit, oatmeal mixed with beer, soups and stews. An occasional porpoise caught by the ship's crew served as a refreshing and nourishing change of menu. Thus the entire Mather family landed safely on the shores of the New World, though a storm threatened to overturn the ship when land was already in sight.

Inward struggles but outward fame

Once in Boston, Mather received so many invitations to pastor churches that he just did not know what to do. As Cotton and Hooker had been instrumental in calling him to the Massachusetts colony, Mather asked them for further advice and it was decided that Mather should form a church at Dorcester as the previous church there had moved with their pastor to Connecticut. Here Mather was to remain for the remaining thirty-four years of his life. Rather than rejoice at reaching a 'Promised Land', Mather became exceedingly depressed on taking up his ministry and was often almost convinced that the Lord had deserted him. This was not much noticed by his friends and church members who were full of praise because of his fervour for the gospel's sake and the soundness of his teaching. Indeed, Mather soon became known in Massachusetts in the words of Hooker as 'a mighty man'.

It was years, however, before Mather received inner clarity concerning his own situation and the reasons for his removal from England. Often, he had grave doubts as to whether his six points truly reflected a difference between the New England churches and his faithful Toxteth church. However, this very trouble of mind kept Mather humble and diligent in the Lord's work.

Mather receives a blessing for the rest of his days

Mather wrote down all his thoughts on the subject and enough have been preserved, quoted in the writings of his son and grandson, to show how earnestly Mather begged in prayer that God would not deny him a heart to bless Him though he should be banned from His Presence. Cotton Mather writes how after several years of wilderness experience 'a glorious light' came into his grandfather's life. Here Cotton is referring to deep spiritual experiences of the presence of God but another great blessing was to come into Richard Mather's life.

John Cotton had died round about the same time as Mather's wife and a year and a half later, the former Mrs Cotton now became the second Mrs Mather of whom Cotton says, 'And her did God make a blessing unto him the rest of his days.'

Richard Mather's syllabus for Christian living
In the summer of 1633 Richard Mather drew up a syllabus concerning his
own behaviour as a Christian which provides a good deal of insight into
the kind of freedom Mather sought in the New World and shows how
private prayer, sound witness, good works and industrious study were the
ingredients of a life of faith in the young colony of Massachusetts. In a
solemn covenant made before God, Richard Mather declared:

> **Promises made to God by me, Richard Mather**. Psalm 66:13,
> 14; Psalm 119:106; Psalm 56:12; Neh. 9:33 with 10:29, 30, 31, &c. 21
> D. 6 M. 1633.
> **I. Touching the *Ministry*.**
> 1. To be more painful and diligent in private preparations for
> preaching, by reading, meditation, and prayer; and not slightly
> and superficially—Jer. 48:10; Eccles. 9:10; 1 Tim. 4:13, 15.
> 2. In and after preaching, to strive seriously against inward pride
> and vain-glory.
> 3. Before and after preaching, to beg by prayer the Lord's bless-
> ing on his word, for the *good* of souls, more carefully than in time
> past—1 Cor. 3:6; Acts 16:14.
>
> **II. Touching the *Family*.**
> 1. To be more frequent in religious discourse and talk—Deut. 6:7.
> 2. To be careful in catechising children—Gen. 18:19; Prov. 22:6;
> Eph. 6:4. And therefore to bestow some pains this way, *every
> week* once; and if by urgent occasions it be sometimes omitted, to
> do it twice as much another week.
>
> **III. Touching *My Self*.**
> 1. To strive more against worldly cares and fears, and against the
> inordinate love of earthly things—Mat. 6:25, &c; Psalm 55:22; 1
> Pet. 5:7; Phil. 4:6.
> 2. To be more frequent and constant in private prayer—Mat. 6:6,
> and 14:23; Psalm 55:17; Dan. 6:10.
> 3. To practise more carefully, and seriously, and frequently, the
> duty of self-examination—Lam. 3:40; Psalm 4:4; Psalm 119:59; es-
> pecially before the receiving of the Lord's Supper; 1 Cor. 11:8.
> 4. To strive against carnal security, and excessive sleeping—
> Prov. 6:9, 10; and Prov. 20:13.
> 5. To strive against vain jangling, and mis-spending precious
> time—Eph. 5:16.

IV. Touching *Others*

1. To be more careful and zealous, to do good unto their souls, by private exhortations, reproofs, instructions, conferences of God's word—Prov. 10:21, and 15:17; Lev. 19:17; Psalm 37:30.

2. To be ready to do offices of love and kindness, not only or principally for the praise of men, to purchase commendation for a good neighbour, but rather out of conscience to the commandment of God—Phil. 2:4; 1 Cor. 10:24; Heb. 13:16.

Renewed with a profession of disabilities in my self, for performance, and of desire to fetch power from Christ, thereunto to live upon him, and act from him, in all spiritual duties—15. D. 6. M. 1636.

> Richard Mather.

Finding a platform for church discipline and order

Mather's own doubts and disappointments were turned to good use in the churches of the colony who were seeking to form themselves into a religious body that was free of the shackles to the state which was so typical of the reign of Charles I, Cromwell and Charles II. Mather soon found that the churches in Massachusetts, though, on the whole, free from British persecution, were frowned upon not only by a number of Anglicans in authority but also by those such as Samuel Rutherford and his Westminster Assembly colleagues who could not be called friends of the Anglican system by any means. His inner fight with his own problems of church government and discipline had gradually enabled him to work out a doctrinal basis for the form, order and activities of a church which, along with Hooker and Cotton, he gradually put down in writing but it was not until 1648 that his influential *A Platform of Church Discipline Gathered out of the Word of God* was published.

Though these godly men were able to set up a church system which gave more freedom to the local pastors and churches and rid them of many externals which were more the product of traditions rather than an expression of Biblical faith, they certainly did not manage to define or rule a pure church which could be accepted by any Reformed Christian. Though the New Englanders rejected the theory of a State being identical with the church and ruled by a monarch who had church authority, they still sought for a *merger* of State and Church and looked upon political franchise as being the right of church members only. Here, indeed, the New England churches practised an intolerance against dissent which, at times, threatened to equal that intolerance in Britain from which they had fled but which during and after the civil war was relaxed and finally abolished in the mother country. This is illustrated by the resignation on October 24, 1654 of Henry Dunster, a successful President of Harvard College whose only mistake it seems as the leading educator of the state was to become a Baptist. Dunster was told to conform or leave and being equally a man of conscience as Richard Mather before Laud, he left. It is interesting to note that the first choice of the New England Puritans, lead by Governor Winthrop, for a man who could equal Dunster yet conform, was the famous Johannes Amos Comenius. This great theologian, linguist and educator had been invited in 1642 to Britain by Parliament to reform British schools and became pastor at Fulneck in Yorkshire for a time. It was then, most likely, that those interested in the New England cause had met him or obtained information concerning him. The New Englanders must have known, however, that Comenius, as a member of the Bohemian Brethren, was probably more a dissenter from their views of church order than Dunster. Comenius received a call to reform education in Sweden and thus was not free to become a colonist.

Difficulties in deciding what a true church is
Nor did the New England churches ever work out a practical, not to mention an infallible, system for admitting new members. They believed wholeheartedly that the children of covenant members were fully accepted within the covenant of promise and that the sign of this covenant was baptism but they still disagreed on what was a profession of faith and how this was to be given. Both Increase and Cotton Mather were far less rigid than Richard Mather and John Cotton on this issue but even this willingness to accept different expressions of faith and conviction resulted in church strife and the founding of other denominations, including the Unitarians. For a time, however, church tests were enacted which demanded an almost stereotype recital of what God had done for the would-be members' souls. As the church situation changed, Mather's views changed and became more tolerant though possibly less Scriptural. Perhaps, in all honesty, it must be said that Mather became less rigid, as his writings show, because he was frightened of shutting out true Christians because of their inability to confess their faith. At first he baptised only families whose heads professed faith in Christ but gradually he extended baptism to all those infants whose parents could show that they had been baptised, even though his conscience told him that the matter was 'dark and doubtful'. Mather still, however, demanded a full confession of faith from adults who wished

to be baptised. Nor did he allow persons, whether baptised or not, to take part in the Lord's Supper unless they made a convincing profession of faith.

The Half-Way Covenant

Thus a two-tier system of membership developed in Massachusetts, known as the Half Way Covenant, which was wide open to criticism from both Anglicans and other Dissenters of all kinds. Robert Middlekauff in his literary and historical master-piece *The Mathers* which won for him the Bancroft Prize, makes out a case for Mather's speedy rejection of this lax attitude to baptism and church membership, arguing that in a moment of temporary weakness, he gave in to the demands of his church. This can hardly be the case as the Dorchester church members did not vote unanimously to adopt the Half Way Covenant until 1677 when Richard Mather had been dead seven years. This was obviously because Mather remained lenient in formal matters of conformity but so great was the converting power of his preaching that he soon had a church which was 'pure' in the strictest Biblical sense, i.e. it became a true body of believers.

Mather finishes his course

By 1660, Mather, now a legendary figure, was the undisputed leader of New England Congregationalism. He became increasingly ill with kidney and bladder trouble, in those days commonly called 'the stone'. For many months before his home-call, Mather could not pass water and he was subject to unbearable pain. As the year 1669 opened, he climbed wearily up the stairs to his pulpit and announced 2 Timothy 4:6-8, 'The time of my departure is at hand. I have fought a good fight. I have finished my course.' When asked how he felt, Mather replied, 'Better than my iniquities deserve.' Seeing that he was dying, Increase asked his father for a final piece of advice. Mather urged his son to practise the Half-Way Covenant but take great care that the rising generation should be brought under the government of Christ. Faithful as Mather had been to the Lord, his son Increase and grandson Cotton were able to carry out his aims to an even greater extent.

HERMAN WITSIUS (1636-1708)

10. Herman Witsius (1636-1708): Man of the Covenant

God covenanted with his Son to save His people

There has always been two ways of viewing God in relation to man. He is seen by some as the God of order, ruling His universe with standards which reflect His eternal nature and which are revealed through the Scripture and which are demanded of man. What man cannot do to keep God's covenant with Adam and his offspring, God accomplishes in His covenant with Christ and His Church. Others see God as acting according to the impulse of the moment, though this leads to completely paradoxical actions. He is a God of contingency, arbitrariness and caprice. The former view was certainly held by the New Testament authors, our Reformers, the Puritans and the leaders of the Evangelical Awakening. The second view was, and still is, held by those such as anti-Calvinist Hugo Grotius (1583-1645) who maintain that God is not bound by Himself and that even the Mosaic Law and God's entire plan of salvation as revealed in both Testaments are merely temporary devices to accomplish transient aims, leaving man with as little true knowledge of God as ever before.

Those who believe that God never changes show how Scripture teaches that God has covenanted with His Son to seek out a people for Himself who will become partakers of His Divine, perfect, unalterable and eternal nature. It became the life's work of Herman Witsius of Enkhuysen, Holland to explain to man how God does this.

A child wonder is born

Witsius was born of believing parents who committed their son to God before his birth. When the puny infant arrived prematurely, the midwives predicted that he would not survive more than a few hours. Mr and Mrs

Witsius prayed in faith, promising to bring their child up in the nurture and admonition of the Lord. He survived to become one of the greatest men of God and men of letters that Holland has ever produced. Young Herman learnt to pray, read and write at a very early age before being sent to a Latin school when five years old. His learned uncle, Peter Gerhard, then took him on as a private pupil and prepared him for university entrance. Gerhard taught Herman History, Dutch, French, Latin, Greek, Hebrew and Science and instilled in the boy a love for the Bible. Because of his proficiency in knowledge, Witsius was accepted by Utrecht at the early age of fourteen. His professors confessed in wonder that there was not much they could teach him. Herman, however, knew that there was one thing still lacking in his education and deepened his Biblical studies. Though taught of God from early childhood, it was as a student that he came to an experimental knowledge of salvation. When one reads that Hoornbek, Voetius and Bogaerdtius were Witsius' professors, one can understand what a heaven on earth Utrecht must have been in those days.

At the age of nineteen, Witsius was set apart for the ministry, called to the French-speaking congregations in Holland. Two years later, in 1657, he was invited to pastor the Reformed church at West Wouden where he remained four years. Meanwhile Witsius' treatise on the Trinity had found European acclamation and he was preaching and lecturing throughout Holland, becoming immensely popular for the gospel's sake. Especially children and young people were led to the Lord by this highly academic young man who could put Divine truths into simple words that even the youngest understood.

Great blessings in a time of political turmoil

In 1660 Witsius married Aletta van Borchorn, a merchant's daughter who always said she did not know which was the greater, her love for her husband or her respect for him. The couple had two sons who died early and three daughters who survived to adulthood. Aletta served the Lord at her husband's side until her death in 1684 after a long and painful illness in which she displayed her deep trust and joy in the Lord. In 1661, Witsius accepted a call to one of Holland's largest churches at Wormeren, a church sadly split into a dozen factions. Witsius' preaching merged them all into one flock and when unity was achieved, he was called to do a similar work in Leuwarden, the capital of Friesland, in 1668. This was the year of the Triple Alliance when the United Dutch Provinces allied with Sweden and England. Dutch believers saw the Alliance as a bulwark against Spain and France, the Pope's two grasping hands for the Protestant pearl of the

United Provinces. When the War of Independence broke out in 1672, Witsius was amazed to find that England, the land of the Puritans, had turned tail and, under Charles II, was supporting Louis XIV of France against the United Provinces. The brave Protestant Dutch swore that they would never bow the knee to a Roman power and prepared to break all their dikes and swamp the entire Provinces, sailing off to found a new Christian state in the East Indies. The Lord of Providence planned otherwise. Just as the Netherlands were about to be trodden underfoot, William of Orange was raised up to save the Dutch from disaster and the English from shame and both Holland and England from a Papal takeover.

Witsius fame as a theologian and writer

In 1675 Witsius gained his doctor's degree and was called to the Chair of Theology at Franeker University. So great was his fame that when he delivered his investment lecture on *De vero Theologo*, he found that an enormous crowd of people had travelled from every corner of the Province to hear him. It was at this time that Witsius realised that God had given him the gifts and the authority to use his pen against the joint enemies of Dutch Protestantisam, i.e. Rome and those Dutch Protestant theologians who, with Grotius, had rejected a *sola scriptura* theology in exchange for an institutionalised, sacramental view of the church based on tradition which they called the *pia antiquitas* and which paved the way back to Rome. Witsius also directed his pen against Socinianism on the one side of Grotianism and Arminianism on the other, arguing that they were public adversaries of Biblical truths who had 'defiled the doctrine of God's covenants' and thus it was 'absolutely necessary to oppose them.' More dangerous than the Socinians and Arminians in Witsius' eyes were the Grotians. They spoke of a 'law' which was not the Law of Moses, a 'satisfaction' which was not through punishment and a 'substitution' which was not of necessity and not vicarious, both using and misusing the language of Biblical theology at the same time. Thus one of the first products of Witsius' professorship was his monumental work on the *Economy of the Covenants* which, next to Calvin's *Institutes* has proved to be one of the main exegetical pillars of Biblical theology and indeed Biblical evangelism. Thanks to Thomas K. Ascol and James I. Packer, the eighteenth century translation published by John Gill and his circle has been recently made available in a two-volumed, bound edition which will prove a godsend to all who feel called to witness for God to their fellow men. James Hervey was sent the Gill edition by John Ryland Sen. in February, 1753 and replied, 'I received your obliging letter, and very valuable present of Witsius,

which I shall thankfully keep as a monument of your friendship, and atten-
tively study as a magazine of evangelical wisdom. May the Lord Jesus
Christ transfer the precious truths from the writer's pen to the readers
heart!' Hervey did indeed experience that transfer and wrote later to another friend concerning the work, 'I wish, for my own sake, that you were
somewhat acquainted with the author, because, if you should be inclined
to know the reason and foundation of my sentiments on any particular
point, Witsius might be my spokesman; he would declare my mind better
than I could do myself.' In his famous work *Theron and Aspasio*, Hervey
calls Witsius work 'the golden pot which had manna; and was outwardly
bright with burnished gold; inwardly rich with heavenly food.'

Witsius draws students from all over the world and becomes an international figure

Though Witsius wrote a number of Christian best-sellers such as his books
on the Apostles Creed and the Lord's Prayer, his work on the covenants
drew students to sit at his feet from all parts of the world and he was able
to persuade the cream of these students to take up teaching posts in the
Dutch universities. After finding a worthy substitute for himself in John
Marck at Franeker, Witsius accepted a call to Utrecht University where, as
in Franeker, he took over the Chair of Divinity (after the death of Professor
Burmann) and pastored the local church. His investment discourse *De
Praestantia Veritatis Evangelicae* made it quite clear that Witsius was
going to stress the evangelical application of academic work. Again,
Witsius soon built up a solid core of evangelical, Reformed pastors and
teachers around him and his lectures were not only visited by his students
but also by the bulk of the teaching staff from every faculty of the university. Witsius' energies were enormous. He would spend his days teaching,
his evenings preaching and his nights studying, writing and preparing so
that his friends affirmed that he never slept at all. Even when middle-aged,
Witsius is known to have often worked through several days and nights
without a wink of sleep. It was no wonder that Witsius' fame led in 1685 to
his being sent as a leading member of a Dutch delegation to the court of
James II of England, whom the Dutch wished to impress with the Reformed
faith. During the months Witsius spent in England he pleased all denominations by treating both Anglicans and Dissenters on equal terms and
had sweet fellowship with evangelicals of both parties. He was made Chancellor of Utrecht University in 1686.

A most fruitful end to Witsius' great life and witness
Now Witsius gained a personal friend in William of Orange and was able to influence him strongly in gospel matters. In 1698 William asked Witsius as a personal favour to take over the Chair of Divinity at Leyden. Old age was now rapidly taking its toll of Witsius' health as he had never spared himself and he felt he should obey the call and now concentrate on preparing men for the ministry, giving up pastoral work. A year later, Witsius was elected Regent of a theological college set up by the Dutch States and West Friesland, and again Witsius found himself with a dual burden as Leyden begged him to stay. Though Witsius was rapidly fading from this world, his fame was still growing and seekers after righteousness and true learning flocked to him from all the Dutch States, France, Germany, England, Poland, Switzerland and Eastern Europe. Even American Indians, converted through the work of Eliot (1604-90) and those who followed him, found their way to Leyden to be trained for the ministry.

Death was not tender to Witsius. His last six years were spent in acute pain and dizziness. He suffered from severe memory lapses and at times he quite lost his powers of thought. After a serious attack in October, 1708, Witsius told those at his side that his home-call had come. He spent the last hour of his life speaking of his blessed hope and heavenly joys before peacefully closing his eyes to be awakened in Glory.

TOBIAS CRISP (1600-1643)

11. Tobias Crisp (1600-1643): Exalter of Christ Alone

Tobias Crisp served the Lord during a time of civil war and ecclesiastical unrest. There were threats of a papal takeover in the Established Church and Amyraldianism, Arminianism, Grotianism and Socinianism were flooding into the country to water down the faith inherited from the Reformers and defended by the Puritans. Crisp found these new religions false as they did not exalt Christ.

Entering the ministry as an unconverted man

This 'holy and judicious' person, as Augustus Toplady describes Crisp, was born into a family of London sheriffs and aldermen and was educated at Eton, Cambridge and Oxford, finishing his studies by gaining a D.D.. He married Mary Wilson, an alderman's daughter, and the couple were blessed with thirteen children. He was ordained Rector of Brinkworth in Wiltshire in the year 1627. It seems that Crisp entered the ministry as an unconverted man. His preaching was highly legalistic, emphasising good works as a means, rather than an outcome, of grace. Yet, he strove earnestly to glorify God in his life and ministry and quickly gained a reputation for popular, forthright preaching. As Crisp delved into the Word to bring comfort to lost souls, his own soul lost the shackles of trust in his own righteousness and he was granted faith in the righteousness of Christ who bore away his sins.

Preaching the whole gospel to the whole man

Crisp now became a seeker and healer of souls second to none in this time of disruption. He preached the whole gospel to the whole man as revealed in the doctrines of grace outlined in Scripture and in the witness of the

New Testament saints. Soon people flocked from miles around to hear him preach. As he had a large family estate which brought him a steady income and also a large rectory, he put all to the service of his flock. After preaching, he would gather together those who had travelled far and make sure that they were well catered for and their horses fed and watered for the return journey. It was not uncommon to find Crisp trotting home from church with scores of riders and dozens of private coaches and wagons in his train, leading his 100 or so guests for the day to their refreshments. Hearers and eye-witnesses testified that Crisp's doctrine was 'spiritual, evangelistic, particularly suited to the case of awakened sinners, greatly promoting their peace and comfort. His method was familiar and easy to be understood by persons of the meanest capacity and was particularly adapted to the condition of his hearers.'

With all his wealth and the political and ecclesiastical influence of his family, opportunities of promotion were regularly offered Crisp who declined them all. He was in his God given element preaching pardon to sinners. Soon there was a marked improvement in his parish through families having their members converted and family prayers becoming a regular feature in their lives. The Lord's Day, rather than being a time of worldly entertainment now became widely respected and observed. Crisp's preaching was highly expository but at the same time thoroughly evangelical with the preacher applying each truth to the situation of the hearer as he laid out his text. His emphasis was on Christ as the only way to salvation and on free grace and especially how to grow in that grace.

A sample of Crisp's preaching
Whenever and wherever one opens Crisp's sermons, one is in for a rich blessing as when reading his words on being quickened in Christ:

Do but look in Eph. 2:4-10, and there you shall perceive how clear and full the apostle is in this business, that Christ is made a way to life absolutely and merely of free gift; 'But God', saith he, 'who is rich in mercy, for his great love wherewith he loved us, even when we were dead in sins, hath quickened us together with Christ; by grace ye are saved: and hath raised us up together, and made us sit together in heavenly places in Jesus Christ, that in the ages to come he might shew the exceeding riches of his grace, in his kindness towards us through Christ Jesus.' Mark how he goes on; 'For by grace are ye saved, through faith, and that not of yourselves, it is the gift of God; not of works, lest any man should boast; for we are his workmanship, created in Christ Jesus unto good works.' Still he runs upon mercy and grace, and works he excludes, that no creature might boast.

If any thing were done on our part, to partake of Christ, we might have whereof to boast. So likewise speaking of Abraham, Rom 4:2, 'For if Abraham were justified by works, he had whereof to glory;' we should have to glory, if we should have the least hand in the participating of Christ; therefore God would give Christ freely unto his creature; because man should have no stroke in participating of him, that so it might be to the praise of the glory of his grace; that we should not glory; yea, 'That no flesh should glory in his presence.' And therefore the same apostle, Eph. 3:12, tells us, that from this grace 'we have boldness, and access with confidence through the faith of him.' In regard that Christ is given unto men to be a way unto the Father, and merely of free gift, hence it is that we have boldness and access with confidence by the faith of him.

Should we regard our own works or qualifications, there would be some mixture of distrust; we should have some fear that God would find out such and such a thought; therefore we could never come with boldness and confidence, if we did not come in Christ as a free gift bestowed upon us: for if there were one condition, and the least failing in that condition, God might take advantage upon that default, and so possibly we might miscarry; and we being jealous and privy to it, that there are faults in all we do, we should be 'subject all our lives to bondage', (saith the apostle), and should fear that God will take advantage of all that which is undone on our part; and so not fulfil what he hath promised on his part. But seeing we have Christ bestowed as a free gift of the Father, 'we come with boldness and access to the throne of grace.' To establish, or a little more to clear this, look (Heb. 10:18-20) 'Now where remission of sin is, there is no more offering for sin; having therefore boldness to enter into the holiest, by the blood of Jesus, by a new and living way that he hath consecrated for us through the veil, that is to say, his flesh.' How come we to have boldness? Through the new and living way made by the blood of Christ; not a new and living way by his blood and our actions, but by his blood; that is, only by his blood, merely by his actions; and so passed over freely to us; this is that which makes us come with so much boldness.

Look into the closure of all the scriptures, you shall find there can be nothing imagined more free; nay, so free, as the participating of Christ to be the way to the Father; nothing so free as this, (Rev. 22:17) 'Both the Spirit and the bride say, come; let him that heareth, say, come; and let him that is athirst, come; and whosoever will, (mark the expression) let him take of the water of life freely.' Hast thou but a mind to Christ? come and take the water of life freely; it is thine; it is given to thee; there is nothing looked for from thee to take thy portion in this Christ; thine he is as well as any person's under Heaven; therefore, you shall find our Saviour exceedingly complain of this, as a great fault, 'You will not come to me, that you might have life;' 'He that comes to me, I will in no wise cast him off;' upon no terms. Thou mayest object a thousand things, that if thou shouldst come, and conclude Christ is thy Christ, he will reject thee, and that it will be but presumption; but, in so doing, thou rejectest thyself, and forsakest thy own mercy; but Christ saith, Whosoever he be, what person soever, 'I will in no wise cast him off, if he come unto me.'[1]

The reasons for Crisp being much more successful than other preachers
Many of Crisp's fellow ministers, including nominal Reformed evangelicals, could not understand why Crisp was so much more successful than themselves. They raised the cry that Crisp was a poacher of souls as their own members were prepared to ride 12 miles and more to hear Crisp rather than walk round the corner to their local church. As this accusation was tantamount to admitting that possibly something was wrong with their own witness, other methods of criticism were devised. Crisp was accused of taking the doctrine of imputed righteousness literally and believing that Christ truly bore our sin and was actually *punished* in our stead. He was also accused, oddly enough by the same people, of denying the need for righteousness and affirming that as one was safe and secure in Jesus, one could live as one wished. The former accusation showed the strong impact of Dutch Grotianism on British Reformed doctrine. Grotius looked upon the imputed righteousness of Christ as a mere metaphor, bringing with it no actual transformation from outside (i.e. from God) into the life of the believer. It was a mere *pro-forma*, arbitrary arrangement between God and man. The latter accusation Robert Traill tells us was made possible because Arminian influence was so strong at the time that it had become

---

[1] *The Sermons of Tobias Crisp*, Tobias Crisp Series: Issue 1, pp. 42-44.

respectable evangelicalism to teach that Christ's atonement merely prepared the way for a salvation which was to be secured by good works. Those who did not believe this were termed 'licentious'. Actually these ideas strongly contradicted each other as Arminians looked upon the Law as reflecting the eternal nature of God and were thus, in this respect, orthodox, whereas the Grotians looked upon the Law as a temporary device of God to exert moral influence on man which in no way reflected God's eternal character. Nevertheless, the two schools of thought combined their energies in denouncing Crisp. He answered these groundless accusations in such sermons as *Free Grace the Teacher of Good Works* and *The Use of the Law*. None of Crisp's works were published during his lifetime, however, and the rumours grew, especially as his critics were slow to check their own prejudiced views concerning Crisp by actually hearing him preach. Those who did hear Crisp preach who had their heart set on heavenly food, learnt how wrong Crisp's accusers were in spreading the evil rumour that he interpreted Christian liberty as allowing him to live a life of sin because God looked on him as sinless whatever he did.

Crisp defends himself against evil claims that free grace encourages licentiousness

In his great sermon *Christian Liberty No Licentious Doctrine*, Crisp argues:

> But some will say, By this it seems we take away all endeavours and employment from believers, the free-men of Christ. Doth Christ do every thing for them? Do they stand righteous before God, in respect of what he hath done for them? Then they may sit still: they may do what they list.
>
> I answer, Will you deny this, that we are righteous with God, and that we are righteous with God by the righteousness of Christ? Or is it by our own righteousness? Then mark what the apostle saith, Rom 10:3, 4, 'They (saith he, speaking of the Jews), going about to establish their own righteousness, have not submitted themselves to the righteousness of God, for Christ is the end of the law for righteousness, to every one that believeth.' Either you must disclaim Christ's righteousness, or you must disclaim your own; for, if the gift of God 'be of grace, then it is not of works, else work is no more work; and, if it be of works, it is no more of grace otherwise grace is no more grace,' Rom 11:6.

But you will say further to me for, except a man be a mere Papist, I am sure he cannot deny but that the righteousness by which I stand righteous before GOD, is the righteousness Christ doth for me, and not that I do for myself, you will ask me, I say, Doth not this take off all manner of obedience and all manner of holiness?

I answer, and thus much I say, It takes them off from those ends which they aim at in their obedience: namely, The end for which Christ's obedience served: as much as to say, Our standing righteousness, by what Christ hath done for us, concerns us in point of justification, consolation, and salvation. We have our justification, our peace, our salvation, only by the righteousness Christ hath done for us: but this doth not take away our obedience, nor our services, in respect of those ends for which such are now required of believers. We have yet several ends for duties and obedience, namely, That they may glorify God, and evidence our thankfulness, that they may be profitable to men, that they may be ordinances wherein to meet with God, to make good what he hath promised. So far we are called out to services, and walking uprightly, sincerely, exactly, and strictly, according to the good pleasure of God; and, in regard of such ends, there is a gracious freedom that the free-men of Christ have by him; that is, so far forth as services and obediences are expected at the free-man's hand, for the ends that I have named, there is Christ, by his Spirit, present with those that are freemen, to help them in all such kind of services, so that 'they become strong in the Lord, and in the power of his might,' to do the will of God. Mark what the apostle speaks: 'I am able to do all things through Christ that strengthens me. Of myself (saith he) I am able to do nothing; but with Christ, and through him that strengthens me, I am able to do all things.' He that is Christ's free-man hath always the strength of Christ present, answerable to that weight and burden of employment God calls him forth unto. 'My grace (saith Christ) shall be sufficient for thee, and my strength shall be made perfect in weakness.' As you are free-men of Christ, you may confidently rest upon it, that he 'will never fail you, nor forsake you,' when he calls you forth into employments. But you that are under the law, there is much required of you, and imposed upon you, but no help to be expected. You must do all by your own strength; the whole tale of brick shall be exacted of you, but no straw shall be given you. But you, that are free-men of Christ, he will help you: he will oil your wheels, fill your sails, and carry you upon eagles' wings, that you shall run and not be weary, walk and not faint. So, then, the free-men of Christ, having him and his Spirit for their life and strength, may go infinitely beyond the exactest legalist in the world, in more cheerful obedience than they can perform. He that walks in his own strength can never steer his business so well and so quickly, as he that hath the arms, the strength, and the principles of the great God of heaven and earth; as he that hath this great Supporter, this wise Director, this mighty Assister, to be continually by him. There is no burden, you shall bear, but, by this freedom you have him to put his own shoulder to it to bear it up.[1]

Twisse and Hervey defend Crisp

Dr William Twisse (1575-1646), moderator of the Westminster Assembly of Divines and author of works on the Christian's moral obligations, on hearing these serious rumours, made a special study of Crisp's teaching and witness, finding him absolutely orthodox. He suggested that the only reason why Crisp was unpopular amongst ministers was 'because so many were converted by his ministry, and so few by ours.' Concerning those who accused Crisp of Antinomianism, Mr Lancaster, his publisher, said 'that his life was so innocent and harmless from all evil, and so zealous and fervent in all good, that it seemed to be designed as a practical refutation of the slander of those who would insinuate that his doctrine tended to licentiousness.'

James Hervey (1714-58) used the edition of Crisp published and edited by John Gill and was full of praise for the great soul-winner, always confessing that it was Crisp who had taught him the value of good works which 'proceed from the SPIRIT[2] of the LORD JESUS, dwelling in our hearts; and then they will be truly good.'[3] Of Crisp's sermons, he wrote to Lady Francis Shirley:

---

[1] *The Sermons of Tobias Crisp*, Issue 2, pp. 73-74.

[2] Many wrote to Hervey complaining that his prolific use of the names of the Trinity might put people off reading his works. Hervey responded by always emphasising the names of the Trinity in captitals. In spite of this his works averaged two editions per year for many decades.

[3] Letter LXXXIV to Lady Francis Shirley, p. 202.

Do not harbour any fear, Madam, concerning the propriety of your sending Dr. Crisp's sermons to Mr. K-. They are, I think, the very discourses which he wants. Especially, if he is inclined to distress of conscience, on account of his spiritual state. I know not any treatises more proper, or more excellently calculated, to administer solid consolation. They are, under the divine influence, one of my first counsellors, and principle comforters. They often drop manna and balm upon my fainting and sickly graces. The LORD JESUS CHRIST grant that your Ladyship may experience the soul-cheering, conscience-healing, heart-reviving power of these precious doctrines!

The Doctor has, as you justly observe, some expressions, which seem to contradict positive commands or peremptory assertions of Scripture. But these expressions, when examined and explained, will generally be found to coincide with the truth that is in JESUS. They are not contrary to the pure Word of the Gospel, but, to our pre-conceived ideas. We have not been accustomed to the joyful sound of grace and salvation—infinitely rich grace, and perfectly free salvation—therefore they are a *strange* language to our ears. O! that We may more frequently hear, and more diligently read, till, like the Colossian converts, we know the grace of GOD in truth![1]

Hervey was referring to the occasional depreciative mention of works of righteousness by Crisp where he is striving to keep his readers from believing that their good works are in any way meritorious. Later critics of Reformed theology have culled these few expression from the entirety of Crisp's writings in order to label their author an Antinomian. Obviously sensitive to such criticisms of Crisp, Hervey wrote again to Lady Francis on the subject, saying:

I do not wonder that, that people object to Dr. Crisp, and such divines as magnify the exalted SAVIOUR, who sits at GOD's right hand; but pour contempt upon the fallen creatures, who dwell in houses of clay: who would represent the divine REDEEMER, as the meridian sun, and all the race of Adam, as glow-worms of the night.—There was a time, when I should have joined, most heart-

---

[1]Ibid, Letter XCIII, p. 221.

ily joined in the opposition. For then I fought to *establish my own righteousness*. I would fain *be* something; would fain *do* something to *inherit eternal life*; and could not brook a total *submission to the righteousness of GOD*. But repeated infirmities, repeated sins, and repeated sorrows, have been the means, under the influence of the SPIRIT, to cure me of this arrogant temper.—It is now the daily desire of my soul, to see more and more the littleness, the insufficiency, the meanness of all that is called my own. But to delight myself in the *unsearchable riches*, and triumph in the transcendent excellencies of CHRIST JESUS my LORD.—And, I do assure you, Madam, that when I wander from this path, I *stumble upon dark mountains*; I fall into briars and thorns; I lose my peace, my tranquillity, my hope.—If this be the case, as it really is, your Ladyship will allow, that I have reason, notwithstanding every contrary suggestion, to adhere inseparably to *this Way*.[1]

The purity of Crisp's practical religion

Crisp's preaching, as his life, testify to his purity of religion. Expounding Matthew 25:44 on the Christian's duty to God and man, Crisp says:

We do not perform Christian duties in order to our being delivered from wrath; but we perform them because we are delivered. A man will work for Christ who has tasted of Christ's loving-kindness: he stands ready to shew forth the praise of that glorious grace which hath so freely saved him. Such a man is as glad to work for Christ's sake, as if he was to work for his own salvation. There are many ingenious persons in the world, who will be more ready to serve a friend that has already raised them; than to serve a master, that they may be raised. This is the true service of a believer. His eye is to the glory of Christ, in regard to what Christ hath already done for him: and not in expectation of anything Christ hath yet to do. He looks upon all, as perfectly done for him in the hand of Christ, and ready to be delivered out to him as his occasions may require. The work of salvation being thus completed by Christ and not to be mended by the creature; the believer having now nothing to do for himself, all he doth, he doth for Christ. . . . Salvation itself, therefore, is not the end proposed in

---

[1] Ibid, Letter XCVI, p. 223.

any good work we do. The ends of our good works are, the manifestation of our obedience and subjection; the setting forth the praise of God's grace and thereby glorifying him in the world; the doing good to others with a view to *their* profit; and the meeting the Lord Jesus Christ in the performance of duty, where he will be found, according to his promise: these are some of the special ends, for which obedience is ordained, salvation being settled firm before.

Crisp also said:

There is no believer who hath received Christ but he is created in him unto good works, that he should walk in them. He that sprinkleth clean water upon them, that they become clean from all their filthiness, puts also a new spirit within them, and doth cause them to walk in his statutes and testimonies. So I say that sanctification of life is an inseparable companion with the justification of a person by the free grace of Christ. But I must withal tell you that all this sanctification of life is not a jot of the *way* of that justified person unto heaven. It is the business a man hath to do *in* his Way, Christ.

The three alleged laws of faith, repentance and sincere obedience

Another cause of criticism against Crisp was the new theology which saw no need to preach the terrors of the Old Law with its call for absolute obedience or eternal destruction, warded off by Christ's perfect righteous sacrifice and His righteousness being imputed to the elect. Followers of such errors, were named Neonomians because they held that 'evangelical righteousness' could be obtained through following the New Law of 'faith, repentance and sincere obedience'. If these three commandments were kept for life, the sinner would be saved. Louis Berkof concludes, 'The covenant of grace was changed into a covenant of works.'

As Crisp preferred God's Law to the New Law he was called an Antinomian—a lawless man. Crisp's enemies had cunningly combined the errors of Amyraldianism, Grotianism and Arminianism to form a new pseudo-evangelicalism. This Neonomian stance split evangelical churches down the middle and the modern cleft between free-gracers and free-willers shows that sadly this cleft remains. On the Neonomian side one finds Presbyterian Dr Daniel Williams (1644-1716), whose views influenced Benjamin Brook's brief biography of Crisp and also the Lorimers' Hall Western Association Baptist Conference of 1704 in which 13 churches denounced Crisp's doctrine of the imputed righteousness of Christ as tending to 'overthrow natural, as well as revealed religion.' On the Crisp side, we find such outstanding evangelicals as Twisse, Traill, Toplady, Hervey, Gill, Ryland Sen., Whitefield, Boston, the Erskines, John Brown of Whitburn, Huntington, those Anglicans who hold Article XIII dear and many modern Particular Baptists, in fact, all true Reformed men.

Crisp resigns his soul to God in confidence and great joy
During the civil war, Cavalier troops forced Crisp out of his rectory and he was compelled to move to London where no less than fifty-two ministers combined together to form a kind of Anti-Crisp Society, doing all in their power to discredit the evangelical pastor. It is interesting to note how their perverted logic developed, showing how even the finest saints can become gossip-mongers through theological prejudice. The critics were convinced that Crisp was an Antinomian. They thus expected him to behave as such. This led them to believe any silly rumour they heard against Crisp and thereafter help to spread it.

Crisp was given strength for the occasion and entered many a public debate with his opponents, proving the better man in argument, testimony and quality of life. The irony of the situation was that slanderers were accusing one of the greatest preachers of righteousness of all time of Antinomianism when they were openly bearing false witness themselves! Crisp was now preaching daily and suffering from great persecution which forced him to spend many a night on his knees praying for guidance. This weakened his physical constitution no end and when in the course of witnessing, he contracted the smallpox, this was the Lord's means of carrying him home. Shortly before his death, Crisp acknowledged that 'as he had lived in the free grace of God, through Christ, so he did, with confidence and great joy, even as much as his present condition was capable of, resign his life and soul into the hands of his most dear Father.' Thus passed away Tobias Crisp, aged 42 years. His son gathered together his literary remains and published them under the title *Christ Alone Exalted* as this was their central theme.

JAMES JANEWAY
(Brother and biographer of John Janeway.)
There is no known picture of John.

12. John Janeway (1633-1657): The Saint Who Lived in Heaven On Earth

An extraordinary pious and gifted young man

This 'Pius and extraordinary' Christian as Benjamin Brook[1] and Erasmus Middleton[2] describe Janeway, only preached two sermons in his whole life and lived to be only 23 years of age but in 1672 Richard Baxter confessed humbly that Janeway had put more into those few years than he, with all his zeal for God, had put into sixty.

John Janeway was born on October 27, 1633 in Lylly, Hertfordshire of believing parents. The rudiments of reading, writing and Latin were taught John by his father until he entered St Paul's School, London where he became especially fond of Arithmetic, Astronomy, Latin, Greek and Hebrew under the care of his teacher, Mr Langley. Apparently even St Paul's was unable to give John the tuition he needed to suit his precocious intellect so he was removed from the school and given several private tutors over a number of years before entering Eton at the age of 13, after amazing the entrance examiners by his skill in Hebrew. At Eton John's biographer says he was 'the glory of the school and the wonder of the age' and this extraordinarily gifted child entered King's College, Cambridge at seventeen, having been the Electors' first choice. John quickly established himself as top scholar in his year. As a young student, Janeway was described as unaffected, of sweet temper and quite free of the usual student vices. Though he was daily praised and admired, he was gifted with such humility that it did not affect him in the least. Yet, there was one thing lacking in his life. James, John's brother put this into words:

---

[1] *Lives of the Puritans*, vol. iii, pp. 271-289.

[2] *Biographia Evangelica*, vol. iii, pp. 362-369.

But all this while it is to be feared that he understood little of the worth of Christ and his own soul; he studied indeed the heavens, and knew the motion of the sun, moon, and stars, but that was his highest; he thought yet but little of God, Who made all these things; he looked but little into the motions of his own heart, and did not as yet employ himself in the serious observation of the wandering of his spirit ; the creature had not yet led him to the Creator, but he was still too ready to take up with mere speculation. But God, Who from all eternity had chosen him to be one of those who should shine as the sun in the firmament for ever in glory, did, when he was about eighteen years old, shine in upon his soul with power, and did convince him what a poor thing it was to know so much of the heavens and never come there; and that the greatest knowledge in the world without Christ, was but empty and unavailable. He now thought Mr. Bolton had some reason on his side, when he said, 'Give me the most magnificent, glorious worldliness that ever trod upon earthly mould, richly crowned with all the ornaments and excellencies of nature, art, policy, preferment, or what heart can wish besides, yet—without the life of grace to animate and ennoble them—he were to the eye of heavenly wisdom but as a dead body stuck over with flowers.' He began now to be of Anaxagoras's mind, that his work upon earth was to study heaven and to get thither; and that except a man might be admitted to greater preferment than this world can bestow upon her favourites, it were scarce worth the while to be born.[1]

Janeway experiences the one thing needed

A fellow student began to take Janeway aside and to tell him of salvation in Christ, putting good books into his hands and taking him to hear good preachers. Baxter's *Saints' Everlasting Rest* was of particular blessing to him. Soon Janeway was confessing that he had found the Creator behind the universe and had met Him in Christ Jesus. He wasted no time in telling his entire family of the change in his life. As one particular relation was in the ministry though he had no faith to administer, Janeway made him a special target, tenderly taking his mind from the cares of this world and pointing him to the gracious Redeemer. Though but nineteen years of age himself, Janeway began to have the care of children at heart and wrote to

---

[1] *Life and Death of John Janeway*, pp. 16-17.

friends and relations, advising them how to lead their children to Christ and how to educate them in spiritual things as if he were a teacher of many years standing. Janeway was made a Fellow of King's College when twenty years old and showed no neglect in either witnessing to his fellow students or using his times of study wisely. Typical of his words of witness are those to a young relation to whom he says:

> You may believe me - for I have through mercy experienced what I say - there is more sweetness in one glimpse of God's love, than in all that the world can afford. O do but try: O taste and see how good the Lord is. Get into a corner, and throw yourself down before the Lord, and beg of God to make you sensible of your lost undone state by nature, and of the excellency and necessity of Christ. Say, 'Lord, give me a broken heart, soften, melt me. Anything in the world, so I may be but enabled to value Christ and be persuaded to accept of Him as He is tendered in the Gospel. O that I may be delivered from the wrath to come. O a blessing for me, even for me.' And resolve not to be content till the Lord have in some measure answered you.

Janeway wrestles in prayer for his family

When at home, Janeway began to catechise his ten brothers and sisters and when he found his eleven-year old brother falling asleep during family prayers, he so preached the terrors of the Lord and the grace of God to him and affectionately pleaded with him to repent and believe that a saving work was effected in the child. To back up his witness both in his family and at college, Janeway conducted open or public prayers twice a day but reserved from three to seven periods a day to pray privately, wrestling with God for the souls of his brethren in the flesh and his students. Janeway's own father, though a minister, had times of great apprehension as death drew near. Janeway took the matter to the Lord, praying fervently that his dear father should be called home in joy and expectancy. He returned to his father's deathbed to find him praising God and saying, 'O son! now it is come, it is come! I bless God I can die: the Spirit of God hath witnessed with my spirit that I am His child: now I can look up to God as my dear Father, and Christ as my Redeemer: I can now say, "this is my friend and this is my beloved!" My heart is full, it is brim-full: I can hold no more. I know now what that sentence means, "the peace of God which passeth all understanding."' Thus after months of severe illness, the Rev. William Janeway crossed triumphantly over Jordan.

Janeway left King's College for a time to look after his mother and family. This period is well documented and reveals Janeway as taking on the duties of a father to his younger brothers and sisters and a son to his thankful mother. His letters of this period show a closeness to the Lord a tenderness of spiritual affection very rarely seen.

Faith and love kiss the Saviour

After returning for a short time to Cambridge, he was recommended by his Provost as private tutor to the son of a Dr Cox. Janeway took up the post but immediately became seriously ill. He was, however, so assured that he was in God's will even in his illness that he felt ashamed to pray for health and life and it is said that all his prayers were praises that he was counted worthy of following his father to glory.

Janeway did recover—for a short time—and returned to his life of intense prayer and witness, telling his students and friends in words such as:

> Dear soul, come near and look upon His face and see whether thou canst choose but love Him. Fall upon Him, embrace Him, give Him thy dearest, choicest love: all is too little for Him; let faith and love kiss Him: you shall be no more bold than welcome. Fix thine eyes again and again upon Him and look upon His lovely sweet and royal face, till thou art taken with this beautiful person.

Learning from Janeway's brief life

What we can learn from Janeway's brief sojourn on earth is best expressed through Baxter's words in his Preface to the first edition of John Janeway's *Life* written by his brother James Janeway.

> Reader, learn by this history to place thy religion in love and praise, and a heavenly life. Learn to keep such communion with God, and to find such employment with thy heart by meditation, as thy strength, and opportunity, and other duties will allow thee; I urge thee to no more. Learn hence to thirst after the good of souls, and to fill up thy hours with fruitful duty! And O that we could here learn the hardest lesson: to get above the love of life, and to overcome the fears of death, and to long to see the glory of Christ, and triumphantly to pass by joy to joy! O blessed world of spirits! whose nature, and work, and happiness is love; not love of carnal self, and interest, and parties, which here maketh those seek our destruction most, who have the highest esteem of our

knowledge and sincerity, as thinking our dissent will most effectually cross their partial interests; but the love of God in himself
and in his saints, checked by no sin; hindered by no distance,
darkness, deadness, or disaffection; diverted by no carnal, worldly
baits; tempted by no persecutions or afflictions; damped by no
fears of death, nor of any decays or cessation through eternity.
To teach me better how to live and die, in faith, hope and love, is
that for which I read this narrative; and that thou mayest learn the
same is the end of my commending it to thee! The Lord teach it
effectually to thee and me. Amen.

Going to the one loved more than life
Friends urged Janeway to spare his energies in his zeal for God so that he
would not be ill so often but the young saint could only say:

> Let us awake, and fall to our work in good earnest: heaven and
> hell are before us, and death behind us. What, do we mean to
> sleep! dullness in God's service is very uncomfortable, and at the
> best will cost us dear: and, to be contented with such a frame, is a
> certain symptom of a hypocrite. O, how will such tremble, when
> God shall call them to give an account of their stewardship, and
> tell them they may no longer be stewards! Should they fall sick,
> and the devil and conscience fall upon them, what inconceivable
> perplexity would they then be in!

Janeway's illness was diagnosed as 'consumption' and he was
plagued by coughing up blood, fainting fits and the loss of his eye-sight.
He told his mother that she should not worry as the only thing that was
worrying him was her grief. 'I am going to him whom I love above life,' he
told her. When the death pangs were upon him, Janeway called his family
one by one to him and gave them wise counsel as to how they should
conduct themselves in the Lord.

A dying testimony to his family
John Janeway's testimony to his brothers and sisters was so strong that at
least three of them became ministers of the gospel, the most well-known of
these being James Janeway (1636-1674) who became his brother's first
biographer.[1] The day before he died, John said to his brother James, 'I

---

[1] My copy, *Invisibles, Realities, Demonstrated in the Holy Life and Triumphant Death
of John Janeway*, London, 1885

thank thee, dear brother, for thy love: Thou art praying for me, and I know thou lovest me dearly: But Christ loveth me ten thousand times more than thou dost. Come and kiss me, dear brother, before I die.' After James had embraced him, John said, 'I shall go before, and I hope thou shalt follow after to glory.' On the following day, shortly before breathing his last, John said to James, 'Brother James, I hope God hath given thee a good heritage. The lines have fallen to thee in pleasant places. The Lord is thy portion. Hold on, dear brother; Christ and heaven are worth striving for. The Lord give thee abundance of his grace.' James did not forget these words of saintly advice and he carried on John's care for and work amongst children, becoming the author of that well-known and well-used book *Token for Children*, still in print after over three hundred years. When Richard Cecil (1748-1810) the Evangelical minister was six years of age, his mother introduced him to James' *Token*. Cecil writes, 'I was much affected by this book, and recollect that I wept, and got into a corner, where I prayed that I also might have 'an interest in Christ', like one of the children there mentioned.'[1]

After addressing each of his dear ones separately, Janeway then told his gathered family:

O that none of us may be found among the unconverted in the day of judgment! O that we may all appear, with our honoured father and dear mother, before Christ with joy; and that they may say, 'Lord, here are we, and the children whom thou hast given us!' O that we may live to God here, and live with God hereafter. And now, my dear mother, brethren, and sisters, farewell. I leave you a short time. I commend you to God, and to the word of his grace, which is able to build you up, and to give you an inheritance among them which are sanctified. And now, dear Lord, my work is done. I have fought a good fight, I have finished my course, I have kept the faith; henceforth there is laid up for me the crown of righteousness. Come, Lord Jesus, come quickly.

Shouting for joy as the time for departure comes

His last moments are portrayed in triumphant detail by James Janeway:

Then that godly minister came to give him his last visit, and to do the office of an inferior angel, to help to convey this blessed

---

[1] *Remains of the Rev. Richard Cecil*, Josiah Pratt, p. 5.

soul to glory, who was now even upon Mount Pisgah, and had a full sight of the goodly land at a little distance. When this minister spake to him, his heart was so inflamed with love and delight as to draw from him tears of joy, amazed to hear a man at the point of death talk as if he had been with Jesus, and came from the immediate presence of God. O the smiles that were then in his face, and the unspeakable joy that was in his heart! one might have read grace and glory in his countenance. O the praise, the triumphant praises, that he put up! And everyone must speak praise about him, or else they did make some jar in his harmony. And indeed most did, as well as they could, help him to praise. So that I never heard, nor knew more praises given to God in one room, than in his chamber.

A little before he died, in his prayer, or rather praises, he was so wrapped up with admiration and joy, that he could scarce forbear shouting for joy. In the conclusion of the duty, with abundance of faith and fervency, he said aloud, 'Amen, Amen'.

And now his desires were soon to be satisfied. Death approached to do his office; his jaws were more and more loosened, and quivered greatly; his hands and feet became cold as clay, and a cold sweat was upon him; but, O how glad was he when he felt his spirit departing! Never was death more welcome to any mortal, I think. Though the pangs of death were strong, yet the far more exceeding and eternal weight of glory made him endure them with much patience and courage. In the extremity of his pains, he desired his eldest brother to lay him a little lower, and to take away one pillow from him, that he might die with the more ease. His brother replied, that he durst not for a world do anything that might hasten his death a moment. Then he was well satisfied, and sweetly resigned himself up wholly to God's disposal; and after a few minutes, with a sudden motion gathering up all his strength, he turned a little on one side, and in the twinkling of an eye fell asleep in Jesus.

And now, blessed soul, thy longings are satisfied, and thou seest and feelest a thousand times more than thou didst upon earth, and yet thou canst bear it with delight; thou art now welcomed to thy Father's house by Christ, the beloved of thy soul; now thou hast heard Him say, 'Come, thou blessed of my Father!' and, 'Well done, good and faithful servant; enter thou into the joy of thy Lord,' and wear that crown which was 'prepared for thee before the foundation of the world.'

O that all the relations which thou hast left behind thee may live thy life, and die thy death, and live with Christ, and thee, for ever and ever ! Amen, Amen.

John Janeway died June, 1657, in his twenty-fourth year; and was buried in Kelshall Church, in Hertfordshire where his father had been minister. Seldom has a saint been permitted to enjoy heaven on earth as he did.

INCREASE MATHER (1639-1728)

13. Increase Mather (1639-1723): Relator of God's Illustrious Providences

A good upbringing helps a 'dull wit'

Increase was the youngest son of Richard and Katherine Mather and was born in Dorchester, Massachusetts on June 21, 1639 after the Mathers had been in New England for four years. He was taught to read on his mother's knee and his father taught him to write, adding Latin and Greek to his home-schooling. Though Increase always felt that he was of mediocre abilities, calling himself 'of dull wit' and could not understand why he was always ahead of his classmates in learning, he may not have realised how much his upbringing at home had done to prepare him for an academic life. This life began very early as Increase passed his university entrance qualifications at 12 years of age. Nowadays one hears so much talk of the low standards of the American university in its early development and how they were run on little more than grammar school lines. This can hardly be the case as when Increase entered Harvard at little over grammar school entrance age, he was expected to be able to read and translate any classical Latin and Greek author on sight, converse freely in Latin and have mastered Greek grammar besides giving evidence of proficiency in writing not only Latin prose but also Latin verse. Furthermore, candidates were expected to have a working knowledge of Hebrew besides Greek as morning and evening prayers from the start of their college lives were accompanied by Hebrew Scripture readings which were translated and expounded in Greek. It would be superfluous to ask what modern 12-year old could cope with equal proficiency in any 'modern' subject. As in modern grammar school courses of vision, however, students were required to study maths and the natural sciences besides geography, history, philosophy, theology and the ancient tongues. Quite unlike most modern universities or schools,[1] examination time was particularly grilling. Before the formal examinations took place, candidates had to present themselves each Monday and Tuesday for three weeks on which days the university governors, experts in various subjects and even the general public were invited in to try and outwit the students and thus show up their knowledge or sad lack of it.

Increase receives a private tutor

Increase's health broke down after six months at college and his father was compelled to withdraw him but put him under the tutorship of their neighbour John Norton who became John Cotton's successor. Norton was born in May, 1606 in Stortford, Hertfordshire[2] in England. After attending Cambridge University he emigrated to Plymouth, New England with Thomas Shepherd and moved via Ipswich to Boston where he died in April, 1663. Norton made a name for himself as a debater on the matter of church government and church discipline and as an opposer of the Quakers, against whom he also wrote. Richard Baxter, whose *Aphorisms of Justification* gave Norton particular offence, also suffered under Norton's pen. Knowing that Increase Mather had been Norton's pupil, Baxter told Increase when they met in England, 'Sir, if you know of any errors in any of my writings, I pray you to confute them after I am dead.'[3] Cotton Mather praises Norton's work *A Discussion of that great point in Divinity, THE SUFFERINGS OF CHRIST: and the Question about his Active and Passive Righteousness, and the Imputation thereof.* Norton also wrote a biography of John Cotton. After Norton's death, he was lovingly referred to as 'Our Orthodox Evangelist'.

A serious illness makes Increase aware of the need to be born again

In 1654 Increase became seriously ill and it was thought that he would be the first member of the family to die. It was during this period that Increase began to have long conversations with his parents about the new birth. The young teenager did not die but the family lost a treasured member in Katherine Mather who died in March 1655. On her deathbed, Katherine

---

[1] It is interesting to note that Cotton Mather often compared Harvard to Uppsala University and indeed, when this author studied there in the sixties such 'public examinations' were still practised in the case of higher degrees.

[2] Cotton Mather gives 'Starford, Hartfordshire' in his biography of Norton in *Magnalia Christi Americana*, vol. i, p.286.

[3] Op. sit. p. 293

Mather spoke to her son about his eternal soul and confessed that it was her prayer to have seen him make a stand for the gospel and become a minister like his father. For months after this experience, Increase lived under conviction of sin and pleaded with God for mercy, behind the locked door of his room for hours on end. Increase turned to his father for counsel and on election day, May, 1655, shortly after the Nortons had left the Mathers' home and Increase could turn to prayer, he received a sense of forgiveness and assurance that the Lord had made him His own. Increase was fit enough to return to college in his final year and graduated with his old classmates as if he had been at the university all the time. There was something of a hitch at the open disputation. Obviously the son of his father, Increase chose to argue on Ramean lines which did not please the college President. As Increase showed such mastery in presenting his case, his bachelor's degree was secured. Little did those examiners know that one day Increase would return to Harvard as its President.

Increase travels to Britain for further studies

Increase helped his father for a year or so in his pastoral work, preparing himself for his Master's degree. It was then that he received a longing to visit the British Isles. Richard had been of two minds for many years about returning to the home country and his family always considered themselves as British colonists rather than Americans. He had thus not complained at all when his son Nathanael left New England and settled down as a pastor in London and a second son, Samuel took over a church in Dublin. Perhaps he was comforted to know that at least one son, Eleazer had accepted a call to a church in the new settlement of Northampton on the Connecticut River and, when Increase announced that he would like to visit his brother in Ireland and finish his studies at Trinity College, Dublin, it appears that Richard felt that Increase, too, would settle down in the old country which they still called 'home'. Increase did not leave his father's house, however, without promising to visit Richard Mather's former Toxteth congregation with whom his father had kept up correspondence, serving as an advisory pastor over the years.

Mather becomes Chaplain to the Guernsey garrison

After studying two years at Trinity, Increase gained his Master's degree. He had received a measure of opposition from within the university because of his puritan views but his scholarship won the day and Increase was offered a fellowship which he turned down, feeling it was now high time to enter the ministry. This was to be somewhere in the British Isles and, after a year at Torrington in Devonshire, Increase, with no plans for returning to America, took up a post on the island of Guernsey as Chaplain to the garrison. With the return of the monarchy in 1660, the future did not seem too bright for the congregational-minded. Charles had pronounced his royal pardon for the puritans in his *Declaration of Breda* with the exception of the individuals directly responsible for his father's execution and with it, the dandy King promised religious tolerance. The Laudians, however, were sure the King could be persuaded to think differently. Already convinced that the King would change his mind, the Commander of the Guernsey garrison began to severely criticise Increase and it was soon obvious that he was preparing a prison cell, if not worse for his Chaplain. Increase was compelled to flee and this time did not hesitate to make his way back to Dorcester where he arrived in the late summer of 1661.

The names of Cotton and Mather are linked

Now begins the story of how the family name of Cotton was linked with the Mathers and how Cotton Mather could trace his descent both from Richard Mather and John Cotton. John Cotton died in 1652 and Katherine Mather almost three years later. The Cottons and the Mathers had been the closest of friends for many years and a year and a half after losing his Katherine, Richard realised that the Lord had provided him with a new spouse in the godly person of Elizabeth Cotton, John's widow. The two were married in August, 1656, shortly before Increase left for Dublin.

When Increase returned from Britain, he was still only twenty-two years of age and unmarried. One of the now enlarged Mather family who greeted Increase on his return was Maria Cotton, aged twenty-one, daughter of John and Elizabeth Cotton and now Increase's step-sister. The two fell in love almost instantly and were married in March, 1662. Increase could not have wished for a better wife. Maria had been brought up in the best of puritan families and had not only become a child of God but had received the best possible instruction in the Word and ways of God. She became a great support to Increase in his ministry and writings and bore him six children of whom Cotton Mather was the first and whose name was chosen to show the union of the two major puritan families.

Cotton Mather was born on February 12, 1663, in Boston, a year before Increase was called to the pastorate of the Old North Church in the town, commonly called The Second Church. Cotton's childhood was even more remarkable for his swiftness in learning than that of his father's and the infant boy learnt to pray, read and write simultaneous with his acquirement of his mother tongue. Though a high degree of intelligence was necessary to learn as quickly as Cotton, this was greatly aided by the tutorship of Richard Mather who ministered another six years before dying in great pain because of the stone. Of course, Increase and Maria were also teachers of great ability. The result was that when Cotton started school, he was already far ahead of his schoolmates both in learning and knowledge of the Lord.

However, we must leave Cotton's story until later and stay with Increase as he had still many fruitful years to live. Though he will also appear from time to time in Cotton's story.

The Second Church in Boston receives a new pastor

In 1664, Increase Mather was installed in the Second Church in Boston as its pastor. The town had changed radically during Increase's life and was now the centre of a large area numbering some thirty-thousand inhabitants. Parts of the town had lost their Colonial look and numerous houses and shops were now hardly different from those in London. The Mathers now lived in part of the double house near Pemberton Square which had belonged to John Cotton, Sir Henry Vane occupying the other half. This was also the house in which Maria Mather was born and also her son Cotton.

Increase's great joy was his library of almost a thousand books and he confessed that he loved to be no place on earth as much as in his study. Besides the ancient writers, Increase had a good collection of theological works including most Puritan authors of note. He had also a surprisingly large number of scientific and medical books. This might explain why Cotton became so interested in science and medicine and so proficient that he became a member of the Royal Academy.[1]

The baptismal and Half-Way Covenant debates

It was not long before Increase became involved in the great baptismal debate and the debate on the Half-Way Covenant touched upon briefly in the essay on Richard Mather. Here, father and son were opposed for some time but this did not seem to affect their families' lives in the least. At first, Increase was totally against relaxing any of the tight rules in the Congregational church system and thus supported John Davenport's written protests at any change. By 1675, however, Increase was openly in favour

---

[1] Kenneth B. Murdock gives several pages of information on Increase Mather's library in the chapters 'Beginnings in Boston' and 'Literary Leader and Spokesman' in his Mather biography.

of the Half-Way Covenant,[1] not against it. Murdock puts this down to the fact that Increase was still a theorist and that 'practical policy replaced theoretical strictness.' Modern American Congregationalists and Presbyterians are still debating whether Increase's move was right or wrong in the circumstances. Murdock points out that two hundred years later, a writer in the pages of the *Congregational Quarterly* saw the Half Way Covenant as the point where 'the decline of Congregationalism was begun, and the seeds of New England Unitarianism were sown.'[2] The matter caused a rift in the Boston churches, however, when Mather's former ally John Davenport, still an opposer of the Half-Way Covenant, became pastor of the First Church at Boston only to find Mather now against him, and half of his own church. Now the first major break with old New England Congregationalism occurred and a third church was founded in Boston by those who rebelled against Davenport and broke from the First Church. The secret of Mather's change of opinion is revealed in his *The First Principles of New England Concerning the Subject of Baptism & Communion of Churches* dated Cambridge, 1675, in which he argues that the rigid ruling concerning church membership was a later development in the colony and he was going back to the teaching of the original Puritan pioneers.

Mather records his innermost feelings in his diary

Affairs of these years throughout the middle and late sixties are minutely recorded in Mather's diaries and we find him a devoted, praying pastor, earnestly seeking the salvation and edification of his flock and being very diligent in his sermon preparation as he took no notes with him into the pulpit. His prayers to God during this time are illustrated by the following entry:

> The threefold wish of the chief of sinners. I wish! I wish! I wish! 1. That I might do some special service for my dear God in Jesus Christ, before I leave this world. 2. I would fain do good after I am dead. I would fain leave something behind me, that may be doing good upon earth, when I shall be in Heaven. 3. After I have finished my doing worke, I would faign suffer and dy for the sake of my dear God, and for Jesus christ. Thus wished IId of IIm. 1670.

---

[1] This topic will be dealt with more fully in the essay on Cotton Mather as Increase worked with his son on this project.

[2] Ibid, p. 83.

I considered with myselfe that if I should write and publish my Fathers life,[1] that would be a service not only honourable to my Father, but acceptable and honourable to the Name of God. And that by enquiring into those controversies which were the present Truth that these churches in New England laboured with, I might do a good service. And that preaching on, and printing some practical subjects would be so too; and that some discourses wherein the Rising generation should be especially concerned, might be made for Gods glory and the good of souls: And that by publishing something in Latin dè[2] the glorious Kingdome which Christ shall ere long possess in the visible world, I might be instrumental in promoting the honor of the son of God. I therefore resolved by his help to sett upon doing those things. Only I thought it my duty to go about them with deep Humiliations, and seekings of the face of God in an extraordinary maner for Guidance and Assistance. Accordingly on March 22. 1670, I thus sett my selfe to seeke the Lord by Fasting and prayer before him in my study.

Causes of Humiliation before the Lord

1. The sins of my unregenerate estate.
2. Failings since, in every place where I have lived, and in every Relation I sustain.
3. The sad divisions in Boston.

Requests to God in Jesus Christ

1. That Hee would furnish me with gifts and graces of his holy spirit, inlarging of me who am a narrow vessell, and filling me with Heavenly Treasure.
2. That Hee would give of his presence to be with me in private meditations and in publick ministrations.
3. That Hee would guide me as to endeavors in order to the accomplishment of the wishes of my soul written down iid of iim.
4. That Hee will please to bless and take care of my Family.
5. That salvation may be sent to his people. God has heard prayer, and does hear. In him I trust that Hee will hear. Amen! dearest Lord, Amen!

---

[1] Published in 1670 as Mather's second published work.

[2] Regarding.

Concerning this day thus spent, I find recorded in my diary
these words, 'In the close of the day especially, my heart was
moved to believe that God would accept of and Answer my poor
prayers. 1. Because I drew nigh to him, therefore his blessings will
draw nigh to me. 2. Because the things which l asked, and the end
why I asked them was for Gods glory. Not for my owne sake, but
for Gods sake. 3. For the honor of his son Jesus Christ. 4. Because
nothing but my sins and abominations which this day I confessed
before the Lord can hinder the Answer of my prayers; but these
can not hinder because they are done away in the blood of Christ;
who has loved me and given Himselfe for me, which I know for I
feele my Heart loveth Him. 5. Because there never was any creature that did humbly seek unto the Lord for such blessings as this
day I prayed for, that was denyed by him. And surely I shall not
be the first whom God will deny. O blessed forever be my dear God
in Jesus Christ who heareth prayer.[1]

The titles of Increase's publications at this time show his spiritual
burdens for his people, *The Folly of Sinning*, *The Glorious Throne*, *The
Excellency of a Publick Spirit*, *The Righteous Man a Blessing*, *Heavens
Alarm to the World* and *Defence of Evangelical Churches*.

Increase Mather asked to lead the colony in demanding a new charter
However, by the late sixties and early seventies, political developments in
New England compelled even the most pietistic of believers to become
politically minded. Increase Mather was called upon by the colony to lead
them in demanding a new charter as the original charter was being ignored
by the British Government and he produced at least five pamphlets anonymously to this end, the most well-known being *Reasons for the Confirmation of the Charter Belonging to the Massachusetts Colony in New England*.[2] Mather's first reason was:

The first Planters in that American Desart, did without putting
the Crown to a penny Charge, inlarge the King's Dominions, in
Confidence that not themselves only, but their Posteritory should

---

[1] Increase Mather's *Autobiography*, entry for January 11, 1670. Reprinted in *American Antiquarian Society*, Vol. 71, Oct. 1961

[2] Mather claimed authorship for this work in his election sermon of 1693.

enjoy those Priviledges which by their Charters were assured to
them. Now when they have performed their part, and been at vast
Charges, whereby the Crown and the English Nation have been
many wayes advantaged, it will seem an hard Case, that those
Priviledges should be taken from their Children. Nor may we suppose that in the dayes of King William they shall be deprived of
what was granted.

In New England politics as in New England theology, Mather always started by asking himself what the Founding Fathers had done. That
Mather was no revolutionary is shown by his seventh reason:

It will be no Prejudice to the Crown, nor to the Kingdom of
England, but the contrary, if Charter-Priviledges be restored, and
Confirmed to his majesties Subjects in New-England. For they
Pray for no Charter, but what shall make them depend on the
Crown, as the Corporations here in England do:[1] Nor to have any
Laws which shall be repugnant to the Laws in England. And in a
particular manner they are desirous to comply with the Acts of
Parliament for the encouragement of Navigastion and Trade, and
that the Transgressors thereof should be punished according to
Law. Since Charters were taken from the Corporations in New-
England, the Crown of England has been put to Charge to maintain the Government, which it never was before: Nor has any
advantage in the least accrued to the Nation or the Publick Rev-
enue thereby. His Majesties Subjects in New England have lately
reduced the French in Acady unto Obedience to the Crown of
England. If the like should be done in Canada, that would be
worth Millions to the English Crown and Nation; not only in respect of the Bever-Trade, but in that the Fishery of those parts
and of New-found-land also, would be entirely in the hands of the
English to the Encouragement of Trade, and the encreasing of
English Sea-men. If his Majesty shall graciously please to restore
his Subjects in New England to their ancient Privileges, that will
encourage them a second time to attempt the reducing of Canada,

---

[1] Mather had the pamphlets printed in England. There was only one printing press in
the colony and as that was under the auspices of Harvard, it was undiplomatic to use
the College facilities for political purposes.

in which if they shall (as in Case they be assisted with Frigats from England, in probability they shall) have good success, a profitable and very considerable Addition will be made to our Kings Dominions.[1]

Becoming the President of Harvard

Mather was eventually sent to England to work out a new charter with the Government and returned with one in his pocket that would have been the envy of any Englishman. Before that, however, Mather had to fight against another negative British custom which limited the number of printing presses that could be set up. Up to this time there was only one major printing press in the colony at Cambridge (i.e. Harvard) but by the time Mather had finished petitioning the Government, he himself and a Thomas Thatcher were given licences to print at Boston. Mather made good use of this freedom, perhaps only being outdone by his son Cotton Mather whose books numbered several hundreds and were issued in editions whose numbers were not heard of before in the colonies. By 1674, Mather was recognised throughout the colony not only as a good pastor but as an academic of unusual powers and he, Urian Oakes and Thomas Sheppard were voted onto the Harvard College Corporation. First Urian Oakes was voted to the Presidency but he declined and then John Rogers was asked but he also declined. Now it was Mather's turn and he said that he would sooner give up his fellowship than take on the task but the corporation asked him to practise 'self denial' and accept the post. Mather appealed to his church in Boston and they unanimously declared that they would not give up their pastor so Mather was spared the post for the time being. Mather persuaded Oakes to accept the post and after him, Samuel Torrey. Mather, however, was almost plagued by his colleagues to accept the post of President and he finally and reluctantly accepted the Presidency in 1685 but did not give up his church.

New England did not develop into a theocracy

Now the colony was at war with King Philip (Metacomet) and Mather, always keen to show the hand of God acting in history, published his *A Brief History of the Warr With the Indians in New-England*. Mather put the blame of the Indians' aggression on the white traders in the colony who had emigrated for gain and not 'having in their Eye the Conversion of

---

[1] *Increase Mather* Bibliography, pp. 450-453.

the Heathen unto Christ.' Mather's book caused quite a stir in England and made him well-known there. Whilst the war was raging, a fire broke out in Boston, destroying the Mather's home but Increase managed to rescue his beloved library, though his books were all soaking wet from the water sprayed by the town's fire engine. Mather became more aware of the dangers of life and also began to realise that New England was not the theocracy the early Puritans had thought it would be. These views are now reflected in the titles of the books he wrote in the seventies and eighties such as *The Times of Men are in the Hands of God*; *Pray for the Rising Generation*; *Returning unto God*; and *A Sermon Wherin is shewed that the Church of God is sometimes a Subject of Great Persecution.*

The baptismal controversy
One book published at this time was on a question now troubling the colony as it had been troubling England since before the Revolution that of believer's baptism as a seal of faith rather than baptism as a covenant sign for believers and their children. Mather thus wrote his *The Divine Right of Infant-Baptisme Asserted and Proved from Scripture and Antiquity* in 1680. It is interesting to note that Mather does not condemn the Baptists for their church order and view of the ordinances, though he thinks them contrary to Scripture and 'the light of nature', i.e. right reason, but for what he takes to be 'their bad Spirit'. Indeed, he emphasises that he does not judge them as heretics as he has met Baptists in England Ireland and New England who were people who were sincerely conscientious whom he would receive with both arms as he believed that they were 'accepted by God'. What he cannot understand about the Baptists, however was their aggressive attitude to fellow Christians in other denominations. Those who were bitter enemies of the Lord's people and snarled at their Shepherds could hardly be the Lord's sheep, was his conclusion. Increase tells the Baptists who maintained that the laws of the land were against them, that for the past 20 years no law against public contempt of infant baptism had been exercised in the colony. Mather, a staunch Congregationalist, but a man of tolerance and vision, nevertheless looked into the matter and campaigned for a 'lenifying' of laws protecting Congregationalist rights to the benefit of the Congregationalists' critics.

The Church of England again receives privileges in Massachusetts
The halcyon days of Massachusetts colony now seemed to be at an end. What with the Indian war, a number of natural catastrophes, and, in 1676,

enforced direct government from England by a group of men specially picked by the King, things looked to be going very badly indeed. Edward Randolf was appointed special messenger of the crown to subdue the highly independent New England colonies and soon he and Governor Andros were even re-establishing the Church of England. Increase did not fear this move but he did protest when he found the Anglican church being put under special Government privileges which the Congregationalists did not enjoy.

Illustrious providences

1684 witnessed the publication of Mather's famous *An Essay for the Recording of Illustrious Providences* which came out in numerous editions of varying contents both in England and New England. The idea to write such a work was started by Matthew Poole (1624-1679) the English Presbyterian with a number of fellow-ministers and a manuscript was drawn up which eventually reached New England and came into Mather's possession.

Increase had long wondered whether he should continue the work as the idea of relating religion with science and interpreting natural catastrophes in terms of theology as well as physics always interested him. Though Mather planned a far more detailed work, he eventually produced a book of twelve chapters on the following topics:

I.   Remarkable Sea-Deliverances.
II.   Remarkable Preservations.
III.   Remarkables about Thunder and Lightening.
IV.   Philosophical Meditations.
V.   Things Praeternatural which have hapned in New-England.
VI.   Daemons and possessed persons.
VII.   Apparitions.
VIII. Several Cases of Conscience considered.
IX.   The Dumb and Deaf...Ways to teach Deaf persons to speak.
X.   Remarkable Tempests in New-England.
XI.   Remarkable Judgments.
XII.   Remarkables at Norwich in New-England.

This book proved something of a best seller as it appealed not only to the Christian reader but also to the scientific world as Mather's research was seen as the most up-to-date on these topics.

Randolf arrests Mather but the people declare him innocent

In 1688, the churches pressed Mather to go to Britain and bargain with James II for better rights for the colony, its churches and Harvard College. As soon as Randolf heard of this he had Mather arrested and put on trial. Though he tried to gather a jury that were churchless and thus possibly anti-Mather, Randolf found that the entire jury he eventually chose, pronounced Mather not only innocent of the various charges brought against him but pronounced that Randolf must carry all court costs. Randolf now took on the role of a deliverer of the colony from the tyrannical hands of the Congregationalists, reporting to England that dissenters from Congregationalism in the colony were being put to death, a state of events which he would quickly stop and grant religious tolerance. The colonists denied such an accusation utterly.[1] Randolf sought for Mather's arrest again but by this time the Congregationalist leader and now speaker for the colonists was on his way to beg audience at James' court where he was graciously received by the King.

At the British court

Mather proved himself an amazingly gifted diplomat and not only found favour with James II and William and Mary who succeeded him but also with the highest Anglican dignitaries who showed Mather far more leniency than his father's generation had shown the Church of England. In particular, Archbishop John Tillotson took Mather's side and urged the King, Queen and Government to give Mather a sympathetic ear. Finally, Mather secured a charter which saw the end of Andros' plans to unite New England under a royal governor, preserved local corporation laws and their enactment in the hands of the colonists and allowed local governments to tax for their own towns' benefits. The churches were able to keep their lands and possessions which more or less meant that Congregationalism would still be maintained but the right of the churches to give political franchise to members only was repelled which caused Mather some criticism back home. As Elisa Cooke and Thomas Oakes joined Mather just as he was putting the finishing touches to the charter, they were able to defend Mather when criticism came. A major victory for Mather was that he was able to secure Sir William Phips as the new Massachusetts Governor, a man who shared very much Mather's doctrines and hopes for the colony.

---

[1] Space does not permit to enter into a discussion as to who was right. The Quakers had fared badly at times but Randolf's major claims were utterly unfounded and yet are still recorded in historical, educational and denominational works as being the truth.

The Salem Witch Trials
When Mather returned to Boston in may 1692, he arrived at the time of the notorious Salem Witch trials. He had already pleaded for lenience and new methods in dealing legally with matters concerning witchcraft in his book *Illustrious Providences* and now he took measures with his son, Cotton Mather, to put an end to the trials. These measures will be discussed in the essay on Cotton Mather. Though Cotton took no part in the actual trials whatsoever, modern America and in particular school literature and Hollywood, still give him the major blame where they should celebrate him as the most liberal-minded defender, with his father, of the accused. Here something has gone seriously wrong with America's popular understanding of her own history.

Mather remains with his Boston church
From now on, Mather busied himself with the needs of his church and Harvard and worked diligently within the Cambridge Association of Ministers to promote true Christian living in the colony. Other churches, including one at Cambridge, called Increase to be their pastor but the shepherd remained true to his original flock. Mather's pen was never idle and he produced one work after the other on theological, devotional and scientific subjects. He also took part in interdenominational debates which produced his *A Vindication of the Divine Authority of Ruling Elders*. Murdock comments on this most interesting work with the words that it 'contains nothing to detain the modern reader.' How wrong he is as this book contains arguments of value as long as churches continue to organise themselves according to Biblical patterns and many of them are very much part of modern debate in the churches.

Cotton allies with Dudley against his father
In 1701 Mather's star waned somewhat when the notorious Joseph Dudley became governor, supported by Cotton Mather. Dudley had been Randolf's right-hand man and an enemy of the new charter. Here we see a traditional situation in the lives of the Mathers. Increase had adored his father as much as Cotton adored his but both opposed their fathers when they thought they were going too far in any direction, without, however, breaking their own fellowship in any way with that of their parents. Cotton, however, lived to regret his opposition to his father's will as did Increase when he opposed Richard. Increase Mather was finally ousted from Harvard by forces which resented his ideas of keeping Harvard thoroughly Christian but indirectly Increase's church had supported their pastor's leaving

the college as they refused to allow him to live in Cambridge which became a college ruling. Dudley, as could only be expected, turned against both Increase and Cotton and the two found themselves once again without the backing of the political powers. Increase and Cotton were asked to assist in the planning of Yale College which many, including the Mathers, hoped would take up Harvard's fallen Congregationalist mantle.

This day thou shalt be in Paradise

Increase now became convinced that his earthly pilgrimage was over, although he was still extremely strong, robust and mentally alert at 80 years of age and carried out his pastoral duties as if he had been a young man. In 1714, his wife of over fifty years had died and, most surprisingly, the old man had married fifty-two year old Ann Cotton a year later. In 1718, he made his will. Perhaps the one event that caused Increase to really feel old was the news in 1722 that Yale was going the way of all flesh and turning from her Christian origins. By the end of the year, Increase was plagued by doubts and was delirious. He asked for the seventy-first Psalm to be read and told his son to pray that he might honour Christ in his death. He had great pain and cried constantly, 'Pity me! Pity me!' Cotton took his father in his arms and said to him, 'This Day thou shalt be in Paradise. Do you Believe it, Syr, and rejoice in the Views and Hopes of it?' Increase Mather had just enough life left in him to answer, 'I do! I do! I do.' He died on Friday, August 23, 1723.

Here we must leave Increase for a while but we shall return to him later when outlining the life of his son Cotton.

RALF ERSKINE (1685-1752)

14. Ralf Erskine (1685-1752): Revealer of Christ's Beauties

No human words more useful than Erskine's

When Mr McMillan of Aberdeen published Ralf Erskine's writings under the above title, he was not thinking of the appearance of the man he admired but of the spiritual gems revealed in his fine sermons and poetry. Gentle James Hervey gave most of his books away but he kept Erskine's *Gospel Sonnets* on his writing desk for constant study throughout his Christian life. Though too weak to write, one of Hervey's last dying tasks was to dictate a Preface to a new edition of Erskine as he had found during his life no human works 'more evangelical, more comfortable, or more useful'.

Son of a father who 'kept conventicles'

Ralf Erskine was born in Monilaws, Northumberland where his Scottish father, Henry Erskine ministered. Ralf's early life was full of disruption as his father refused to renounce the Solemn League and Covenant which caused his expulsion from the Church of England and the Scottish Assembly looked down their noses at him as he 'kept conventicles'. Thomas Boston, famous for his *Human Nature in its Fourfold State* was one of Henry Erskine's converts. Ralf experienced marvellous answers to prayer as a small child and penned in his exercise book, 'Lord, put Thy fear in my Heart. Let my thoughts be holy, and let me do for Thy glory all that I do. Bless me in my lawful work. Give a good judgement and memory—a firm belief in Jesus Christ, and an assured token of Thy love.' With this background, Ralf made excellent progress at school and entered Edinburgh University at the age of fifteen to study Divinity. During his holidays, Ralf stayed with his brother Ebenezer who ministered at Portmoak though unconverted. In old age, the more famous Ebenezer spoke of the two advantages his younger brother had over him. He came to know the Lord earlier and went to be with the Lord earlier. After qualifying, Ralf worked as a private chaplain to his relative Colonel John Erskine. The Colonel wrote to Ralf, saying, 'I beg earnestly, that the Lord may bless your good designs to my children; and am fully persuaded, that the right impressions that children get of God and the ways of God, when they are young, is a great help to them in life.'

Called to be a minister of the gospel

By 1709 Ralf was old enough to be licensed as a preacher but he felt unworthy of the task. The Colonel did all in his power to persuade him and after Ebenezer had secretly heard Ralf practise preaching, he gave his brother every encouragement to enter the ministry. The Dunfermline Presbytery put Erskine 'on trial' and became convinced that he was a man sent by God to preach the gospel. It was in Dunfermline that Charles I of England was born and it was in this town that Ralf pastored his first flock. Once Erskine was called to the ministry, he was filled with grave doubts as to his Christian witness and calling and scoured the works of godly men to find comfort. On reading Boston on the Covenant, he was able to plead the promises of God and regain peace of heart. He now went through a period of great energy. So intent was he on studying the Word, praying and preaching that he ignored sleep and could be still found at his desk long after midnight. His motto became, 'In the Lord have I righteousness and strength.' Erskine's view of himself as shown by his diary at this time, is highly instructive. He writes, 'This morning, after reading, I went to prayer, under a sense of my nothingness and naughtiness, vileness and corruption, and acknowledged myself 'a beast before God'.' He could nevertheless add, 'Yet looking to God as an infinite, eternal and unchangeable Spirit, who from everlasting to everlasting is God, and always the same, and who manifests Himself in Christ ... I think He allowed me some communion with Him in a way of believing, and I was made to cry with tears, "Lord I believe, help Thou mine unbelief." I was led, in some suitable manner, under a view of my nothingness, and of God's all-sufficiency, to renounce all confidence in the flesh, and to betake myself solely to the name of the Lord, and there to rest and repose myself.'

Erskine's family life

Erskine was united in marriage to Margaret Dewer, a gentleman's daughter, in 1714. Margaret was noted for her kindness and care and served at Ralf's side for 16 years, bearing him ten children, five of whom died in infancy. Telling a friend how Margaret died, Erskine said, 'Her last words expressed the deepest humiliation, and greatest submission to the sovereign will of God, that words could manifest, and thereafter, she shut up all that,—"O Death, where is thy sting! O Grave, where is thy victory! Thanks be to God who giveth us the victory through Jesus Christ our Lord!"—which she repeated two or three times over. And yet, even at this time, I knew not that they were her dying words, till instantly I perceived the evident symptoms of death; in view whereof I was plunged, as it were, into a sea of confusion, when she, in less than an hour after, in a most soft and easy manner, departed this life.'

Some two years later Erskine was married to Margaret Simson of Edinburgh and in June 1732 we find him writing, 'I was made to bless the Lord for his goodness in providing me a wife whose temper was so pleasant and peaceable.' Erskine experienced great blessing as he and his wife taught their children of the mercies of God in Christ but their faith was tried many a time as one child after another died.

True revival follows Erskine's ministry

Erskine's ministry was so blessed that revival broke out and the worshippers filled the church and churchyard. After the service prayer and thanksgiving went on in small groups sometimes all night long. One seeker arose at two in the morning to pray in secret and found the whole town on its knees so that the entire countryside hummed like a gigantic hive of bees as hundreds of penitent sinners poured out their petitions to God under the dome of heaven. The seeker writes marvelling at the fact that he could hardly find a place to pray though it was raining steadily.

Professions were so numerous and the Lord's Table so crowded that Erskine and his fellow pastors began to soundly catechise the people to remove the chaff from the wheat, only to find the former hardly present. Erskine's sermons are extant in which he portrayed hell so that his hearers felt they were already there and then he portrayed heaven's open doors in Christ and admonished his hearers to flee from the wrath to come. This method produced genuine conversions.

The Marrow Controversy

All was not plain sailing for Erskine. The error prevailed that all men receive a common grace to be improved on. This could develop into saving grace which, in turn, could be neglected and rendered ineffectual. This view was coupled with Neonomianism, the teaching that faith became savingly effective through keeping the New Law of 'sincere obedience'. When Edward Fisher's *Marrow of Modern Divinity* was re-published, men such as Hog, Boston, Wilson and the Erskines saw in it a refutation of these errors. The Scottish Assembly regarded the book as a plea for Antinomianism and branded those who supported its teaching, popularly called the Marrow Men, as heretics. Then the Assembly legalised the appointment of ministers via patrons rather than the vote of church members and as the Marrow Men protested against this move they were gently but firmly thrust out of the denomination. Both sides accused the other of acting contrary to the church confessions. The Assembly genuinely thought the Marrow Men were making justification the goal of faith rather than Christ and showing disrespect to those placed in authority. They, in turn, felt that the Assembly mistook anti-Baxterism and anti-Neonomianism for Anti-nomianism and showed too much respect for 'persons of quality'. After much inner conflict, Ralf Erskine believed he ought to identify himself with the Secession and entered into his diary on Wednesday, February 16, 1737, 'I gave in an adherence to the Secession, explaining what I meant by it. May the Lord pity and lead.' The great majority of Erskine's congregation wasted no time in leaving the Established Church with Erskine and erecting a new place of worship.

The quarrel with Whitefield
The next unhappy chapter in the Erskines' lives was their quarrel with evangelist George Whitefield. Most likely because of the difficulties the Erskines had with the Assembly, they began to develop most rigid views of church government so that when Whitefield came to preach around 1742, the Seceders refused to support him because of his supposed laxity in matters of church order. Whitefield's biographer Middleton comments, 'Most certainly, he did not care for all the outward church government in the world, if men were not brought really to the knowledge of God and themselves. Prelacy and presbytery were indeed matters of indifference to a man, who wished "the whole world to be his diocese" and that men of all denominations might be brought to a real acquaintance with Jesus Christ.' Sadly however, in campaigning for their own right to Dissent, the Erskines refused Episcopalian Dissenters any right to that same freedom.

Driving, drawing, winning, compelling and filling work
Happily, such times of controversy were seldom as most of Ralf Erskine's life was taken up with winning souls and training young ministers. His literary works were so treasured that as late as 1879 they were still the best

selling religious books in London. Typical of Erskine's exposition is that of Luke 14:23 on the compelling duty of ministers. 'Their work is not only driving work, while they preach the law as the schoolmaster to lead to Christ; but it is also drawing work, while they preach the Gospel of Christ, who was lifted up to draw men to Him by His love and grace. Their work is winning work, seeking to win souls to Christ, compelling them to come in; and their work is filling work, that their Master's house may be filled; and that every corner, every seat, every chamber, every storey of His house may be filled. As long as the Gospel is preached, His house is filling; and as long as there is room in His house, there is work for the minister; his work is never over, so long as His Master's house is empty; compel them to come in, that my house may be filled.'

For ever a debtor to free grace

In the autumn of 1752 Erskine's wife begged him to slow down his pace of work and spend more time with the family. He promised to do so and in October received a strong conviction from God that his work was at an end and he could prepare himself to depart in peace. That departure came very quickly. Death struck Erskine in November of the same year whilst carrying out his duties though suffering from a heavy fever. His deathbed message was difficult to understand as it was spoken in great weakness. Those around him caught the words 'I will be for ever a debtor to free grace.' As God called him home, Erskine's last utterance rang out crystal clear for all to hear, 'Victory, victory, victory!'

COTTON MATHER (1663-1728)

15. Cotton Mather (1663-1728): New England Pietist

Difficulties in depicting Cotton Mather's life

Most biographers are faced with an enormous difficulty in portraying Cotton Mather's life. He was so versatile and so productive that whatever one writes about, one seems to be only covering a fraction of the real Cotton Mather. This has given rise to many most one-sided, if not lop-sided views of this Puritan minister. Also, in striving to portray Cotton Mather accurately, many biographers have back-projected on to Mather views which have developed over the years and taken on the proportions of fairy-tales, legends and myths. Indeed, Hollywood, the stage and even school and college text books for many decades now have used Cotton Mather as a basis for stories of 'blue laws', bravado, scandal, intrigue, immorality, holocausts, and apocalyptical madness which quite equal tales from the Old World of Nostradamus, Robin Hood, Rasputin, Cardinal Richelieu, General Cortez and even Don Juan. Even prize-winning authors and brilliant writers such as Robert Middlekauf interpret matter of fact statements of Cotton Mather in terms of constant vials of wrath being poured out by ever-present eschatological riders, whilst Perry Miller seems to think Mather was stark staring mad. This author is obviously influenced by Unitarian enemies of orthodox Christianity who began to concoct a Mather mythology almost a hundred years after the man of God was buried. New myths which have surrounded new events such as the Ellis Island cleansings have been back-projected onto Mather and given Arthur Miller the idea of viewing him as a seventeenth century McCarthy, claiming that he was the proto-type of 'absolute evil'. Thus over the almost three hundred years which have separated us from the life of Cotton Mather, interpretations of the foundation fathers of the earliest colonies have taken on characteristics which reveal more of the times of the biographers than those of the Mather family.

A further embarrassment for the would-be biographer is that Cotton Mather wrote over 400 works for publication himself and for every work there seems to be a veritable library of secondary literature to comment on them. The amount of literature on Cotton Mather is sheer mind-boggling. Perhaps no other character has had so much written about him by such a wide spectrum of writers as Cotton Mather. Nevertheless, I feel that not half of what could be said about Cotton has been said and much that has been said does not relate in any way to this fine Christian man. I thus feel that it is still worth the attempt to separate the man from the myth.

A child of remarkable abilities

Cotton Mather, grandson of the American Puritan pioneers John Cotton and Richard Mather, was born on February 12, 1663, in Boston, Massachusetts, the first child of Increase and Maria Mather. His life was remarkable from the beginning as he started to pray, read and write simultaneously with his acquirement of his mother tongue so that when he started school, he was already far ahead of his schoolmates both in learning and knowledge of the Lord.

Cotton absorbed his parents' Christian teaching diligently in his earliest years. He learnt to read the Classical authors and study the Greek New Testament whilst other children were still struggling to read Aesop's Fables in English. Before his eleventh year, he was working hard at Hebrew, writing a catechism to instruct his school-mates and composing prayers for those who wanted to follow his Christian zeal but lacked his literary abilities. During these youthful years, Cotton kept a diary of his spiritual experiences and recorded the books he read and their effect on him. He was sent to Harvard aged eleven as the ordinary schools could no longer teach him anything.

Suspected to be an insufferable young prig

Harvard was a sore trial. Many of Cotton's older fellow-students considered him an 'insufferable young prig'. When it became apparent how intelligent he was, Cotton received many a beating from youths who tried to prove their superiority with their fists rather than with their brains. Matters grew worse when it became obvious that Cotton was the darling of his professors. Nonetheless, the boy maintained a firm witness at college, at times spending whole days in fasting and prayer for his fellow-students. He gained his Bachelor of Arts at fourteen and was a Master of Arts by the time he was eighteen. He was moved to join his father's church in Boston as a communicant member at sixteen when he preached his first sermon. Increase advised his son to fill his sermons with Christ and not with displays of academic knowledge. This is one piece of advice Cotton always kept. Indeed, it is said that Cotton obeyed the Fifth Commandment with more devotion than any other.

Cotton joins his father in pastoring their Boston church

In 1681 Cotton was called to the pastorate of New Haven Church but felt he should stay and help in his father's growing work. When only nineteen, he was unanimously called to the co-pastorate of the North Church[1] but would not allow himself to be ordained until he reached the age of maturity (then 21). Soon afterwards, Increase was sent to England to bargain at the Court for a better constitution for the Massachusetts colony and remained there for almost five years, having to start negotiations all over again after William and Mary succeeded James. Meanwhile the North Church grew at the rate of 25-49 new members per year through Cotton's pastoral work.

In his ministry Mather fought fiercely against superstition and a belief in witchcraft which was growing throughout the colony. He blamed this on the poor education of the day, especially that of women and slaves, and drew up curricula for their education and even wrote textbooks for female pupils and handbooks for their teachers. All in all Mather wrote some 450 books in several different languages to combat ignorance and unbelief.

Tumult in Massachusetts

In 1692, New England was in a tumult. Within a matter of weeks no less than 150 suspects had been charged with witchcraft and in the Massachusetts colony frightened men, women and children believed that the devil was on the loose. The epicentre of this wave of evil which was to alienate children from their parents, churches from their pastors, servants from their masters and even wives from their husbands was the small community of Salem several hours ride on horseback from Boston. When the courts decided to arrest and charge those suspected of witchcraft, Mather begged them to re-consider, offering to look after those concerned in his own home. This request was refused. A. P. Marvin in his book *The Life and Times of Cotton Mather* says that if Mather's methods had been 'studied and imitated, it is possible, if not probable, that the whole awful

---

[1] Also called the Old North Church or The Second Church.

tragedy of blood, in 1692, would have been averted.' When Increase returned, he joined his son in condemning the fact that a secular court was
sentencing people to death on the grounds that they were attacking the
innocent by means of spectres or visions. The judges refused to listen.
Eventually the Mathers received the backing of the new Governor and the
trials were ended but not before nineteen people had been hanged and
one old man crushed to death.

A shocking travesty of justice

The Salem Witch Trials, were, on the whole, a shocking travesty of justice.
They were conducted by men who were completely out of their depths,
who thought that spiritual problems were a matter for the law courts. Their
action is a constant reminder to all that when God's Word is not respected
and superstition and worldly wisdom are used as substitutes, any evil
might happen. Sadly American school books still condemn the Mathers
for attempting in the name of justice to interfere with the secular courts.

Thus Salem, though of very insignificant size, has received an over-
proportioned importance in American 'popular' history as an example of
how the Puritans strove to purge a town of its sin by burning its evil-
doers.[1] To a balanced Christian mind, Salem ought rather to be an example
of how superstition and lack of spiritual insight can so blind secular authorities and social critics that they see the very men who were gifted by
God to end the misguided witch-purging as being the very instigators of it.
Thus Puritan giants of the faith such as Increase and Cotton Mather are
held up to ridicule by politicians, historians and writers alike as the men
who, in their twisted religious zeal, sent dozens of innocents to the scaffold. Arthur Miller, the self-styled moral reformer and author of *The Crucible*, a dramatised account of the Salem Witch Trials which the author
claims is historical, sums up all the antipathy poured out against the Mathers
by declaring that Cotton Mather incorporated 'absolute evil'. Elsewhere
he speaks of Mather's doing his uttermost to have the witches hanged in
spite of the opposition of the populace, saying, 'There is and will always
be in my mind the spectacle of the great minister, and ideological authority
behind the persecution, Cotton Mather, galloping up to the scaffold to
beat back a crowd of villagers so moved by the towering dignity of the
victims as to want to free them.'[2]

---

[1] There were no burnings in Salem. The numerous novels and films dealing with these
'burnings' are pure flights of the imagination.
[2] *Theatre Essays*, page 157.

The two sides in the conflict

Many modern commentators, such as Arthur Miller and Shiela Huftel,[1] believe that those accused of witchcraft in Salem were the poor, illiterate and oppressed who began to stand up for their rights only to be accused falsely of witchcraft by the wealthy Puritan businessmen who either employed them or let land to them. The trials were thus a typical example of class warfare where the 'bosses' suppressed the 'workers'. This is a travesty of the truth for two reasons. Firstly, both the accused and the accusers included all classes from slaves to Harvard graduates and rich landowners. Secondly, if one has to generalise about the accused and the accusers it must be noted that Salem was rapidly developing into two separate communities. There were the 'villagers' and the 'townspeople' each group campaigning for a different form of local government. The 'villagers' eventually formed themselves into Salem Village which is now called Danvers, the 'townspeople' forming themselves into Salem Town, which still bears that name. The accusers were on the 'village' side and the accused on the 'town' side. It is interesting to note that when one compares the total education of the accusers with that of the accused one sees how up-side-down Miller's and Huftel's theory is. On the whole, the accusers' education was lower than that of the accused. This was because most of the accusers were either women (of various classes), children or slaves.

Mather's part in the witch trials analysed

Cotton Mather is a man whose reputation has been smeared for three hundred years by the abuse and harsh criticism of a legion of know-all antagonists. A closer look at his character will show how ill-founded such criticism is. Mather was still in his twenties in 1692 and assisted his father, Increase Mather, aged fifty-three in his Boston church—miles away from Salem. Young as he was, Cotton Mather had a great deal of experience with witches. He had studied a huge amount of material concerning witchcraft in Europe and the North American colonies and was particularly influenced by reports from Sweden where prayer, counselling and intense care had led to cures. At 25 years of age Cotton felt that he now knew enough about witchcraft on the theoretical side and felt called of God to start a practical ministry to those involved. His first 'patients' were four children who had come under the influence of an elderly Irish Roman Catholic woman who openly professed to be in league with the devil. Under the

---

[1] Shiela Huftel in her *Arthur Miller: The Burning Glass*, N.Y., 1965.

'spells' of the wicked woman the children became very violent, went into terrible fits and lost the use of their senses. All four children suffered from inexplicable and agonising pains. The Irishwoman claimed defiantly to be a witch even when threatened with the death penalty. She was subsequently condemned to death but shortly before her execution she boasted that the four children would continue to be bewitched as the devil had other helpers to replace her.

Mather discussed the children's cases with them and prayed with them about their condition. As they were obviously undernourished he arranged for them to be put on a special diet and appealed to the whole church to support him in prayer and help him care for the children. The youngest children soon became normal again but the eldest daughter was in too bad a condition for her widower father to look after her so Mather took her to live with his own family. The girl was given good books to read by Puritan and Quaker authors but also supplied with books of humorous stories. The girl, too, was speedily cured and Mather then opened his home to at least six other people who were said to be in league with the devil or under an evil spell. In every single case Cotton Mather was completely successful in assisting those in his care to return to a normal healthy life both in body and mind.

Mather's reasons why witchcraft was spreading

Mather gave solid reasons why superstition and witchcraft were spreading in the New England communities, as referred to previously. However, striving to educate the community almost cost Mather his life. The small pox took its toll of the Massachusetts colony and Mather started a rigorous inoculation campaign. This caused a great uproar amongst the superstitious in the colony. Word went round that as cow-pox serum was used in the inoculation, those inoculated would grow horns and start to moo. Thus, instead of thanking Mather for seeking only their health and general welfare, the mob thought Mather was trying to shape them into a race of mutants and the cry went up that Mather must be lynched. Indeed, the pastor narrowly escaped being blown to pieces by a bomb someone threw through his window.

Mather was also strong in his criticism of the churches in the colony. He felt they were becoming slack in their responsibility to call 'officers appointed by the Lord Jesus Christ' to shepherd them. His advice went unheeded and by 1692 one church, for instance, had given the pastorate to an ex-merchant who had gone bankrupt and was looking for a comfortable job. This man turned out to be a real burden to his church and was one of the chief accusers in the trials. Another church, apparently impressed by the great strength and loud voice of a man, allowed him to pastor them although he was not ordained by any church body and had a history of violence and immorality behind him of which he boasted rather than repented. This man was accused of crimes committed as a witch and subsequently executed. Indirectly and tragically, it was the tolerance of the Mathers which paved the way for the low spiritual state of many a church. Increase, with Cotton's support, had introduced what came to be known as the Half Way Covenant into the churches. This system allowed for 'people of good will' to become church members without any true profession of faith. The outcome was that churches became more and more social bodies rather than the local communion of the saints as signs of conversion were no longer expected of members. By 1692 the tares had spread so rapidly amongst the wheat in the churches that the wheat was being choked.

A people who would not be ruled

Mather taught that worldly powers were ordained of God and he reprimanded his hearers for their lack of respect to those who governed the colony. Mather was not campaigning for an uncritical acceptance of Crown rule but he complained about a people who would not be ruled at all. Before one can attempt to understand the Salem Witch Trials one must realise that the whole colony was in a state of rebellion because of the instability of the Stuart cause and the impending Glorious Revolution. The colonialists refused to accept the Governor, Edmund Andros, because of his links with the old regime and his close allegiance to the Church of England. This is why the colonialists sent Increase Mather to England to bargain for a new charter. They hoped for semi-independence from the Crown and the right to make their own laws. Increase returned in the late spring of 1692 with the new, liberal charter in his pocket and accompanied by Sir William Phips, the new Governor, appointed by William and Mary. The document that Increase Mather had worked out with both their majesties gave the colonists a freedom that Englishmen in England could only dream of. The penal code, however, was not repealed and the colony was still bound to try suspected criminals, including witches, according to English law. This did not suffice to calm down the populace, particularly because Phips, as soon as he arrived in Massachusetts, was called away to deal with troubles between settlers and the Indians and left the government in the hands of untried and partly unsuitable administrators.

Mistakes often made in judging the situation

Critics of the Mathers make two major mistakes in judging their supposed part in the Salem Witch Trials. They emphasise Increase's alleged co-responsibility with his son, a historical impossibility as Increase was in England when accusations of witchcraft were raised and the first imprisonments occurred. They also emphasise that it was specifically New England Puritan influence that damned the accused. Again, this is historically false. The Salem Witch Trials were conducted by an Oyer and Terminer Crown Court holding the legal powers of the day and an English lawyer, Mr Newton, was present to act as King's attorney. *Dalton's Justice*, which was the accepted legal guide, was used as a basis for examining both the accusers and the accused. The English law of the day was quite complicated in its relation to witchcraft. Professing to be a witch was not *ipso facto* a crime. If witches were brought to court it was because they were accused of committing crimes through the agency of witchcraft. Thus renegade Pastor Burroughs was arrested for allegedly boasting that he had murdered one of his previous wives by means of wizardry. He was also charged with brutality against other women. Torture was allowed by English law in order to gain confessions. John Proctor, one of the accused, wrote to Increase Mather complaining that three of the defendants, including his own son, had been tortured. Giles Cory, an old man, who refused to plead, was tortured to death. Cory had accepted this brutal death to ensure that his sons would inherit his farm. If he had pleaded 'not guilty' yet was found guilty, his property would have been confiscated by the court. This all sounds brutal and inhumane but it was the law of the land at the time. It had nothing to do with the New England Puritans and certainly nothing to do with the Mathers. On the contrary, it was the product of a regime, on the whole, opposed to Puritanism, and if the courts had listened to Cotton Mather from the start, there would certainly have been fewer hangings if any at all. Indeed, because of its Puritan inheritance, New England can be shown to have had far fewer witch trials than European communities of a similar size, during the same period. There were also far more reprieves than condemnations—even in the case of the Salem Witch Trials where legal blunder after blunder was made.[1]

A lamentable want of regeneration

Mather blamed the increase in superstition in the colony on 'the lamentable want of regeneration in the rising generation'. He thus used all the

[1] For a detailed report and analysis of the trials see the Massachusetts Historical Society's papers for 1883.

influence he had to make sure that true men of God were called as pastors. This, however, made Mather very unpopular amongst his ministerial brethren who had a lower view of regeneration. A number of Mather's clerical colleagues looked upon him as over-pedantic because of his strict adherence to sound puritan doctrine. Nothing daunting, Mather started to form educational projects and youth clubs throughout the colony to care for the physical, mental and spiritual needs of young people according to Scriptural principles. Benjamin Franklin was one of the youths who came into Mather's care and when he reached high office, he testified to the teaching of Mather which helped him to remain humble whilst carried along on the wings of fame.

Playwrights who are mythwrights

Readers will begin to suspect that even Cotton Mather had very little to do with the Salem court proceedings. This is quite true. Arthur Miller and his witch-hunting playwrights are mythwrights. Neither Increase nor Cotton had any ecclesiastical or legal jurisdiction in Salem nor were they ever present at the Salem Witch Trials although Cotton did visit Proctor, one of the accused, when he was imprisoned for a short time in Boston. He may also have visited Burroughs, the self-styled but unordained minister, when he was imprisoned in Salem. The truth is, that though Cotton Mather protested strongly against the methods of the court and his father joined with him in these protests when he returned from England, their protests, whilst the governor was absent, fell on deaf ears.

Relying on evidence outside the realm of the law

The Mathers' main objection was that the secular court was trying the accused on evidence outside the realm of the law. The witch-hunting apparently started when children complained that they were being tormented by the spectres of people who, to a great extent, were seen as respectable citizens and sound Christians. Vice-Governor Stoughton, who led the judges, was quite at a loss in dealing with the situation and maintained that good people could never be used by the devil to harm other people. Thus if anyone were tormented by a spectral vision, the person appearing in that vision must be in league with the devil. Increase pointed out that such a view was contrary to Scripture and common-sense and spectral evidence could in no way be used as evidence in court. Furthermore the court believed that asking suspects to recite the Lord's Prayer would show who was innocent and who was guilty. They naively believed that innocent people would recite the Lord's Prayer without faltering, but guilty people could not. Cotton protested strongly against such a superstitious practice but the court closed their ears to his protests.

Thus the Mathers had to stand back and see old ladies being 'ducked', to gain confessions, old men being crushed to death if they refused to plead and women being accused of witchcraft merely because they had malformed breasts.

After Cotton was refused permission to look after the accused, Increase prepared a pamphlet entitled *Cases of Conscience* for general distribution. In it he argued that evidence against witches should be obtained in exactly the same way as evidence in the case of those charged with other crimes. Torture and duckings should be abolished and the evidence of single accusers rejected. Only evidence substantiated by two witnesses at least should be accepted. Increase actually wrote, 'It were better that ten suspected witches should escape, than that one innocent person should be condemned'.

How the Mathers were placed under suspicion

Again the question must be asked, if this is all true—and the records are still there to vouch for the validity of the above statements—how could it be possible for Increase and Cotton Mather to be castigated by generations as the perpetrators of the very abuses of law which they strove to abolish? The records come to our assistance here, too, and show us how the truth has been distorted by enemies of the Gospel.

In September, 1692, the trial judges were required to write an interim report for the Governor which was to be sent to England. The judges by this time were very sensitive to the fact that public opinion was moving against them and they decided to choose someone to write the report who had played no part in the court proceedings. Their choice fell on Cotton Mather who agreed to the undertaking. He felt that the task might help him to exert the influence on the court for the good of the accused that had been denied him. Cotton thus chose five cases out of over a hundred that had been dealt with by the court. These were the few cases in which, in Cotton's opinion, crimes had been detected by convincing and lawful means. In this way Cotton strove to show the court how they should have behaved in the other cases and how little respect he had for their findings in general.

Now the Mathers had made many enemies amongst free-thinkers, sceptics and Deists in the colony and this report fell into the hands of a Boston weaver named Robert Calf who detested the Puritan faith. Without consulting either the court or Mather, Calf combined Cotton's work with imaginary, and quite scandalous, accounts of his own fabrication and published the whole under the name of Cotton Mather. Calf, who otherwise used the name 'Calef'[1] in his writings, even went to the extreme of claiming that both Increase and Cotton had behaved immorally with one of the female victims of witchcraft in their care, in full view of a number of onlookers.

Cotton had produced a scientific work called *Wonders of the Invisible World* so Calf, wishing to bring Cotton further into disrepute, produced a 'sequel' to the volume calling it *More Wonders of the Invisible World*. In the work, he disclosed hitherto 'unpublished' sayings of Cotton which Calf, of course, had merely made up. Calf was well-known as a public liar and no one took his scandalous works seriously at the time. The rogue eventually showed signs of repentance and wrote a contrite letter which stopped Mather from taking the matter to court. Calf also wrote libellously against another minister, Samuel Willard, whose friends urged him to sue Calf. Willard replied that the only adequate way to deal with his adversary was according to Proverbs 26:4 which reads 'Answer not a fool according to his folly, lest thou also be like unto him'. When one reads the works of many a modern critic of the Mathers, it is clear that they are using Calf as he is the only source for many of the adverse statements that they repeat as being 'substantially true'. Arthur Miller, for instance, teaches that the records prove that Cotton Mather beat back the crowds who wanted to free the witches. Calf is the only source for this piece of misinformation.

Deistic and Unitarian opposition to the views of the Mathers
By the nineteenth century Deistic and Unitarian churches had become relatively numerous in the colony and their ministers looked on the Reformed, Calvinistic faith of the Puritan fathers as absolute evil. These false witnesses began to systematically rewrite the history of the New England churches. They were very careful to fan the flames of controversy against Christian denominations by alluding to Calf's works as the standard books on the Puritan divines. In 1831, a pastor of the Unitarian Church in Salem, Charles W. Upham, gave a series of lectures on the witch trials and eventually published his notes under the title *Salem Witchcraft*. Knowing that Cotton Mather detested Unitarianism, Upham severely criticised the Puritan and gave him the full blame for the trials. The 'proof' he gives is highly

---

[1] Mather has been criticised for calling Calf by that name and not 'Calef'. The latter name, however, was a misspelling in one of Calf's publications, which Calf adopted as a better version of his name. Calf's wife, however, always signed herself 'Calf'.

speculative and of a very strange logic. It is impossible to believe, he
argued, that Mather, who put his nose into everything and tried to manage
everything, did not take part in the trials. It can thus be safely taken for
granted that he was there. As we must suppose that Mather was there and
yet he did not stop the trials, he must have not only condoned them but
also encouraged them. Thus Upham can conclude that Cotton Mather
was 'the leading champion of the judges'.[1]

Upham's portrayal of Mather, which leans heavily on Calf's, is a
parody of the man. One of the reasons why Upham gives Cotton Mather
the full blame for the trials is that the entire government of the colony and
the judges were his 'creatures'. This does not fit the facts. Increase Mather
had far more authority and influence than his son who was merely his
assistant yet of the 28 Councillors in office in 1692 only three were members of the Mathers' church. Of these three, one, Governor Phips was
away fighting the Indians throughout most of the trials. Another member,
Judge John Richards, fought against his pastor's views and almost split
the church in his fierce opposition to both Increase and Cotton. There are
letters extant in which the Mathers urge Richards to stop judging the
accused on the grounds of spectral evidence but Richards refused to be
influenced by his pastors thus showing that he was certainly not their
'creature'. Even if the Governor himself were Cotton Mather's 'creature',
this would only have spoken well for Cotton as when Phips returned from
fighting on the border to take an active part in the trials, he quickly gave
the judges a piece of his mind and reprieved all those impeached. His
action, however, came too late to save 20 of the accused from the scaffold,
being crushed to death or dying in prison awaiting the gallows. Thus fine
Christians such as Rebecca Nurse and John Proctor were hanged along
with obvious criminals. Proctor's last words were to ask Cotton Mather as
his 'comforter and friend' to pray with him and he died asking God to
forgive his false-accusers.[2]

Mather's fame at home and abroad

Cotton Mather's theological and scientific works had now made him famous and soon he was corresponding regularly with at least 50 learned
men all over the world. The University of Glasgow made him a Doctor of
Divinity in 1710 and he became a Member of the Royal Academy in 1713.
He was on especially good terms with August Hermann Franke in Ger-

---

[1] See *Historical Magazine*, Sept. 1869, vol. VI, Second Series, especially p. 161.
[2] See *North American Review*, No CCXIII, April 1869, pp. 385-6 for an account of
Proctor's brave death.

many and the Austrian Bartholomaeus Ziegenbalg and supported their missionary plans for India, exchanging letters with them of up to 70 pages. He, however, became appalled at the decay he found in European evangelism, putting it down to the rationalistic duty-faith preaching of those who neglected the doctrines of the indwelling of Christ in the believer and His imputed righteousness. He criticised Isaac Watts strongly believing that his low view of Scripture led to shallow evangelicalism and Arianism. Perhaps Mather called his own faith 'American Pietism' to distinguish it from this contemporary European down-grading.

It seems that Mather never knew, or needed, such a thing as relaxation. Charles Chauncey said that he was the greatest redeemer of time that he ever knew. Much of Mather's earlier work was on experimental Christianity but those were the days when there was no Socinianism, Deism or even Arminianism in New England. During the last decade of the seventeenth century, these heresies invaded the colony and Mather found himself taken up more and more with expository theology. Mather gave much of the blame to the Anglican *Society for the Propagation of the Gospel* which he called the *Society for the Molestation of the Gospel in Foreign Parts*. He was amazed to see one old friend after another in England such as William Whiston go the way of all flesh and deny their Saviour. As Arianism swept through the English churches, he advised his students: 'Among all the Subjects, with which you Feed the People of GOD, I beseech you, Let not the true Bread of Life be forgotten; but exhibit as much as you can of a Glorious CHRIST unto them: Yea; Let the Motto upon your whole Ministry, be CHRIST IS ALL.'

Mather's theology

Mather loved to point out that Paul said, 'I determined to know nothing among you, save Jesus Christ, and Him crucified' and always remained christo-centric in his own theology, teaching that Christ is the golden key to unlock all the oracles of the sacred Scriptures. In 1702 Mather soundly attacked what he called 'English heresy' before the General Convention of Ministers at Boston stressing the total depravity of man, conditional election through God's mercy, the effectual calling of the elect through irresistible grace, the bondage of the unregenerate will and justification by faith through the imputation of Christ's righteousness. He insisted that failure in evangelism was due to not 'preaching the value of the doctrine of election for practical godliness, for comforting the believer and for breaking down resistance to the divine Lordship.' By suppressing the facts of election, he argued, contemporary over-cautious evangelists were substituting the Gospel of the God of justice, wisdom and grace for a picture of a 'nice', benevolent God who could never say 'no'. 'We find,' he preached, 'the Doctrine of PREDESTINATION Proposed by our Lord, and His Apostles, with a very frequent inculcation; We find, that it hath a wondrous Tendency to the Edification of the Faithful.'

Hard times at life's end

Cotton Mather's last few years were, humanly speaking, sad ones. His beloved father died in 1723 and his son, named Increase after his father, was lost at sea in 1724. Mather's third wife became permanently deranged and extremely violent. Her family accrued large debts, giving Mather's name as their creditor so that, at one time, it seemed that Mather would die in a debtor's prison. Nevertheless, Mather looked forward to his home-call, stressing that he was 'on the borders of paradise' longing to enter the promised land. His constant plea was revealed in his last major work *Suspira Vinctorum*: to be able to labour in constant prayer for a worldwide revival, to have decayed piety revived and to feel the quickening Spirit within. When the hour of death came, Mather was in a state of calmness and expectant joy. He told his loved ones, "I am not afraid to die: if I was, I should disgrace my Saviour. I am in His hand, where no ill can befall me." His son Samuel asked the dying man for a last word of counsel. Mather had breath left to utter just one word, *Fructuosus*. To be fruitful and useful in the spread of the Gospel had always been Mather's calling.

JOHN GILL (1697-1771)

16. John Gill (1697-1771) and the Cause of God and Truth

The good work of 18th century Baptists often overlooked
So often when speaking about the work of the Holy Spirit which infused the churches with new life in the 18th century, mention is made of Anglican stalwarts such as Whitefield, Hervey, Toplady and Romaine. The works of these men through God's sovereign grace cannot be praised enough but the fact that recent biographers have highlighted their activities has tended to give the impression that other denominations, such as the Baptists, were quite inactive during this period. This is by no means the case as the testimony of John Gill shows.

John Gill was born in 1697 in the town of Kettering and became a member of the Particular Baptist church there before being called to the pastorate at Goat Yard Chapel, Horselydown, London. This church, now known as the Metropolitan Tabernacle, is famous in Baptist history for being pastored by such prominent men as Benjamin Keach, Benjamin Stinton, John Rippon and Charles H. Spurgeon besides Gill.

John Gill introduces sound Baptist principles
When Gill took over the Goat Yard church, its doctrines and methods of church government were far from Biblical. Too much emphasis was placed on the supervisory rights of extra-church affiliations which robbed local churches of their sovereignty. An association of ministers who met regularly at a Coffee House, of all places, had set themselves up as joint elders of the Particular Baptist churches in London claiming the sole right to ordain pastors and deacons. Indeed, an influential minority in the churches maintained that they had no rights of their own regarding the choosing of deacons as this was entirely the task of the Coffee House fraternal. In effect, what came to be known as the Baptist Union was here in its infancy.

Gill treated such a movement as a changeling child and no true offspring of the Gospel.

Once Gill was established in his new church, he denounced the assumed powers of the Coffee House clique and saw to it that his church chose and ordained its own deacons. Confronted with much anti-creed opposition, he bravely drew up a statement of faith which was thoroughly evangelical in its scope and thoroughly Calvinistic in its doctrine. This step was necessary as, along with lax ideas of church government, doctrine was being downgraded and heresies concerning the Trinity and the eternal sonship of Christ were being fostered in the churches. Once Gill put his church back on a Biblical footing, membership at Goat Yard grew by leaps and bounds and the church, which moved to Carter Lane for larger premises, became one of the most influential congregations in the country.

Gill's gifts as an evangelist

The brethren at Horselydown had been initially drawn to Gill because of his evangelistic gifts and now Gill began to systematically evangelise the Southwark area. His method was to divide the district into four parts and assign two brethren to each sub-area who were to visit and instruct the members. What started as a work amongst his own flock soon spread to a wider work and evangelical ministers of all denominations gave Gill their support. Soon Anglican pioneers of the Revival such as Hervey and Toplady were full of praise for the help they received through Gill's sermons and publications. Hervey was particularly fond of Gill as he taught the sinner's need of the imputed righteousness of Christ and Toplady loved Gill for the way he convicted Arminians of their faulty view of man. Hervey wrote of Gill who, 'presents us with such rich and charming displays of the glory of Christ's person, the freeness of His grace to sinners, and the tenderness of His love to the church.' What better report could be given of a Christian evangelist?

In order to give Gill more access to a wider field of hearers, denominational leaders begged him to give a weekly lecture at Great Eastcheap. This series, which was to last almost thirty years, was opened in 1729 by Gill preaching on Psalm 71:16, 'I will go in the strength of the Lord God; I will make mention of thy righteousness, even of thine only.' Many of these sermons formed the basis of Gill's fine book *The Cause of God and Truth*. The Great Eastcheap experiment proved a huge success and soon Baptists, Anglicans and Independents were subscribing to hire other halls so that Gill could give regular lectures there.

Gill recognised as an ardent evanglist

Contemporary evangelical authors looked on Gill's work with admiration writing how his message of joyful Christian experience spread far and wide amongst the Baptists and even influenced, as one missionary minded contemporary commentator put it, 'all the evangelical denominations at home and abroad'. This was to be expected as Gill had worldwide evangelism as his goal. Two of Gill's favourite texts were Isaiah 24:16 'Look unto me, and be ye saved, all ye ends of the earth', and 2 Chronicles 16:9 'For the eyes of the Lord run to and fro throughout the whole earth, to shew himself strong in the behalf of them whose heart is perfect towards him.' Preaching at the induction of John Davis, Gill told him, 'Souls sensible to sin and danger, and who are crying out, What shall we do to be saved? you are to observe, and point out Christ the tree of life to them; and say,— "Believe on the Lord Jesus Christ and thou shalt be saved."' He went on to say, 'Your work is to lead men, under a sense of sin and guilt, to the blood of Christ, shed for many for the remission of sin, and in his name you are to preach the forgiveness of them.' Perhaps having in mind those Arminians who told him mockingly that he could not believe in the need for repentance if men were predestined to believe, he told his hearers with Spirit led power, 'Be faithful, labour to shew the one and the other their wretched state by nature; the necessity of repentance towards God, and faith in our Lord Jesus Christ, in his blood, righteousness, and atoning sacrifice, for peace, pardon, justification, and salvation.'

Wesley's clash with Gill concerning Christ's righteousness

It was inevitable that John Wesley would clash with Gill and their debate on the question of the perseverance of the saints filled several books on both sides. Wesley claimed, 'I believe a Saint may fall away; that one who is holy or righteous in the judgement of God himself, may nevertheless so fall from God, as to perish everlastingly.' He further stated that 'He who is a child of God today, may be a child of the devil tomorrow.' Gill answered him by saying, 'Those who are truly regenerated, effectually called, and really converted, and internally sanctified by the Spirit and grace of God, shall persevere in grace to the end, and shall be everlastingly saved; or shall never finally and totally fall, so as to perish everlastingly.'

Wesley's mistake was that, as he did not believe in the imputed righteousness of Christ, he could not accept that Christ was indwelling the believer and preparing him for eternity. Quoting Job 17:9 'The righteous also shall hold on his way; and he that hath clean hands shall be stronger and stronger!' Gill tells Wesley, 'By the righteous man is meant one that is made truly righteous, by the righteousness of Christ imputed to him, and which he receives by faith; in consequence of which he lives soberly and righteously: and by his way is meant, Christ the way; in which he walks as he has received him, as the Lord his Righteousness.' Gill argues that as it is Christ who makes a man righteous by imputing His own righteousness to him, so it is Christ who keeps the righteous one in that righteousness. It thus follows that even if the righteous one slips, falls or stumbles because of the inner fight within all Christians, he cannot slip or fall or stumble out of fellowship with Christ as it is Christ who maintains that fellowship not the man himself. It is, after all, Christ who is our right-eousness, not our own works.

The holiness of the law and good works

Dr Abraham Taylor argued that Gill could not possibly, as a Calvinist, believe in the holiness of the Law and in good works. Though the Principal of a theological college, he had no idea what Calvinism really was. Gill told him:

> Though we say, that works are not necessary to salvation; do we say, that they are not necessary to anything else? Do we say, that they are not necessary to be done in obedience to the law of God? Do we say, that the commands of the law are not to be regarded by men? That they are things indifferent, that may be done, or not done? No; we say none of these things, but all the reverse. Do we make void the law through this doctrine? God forbid: Yea, we establish the law, as it is in the hands of Christ our Lawgiver; to which we desire to yield a cheerful obedience; to show our subjection to him as King of saints, and to testify our gratitude for the many blessings of every kind we receive from him.

Gill and Arminianism

Gill's emphasis on the insensitivity of the unsaved to his own state and his spiritual inability angered many an Arminian. One day Gill was preaching on the total depravity and spiritual inability of man when a hearer became deeply offended. The man decided to give Gill a piece of his mind. 'You have degraded man and laid him much too low,' he told the preacher. 'Pray, sir, how much do you think men can contribute towards their own conver-sion and salvation?' Gill asked. This was the cue the man had been waiting for and he promptly gave Gill a long list of all that man could do to vouchsafe God's eternal favour. Gill listened patiently and then said, 'Have you done all these things for yourself?' 'No, I cannot say that I have,' replied the man. Gill looked at him with some surprise and said, 'If you really have all these things in your power and have not done them for yourself, you deserve to be doubly damned, and are but ill qualified to stand up for that imaginary free will which, according to your own confession, has done you so little good. However, after you have made yourself spiritually whole (if ever you find yourself able to do it), be kind enough to come and let me know how you went about it; for at present I know but of one remedy for human depravation, namely, the efficacious grace of him who worketh in men both to will and do of his own good pleasure.'

Efforts made to silence Gill

Great effort was made to silence Gill by a number of his free will enemies and he was often cautioned by his own people to be less rigorous when preaching the truth. Spurgeon, who found a downgrade controversy on his own hands similar, though broader in scope, to the one Gill corrected, must have been greatly indebted to him. Spurgeon says of his 'eminent predecessor', 'Dr Gill, was told, by a certain member of his congregation who ought to have known better, that, if he published his book, *The Cause of God and Truth*, he would lose some of his best friends, and that his income would fall off. The doctor said, "I can afford to be poor, but I cannot afford to injure my conscience." Spurgeon then added, "and he has left his mantle as well as his chair in our vestry."'

Sadly the downgrading of doctrine amongst the Baptist Union churches during the time of Spurgeon got out of hand and Spurgeon's fight against it proved in vain. There is nothing new under the sun and the follies of Gill's times as those of Spurgeon's days are with us again, or rather with us still. This writer must confess that in reading Gill he has found a compendium of sound theology second to none which serves as a God given armour against the downgrading going on in evangelicalism today.

Giving knowledge of salvation to His people by the remission of their sins

Gill's very last preaching wish was to expound the song of Zacharias, going on through Luke until he came to the *Nunc Dimittis* in Chapter Two. The old scholar-preacher did not get that far but ended his fifty-one years in the ministry by preaching on the text 'To give knowledge of salvation unto his people by the remission of their sins, Through the tender mercy of our God; whereby the dayspring from on high hath visited us, To give light to them that sit in darkness and in the shadow of death, to guide our feet in the way of peace.' What better note could a true evangelist end on?

During these months Gill was wracked with violent pains in his stomach and he lost his sense of taste, eating merely out of duty. Middleton records how, 'He bore his visitation with great patience, composure, and resignation of mind to the divine will; without uttering the least complaint; without ever saying to God, What doest thou?'[1] During such bodily discomfort, a fortnight or so before his death, Gill's nephew of the same name,[2] who was a pastor himself, asked his uncle how he was feeling. How many would have taken the opportunity to moan in self-pity?

A dying man's dependence on the everlasting love of God
Instead, as an answer, Gill preached a regular sermon to his dear-one, outlining his hope in the Lord, saying:

> I depend wholly and alone upon the free, sovereign, eternal, unchangeable and everlasting love of God; the firm and everlasting covenant of grace, and my interest in the persons of the Trinity; for my whole salvation and not upon any righteousness of my own, nor any thing in me, or done by me under the influences of the Holy Spirit; nor upon any services of mine, which I have been assisted to perform for the good of the church; but upon my interest in the persons of the Trinity, the person, blood and righteousness of Christ, the free grace of God, and the blessings of grace streaming to me through the blood and righteousness of Christ; as the ground of my hope. These are no new things with me; but what I have been long acquainted with; what I can live and die by. And this you, may tell to any of my friends. I apprehend I shall not be long here.

To other enquirers, Gill was more brief. When one visitor asked him of his wellbeing, shortly before he passed away, Gill merely replied, 'I have nothing to make me uneasy.' and quoted a verse from Isaac Watts:

---

[1] *Biographia Evangelica*, vol. vi, p. 457.

[2] The Rev. John Gill was also a pastor for over 50 years, serving mostly in St Albans. When he died in March, 1809 aged 79, his funeral sermon was preached by John Sutcliff of Olney. Mary Gill, Dr Gill's daughter, had been in membership with her cousin's church since May, 1764.

> He rais'd me from the deeps of sin,
> The gates of gaping hell;
> And fixed my standing more secure
> Than 'twas before I fell.

This again showed how steadfast to the last Gill was in stressing the need for a better covenant bringing with it a better hope and a better righteousness which he faithfully believed God had made with him. Thus when the time came for John Gill to depart and be with his Lord, he went without a sigh or a groan but with a look of inward joy and peace on his face and the words 'O my Father! my Father!' on his lips. Blessed are they that die in the Lord!

PHILIP DODDRIDGE (1702-1751)

17. Philip Doddridge (1702-1751): The Rise and Progress of Religion in the Soul

A nigh tragic birth

It was June 26, 1702. After thirty-six hours labour, Monica Doddridge gave birth to her twentieth child. It was obviously stillborn and Monica's hopes were dashed. Eighteen of her children had already died in infancy and she had so wished to have a brother for her only surviving child Elizabeth. The midwife picked up the pale corpse to put it out of sight of the sorrowing mother. Suddenly her heart fluttered. Had she not seen a slight movement in the breast of the tiny boy? She began to slap the infant in an effort to wake him to life and, sure enough, soon the wee child gave out a large cry as if he had the lungs of a robust, healthy child.

Such was the nigh tragic birth of Philip Doddridge, son of oil-merchant Daniel Doddridge, who, rather than walk in his father's footsteps, was to combine the professions and callings of both his grandfathers. John Doddridge was a well-to-do minister of the Established Church who found himself without a parish as a result of the 1662 Act of Uniformity. He subsequently became pastor of a Dissenting church in Twickenham where he gained a reputation for being 'an ingenious man and a scholar; an acceptable preacher, and a very peaceable divine.' John died in 1689, so did not live to see his illustrious grandson. Philip's maternal grandfather, John Bauman was a Hussite Protestant of great academic ability and qualifications who had to flee from Bohemia in disguise, hunted by the Roman Catholic forces who had ejected Frederick the Protestant Elector. He eventually arrived in England via Germany, accompanied by his leather-bound Luther Bible which became the treasured possession of his grandson. Bauman founded a grammar school at Kingston-upon-Thames and died in 1668, leaving behind his teenaged daughter Monica.

Teaching at the fireside

The Doddridges provided a private tutor for Philip but the lessons he remembered best were those taught by his mother. The large fireplace in the sitting room was framed with Delft tiles illustrating the history of the Bible. Monica would sit Philip on her knee and go through the Lord's dealings with his people tile by tile so that her son might grow up to understand the ways of God with man.

Monica died when Philip was eight years old. He was then put under the care of Daniel Mayo of Kingston, an ejected, now Dissenting, minister who also ran a private school. Mayo brought Philip to an understanding of the gospel besides providing him with an excellent education. In 1715 Daniel Doddridge died, leaving Philip an orphan. A work of God, however, had begun in his life and the young boy could write in his diary that though he had lost his earthly parents:

> God is an immortal Father, my soul rejoices in Him; He hath hitherto helped me and provided for me; may it be my study to approve myself a more affectionate, grateful, and dutiful child.

Living for God alone

Philip then came under the guidance of the Rev. Samuel Clark, who helped him to gain an experience of saving faith before he was sixteen years of age. Philip's guardian (his father's former business partner) declared himself bankrupt and young Philip had to sell the last of his family heirlooms, with the exception of his grandfather's German Bible, to save him from the debtor's prison.

Philip was destitute but his sister Elizabeth, now married to a clergyman, offered him a home. He felt called to the ministry but all chances of finishing his education had gone. The Duchess of Bedford decided to finance his entire education providing he promised to become an Anglican clergyman but Doddridge was set on becoming a Dissenting minister. Samuel Clark came to the rescue and offered to finance Doddridge's studies, obtaining for him a place at a Dissenting college at Kibworth, Leicestershire run by John Jennings.

Doddridge now resolved to live for God alone and worked hard to improve himself spiritually and academically. He made it a point to study no book more diligently than the Scriptures but his wide reading was still enormous by any standards and he never seemed to waste a minute of prayerful study, even praying whilst getting washed and dressed. Such a testimony to a godly life was probably the reason why Jennings, who usually forbade his students to preach outside the college, made an exception in Doddridge's case. Shortly after Doddridge graduated, John Jennings died and his church called Doddridge to the pastorate on a salary of £35 a year.

Doddridge's Academy

Jennings' academy closed down for a time but in April 1729 Isaac Watts and several other ministers met at Lutterworth for a day of fasting and prayer and felt moved to invite Doddridge to reopen the academy in Market Harborough. Soon after the reopening, Doddridge was put under great pressure by parents, students, local politicians and the Castle Hill church to move his work to Northampton. This step was eventually taken in January 1730 when Doddridge set up his academy in Marefair, Northampton, becoming at the same time pastor of the Castle Hill church. Doddridge was still only twenty-seven years of age and about to be married to Mercy Maris who was twenty-two.

It was not long before Doddridge's academy became quite famous and even Church of England ministers sent their sons there rather than have their morals corrupted at the universities. At first the students complained that, though their tutor's lectures were excellently organised, his sermons were quite chaotic so Doddridge began to take great care with his preaching. Soon, the students were rejoicing because Doddridge's sermons touched their hearts and pointed them to God. He had determined to 'preach experimentally man's fall, sin, and misery; the necessity of regeneration; the imputation of Christ's righteousness; the necessity of holiness, as the evidence of acceptance before God; and the absolute need of the Holy Spirit to begin and carry on a saving change in heart and life.'

Doddridge's students were even more influenced by the prayers of their tutor than his sermons. He could spend up to five hours in his own private prayers and when praying in public, he had an extraordinary gift of echoing the thoughts and longings of his fellow worshippers so that they inwardly prayed with him when he acted as their spokesman before God.

Many of his church members came from far off villages, so Doddridge, assisted by his students and church elders, took the gospel to them regularly and introduced daily family worship amongst them. The elders' major duty was to catechise members at their homes and distribute Christian literature such as Doddridge's *Family Expositor* and his famous *The Rise and Progress of Religion in the Soul*. The elders also helped in church discipline when drunkardness, bankruptcy and quarrelling amongst members' families marred fellowship in the church.

Doddridge's theological position

Doddridge's theology has been criticised in recent years because of his association with several believers such as Isaac Watts whose Christology was somewhat unorthodox, if not erroneous. This, I believe, is merely a matter of condemnation by association. Doddridge's theology can be compared with that of his contemporary John Gill, whom most scholars believe was a very 'high' Calvinist. Yet Doddridge was certainly far 'higher' than Gill in his doctrine of election and reprobation, though he disagreed with Gill on eternal justification, though not radically so. He agreed fully with Gill concerning the scope of the atonement as being limited savingly to the elect and that Christ's death nevertheless provides universal benefits. Doddridge urged that, 'there was a sense, in which Christ might be said to die for all; as all men partake of some benefits by his death, and such provision is made for their salvation, as lays the blame of their ruin, if they miscarry, entirely upon themselves: but it was in a very peculiar and much nobler sense, that he died for the elect, intending evidently to secure for them, and only for them the everlasting blessings of the gospel.' This stance is identical with that taken at the Synod of Dort which laid the foundation for what has become known as 'Calvinism'.

Doddridge was freer in his comments on Calvin than most Calvinists, telling his students 'Calvin has a multitude of judicious thoughts; but they are generally intermingled with a great many that are little to the purpose.' This criticism has hurt many Calvinistic commentators who feel that their idol has thus been removed from its pedestal. They retaliate unfairly by pointing out that Doddridge's theology must have been shaky as a number of his pupils turned liberal. This is a weak argument, indeed. Doddridge maintained an open college and several charity schools for anyone seeking a general education, so he can hardly be blamed if some of those under his care did not honour the gospel. The truth is that anyone looking for metaphysical speculations, theological systems and philosophical applications in Doddridge's works will be utterly disappointed. Those who wish for a deeper interest in Christ and are prepared to accept an evangelical and experimental exposition of the good 'old-time religion' cannot do better than read Doddridge's works.

Dissenters such as Isaac Watts criticised Doddridge for supporting George Whitefield and exchanging pulpits with him. He was also criticised for his close friendship with Anglican James Hervey and for his practice of open communion with Baptists. Whatever Doddridge did or said was interpreted by the hyper-orthodox as liberal and by the liberal as ultra-conservative. Doddridge simply maintained that revival of religion was the task of the Holy Spirit within the work of the universal church in which true Christians, whatever their denominations, should work together. This is perhaps why Doddridge's works are still popular throughout the denominations and have been translated into so many different languages including Tamil and Syriac. In fact, during the eighteenth and nineteenth centuries no works were translated as often as Doddridge's. They had a worldwide, inter-church appeal.

Transporting views of heaven

Doddridge was never in good health and was always so thin that he could best be described as 'a bag of bones'. Yet he was often compared to a hare, always running hither and thither for the Lord. By the time he was forty-eight years of age, he was a worn out man. In 1751, he knew that the Lord was calling him home and began to prepare his church and college for the event. Friends from all denominations rallied around the dying saint and some £500 was raised, mainly by Anglicans and the Countess of Huntingdon Connexion, to send Doddridge to Lisbon for a change of air. Benjamin Forfitt had wished Doddridge, 'When the solemn hour comes, may you enter into the port of bliss, like a gallant ship laden with the spoils of victory.' On the sea journey, which was to be his last, Doddridge confessed, 'Such transporting views of the heavenly world is my Father now indulging me with, no words can express.'

On arriving at Lisbon Doddridge was met by cold, rainy, windy weather exactly like the weather he had fled from in England. Doddridge, full of joy, knew that the climes of eternal Canaan were beckoning him and told his loving wife, 'So sure am I that God will be with you and comfort you, that I think my death will be a greater blessing to you, than ever my life hath been.' Doddridge passed over Jordan on 26 October 1751. The *Northampton Mercury* recorded that 'His Piety was without Disguise, his Love without Jealousy, his Benevolence without Bounds . . . He had no Equal.'

WILLIAM GRIMSHAW (1708-1763)

18. William Grimshaw (1708-1763): Apostle of the North

The benefits of viewing a subject against a familiar background

When writing historical biography, it is essential that the author knows something of the background of his subject and the local colour of the area in which he lived. This has always been an embarrassment to me as many of my subjects have been British and I do not know that country well having spent almost my entire adult life and even some of my childhood on the European Continent. I feel no embarrassment whatsoever when tackling the story of Haworth's greatest saint. Evacuated to the Haworth district around 1939-40, I took my first steps in my little clogs on the steep cobbled streets of Worth Valley and the language I learnt was in the expressive words of a Norwegian-Celtic language now almost extinct. My deep memories of that town of black millstone grit are scenes of irate mothers coming home from the mill and working off their wartime frustration on their key-on-a-string-around-their-neck children, crying out, 'Lewk aht, mi barn, tha peyswarth, a tells thi. Tha moänt deä tha' or a'l biff thi yan wi' mi kneëv.'[1] I also remember the evangelical minister of Howarth Church in my teens and how we, 'Kaad es senz dahn an a 'ed a reet grand po'a chaa en a kall wi' t'awd paahsen, 'doy.'[2] My first major hikes as a ten or eleven year-old were 'owwer 'top' of the wild Yorkshire, snow-clad moor, passing the enemy border of Lancashire and progressing on to Colne, spending the night at Jerusalem Farm on the way. How well I remember getting up at six o'clock on a pitch-black December morning and having to

---

[1] 'Watch it, my child, you pea-pod, I tell you. If you do that I will give you a back-hander.'

[2] 'Sat down and I had a really good pot of tea and a chat with the dear old parson.'

strip in the cold and wash under the outside pump. Not that the picture was much different in summer. I have walked over the moors at the end of June when it was dark as a December night at noon and the snow lay thick. On such occasions, we marched passed the old, large, empty mansion called Withens[1] made famous as the background for Emily Brontë's *Wuthering Heights*. Emily was the daughter of another Evangelical Haworth clergyman, Patrick Brontë, the friend of Hugh Martyn the missionary and Charles Simeon of Cambridge, and she was a fine Windhill speaker. I was introduced to the Brontës' lives and works before Grimshaw's and was impressed by Patrick's view of preaching which he practised at Haworth, thus filling his church almost as successfully as his predecessor did:

> I do believe that no preaching is good or calculated to profit except that which is truly apostolical…Let the minister hold up Christ and he will draw all men after him. Let him preach the doctrines of the gospel faithfully and plainly, and his church will be crowded.[2]

My own childhood memories and the reading of my youth thus make it easier for me to understand the conditions under which Grimshaw lived and worked. They also remind me that I was then like Emily Brontë's anti-hero Heathcliff—a degenerate soul.

Young Grimshaw: Spiritually every inch a Heathcliff

William Grimshaw was born on September 3, 1708 in Brindle near Preston, Lancs. He was educated at the Free Grammar Schools in Blackburn and Heskin. We know nothing of Grimshaw's parents but they were obviously comfortably situated and at least tolerant of the Christian faith otherwise they would not have sent young William to Christ's College Cambridge to be trained for the ministry. The little we know of William's life at Cambridge, suggests that he was spiritually every inch a Heathcliff. Yet, Grimshaw returned home to Lancashire in 1731 to become curate at Rochdale Parish Church. His Vicar, Dr Dunster, a true man of God, gave his young curate copies of Brooks' *Precious Remedies Against Satan's Devices* and Owen's *Justification* to help care for his soul. Soon after, Grimshaw moved to Todmorden a place, I remember, called depreciatingly by its inhabitants 'T'oils' or, 'The Holes' and what a cold windy hole it was! Here Grimshaw

---

[1] The local language for 'The Willows.'

[2] *The Maid of Killarny*, 1818, p.13.

put aside his Bible, Brooks and Owen and wasted his time card-playing, hunting and fishing, rolling home at nights totally inebriated and sleeping off his hangovers until almost midday. His only hireling's advice to his sheep was, 'Put away these gloomy thoughts; go into merry company; divert yourself; and all will be well at last.' Such was his life and such was his message as a minister of the Gospel.

A reforming work starts in Grimshaw's life

This life lasted for three years after which, though not converted, Grimshaw began to reform his ways. He gave up his cards, his weapons and his strong drink and began to pray four times a day, a practice which he never gave up. Gradually a strong feeling of guilt overcame his soul. At this time, around 1734, he married Sarah Lockwood of Ewood Hall and she became his sole joy in life. Sarah died five years later leaving Grimshaw so heart broken that he, too, wished to be gone from the world for ever. He made his will, believing that Sarah's funeral bells had also tolled for him. An acquaintance committed suicide, which gave Grimshaw the idea of escaping from his misery in the same way. The next three years were a taste of hell for the hopeless pastor and it was then that he turned in desperation to read Brooks' *Precious Remedies* and to consult Owen on how to be declared just by God. Then he discovered the Bible which opened God's mercies to him on every page. He saw that God's grace was all that he needed. God was gently calling him to partake of such and return as the prodigal son to have the new garment of Christ's righteousness clothe and protect him. Grimshaw told his friend Henry Venn, 'I was now willing to renounce myself: every degree of fancied merit and ability: and to embrace Christ for my all in all. O, what light and comfort did I now enjoy in my soul, and what a taste of pardoning love of God!'

Taking on a church with but a dozen hearers

Grimshaw received a call to Haworth, in the vast parish of Bradford, in 1742. He took over a newly enlarged church with a congregation that had sunk to a dozen. The main employment in the tiny town of perhaps two thousand inhabitants was sheep farming on the common ground of the moors above and spinning, doffing, weaving, burling and mending in the tiny, dark rooms of the cottages below.[1] Most houses had a 'pig-middin' and 'hen-run' as well as a 'muck'oil' or 'ash'oil' for rubbish and compost. The stone sink, pump and closet were usually outside, the poorer inhabit-

---

[1] I am thinking of Haworth in the wider sense here, including Oxenhope and Denholm.

ants having to share all water and sanitary arrangements with several households. Most houses were owner-occupied. Each cottager was thus his own boss as this was before the social curse of the industrial revolution that as good as erased independent labour and enslaved the poor.

The newly awakened pastor gathers a great flock

As soon as newly awakened Grimshaw began to preach from his redeemed heart, souls were saved. One might even say that there was a mass exodus at Haworth from the world of sin into the kingdom of Heaven. Soon the dozen worshippers became a hundred and then grew quickly to a thousand or more. Within a year, the church had to be extended to make room for the growing congregation. The pulpit was placed near a window, kept open so that Grimshaw could be heard by the crowds standing outside. Grimshaw received sure signs that the Lord was blessing his ministry spiritually and not merely in numbers when visiting the terminally ill. Of the average eighteen deaths per year, Grimshaw found that sixteen of the deceased left this life with a steadfast trust in their Saviour. Another major sign was the presence of believers at the Lord's Supper.

In 1749, word had reached the Archbishop of York that Grimshaw had become a Methodist and was guilty of exercising an unlawful ministry in the barns and cottages of the West Riding. The senior clergyman decided to investigate himself and pay Grimshaw a surprise visit. Grimshaw was asked how many communicants he had when commencing his Haworth ministry, and the Archbishop received the answer, 'Twelve.' The next inevitable question was, How many have you now?' To which Grimshaw answered, 'In winter, between three and four hundred, according to the weather. In summer sometimes nearer twelve hundred.' On hearing this, the Archbishop said, 'We can find no fault in Mr Grimshaw, seeing that he is instrumental in bringing so many to the Lord's Table.' It must also be noted here that the normal Anglican practice at the time in more rural parishes was to celebrate Holy Communion six times a year whereas Grimshaw held communion at least monthly. Soon the number of communicants grew even more and the year after the Archbishop's visit we know from Whitefield's testimony that the church was filled three times on Sundays with communicants. Five years later, Whitefield reported that Grimshaw was preaching to many thousands. Such preaching was not a mere Sunday activity for Grimshaw as he expounded the Scriptures twice a day in his church and two to three times per day elsewhere in a radius of some forty miles. Thus preaching over thirty times a week became his practice for twenty-one years, missing only one preaching engagement through illness in all that time. This mighty record of Christian witness does not include his house-to-house visitations, his catechising and his long talks and discussions with seekers in the Parsonage, and his support for other churches be they Anglican, Presbyterian, Congregationalist, Methodist or Baptist. All heard Grimshaw gladly and all were often relieved of financial needs from Grimshaw's own pocket. Modern Baptist might do well to take note that at least two large Baptist churches were set up in the Haworth area as the fruits of Grimshaw's ministry and generosity.[1]

A miracle of grace

All this certainly displays the fact that Grimshaw was a miracle of grace. When meeting him, however, strangers never imagined that he was a clergyman as he had none of their usual airs and graces. His appearance was most ordinary and he was usually taken for one of the poorer farmers or weavers amongst whom he lived. When Grimshaw's friend John Newton was asked to explain the Haworth pastor's great skill in winning men and women for Christ, he felt he could best describe the phenomenon by quoting the old adage, 'The best cat catches the most mice.' He did not mean this irreverently but explained that God had so equipped the man that all who scoffed at him would come back to pray with him. Even if his hearers refused to believe what he said, they trembled at the consequence of knowing what would happen to them if they did not. Truly his message was a savour of life unto life for many but came as a solemn warning to others and was experienced as such.

Grimshaw's doctrines

The stories which adorn most biographies of Grimshaw concerning the imaginative methods he used to coax (some would say tricked, others would say even whipped) the crowds into his church are legend and probably well-known to our readers. I would like to comment, however, on a subject which is often absent from sketches of Grimshaw's life, namely his doctrines. The Haworth minister lived peacefully as a co-worker with both John Wesley and George Whitefield, which is something of a wonder in itself. Indeed, there is not a word anywhere to indicate that Grimshaw ever fell out with a brother be he Anglican, Inghamite, Methodist, Presbyterian or Baptist. Indeed, when Newton joined Grimshaw on his preaching tours, he found that half of his believing hearers were Methodists and half Bap-

---

[1] William Hartley's chapel at Haworth and Richard Smith's and John Fawcet's at Wainsgate.

tists. Even the local Baptist minister was a convert of Grimshaw's and a lasting friend. This does not mean that Grimshaw was wishy-washy on doctrine but that he was able to live in peace especially with those who had the glory of God and the needs of mankind at heart. In those days, denominational differences amongst evangelicals were far less than to-day. One Presbyterian I know will not accept Baptists as Christian breth-ren, another says that all Arminian Methodists will rot in hell, another calls my favourite Puritans 'mere civil servants' to my face because they were Episcopalians whom he detests. I know a Baptist who will not accept the baptism of anyone but that of himself and a few chosen friends in his tiny denomination. Anyone joining his church must be re-baptised! There are present day so-called Reformed writers who will not accept Grimshaw as a Christian. We are living in a sinful, theological and denominational time of Babel! Those times of blessings in Grimshaw's day were, on the whole, far different. They were the days when the Anglican Vicar of Bradford and his curate, when they heard that Baptist William Carey had no money to pay for his journey to India, dug into their pockets and each gave a guinea, which for the curate at least, meant three weeks' wages. Those were the days when the Christian poet William Cowper prayed that the 'dipp'd and sprinkled' would live in peace and not break up the family of God and his friend John Newton wrote the curriculum for William Bull's Independent Academy. At that time, William Grimshaw, John Gill, James Hervey, William Hartley, Augustus Toplady, John Ryland Sen., George Whitefield, and John Fawcet fought the good fight side by side.

Grimshaw's twenty-six Articles of Faith

In December, 1762, shortly before his death, Grimshaw wrote a long letter to his London friend William Romaine who had reminded him of his prom-ise to write down his personal creed. In his reply, Grimshaw drew up twenty-six articles of faith which are remarkable for their combination of independ-ence of thought but absolute Scriptural veracity. They are very different from the usual Reformed statements but those who possess a Reformed heart cannot but testify that they are sweet and comforting doctrines which delight the soul. The difference is that Grimshaw does not so much dwell on the destiny of man in his life of rebellion from or walk with God so much as with the justice, righteousness and mercies of God from which man has rebelled and to which he may be drawn. Grimshaw shows his independence in his first article on the creation of man. The modern debate centres around the natural and moral abilities of man, speculating on which of these he lost at the fall and which will help him return to His Creator as

His child. Some say man lost all his abilities at the fall, others say only his moral abilities. This is idle speculation to Grimshaw who maintains that man had never possessed any natural or moral abilities at all. He was what he was purely by the upkeep of the Holy Spirit to whom he was united and who made him upright. Once man preferred to follow the serpent rather than the Spirit, he became Ichabod, which means the glory departed from him and left him 'a dead, dark, helpless, guilty, miserable mortal', begetting children of the same kind. Though man has lost all claims on God and even all powers to seek Him and obey Him, yet God has not lost His power and claim to that man's obedience. Nor has He lost His justice and holiness to demand it. Yet even before time was appointed, the Eternal Trinity had worked out a method whereby God's justice could be met and God's will obeyed. This was only if He met them Himself on behalf of man thus causing justice to be done through mercy. This is why Jesus Christ the Son of God became the God-man, God manifested in the flesh, and placed Himself in our law-place and both suffered the penalties and curse of the law for those on whom He would have mercy and set Himself under the law to obey it on behalf of the same. This, Grimshaw calls the New Covenant as opposed to the Old Covenant of Works, saying in Article Thirteen:

> I believe that God the Father required, that in the New Cov-
> enant, the Old Covenant should be fulfilled, the breach repaired,
> His violated law made honourable, the curse thereof removed, His
> justice satisfied, His wrath appeased, and His holiness revered,
> and this too (though no one in heaven or earth, save His only
> begotten God-co-equal Son was competent of) by the very na-
> ture, strange to tell, that had transgressed; and this, glory be to
> God, was regular, lawful, right and just.

Speaking of God's righteousness as revealed in Christ, Grimshaw says it is sufficient to redeem all mankind. Let us not misinterpret such words. Let us not compare the ridiculous with the sublime. Here, Grimshaw is not speaking of hypothetical universalism, that bogey of modern debate. He is speaking of the unique, all-holy, all-sufficient, righteousness of Christ. That this righteousness is sufficient for the redemption of any or every man is a Biblical and theological fact. That Christ's blood was meant to redeem every man is pseudo-theological speculation and the wishful thinking of those who believe in works-righteousness. Christ's righteousness, Grimshaw teaches in his articles, is imputed by free grace to those on whom God has mercy because He would have mercy. By this means, and this only, he argues, every believer stands 'complete, irreprovable and acceptable in God's sight.'

Grimshaw goes on to explain how Adam lost the Holy Spirit and without Him we are none of His. The new birth is to receive the Spirit lost by Adam which now testifies to us of the work of Christ done for us so that, this time, we cannot fail because we are in Christ who cannot fail. It is when Grimshaw is outlining his doctrine of the Spirit in the New man that he touches on two doctrines which have been radically altered in much modern Reformed teaching. These are the doctrines of the old man and the doctrine of Christian knowledge. A careful study of Grimshaw's twenty third article would help us gain a balanced view of these doctrines:

> I believe that it is by the Spirit that we are enabled, not to eradicate, as some affirm (for that is absurd) but to subjugate the *old man*, to suppress, not extirpate, the exorbitance of our fleshly appetites; to resist and overcome the world and the devil, and to grow in grace gradually, not *repentively, i.e. suddenly, or all at once*, upon the perfect and eternal day. This is all I know or acknowledge, to be Christian perfection, or sanctification.

Recent would-be Reformed literature teaches that the old man is eradicated and extinct in the believer's life, that Paul's 'wretched man' is a thing of the past. We read also that, 'Just as one who does not have faith is not saved, one who does not have knowledge of the truth of salvation is not saved.' We are told that full faith and full knowledge of the doctrines of grace are the immediate results of conversion. This is Arminian perfectionism at its worst. The best believer is but an ignorant sinner at best, Grimshaw tells us, and all our supposedly holy deeds are riddled with iniquity. Christ alone is the author of our faith and it is in His wisdom and knowledge and not our own that we rest. Christ dwells in our hearts by faith and His love constrains us in a way that surpasses knowledge.[1] Grimshaw's final article has to do with the Christian's security:

> I believe, lastly, that God is faithful and unchangeable, that all His promises are yea and amen; that He will never, never, never forsake me; but that I, and all that believe, love and fear Him, shall receive the end of our faith, the salvation of our souls.

---

[1] Ephesians 3:17-19.

Thoughts on death

After writing out his creed, Grimshaw turns to the topic of his death though he could not possibly have realised then that he would be dead in a few months. He wrote:

> Christ alone has purchased for us what grace in heart and life makes us meet for. What have we to boast of? Or what have we that we have not received? Surely, by grace we are saved. When I die I shall then have my greatest grief, that I have done so little for Jesus; my greatest joy, that Jesus has done so much for me. My last words shall be 'Here goes an unprofitable servant.'

In the early part of the following year a 'putrid fever' spread rapidly through Haworth resulting in many casualties. Grimshaw continued with his ministry and visitations as usual but was quickly struck down with the disease and his situation worsened rapidly. He would allow no one to see him as his visitors would have been at great risk of infection. Benjamin Ingham and Henry Venn were allowed in to pay their last respects to their friend. Grimshaw asked Venn to take his burial service and preach on Philippians 1:21, 'For to me to live is Christ, and to die is gain.' Grimshaw had much to tell his friends and it was as if he were comforting them rather than the reverse. He told them that he had just experienced such a sweet visit from God of an intensity that he had never experienced before. When Venn asked Grimshaw how he felt, the saint answered, 'As happy as I can be on earth and as sure of glory as if I was in it.' He told his servant, 'My flesh has been as it were roasting before a hot fire. But I have nothing to do but to step out of my bed into Heaven, I have my foot on its threshold already.'

On April 7, 1863, at fifty-five years of age, Grimshaw's left foot followed his right and he entered into glory with the words on his lips that he had planned, 'Here goes an unprofitable servant.' But what a profit this man's life and this man's letters have been to countless thousands of others, this writer included! Romaine, commenting to his own flock at St Dunstan's in a memorial service, said that Grimshaw had reached more souls with the message of salvation since the gospel first came to England than any other preacher. Over thirty sermons a week for over twenty years must have been a record. He told his congregation that whenever friends tried to slow Grimshaw down or urge him to take a rest, he would merely say, 'Let me labour now; I shall have rest bye and bye. I cannot do enough for Christ, who has done so much for me.' This led Venn to say in his

funeral sermon, 'In this work no roads were too dangerous, no refreshment too coarse, no lodging too hard, no discouragement too great. His
work was the wages of itself as much as he desired.'

Dear Christian friends, Christ has done exactly as much for us as
He has done for His servant William Grimshaw. Ought this not to mean that
we should be living our lives in the same way, not counting the cost but
labouring on more diligently in the Lord's harvest field, knowing that we
shall have rest by and by? May our work be to us, so precious that it is
wage enough in itself.

JAMES HERVEY (1713-1758)

19. James Hervey (1713-1758): The Prose Poet

Few Gospel ministers have lived as close to Christ as James Hervey,[1] the Poet of Prose; called such because the beauty of his language matched the beauty of his life.

Hervey's early education

Hervey, a country parson's son, was born at Hardingstone near North-ampton and received his first education from his mother who taught him his letters by means of a horn book with a passage of Scripture written on it. When James was seven years of age he was sent to the Grammar School at Northampton where he made excellent progress in Greek grammar, soon wishing to tackle the Classics. His teacher, however, had a very dull son and he would not allow his pupils to progress beyond his own son's standard. Thus the bright pupils such as James fought boredom on the sportsfield until the slow-coach learnt his lessons.

In 1731, Hervey, now seventeen years old, entered Lincoln College, Oxford on a scholarship of £20 a year. His tutor, Richard Hutchins, intro-duced him to Hebrew, guiding him carefully through Genesis. John Ryland, no mean Hebraist himself, reported that Hervey quickly became one of Europe's leading experts in Biblical Hebrew. Nevertheless historians tell us that 'Scriptural, experimental religion was become quite unfashionable' at Oxford and for two years Hervey showed no spiritual interest, merely studying science, medicine, natural history, poetry and the Classics.

Initial ideas of personal holiness and acceptability with God

By 1733 Hervey had begun to think more seriously and became eager to reform his soul as well as his mind. Through reading books on science, he

---

[1] Hervey's surname is pronounced 'Harvey'.

was moved to think about creation and the Creator. He informed his sister of his new 'religious' ideas:

> What sweet complacency, what unspeakable satisfaction shall we reap from the contemplation of an uninterrupted series of spotless actions: No present uneasiness will prompt us impatiently to wish for dissolution, nor anxious fears for futurity make us immoderately dread the impending stroke; all will be calm, easy, and serene; all will be soothed by this precious, this invaluable thought, that, by reason of the meekness, the innocence, the purity, and other Christian graces which adorned the several stages of our progress through the world, our names and our ashes will be embalmed, the chambers of our tomb consecrated into a paradise of rest, and our souls, white as our locks, by an easy transition, become angels of light.

Hervey, still a teenager, had become a religious snob, trusting in his frequent good works to transform him into an angel. His new tutor John Wesley encouraged him in these thoughts and together they read the notorious *Whole Duty of Man* to improve their morals. Another friend, Risdon Darracott, was more useful. He had found Christ through Dr Doddridge's ministry and began to turn Hervey's gaze away from his own righteousness to the righteousness of Christ, putting him in touch with godly writers such as Walter Marshall.

The Holy Club

Marshall, however, was left unread for some time as Hervey had joined a group of students who had become dominated by his new tutor's views on the perfect life. Hervey's friend John Ryland says of these members of the so-called Holy Club:

> These men became his spiritual physicians; and foolish physicians they were: their religion consisted in a set of outward observances, and a punctilious regard to rules of their own devising—rising at stated hours—fasting several times in the week—giving the food they saved by fasting to the poor—saying prayers at certain hours—visiting the prisoners in the jails—frequent attendance upon the sacrament—binding themselves by vows and covenants, to certain virtues and practices. This was the sum total of their religion: they had no spiritual perception of the per-

son of Christ: no understanding of his glorious righteousness for our justification: no acquaintance with the spirituality and vast extent of God's law : no sense of the immaculate purity of God: no conviction of the plague of their own hearts; no deep discernment of the power, deceit, and malignity of indwelling sin: no sight of the absolute necessity of regeneration by God the Holy Spirit: no knowledge of his divine person, and the infinite impor- tance and necessity of his operations in the scheme of our salvation: no experience of the pleasures of vital religion.

As a result of this reckless living, one student died and, though once a strong and robust sportsman, Hervey's health broke and left him an invalid for the rest of his short life.

A clergyman still 'righteous overmuch'

After five years at Oxford, Hervey took his degree and was ordained a deacon of the Church of England. He had no idea of the Gospel and was still 'righteous overmuch' in his own estimation. But God was already preparing the mind and heart of an unlettered farmhand in order to humble him.

Because of his poor health, the doctors advised Hervey to accompany a ploughman over the fields as the fresh air and odours of the newly-turned soil would do him good. For one who had his nose in a book night and day, it was obviously sound advice, so Hervey decided to follow it.

While Hervey was walking alongside the ploughman, he decided to catechise him. He began with the question, 'What is the hardest thing in religion?' The ploughman replied, 'I am a poor illiterate man, and you, Sir, are a minister. I beg leave to return the question.' Taking up the cue, Hervey said, 'The hardest thing is to deny sinful self.' He was thinking of the Lord's words in Matthew 16:24 'If any man will come after me, let him deny himself, and take up his cross, and follow me.' Hervey then lectured the labourer on self-mortification. The son of the soil soon realised what was lacking in Hervey's view of sanctification. 'There is another instance of self-denial,' he said patiently, 'to which the injunction extends, is of great moment, and is the hardest thing in religion, and that is, to deny righteous self.' The simple man had seen that Hervey's own righteous self, his own self-righteousness, was standing between him and a saving knowledge of Christ. Whilst Hervey was taking this in, it was the ploughman's turn to lecture his clergyman friend. 'You know,' he continued, 'that I do not come to hear you preach, but go every Sabbath, with my family, to

Northampton, to hear Dr Doddridge: We rise early in the morning, and have prayers before we set out, in which I find pleasure. Walking there and back I find pleasure; under the sermon I find pleasure; when at the Lord's table I find pleasure. We read a portion of the Scriptures and go to prayers in the evening, and we find pleasure; but to this moment, I find it the hardest thing to deny righteous self. I mean the instance of renouncing our own strength, and our own righteousness, not leaning on that for holiness, not relying on that for justification.'

Hervey looked at the man with pity, thinking 'What an old fool!' but God had begun a work in his heart. He found himself thinking of Christ's holy life. Suddenly, he felt that he hated Christ's righteousness as it stood in the way of a trust in his own. Nevertheless, Hervey could not forget this experience and was soon led to see that he had been the ignorant fool and the uneducated farmhand had taught him solid sense and godly wisdom.

God's strategy in bringing Hervey to Christ

Hervey's letters over the next five years show how a work of grace was taking place in the young minister's life. He now tells his sister, "Let us remember, and remembering, let us acknowledge, that we are nothing, and have nothing, and deserve nothing, but shame and contempt, but misery and punishment." For the first time in his life, Hervey saw his own sinfulness and nothingness before God.

George Whitefield had entered Lincoln College the year after Hervey and became the first of the Holy Club members to find Christ. By the end of 1735 he had joined Darracott in witnessing openly to Hervey, saying that he would never find righteousness unless he was clothed in the righteousness of Christ. Hervey accepted the point but was too ashamed to reply. He began to study Walter Marshall's *Gospel Mystery of Sanctification* and Jenks on *Submission to Christ's Righteousness* and, slowly gained insight into the need for a new birth.

Whitefield's sermon 'What think ye of Christ?' was the final link in the chain of divine providence that granted Hervey repentance and faith and caused him to shed all trust in his own righteousness. He was quick to inform Whitefield of the news, saying:

> I now desire to work in my blessed Master's service, not for, but from salvation. I believe that Jesus Christ, the incarnate God, is my Saviour; that He has done all which I was bound to perform; and suffered all I was condemned to sustain; and so has procured

a full, final and everlasting salvation for a poor damnable sinner. I would now fain serve Him who has saved me. I would glorify Him before men, who has justified me before God. I would study to please Him in holiness and righteousness all the days of my life. I seek this blessing, not as a condition but as a part—a choice and inestimable part—of that complete salvation, which Jesus has purchased for me.

Hervey's pastoral work

Hervey took over his late father's work amongst a very faithful flock. The poor walked as much as twelve miles to the Lord's Day services, and the rich drew up in their coaches from far wider afield. Though marked by illness and often only able to recline on a couch whilst preaching, Hervey always had a full church. His portrayals of Jesus and His salvation were so moving that his hearers longed to depart from this life and be with Christ for ever.

Hervey started work before six in the morning, writing his best-selling books or preparing sermons. At eight, he called his servants, his family and visitors to morning devotions. They were questioned on the texts expounded the day before and given additional instruction. Prayers were then conducted until breakfast for all at nine. During the rest of the morning and early afternoon, Hervey would either work in his study without a break for lunch, or visit his flock whom he catechised on doctrine and the Scriptures.

He also distributed Bibles, books, household goods and clothing to the poor, rather than distribute money. If he discovered, however, that a family was in financial straits and had medicine bills etc. to pay, he would dig deep into his own pocket and settle the bills.

Though Hervey earned a huge sum on *Meditations* and *Theron and Aspasio* alone, he gave it all to the poor. He paid particular attention to the health of his flock, consulting the best doctors on their behalf. Whenever a prominent doctor was in the vicinity, Hervey sent messengers to him, begging him to visit his sick parishioners, promising to meet all expenses himself.

In the late afternoon Hervey had a cup of tea and then gathered his family and servants around him to hear verses of Scripture expounded from the Hebrew or Greek Testaments. The remaining hours until the main evening meal were usually taken up by study and preparation. At eight he would dine and at nine expound the Scriptures again to his family and his numerous visitors.

Called home early

Hervey's prolonged illness and his death at the early age of forty-four were such glorious testimonies to the Grace of God that James Stonehouse, his doctor, became converted and, as Hervey passed away in his arms, received a call to take up Hervey's mantle and become a minister of the Gospel. Hervey's last words were 'Precious salvation. Precious salvation.'

WILLIAM ROMAINE (1714-1795)

20. William Romaine (1714-1795): Evangelical Pillar

A main pillar of evangelisation

When paying tribute to the memory of William Romaine, Philip Schaff, the church historian, said that he 'stood forth as the main pillar of Evangelization, which was reviving in the Church of England after the reaction against Puritanism consequent upon the Restoration a hundred years before.' This is no exaggeration as whatever Romaine preached, lectured, wrote or said in conversation witnessed to blessings in Christ. Imagine, for instance, attending a lecture by Romaine in his capacity as Professor of Astronomy and hearing him declare, 'Were dying sinners ever comforted by the spots on the moon? Was ever miser reclaimed from avarice by Jupiter's belts? or did Saturn's rings ever make a lascivious female chaste?' Well might the secular historian W. H. E. Lecky say in his history of the eighteenth century, 'Few contemporary clergymen exercised a deeper or wider influence, or displayed a more perfect devotion to the cause they believed to be true.' Both Schaff and Lecky agree that Romaine's contemporary fame 'rests chiefly on the extraordinary popularity of his preaching'. J. B. Owen goes even further and says that as a preacher and writer 'none ever attained a greater popularity; and, what is infinitely more important, none were ever more signally blessed with proofs of usefulness in his ministry.' Yet this man who was mightily used of God to open the doors of the Great Revival and usher in the work of the Spirit in the Metropolis is almost unknown amongst present day evangelicals who rest on his laurels.

Divine revelation and grace the only true religion

William Romaine was born in Hartlepool in 1714, the second son of believing parents. His father was a Protestant refugee who had fled to England after the revocation of the Edict of Nantes. His industry soon made him a leading merchant and member of the town corporation and he was thus able to give William the best of education. William attended Bernard Gilpin's Grammar School at Houghton-le-Spring. He was ordained as an Anglican minister in 1736, a year before obtaining his Master's degree at Oxford. Romaine became chaplain to Sir Daniel Lambert and through him gained access to the pulpit of St Paul's Cathedral where, at 27 years of age he preached a sermon on Romans 2:14 ff. against Latitudinarian ideas of natural religion and reason, stating plainly that the only religion suitable to his hearers' fallen condition was the religion of Divine revelation and grace. Romaine's biographer Cadogan tells us that Romaine was converted as a child and this, Romaine's second sermon printed, shows truly the mind of a converted man and must have brought great surprise to this centre of Restoration religion.

A sure and certain calling comes to Romaine
After working on a Hebrew lexicon for a number of years without finding a church to pastor, Romaine fought with his own pride, finding that 'the Holy Spirit will glorify nothing but Jesus.' He committed his life fully to Jesus, come what may, and in 1748 decided to sail from London back to the North, should nothing intervene. His trunks were already stored on board when a complete stranger approached him and asked him his name. It turned out that the man was an old friend of William's father and had seen the likeness in his son. On hearing of Romaine's situation, the stranger said that the joint lectureship of St George's, Botolph Lane and St Botolph's, Billingsgate was vacant and he could perhaps obtain it for him. The young clergyman took this as the sign he had been praying for, stayed in London and received the lectureship, adding another to it the following year. These lectureships were mainly based on public subscription but Romaine refused to canvas for money and lived very frugally for many years on £18 per annum. This did not prevent him, however, from raising hundreds of pounds a year for charity. Romaine was so sure that this was God's will that he refused Whitefield's offer of a church in Philadelphia with a salary of £600 a year.

The common people heard him gladly
Romaine became immensely popular in his new form of preaching, telling sinners that it was useless looking to a right use of their own senses to comprehend and accept Christ's salvation. They must accept their complete and utter impotence and, in this state of inability, draw near Christ who accepts all those who bring their yoke to Him. Much as the common

people were glad to hear that there was hope in Jesus, the office-bearers in the churches where Romaine lectured were appalled. Here was a learned man telling the people frightening Bible stories instead of patting them on the back and informing them that God had given them the privileges of reason and natural ability so that they might assist Him in the moral rule of His world and thus earn eternal rewards. They strove to hinder Romaine in every way possible, at times preventing him physically from entering the pulpit and at times locking the doors of their churches so that the vast crowds could not enter. Though Romaine won the backing of his Bishop, these false ministers refused to lighten up their churches on winter evenings so that Romaine preached holding a candle whilst his large congregation sat and stood in physical, but by no means spiritual, darkness.

In 1750 Romaine was appointed assistant morning preacher to St George's, Hanover Square, one of the most fashionable churches in London. For five years he 'preached Christ crucified among those who are least disposed to receive him.' His sermons carried titles such as *A Method for Preventing the Frequency of Robberies and Murders*, showing how the reformation of manners demanded by the Latitudinarian clergy could only be accomplished by converted men and women. Soon the rich left the church and the poor took their place and the clergy were once more up in arms. One nobleman said that the theatres were only too glad to welcome the rich but the Church did their best to ban them. Romaine was also banned in 1755, the year he married. In 1752 he had been appointed Professor of Astronomy at Gresham College but as he was very free in finding loopholes in the Newtonian view of the cosmos which was held as 'gospel' by scientists, he soon lost this appointment. Romaine also preached at Oxford University but, though welcomed by the students, the Vice-Chancellor was 'deeply offended' by his words and dismissed him in 1757. Such events never seemed to weigh Romaine down. As one door closed, he waited cheerfully and calmly until the next one opened.

Though forty years of age, still only a curate

Now Romaine became curate to St Olave's, Southwark, in an area supporting a dozen Dissenting churches, including John Gill's, only a matter of yards away. Indeed he took it in turns with Gill to visit ailing James Hervey in Mile Lane who became a firm friend of both. Now supported by a wife, Romaine kept an open breakfast table where all could join in the meal and share in Romaine's message. Though over forty years old, he was still only a curate but the younger clergy who came to visit Romaine looked upon him as a father in Israel.

The 1757 call to prayer

The year 1757 was a notable one for Evangelicals as Romaine sent out the first of three calls for prayer. A weekly hour of prayer was to be set up nation-wide for the spread of the gospel, to 'advance the fame of Christ' and support Evangelical ministers who were prayed for by name. At first, Romaine knew of only eight Evangelicals in all Britain but when he issued his second extended call in 1779 at least 80 Evangelical ministers were preaching the true gospel up and down the country. Romaine circulated a tract listing seven reasons why the prayer life of the Church was of vital importance in the cause of revival.

Called to the rectorship of Blackfriars

Soon Romaine was moved on again and ministered a short time at St Bartholomew's and Westminster Chapel besides doing itinerant work all over the country, in particular in Yorkshire. Wherever he went, Romaine was adored by the poor and hated by the senior clergy who used rights of patronage to get rid of him. Finally in 1764, though he refused to canvas as the other nominees, he was chosen by a great majority of the parishioners to the rectory of Blackfriars. The two candidates who lost pressed for a second election, which also turned out in Romaine's favour. They then took their unworthy cause to the courts who confirmed the result of the election. Romaine told his new church that he looked upon them as a nursery which it was his duty to water and feed until they could be planted out and work for Christ in their various spheres. He confessed openly that it was his duty to create in his flock a knowledge of themselves—their vileness, and a knowledge of Jesus—His glory.

Finally settled down in his own congregation, Romaine's work prospered and his church had to be extensively enlarged. As most of his parishioners moved out of the city in the summer months, Romaine found time to do itinerant work throughout the country. He is said to have never avoided an opportunity to preach nor to have failed to take on an appointment because of illness.

Romaine's life of faith

Romaine published little, his main calling being to preach. He did however produce one book on the *Life, Walk and Triumph of Faith* which has become a Christian classic. Some critics see in this book an exaggerated stress on the work of Christ in these areas of faith to the detriment of man's responsibility. It must be remembered, however, that Romaine's calling was to a denomination that had tended to ignore the Biblical doctrines of imputed righteousness and the inner work of the Holy Spirit; in fact all that had to do with living a holy life through the indwelling Christ. This had been substituted by the teaching of Grotius, Toland and Tillotson with their high view of man as one who, though fallen in part, is not subdued by sin and has the natural capacity to climb to his former glory. This is pseudo-holiness at its worst. Any reservations one might have in thinking Romaine leaves out human responsibility are put to flight when one reads his published letters which are packed with experimental, practical advice concerning how to walk with and serve the Lord. As Cadogan says, Romaine's writings are 'the effusions of a good man, full of faith and the Holy Ghost, and as a little history of heaven upon earth.'

Romaine had enjoyed all that was worth enjoying

When Romaine realised that his earthly tabernacle was to be replaced by a heavenly eternal one, he wrote 'I have lived to a blessed time. All that is worth enjoying has been freely given to me. By the quickening grace of the Spirit, brought into oneness with Jesus, and to partake of the Father's love in Him,—all is mine ... These are the prospects which faith, looking back, opens to the christian with delight; and thereby renders my present condition a subject of praise and thankfulness.' Romaine caught God's chariot to his new home on July 26, 1795, fully satisfied with all that was past and all that was before him.

DAVID BRAINERD (1718-1747)

21. David Brainerd (1718-1747): God's Hiawatha

A prophet to the Indians

During my youth, two things fought for pre-eminence in my imagination; the call of the wild and my flights of fancy on the wings of poetry. I loved to follow in my mind's eye the adventures of Pathfinder and the Last of the Mohicans. Even more enrapturing were the true American backwoodsman tales of Horace Kephart who enticed me so often 'far from the madding crowds' ignoble strife'. Similarly, it was the adventurous tales of the Land of the Wig-Wams in the poetry of the Indian's friends Henry Wadsworth Longfellow and John Greenleaf Whittier which made my joy complete. Few boys who have read such tales can complain that they have been bored and still speak from their heart. Who has not been thrilled by the throbbing rhythm of courageous Hiawatha and the tom-tom beat of Nauhaught, the Indian deacon who strove to put 'a convert's faith' before 'Indian lore of evil blending'?

Whilst writing *Hiawatha*, Longfellow knew that there was one thing lacking in his hero's life. It was that which he treasured most himself—peace with God. He therefore preached to the American Indians and spoke to his own soul in his poem in words as from God:

> I will send a Prophet to you,
> A Deliverer of the nations—
> Who shall guide you and shall teach you,
> Who shall toil and suffer with you.
> If you listen to his counsels,
> You will multiply and prosper;
> If his warnings pass unheeded,
> You will fade away and perish!

Both Longfellow and Whittier knew that God had sent a number of messengers of deliverance to the Indians. The Essex schoolmaster John Elliot pioneered the work and David Zeisberger with his Moravians friends followed him. American-born Jonathan Edwards and his son of the same name also toiled for God under the shadow of the totem-poles. Nevertheless, one name, that of David Brainerd, stands out above all others as the youngster who followed the call of the wild because it was God's call. He lived to die bringing the gospel to the Indians. His testimony shows him to be Longfellow's ideal Hiawatha and this is how I have always viewed him.

Striving to be a Christian without Christ

David Brainerd, of Connecticut, was of British Puritan stock, his ancestors having come over with the earliest settlers. Heziekiah Brainerd, David's father, was a King's Councillor but died whilst David was a small child. His mother, Dorothy, a minister's daughter, left a her son an orphan at the age of fourteen. David was a sickly, melancholy child, often convicted of sin. At the age of thirteen a severe epidemic plagued his town and David felt he would die without having made his peace with God. This drove him to read Janeway's *Token for Children* which made him strive to follow Christian duties without knowing Christ.

After working on a farm, David went to study under a minister, Mr Fiske, who encouraged him to read the Scriptures and follow Christ. He made many friends amongst serious young men and believers and they met regularly together for prayer and mutual exhortation. Mr Fiske died and David still confused Christianity with being 'consistent in religious duties'. It was whilst performing these duties in 1738 that David received a deep sense of the wrath of God, his fine opinions of his own efforts fled and he felt sure that God's vengeance would overtake him. He was now plagued continually with an inner voice telling him that it was too late, he had done his worst and could not now be saved.

Brainerd's conversion

On July 12, 1739 on a Sunday evening, light dawned. After half an hour of duty-prayer, a sudden sense of unspeakable glory flooded his heart and all his fear and apprehension fled. It was a new and mighty experience and as fast as his fears disappeared, he was filled with unspeakable joy. David saw God no longer as a 'do this or die' taskmaster but says, 'My soul was so captivated and delighted with the excellency, loveliness, greatness, and other perfections of God, that I was even swallowed up in Him, at least to that degree that I had no thought that I remember at first about my own salvation, and scarce reflected that there was such a creature as myself.'

Brainerd became a student at Yale but was again seriously ill. This time, he could trust in God in the face of death. After recovery, he made excellent progress at college but his efforts to witness did not always reflect godly wisdom. Once, when talking to a friend, he was asked what he thought of a certain tutor named Mr Whittesley. 'He has no more grace than this chair,' answered Brainerd. This news flashed through the college like lightening and soon Brainerd was called before the disciplinary committee at Yale and ordered to make a public confession and 'humble himself before the college'. He refused to do this and though he was first in his year and about to receive an honours degree, he was expelled with no recognition of his scholarship whatsoever.

Months of depression followed but Brainerd was gradually pulled out of the doldrums by an awareness that whilst he was overcome by self-pity, heathens were dying in their sins. He thus obtained a licence to preach and received an opportunity to witness to the Indians. There was an immediate thirst for the gospel in their reception and Brainerd grew in grace in proportion to the fruits he harvested. His prayer-life strengthened and he was filled with joy at being counted worthy to draw men to Christ. The news of his success spread and soon the Scottish Society for Promoting Christian Knowledge requested details of his Christian experience and calling with a view to appointing him as their missionary to the Indians. Brainerd was interviewed and asked to preach. He felt such a sense of his own vileness, ignorance and unfitness for the task that he wondered why the society was bothering about him. Brainerd's examiners saw only a man sent from God with a zeal for souls and promptly appointed him to his life's work.

Now Brainerd sold all his inherited property, giving the proceeds to a penniless theological student. Then, forsaking all, at a time when Pale-faces and Redskins were at war and life was always in danger, Brainerd set off to track down the Indians in the dense forests of Kaunaumeck and on the shores of the Delaware. At first he felt that Christ was hiding His face from him and he was often completely exhausted and ill from the hardships of the wild and from riding literally hundreds of miles at a stretch. Bivouacking in the summer woodlands may seem romantic to some, despite the mosquitoes, grizzlies and the odd scalp-hunter, but sleeping out in the winter outback was a nightly duel with death.

Just as he was beginning to think that the chances of converting the Indians were as black as midnight, he felt moved to disturb a well-attended pow-wow and preach the gospel to the prancing medicine-man and braves who, instead of martyring Brainerd on the spot, stopped in their tracks to listen in amazement. After this experience 'a most surprising concern' was shown by the entire Indian population along the banks of the Susquehannah and the Spirit of God came down upon them like a rushing mighty wind. Soon the very old and the very young, drunkards and warrior braves were all crying out for mercy and the forgiveness of sins. White men who came to scoff were caught up in the work of the Spirit and remained to pray with their Redskin brethren. The Deliverer of the Nations had come. Soon a widespread cry went out to God 'Guttummaukalummeh weehaumeh Kineleh Ndah' 'Have mercy upon me and help me to give you my heart.'

Brainerd found it difficult to teach the Indians sound theology as they had no Christian culture to lean on. In particular the doctrine of redemption was foreign to their ears as they had no legal system to speak of and the idea of someone being condemned, forgiven and acquitted was quite new to them as was commercial language such as being bought with the blood of Christ. This came at a time when even some Christians with Puritan and evangelical roots were giving up the Biblical language of debt, payment and surety to talk with the Dutch Grotians and British Deists and Latitudinarians of salvation being solely a matter of duties and moral influence.

Brainerd kept to the language and truths of the Bible, demonstrating total depravity by convincing the Indians that they had no need to teach their children to lie and rebel as they did so by nature. As the Indians treasured gold, Brainerd taught them how the more precious things have the greater purchasing power and how debt, which they understood, could be accrued and settled before leading them to the redemption which is in Christ Jesus. Actually, Brainerd did not need to rationalise with the Indians much at all as, during the times of revival which he experienced, conviction and salvation came hand in hand with expounding the Word of God. Brainerd was astonished at the results and could only give the explanation, 'God himself was pleased to do it.'

As light spread, Brainerd increased his efforts. He confessed 'I am in one continual, perpetual, and uninterrupted hurry, and Divine providence throws so much upon me that I do not see that it will ever be otherwise.' Though plagued with illness and bodily weakness, he remained faithful to his calling until severe tuberculosis began to slay him. In May, 1747, only just 29 years of age, we find Brainerd approaching Northampton, propped up on horseback, to visit his friend Jonathan Edwards and consult Dr Samuel Mather. The Christian physician examined the young preacher's pain-wracked frame and shook his head. 'You have not the least chance of living more than a few months,' was the sober diagnosis. How would Brainerd take the news? His next diary entry reads, 'My attention was greatly engaged and my soul so drawn forth, this day, by what I heard of the exceeding preciousness of the saving grace of God's spirit, that it almost overcame my body in my weak state.' Brainerd was so caught up with the wonders of Christ's love that life and death were secondary to him. Instead of taking to his bed and awaiting the end, Brainerd mounted his horse and crying that there was no rest for the Christian until he rested in Heaven, he continued his life bringing preaching to the Indians, hardly dismounting from the saddle until his triumphant departure from this life came in October, 1747.

Jonathan Edwards, in whose home Brainerd died, preached the funeral service on the subject, 'True Saints, When Absent from the Body, are Present with the Lord.' The New England pastor, who had also, as Brainerd, seen great revival under his own ministry, ended his heart-felt tribute with the exhortation to posterity, 'Oh that the things that were seen and heard in this extraordinary person, his holiness, heavenliness, labour, and self-denial in life, may effectually stir us up to endeavour that in the way of such a holy life we may at last come to so blessed an end.'

Dr Doddridge's House in Northampton
(Where Risdon Darracott studied.)
There is no known picture of Darracott.

22. Risdon Darracott (1717-1759): The Poor Man's Preacher

A sufferer for Christ's sake

It was October 21, 1736 and Risdon Darracott was urgent in prayer. Though but a young theological student, and always in poor health, he had been sent by his tutor Philip Doddridge to preach in the surrounding villages of Northampton to experience at first hand the proof of his calling. Now he had arrived at Brixworth and was sitting in William Beck's humble cottage waiting to preach. Darracott had discussed his text with Doddridge and was sure of what the Lord had called him to say. His anxious prayer was because, only the week before, fierce anti-Dissenting riots had broken out in the village and threats to life and limb had been made to Dissenting preachers. This evening was to be Darracott's baptism of fire, commencing a short life of spiritual warfare in which he knew no defeat.

It was time to start. Darracott stood up with his back to a window and faced the eager cottagers cooped together in front of him. Loud shouts were suddenly heard in the street and a gang of thugs rammed the cottage door down in a matter of seconds. Stones crashed through the windows. Then the violent mob poured in through the open doorway with one cry issuing from their drunken throats, 'Lynch the preacher!'

Violence had been feared, yet the worshippers were taken by surprise at its ferocity. Some were pelted with filth and beaten with sticks and stones. Others were brutally knocked down and rolled in the mud outside accompanied by the cheers and jeers of the enemies of the Gospel. When the mob charged, Darracott, almost without thinking, had dived through the window behind him and fled as the missiles flew. The rioters were beside themselves with rage on finding that the preacher had escaped, so they vented their wrath on William Beck. After being covered in mud,

Beck's garments were torn from his back and he was towed backwards and forwards in the village horsepond until the beasts in human form thought they had drowned him.

Walking in the steps of his father

The experience strengthened Darracott's call to finish his five-year course and become a full-time minister of Christ. He was not even deterred when Doddridge brought the rioters to court but the judges treated the Dissenters as if they were the criminals instead of their attackers. His example in all this was his own father who had suffered much for the Gospel's sake and spent all his energies combing the highways and bye-ways for lost sinners so that his strength and life ebbed out in his fortieth year.

Darracott had entered Doddridge's Academy with a fine knowledge of Latin but now worked hard to master Greek, Hebrew and French. Doddridge insisted on his students taking basic courses in natural sciences, mathematics, history and anatomy before taking up theology. Unusual also was his stress on 'Pneumatology'(psychology), as a compulsory subject. Doddridge's ability as a teacher was enhanced by a system of shorthand he invented which was of great use to his students not only whilst note-taking in college but in their occupational duties afterwards.

Besides preaching in the surrounding villages, Darracott was called to start a work amongst students. Through this work he met the young Anglican theological student, James Hervey, who was staying for the summer break at nearby Weston Favel where his father ministered. Hervey misguidedly thought that his own righteousness was so untarnished that God must be very pleased with him. Darracott gave his over-righteous friend a number of books, including Walter Marshall's *Gospel Mystery of Sanctification* and slowly but surely over a period of six years and with the help of another friend, George Whitefield, brought Hervey to the point where he was able to rely on Christ's righteousness. Darracott was to always stress in his preaching that pride was the mark of a fallen man and that the only righteousness acceptable to God was Christ's own in the believer.

The scope of Darracott's work

Darracott formed his Christian society for students on three principles; to glorify God by honouring Christ, to be quickened and confirmed in the faith and to be useful in evangelising the neighbourhood. The basis of Darracott's teaching was what he called 'covenant theology' whereby the believer is brought into a covenant with God in Christ and this covenant provides sure and eternal salvation, kept by the Covenant-Maker for both parties. He was so successful in his work amongst students that when Hervey was converted, he joined him in founding similar societies. The rules the friends made are still extant and remind one of a combination of Paul's words to Timothy and Titus and Baden-Powell's excellent advice for young people in *Scouting for Boys*. Later Hervey expanded the rules for various 'Improvement Societies' and sent them to Walker of Truro who was busy founding similar societies. Soon a number of churches, not directly connected with Wesley's similar work, were using the rules and thus helping to spread the Evangelical Awakening amongst Anglicans, an awakening which had been helped in its infant stages by a devoted young Dissenter. One feature of Darracott's vision not shared by Hervey and Walker was that he opened God's word in his societies to Dissenter and Anglican alike but Hervey and Walker limited membership to Anglicans. This was because of their sensible insistence that the societies should be church based but one cannot help thinking that a chance of a wider evangelism was missed by this added rule. Perhaps it was the fact that Risdon Darracott was one of the very first the Lord chose in pioneering the great work of the Spirit in the eighteenth century revivals that moved John Gillies to include several brief accounts of his work in his *Historical Collections of Accounts of Revival* republished lately by the Banner of Truth.

A great work started at Wellington

Darracott finished his studies in 1738. After pastoring a work in Penzance for two years, seriously hindered because of acute bleeding in his stomach, he was called to Wellington in Somersetshire and took over a very neglected, poverty-stricken congregation with only 28 communicants. He was shocked to find that the members, though professing Christians, had not the faintest idea of the Christian religion. Darracott worked out a pastoral system whereby the entire neighbourhood was visited and received good Christian teaching, whatever their religious confession. To help him in his work, Darracott spent his last pennies on Bibles and Christian books which he freely distributed. He became a witness at large for God, intent on winning souls for Christ, whatever denominational brand-name they would take on afterwards. Part of this witness was to gather the children in the neighbourhood and see that they were clothed and fed both bodily and spiritually.

So intense was Darracott's work for the Lord that it became a common saying amongst onlooking neighbours that he served Christ 'as if the devil were in him'. Soon Darracott found himself catechising a hundred children and membership of the church rose to well over 200. Many of those visited were so thankful for the kindness the young Dissenter showed them that they went to hear him preach, became converted and became church members although their backgrounds were Church of England. It was not long before the tiny chapel was overcrowded and had to be extended several times. Darracott's fame, which was entirely due to his faithful witness, preaching and godly life, spread far and drew in many from the surrounding districts. When John Cennick visited Darracott after attending a Calvinist Methodist association meeting in Bristol, he found 'a congregation made up of Church people, and several sorts of Dissenters.'[1]

Darracott joins with other great men of the Awakening

So great were the crowds that poured in from miles around to hear Darracott's simple sermons on the ruining effects of sin and the eternal merits of a Saviour's love that he feared for the health of his starving flock who returned home exhausted on a Sunday night after a ten mile walk on an empty stomach. Though hardly any stronger in body himself, Darracott decided that as he could not allow his members to walk so far, he would walk to them. He then took out preaching licences for the surrounding districts, taking services in any building he could find in a wide radius around his home church. It is significant that it was to Darracott that Whitefield first used the words 'The whole world is now my parish.' He knew his friend, for whom he occasionally preached, had the same vision. Darracott's support of George Whitefield caused quite a stir amongst the Independents. Mr Nathaniel Neal, an eminent attorney and son of Daniel Neal the church historian, complained to Doddridge because he had opened his pulpit to Whitefield and also complained about Darracott and another former student, Fawcett, for associating with the Anglican revivalist. Doddridge told Neal:

> I had heard before of the offence which had been taken at two of my pupils in the west, for the response they shewed to Mr. Whitefield: and yet they are both persons of eminent piety. He whose name is chiefly in question, I mean Mr. Darracott, is one of the most devout and extraordinary men I have ever sent out, and a person who has, within these few years, been highly useful to numbers of his hearers. Mr Fawcett labours at Taunton; and his zeal, so far as I can judge, is inspired both with love and prudence.

---

[1] Tyerman's *Life of Whitefield*, vol. 2. p. 113.

Yet, I hear these men are reproached because they have treated Mr. Whitefield respectfully; and that one of them, after having had a correspondence with him for many years, admitted him into his pulpit.[1]

Whitefield on Darracott
Whitefield's high opinion of Darracott is witnessed by the following letter sent by Whitefield to the Countess of Huntingdon:

PLYMOUTH, *February* 25, 1750.

The day after I wrote my last letter to your ladyship, I preached three times, once at Kingswood, and twice at Bristol. It was a blessed day. The next morning, I came on my way rejoicing. At Taunton, I met with Mr. Pearsall, a Dissenting minister, a preacher of righteousness before I was born. At Wellington, I lay at the house of one Mr Darracott, a flaming successful preacher of the gospel, and who may justly he styled, ' the star in the West'. He has suffered much reproach; and, in the space of three months, has lost three lovely children. Two of them died the Saturday evening before the sacrament was to be administered; but weeping did not hinder sowing. He preached next day, and administered as usual; and, for his three natural, the Lord has given him above thirty spiritual children. He has ventured his little all for Christ ; and last week a saint died, who left him £200 in land. At his place, I began to take the field for this spring. At a very short warning, a multitude assembled. The following evening, I preached at Exeter; and last night and this morning I have preached here. This afternoon, God willing, I am to take the field again.[2]

Working with the Anglicans
Darracott was greatly supported in his work by Doddridge who visited his one time pupil, now firm friend, often and preached at his chapels. Surprisingly, both Darracott and Doddridge experienced little criticism from the Established Church though they regularly 'poached'. On the contrary, many gifts were sent to the Dissenting friends' work from their Anglican . fellow-labourers. Darracott worked hand in hand with nine Anglican clergymen who gave him a large say in the organising of Parish matters and

---

[1] Ibid, pp. 75-76.

[2] Ibid, p. 250.

the enforcing of laws against profaning the Sabbath. The Countess of
Huntingdon sought Darracott's advice and supported him in his work.
When Doddridge was gravely ill, Anglican friends contributed funds, in-
cluding £100 from the Countess, so that he could visit milder Lisbon.

Once, shortly before his death, Doddridge called on the Countess
on his way to paying his friend Darracott a last farewell. The Countess was
most concerned about her friend's health, especially when she heard
Doddridge weeping in his room. On asking him what was wrong, Doddridge
replied that he was the happiest man alive and said:

> I am weeping, madam, but they are tears of comfort and joy. I
> can give up my country, my relations, and friends into the hand of
> God; and as to myself, I can well go to heaven from Lisbon as from
> my own study at Northampton.

Doddridge was soon to 'go to heaven' and Darracott followed a
few years after, experiencing many conversions during his last months of
service. Doddridge died before reaching the age of fifty and Darracott was
only forty-two. The doctors were unanimous in believing that the two
friends had worked themselves to death.

A glorious homecall

Few deaths have been as triumphant as Risdon Darracott's. He really and
truly enjoyed dying. Never one to neglect a chance to help stray sheep
return to the Good Shepherd, he even told those standing around his
deathbed, 'I charge you see to it, that you meet me at the right hand of God
at the great day.' When friends told him to conserve his energy, he replied,
'You must sew up my lips, or tie my tongue, if I must not speak of Christ.'
When the doctor told him he was breathing his last, Darracott replied, 'It
cannot be, it is too good, it is too good.' He then opened his arms wide and
said in a strong voice, 'What a mercy it is to be in Jesus. He is coming, he
is coming. But surely this cannot be dying, cannot be death. Oh, how
astonishingly is the Lord softening my passage. Surely God is too good to
such a worm. Oh speed thy chariot wheels. Why are they so long in
coming?' Darracott then whispered, 'Faith and hope.' The chariot had
come.

JOHN COLLET RYLAND (1723-1792)

23. John Collett Ryland (1723-1792): Evangelical Educator

John Ryland's name is forever linked with those of his closest friends Hervey, Gill, Brine, Toplady and Doddridge doing much of the spadework which brought about the revival of true religion in eighteenth century Britain.

A strict, though indulgent father

Ryland was born at Burton-on-the-Water, the son and grandson of staunch yeoman Dissenters. Like his contemporaries Cowper and Newton, Ryland's mother died in his sixth year. Of his father we only know that he gave twelve year-old Ryland a good beating with a stick for perpetually begging him for a gun. He then gave him the gun to make up for his display of temper. Ryland showed how ill-fitted he was for the weapon by playing with it in the house, narrowly missing blowing his own brains out, though he did manage to blow a large hole in the ceiling. In 1741 Benjamin Beddome's preaching was reaping great blessings in Bourton and young Ryland was converted with thirty-nine other sinners at this time and was promptly baptised and became a church member. Beddome recognised Ryland's talents and secretly corresponded with President Bernard Foskett to have Ryland entered at the Bristol Academy. Ryland entered the college in 1744, but, on commencing theological studies, he was gripped by a period of darkness, doubting his own salvation and the existence of God. He found some comfort in reading Henry and Owen and in intensive prayer. Determined to discover the truth, he recorded in his diary, 'June 25, evening 10, 1744, æt. 20 years, 8 months, 2 days. If there is ever a God in heaven or earth, I vow and protest, in his strength, or that God permitting me, I'll find him out; and I'll know whether he loves or hates me; or I'll die and perish, soul and body, in the pursuit and search.'

Thoughts on a poor education

During the next two years, Ryland slowly received a conviction that the Lord, indeed, loved him and he was able to comfort a number of friends who were going through a similar time of darkness. Ryland came through the ordeal with all his pride gone and he looked forward to his ordination to the ministry with fear and trembling. The unanimous call to pastor a church in Warwick came when Ryland was seriously ill with the small-pox and was unable to continue his studies. On recovering, Ryland felt that he ought to follow the call and not try to make up for lost time at the Academy. His disappointment with his theological education, made him determined to do better himself at the business of educating students to live a life pleasing to God. In old age he wrote, 'Foskett should have spared no pains to educate our souls to grandeur, and to have enriched and impregnated them with great and generous ideas of God in his whole natural and moral character, relations, and actions, to us and the universe. This was thy business, thy duty, thy honour, O Foskett! and this thou didst totally neglect.'

Friendships with Hervey and Doddridge

Shortly after taking up his post at Warwick, Ryland married Elizabeth Frith, daughter of a Dissenting schoolmaster who taught his pupils in Dr Tate's Vicarage rented for the purpose! The young couple formed a firm friendship with James Hervey, often spending their holidays with him at Weston-Favell and exchanging numerous letters and books.

After almost ten years at Warwick, Ryland felt called to move to Northampton and follow in Doddridge's footsteps and found a college there. His church took the move coldly and in their letter of dismissal wrote that Ryland had been a member for several years 'and as far as we know, has not acted altogether inconsistent with the grace of God and the profession he made among us.' Much of this coldness was also because of Ryland's openness to evangelicals of other denominations and his conviction that the Lord's Supper should be shared by all who loved the Lord.

Ryland highly successful at Northampton as a minister and teacher

Immediately on taking up his duties in Northampton, Ryland's church of which he held the oversight, prospered and grew so that the building had to be enlarged twice and twenty neighbouring villages were evangelised. Ryland busied himself as an author for the edification both of church and school and his output was enormous. Works on science, literature, history, geography and languages besides theology poured from his pen. It seemed that as soon as Ryland increased his own knowledge he hurried to the press to have it put into a text book. All his brains, his friends said, were like fish-hooks and he had an unquenchable thirst for knowledge and for passing on that knowledge. If he had any weakness at all, those same friends said, it was the printing-press. His biographers are agreed that he would have done more had he printed less but Ryland was filling an enormous vacuum in general education. He argued that good books were a necessity as there were not ten of them in the whole Bodleian Library!

Sadly, Ryland had no head for finance and, although £25,000 passed through his hands to support his school, he found himself in severe financial difficulties. This spoilt his testimony, though friends, including his children, were always there to help him out of difficulties.

Ryland moves to Enfield

Elizabeth Ryland died in 1779 and Dr Erskine of Edinburgh wrote recommending Flavel's *Token for Mourners* to him. Three years later Ryland married a Mrs Scott, the widow of a military officer and the Rylands moved school and staff to Enfield, near London where they catered for some eighty pupils. Now, however, Ryland was in poor health and spent only two mornings teaching Scripture, leaving his partner, Mr Clark, who had married into his family, to direct the other teaching. He still took care of interviews and parental visits and, as he had now no pastoral charge, he assisted at a Countess of Huntingdon church.

It is from this period that tales of Ryland's eccentricity spread such as his always dining alone, and never more than for seven minutes, and his wearing a large brown gown and a wig 'seven stories high'. Ryland's dining alone was certainly because his concentration and memory were failing and any disturbance broke his train of thought and he could then not work efficiently. Perhaps Ryland wore his strange regalia to attract attention when sitting on top of his coach preaching to the masses, otherwise intent on their Sunday sports and pastimes in the open air. On Ryland's awesome appearance the common people would call out 'There is a bishop to speak to us' and when Ryland cried out in his tremendous voice, 'Friends, and fellow-countrymen' such a silence ensued that he could preach unhindered.

The Modern Question

Ryland's old age brought loneliness. The friends of his youth were all dead and ill-winds of change were blowing amongst evangelicals that boded no good. The old paths were being eroded by the so-called New Divinity with its high view of man and its low view of the Law, sweeping along many evangelicals, including members of his own family. There was a time, in the 1780s when it seemed that Ryland would also be carried along with the blast of Bellamy's rationalism and the anti-Scriptural philosophy of Hugo Grotius but Ryland rallied and though very weak bodily in the last year of his life, he began to emphasise, as in his younger days, the penal vicariousness of Christ's death, the need for Christ's righteousness and the inability of man to reason himself into Heaven.

These were the days when the so-called *Modern Question* was being looked on as the key to evangelicalism, taking the preacher's mind away from his divine task of expounding the whole gospel to the whole man. The question was, 'Should not the basis of gospel preaching be to emphasise the sinner's duty to believe savingly?' Those who answered the question in the affirmative claimed that the emphasis of gospel preaching was to bring the sinner to an awareness of such duties. They did so because they believed that the sinner had the physical, rational, moral and spiritual powers to give him this awareness on hearing the Gospel. The aged Ryland looked sadly upon the emphasis of Andrew Fuller and the two Robert Halls in making the *Modern Question* the centre of their teaching and said, 'The devil threw out an empty barrel for them to roll about, while they ought to have been drinking the wine of the kingdom. That old dog, lying in the dark, has drawn off many good men to whip syllabub, and to sift quiddities, under pretence of zeal for the truth.'

The gospel a gift not a natural right

Ryland emphasised that election, an essential part of the gospel, is God's will to make us happy by making us holy and until that electing gift was man's, he could have no awareness of anything savingly. He felt the *Modern Question* enthusiasts had not only got their emphasis wrong but also their vocabulary as, following Bellamy, they refused to talk about the gift of salvation and spoke merely of the offer of salvation as if man had a natural right to it. Ryland, on the other hand, taught diplomatically but firmly:

> The word offer is not so proper as declaration, proposal, or gift. The gospel is a declaration of the free grace of God. It is a proposal of salvation by Jesus Christ, and it proclaims Christ as the free and absolute gift of God.

Ryland saw this gift worked out in practice by recognising that 'Love to Christ's righteousness includes conviction of our need of it; dependence upon it; renouncing all other righteousness; and thankfulness for it.'

The gospel preached must be a full gospel

Ryland was concerned that the gospel should be preached to all but it should be a full gospel, including the terrors of the Law, which he felt the modern generation were neglecting by emphasising, in Fuller's words, the duty to 'love Christ as if they had never apostatised'. Preaching to his startled congregation shortly before his last illness and at the time of the greatest natural catastrophes in human memory, Ryland proclaimed 'Some high Calvinists neglect the unconverted; but Paul left no case untouched. He spoke properly and suitably to Felix, as well as to Timothy. Some neglect to preach the law, and tell their hearers to accept Christ. O sinners, beware! If Christ says, "Depart", 'tis all over. Depart into a thousand Ætnas, bursting up for ever and ever. Your souls are now within an inch of damnation. I am clear of your blood. If you are condemned, I'll look you in the face at judgement, and say, "Lord, I told that man—I told those boys and girls, on the 29th of August, 1790—I warned them—they would not believe—and now they stand shivering before the bar!"'

A happy death

Ryland, whose last request was to be buried at the side of his dear friend John Brine, had begged the Lord that when his time came, he might slip out of this world as an acorn from its shell. The Lord granted him his wish. On Tuesday, July 24, 1792, as he slipped out of his shell, his lasts words were, 'Happy, happy, happy. Oh, what ease of body—oh, what ease of soul!'

JOHN GANO (1727-1804)

24. John Gano (1727-1804): Preacher in the Spirit of the Gospel [1]

The significance of Gano's life for the American public

American writer and publisher Terry Wolever did the churches good service in compiling and editing the works of British Particular Baptist Joseph Kinghorn and now he has delighted his readers again by publishing the biography and writings of John Gano, one of Kinghorn's American counterparts. This work is most significant as American Baptists perhaps know more about their British roots than about the great Particular Baptists during the birth of their own republic who in no way lagged behind their British counterparts for soundness of doctrine and evangelical outreach. Gano, of course, has gone down in history as the man who baptised General Washington but sadly, little more is known of this great man of God on either side of the Atlantic.

Of Huguenot stock

Gano, or Gayneau as his name was originally spelt, was of French Huguenot stock who had fled to the Channel Islands from persecution and eventually settled in the New World. He was born in Hopewell, Hunterdon County, a name which became significant for his own faith and his subsequent ministry. Gano's parents were sincere Presbyterian believers and brought their eight children up to seek salvation in Christ. Gano went through years of such seeking, receiving abundant signs of Christ's electing love until the decisive call came to bid Gano receive a new heart when he was listening to a sermon on Canticles 3:11 *'Go forth O ye daughter of Zion, and behold King Solomon ... in the day of the gladness of his heart.'*

---

[1] 'His preaching was in the Spirit of the Gospel. Their hearts were opened.' Robert B. Semple, *A History of the Rise and Progress of the Baptists in Virginia*, pp. 65-66.

Hardly an evangelistic text, one might say, but it was used of the Spirit to point out the hardness of Gano's heart, in spite of his Christian upbringing.

Appropriating God's mercies in Christ

Now Gano was convinced how God had a just right to condemn him but how to be justified before God was still unknown to him. He testifies to the change that now came over him by saying:

> In this state, I remained for some time. And it was some satisfaction to my mind, that God would secure His own glory, and the honor of His Son. In this temper of mind, the way of salvation, through the life, death, and mediation of the glorious Saviour, appeared plain. I contemplated on the amazing wisdom and goodness of God, and the condescension of Christ. My soul was enraptured, amazed, and confounded, that with all my ingratitude, I could still be saved. My mind was enlightened, and my guilt and fear of punishment was removed. Yet, notwithstanding the alteration I felt, I am not sensible that I thought of its being a real conviction; I was afraid my convictions would not be lasting; and I prayed for a continuance of them. I was constrained at times to rejoice in God and His salvation; and in this state continued some time, until a sermon from these words, with light and power fastened on my mind: '*Jesus, thou Son of David, have mercy on me.*' I trust they were so applied, that I could not put them from me. They opened the way of salvation, the suitableness, fullness and willingness of God; and I was enabled to appropriate them to myself, and rejoice in Christ.

Gano and Gilbert Tennent

Gano quickly gathered like minded young men around himself and they encouraged one another in the faith. His mentor at this time was none other than Gilbert Tennent who was used so mightily of God in the Great Awakening. Tennent guided Gano well into the ways of the Lord but failed to convince him of the Biblical nature of covenant baptism as practised by the Presbyterians. This moved Gano to seek fellowship with the Baptists and eventually, after much soul-seeking over several years, he became a member of a Baptist church and was called from within their midst to be a preacher of the gospel. From the start, Gano felt he must preach the whole gospel to the whole man which thus included election, total depravity, regeneration by grace alone, submission to the righteousness of Christ and the final preservation of the saints. Wherever he went, he found the Lord's people who felt that they were sheep without a shepherd and they heard his full-gospel message gladly. Preaching in Hopewell, Morristown, Opocken and Charleston, young Gano found that the Lord had given him a gift of uniting the brethren, even in places where pastor and people had been of two minds and even families had become divided. Gano was also blessed in preaching the doctrines of grace in free-will Baptist churches and seeing men and women coming to Christ. On one occasion, whilst itinerating, the young preacher, yet without a pastorate, was called on to address a most wealthy and well-educated congregation with twelve pastors sitting amongst them, including George Whitefield who was on his fifth visit to North America. Believing that he had none to fear and obey but the Lord, Gano preached to them with his Lord's power.

Gano under suspicion of being a French spy

It was the time of the final phase of the French and Indian War (1756-63) which ended France's days as a North American power and Gano heard that he was under suspicion of being a spy by the colonel of the local regiment because of his French name and that he was in for a 'chastisement'. Without hesitating, Gano sent a message to the commanding officer, who was to muster new troops in the area the following Monday, saying that he would visit the enrolment place at 10 o'clock and preach to the recruits before their military duties commenced. Gano duly preached and found the critical colonel calling the one man to order who refused to listen respectfully. Afterwards, the colonel shook hands with Gano and thanked him, giving him a further opportunity to preach. Gano commented, 'Thus ended my chastisement and the fears of my friends.'

Becoming a self-supporting Baptist pastor

Whilst still itinerating, Gano married Sarah the daughter of John Stites who was mayor of Elizabeth Town. The Ganos bought a farm and settled down to ministering at an infant Baptist church. In those days, it was the custom of Baptist ministers to provide for their own livelihood and a professional ministry with a college trained pastor was frowned upon. Soon Gano found that he was ministering to a number of small and scattered churches who were without shepherds and had to make journeys throughout New Jersey and North Carolina. One of Gano's converts at this time was Hezekiah Smith (1737-1805) who became a noted minister. Now Gano was receiving calls from a number of churches to be their pastor and, after discussing the matter with his home church, felt that he should take on a church at Yadkin in North Carolina which was more destitute. Today, we often hear of pastors accepting calls to churches who can pay larger salaries and offer children a better education but John and Sarah and their young son felt that calls should be answered where the needs were greatest. The journey to Yadkin was long, tedious and expensive, taking five weeks. Within a few months of his arrival, Gano had built a meeting house at Yadkin and a regular ministry was maintained amongst Christians with various denominational backgrounds in the neighbourhood as this was the only chapel and Gano the only pastor for miles around. Gano was careful to appoint trustees from each denomination who gradually provided for separate buildings as time went on. As many of the new converts and older believers were led to accept believers' baptism, a Baptist church was constituted before little more than a year had gone by.

Difficulties caused by the Cherokee War

After two years, Gano, had to leave Yadkin because of the Cherokee War which ended with the surrender of the Cherokees in 1761 and their being pushed westwards from the Carolinas and Virginia. This was the time of Daniel Boone who left his North Carolina home on the Yadkin River in search of the Kentucky El Dorado, the settlement of which robbed the Cherokees of further territories. Driven from their own land, the Cherokees were forced onto Shawnee territory which caused a further war between the two tribes. Then Virginia decided to claim Shawnee territory and the slaughter of more Indians was programmed. As Gano was a commissioned reservist, he had feared that his pastoral activities would come to an abrupt end but he was not put on active service and thus accepted a call to pastor churches in New York and Philadelphia, the latter temporarily until their new minister, Morgan Edwards came from England. Again, it was the fact that the churches were destitute that drew Gano and, though he and Sarah had now two children, they felt that they should take on the strenuous task of moving fortnightly between New York and Philadelphia. Both churches grew, even though Gano felt duty bound to visit his former and now scattered Yadkin flock from time to time. Edwards was delayed considerably and Gano found a successor at Philadelphia in Samuel Stillman until Edwards arrived and concentrated on the work at New York. Just as Gano's church was prospering, a man named John Murray arrived from England and began preaching universal salvation which drew some hearers away for a time. Two other Englishmen came and began a policy of sheep-stealing, aiming all their darts at Gano instead of the devil. However,

Gano's church prospered and a good number of men were called to the ministry through Gano's preaching. Sadly, in 1765, the Ganos' eldest child, John, who had professed faith in Christ, died after a nasty fall. A year later, another son was born to the Ganos and received the name of John after his deceased brother.

War with Britain breaks out

Again war broke out, this time with the British, and the people of New York were scattered. Gano was called up but was invited to become army chaplain, a call which he accepted. New York soon fell to the British. It was then that Gano joined Washington's troops at the Battle of White Plains. The Hanoverians had pitted their Hessian troops against Washington, eleven hundred of whom he took prisoner. With but a handful of men, Washington repelled the British and Germans time and time again for a full year, though most of his stout-hearted Americans were irregulars and had only volunteered for a few weeks. Gano found himself ministering to men in the thick of battle with musket balls falling like hail. Though it was the Americans who were besieged, at the end of Gano's first taste of battle, the British counted eleven hundred dead whereas all the American casualties, including those taken prisoner, amounted to three hundred. The British and German professional soldiers were just no match for the hardened colonists who were fighting for family, home and freedom.

Gano made General Clinton's Chaplain

Now General Clinton made Gano Chaplain to his brigade. The troops clamoured to hear Gano's preaching, though some did ask him to put a little more politics in his message so as to give them some hope for the country's future. Gano replied to these people by preaching on 1 Samuel 22:23, 'Abide thou with me, fear not: for he that seeketh my life seeketh thy life: but with me thou shalt be in safeguard.' We may be sure that Gano stressed the surety of Christ for those who trust in Him. Gano always chose a text fitting for the moment. Before one battle, he preached on 'This day shall be a memorial unto you throughout your generations.' Another time when Sabbath rest was ordered, he preached on 'Being ready to depart on the morrow.'

Many of the Indians allied with the British who promised them equality with the whites and annuities. Equality was hardly ever gained but many of the tribes drew pensions from the British for many years to come even though the King's men lost the war and the tribes had to march annually to Canada to receive their annuities and presents. The discipline of the Americans was amazing at this time. When the troops were put on half-rations so that they would not waste time tracking down the Indian enemy they all cried out 'Huzza'[1] in agreement. One Irishman present said that he had served for years under both the British and the Americans but had never heard soldiers crying out 'Huzza' before because they were put on half-rations. General Clinton forbade his men to harm the Indian women.

Preaching Christ in the heat of battle

In the heat of the battle, soldiers' hearts were troubled and Gano had enough opportunity to point these men to Christ. The senior officers were also very anxious that the men should have spiritual comfort and often spoke with Gano about their own spiritual state. Meanwhile the churches were left without pastors and elders and the Baptist church at Philadelphia begged Gano to come over and rally them again. Gano showed the letter to General Clinton who gave him leave of absence for several weeks. Gano was also able to contact his family and to make plans for gathering his scattered New York flock should the British be defeated. Such a defeat now seemed inevitable as Washington, assisted by the French who were eager to revenge themselves on the British for the last Seven Years' War, suddenly ordered his now vast army on New York. Even Gano was taken totally by surprise and had to move with only the clothes he stood in. The British capitulated. Gano started searching for his family and found them well and larger than he had last left them as a son, William, had been born. Gano was soon back with the army and was given leave to preach three times on the Lord's Day to the now victorious troops. By the next Spring, all the British had moved out of New York and such as Gano could re-inhabit their now ruined houses. Of the two hundred members of Gano's church, only thirty could be traced, most of the others having been killed in the war. Gano set his church rebuilding and he built his members up in the faith in next to no time and soon membership was higher than before New York was taken by the British.

Not called to a comfortable, prosperous pastorate

Gano was on the way to becoming a prosperous, respected pastor of a prosperous and respected church, but this was not his calling. On hearing that his Association was looking for a volunteer to do a year's pioneer work as a missionary, Gano offered his services. His destination was to be Kentucky, now opened through the discoveries, escapades and adven-

---

[1] The equivalent of the modern 'three cheers'.

tures of Daniel Boone. This time, however, Gano's plans were not entirely free from material cares. He had accrued debts as a result of his rebuilding activities after the British capitulation and now felt that he should sell his property in order to free himself of such a burden. The Kentucky brethren had also promised him that they would look after his family's material needs. As soon as they heard his plans, the New York church offered Gano a substantial salary but they left the final decision to him. After a dangerous and exhausting voyage down the Ohio River during which a boat with much of his property capsized, Gano arrived in Kentucky during June, 1788. As soon as Gano reached his destination, he preached to his fellow-travellers on the words referring to Paul's shipwreck on the island of Melita, 'So we got all safe to land.'[1]

Hard times ahead

Now a great time of testing set in. The Ganos had already lost their most cherished possessions on the Ohio River but John was to face a far greater loss. Whilst looking for a site to set up a home, Sarah fell from her horse and her broken bones would not set correctly. She then contracted the pleurisy and died. She was resigned, indeed cheerful, to the end and safely entered, as Gano testified, to the 'house not made with hands, eternal in the heavens.' Then Gano heard from a friend that the person who had bought his property refused to pay, arguing that Gano had sold land to which he had no right. It was as if the trials of Job were now descending on Gano's head. Happily, Gano had not lost the deeds and papers he had signed on buying the land under question and, at great expense and after a fatiguing journey, he was able to settle the matter. Gano's reputation had suffered because of this matter and he felt that it must be cleared up for his testimony's sake.

Still not really settled in Kentucky though several years had passed, Gano found another Sarah, this time Sarah Hunt Bryant with whom he was married on April 15, 1793. Sarah had many matters to settle in North Carolina before accompanying her husband to Kentucky and the problems arising from these matters just could not be solved. Meanwhile, Gano did itinerant work around the Charleston area, visiting the places of his former labours and assisting Richard Furman in his work. As Mrs Gano's business matters had not been solved by the following September, Gano returned to Kentucky alone but had difficulty settling down there and again did itinerant work in North Carolina, New York, New Brunswick, Rhode

---

[1] Acts 27:44.

Island, Philadelphia, Maryland and Virginia. Almost a year and a half after their marriage, the couple reached Kentucky together but Mrs Gano had difficulties adjusting herself to the fact that she was now the step-mother of children who had families of their own and those children found difficulty in accepting a mother who was a total stranger.

The way to heaven provides further trials

Gano now concentrated his itinerary preaching efforts on Kentucky, though he frequently supplied for the Town Fork Baptist Church where he was a member. He also preached regularly at the State House in Frankfort where a gathering of Christians without denominational affiliations met. In the autumn of 1798, Gano fell from his horse and broke a shoulder blade which left one arm useless. Shortly afterwards he received a paralytic stroke down one side which left him blind in one eye, deaf in one ear and unable to speak correctly or move about with ease. Then, his son William, born in 1781 and the apple of his father's eye, died of a fever at the age of seventeen, professing faith in the risen Lord. This event, and the sad affairs preceding it, made Gano wonder whether his appointed work was at an end. He wrote:

> I see nothing worth living for; but to be more devoted to God, and the advantage of my family, and the church of God. And indeed it appears to me latterly, that I have lived beyond my usefulness; but I know I must wait for God's time, when he will unravel all the mysteries of His Providence. I sometimes wonder, why God ever conducted me to Kentucky, when so little fruit or good effect of my poor labours have appeared, at least to myself! why in this half dead condition, I am yet continued in life! Yet, I have more cause to wonder, that ever God made me instrumental of good, at any time of life; or any where in the world; and that now I should be laid by, as an instrument out of use.

Ah, lovely appearance of death

Gano continued to preach as best he could for a further six years, supported in his bed or sitting in a chair. When he realised that his earthly end was near, he told his family to shed no tears as he was going home and asked for the hymn 'Ah, lovely appearance of death', to be sung at his funeral. Whilst Gano was preparing for his home-call, news reached him that a great work of the Spirit was spreading through Kentucky and this increased his final joy. With his cup full and running over, Gano departed from this life on August 10, 1804, aged seventy-seven.

I have purposefully retold Gano's story more from his humble point of view than from that of those who were blessed by his ministry. Needless to say, others had a far more positive view of the life the Baptist saint lived and the great success of his ministry. This is all outlined in great detail in Terry Wolever's new book which includes numerous eye-witness testimonies to his work. Wolever also provides documentary backing for Gano's biography in great detail, and gives many evidences of the saint's great spirituality from his sermons. There is also a fine chapter on the Particular Baptists of North Carolina and a relatively large section on the histories of Gano's children, several of whom became notable ministers and public figures. Volume II will include a detailed account of Gano's pastorates, his diary account for the year 1773-1774, his associations with George Washington and various wills and legal documents belonging to the Gano family. In all, this is a feast of good things for those who read for edification. Those also who are interested in doing research into this period of great spiritual blessing in the history of the United States, on reading these volumes, will find that their time is far from wasted.

WILLIAM COWPER (1731-1800)

25. William Cowper (1731-1800): Christian Campaigner

Social reform pioneered by evangelical Christians

Atheistic sociologists and Marxist orientated humanists persist in telling their followers that Christians have always been on the side of the 'capitalist oppressors' and have done little to alleviate the needs of the poor. We are therefore in danger of forgetting how much social reform was pioneered by Christian men and women.

The 150th anniversary in 1983 of the emancipation of the slaves reminded us of the untiring efforts of frailbodied, evangelical William Wilberforce and helped greatly to bring this fact again to the public eye. But Wilberforce was not the only evangelical to work for the slaves. William Cowper is well known for his poetry and his hymns—such as 'Hark, my soul! it is the Lord', or 'God moves in a mysterious way'. Even this recluse of a man, however, did much pioneer work for the gospel in bringing spiritual and material comfort to the poor and in taking up the cause of the oppressed at home and abroad in the latter half of the eighteenth century. Before going on to examine Cowper's works, it may assist the reader to know something of his birth as a son of Adam and his re-birth as an adopted child of God.

William Cowper's birth and family background

Our subject was born on November 15, 1731, the child of parents of noble birth who numbered Kings, Lord Chancellors, Chief Justices and bishops in their family. Cowper's father was the Rev. John Cowper, D. D., fellow of Merton College, Cambridge, Chaplain to the King, Commissioner of Bankrupts and Rector of Berkhamsted. His wife, Anne, née Donne, was related to the Boleyns, the Careys, the Howards, the Mowbrays and Sir Thomas

Moore. Cowper, however, made nothing of his background save for the fact that his parents were both evangelical believers who had seen a work of real grace in their lives. This was all important for Cowper who testified long after both parents were dead:

> But oh the thought, that thou art safe, and he!
> That thought is joy, arrive what may to me.
> My boast is not, that I deduce my birth
> From loins enthron'd and rulers of the earth,
> But higher far my proud pretentions rise—
> The son of parents pass'd into the skies.[1]

Born into a family of poets

Important, too, for Cowper was the fact that both his parents were lovers of poetry, his father and paternal relations having published several volumes of poetry. Even Pope the famous poet, seldom given to modesty, praises Cowper's Great Uncle in his poem *Dunciad* and confessed that Cowper's Aunt Judith's poetry was of a greater standard than his own. Anne Cowper was reputed to be a direct descendent of John Donne, a fact which often overcame Cowper's basic modesty and made him very proud of the connection.

Anne Cowper died six days after giving birth to another boy when William was scarcely six years of age. She was only thirty-four. William felt the loss of his mother greatly and treasured every memory he had of her, assisted in later life by a portrait of his mother which he received from an aunt. This gave rise to his very beautiful, but very sad poem *On the receipt of my mother's picture*. In this poem, Cowper, now the foremost poet in the kingdom, looks back to the day of his mother's death and writes:

> My mother! when I learned that thou wast dead,
> Say, wast thou conscious of the tears I shed?
> Hovered thy spirit o'er thy sorrowing son,
> Wretch even then, life's journey just begun?
> *Perhaps thou gav'st me, though unfelt, a kiss:*
> Perhaps a tear, if souls can weep in bliss—
> Ah, that maternal smile! it answers—Yes.[2]

---

[1] *On the receipt of my mother's picture*

[2] Ibid.

Anne's foolish but well-intentioned maids tried to keep the news from William and, creating a make-believe lie, told the poor boy that his mother had gone on a journey and would soon be back. William, however, had understood more than the maids realised. Looking back on those unhappy days Cowper wrote:

> I heard the bell tolled on thy burial day,
> I saw the hearse that bore thee slow away,
> And turning from my nursery window, drew
> A long, long sigh, and wept a last adieu.[1]

Cowper meets up with the school bully

John Cowper remarried after several years but Cowper never really got on with his stepmother. This was perhaps because he was seldom at home as he was sent to boarding-school from the age of six or seven until eighteen. At his infant prep school 'Old Vicarage', Cowper had his first experience of bullying and first experience of the Lord's deliverance. A fifteen-year-old lout, who was still at the school because of either his lack of interest in learning or lack of mental ability, took a perverse delight in tormenting and even torturing small boys. When he met gentle, refined seven-year-old William with his quick wit and obvious superior intelligence, the bully realised that he had found an ideal victim. Day after day, week after week he tormented Cowper so cruelly that the poor boy dared not look him in the face, so frightened was he of this cowardly monster. Later the poet wrote, 'I well remember being afraid to lift my eyes upon him higher than his knees, and that I knew him by his shoe buckles better than by any other part of his dress.'[2] It is typical of Cowper that he goes on to write, 'May the Lord pardon him and may we meet in glory!' Cowper had, however, been taught many a passage of Scripture at home and had learnt to pray. This was to be God's way of delivering the small boy from his tormentor. Cowper tells how it happened:

> One day I was sitting alone upon a bench in the school, melancholy and almost ready to weep at the recollection of what I had already suffered at his hands and at the apprehension of what was yet to come, expecting at the same time my tormentor

---

[1] Ibid.

[2] *Adelphi*, King and Ryskamp, vol. 1, page 5.

every moment, these words of the Psalmist came into my mind, 'I will not fear what man can do unto me.' I applied them to my own use with a degree of trust and confidence in God that would have been in no disgrace to a much more experienced Christian.—Instantly, I perceived in myself a briskness of spirits and a cheerfulness which I had never felt before, and took several paces up and down the school with a joyful alacrity, his gift in whom I trusted.[1]

What started as an ordeal for Cowper ended in a triumph of grace and an exhilarating experience the poet never forgot. There was no more bullying. Shortly after this incident Cowper's antagonist was found out and expelled. Cowper related this years later after his conversion to show how the hand of God was on him even as a child. The poet often complained that his eyes had often been turned to God in childhood when in need, but his heavenly father was forgotten when things went smoothly. All of us, with shame, know what Cowper meant.

Fame lay at Cowper's feet but his life fell apart

After the Old Vicarage, Cowper went on to do very well at the renowned school of Westminster both in academic and sporting pursuits. He became School Captain and when he left Westminster he had received his colours in both football and cricket. After Westminster, Cowper studied law at the Inner Temple and published his first works which were mainly of a satirical nature. He was one of the founders of the famous Nonsense Club, to whose members the satirical painter and engraver William Hogarth belonged as also the notorious politician John Wilkes, 'the Falstaff of his age', Charles 'Toby' Price, the famous lawyer Joseph Hill and Bonnell Thornton and George Colman, editors of the fashionable *Connoisseur*. Several joint publications came from the pens of these men. As James Boswell called Cowper and his fellow members 'the London Geniuses', the Nonsense Club seems to have made a name for itself. At this time, Cowper was called to the Bar and fell in love with his cousin Theadora Cowper, daughter of Ashley Cowper who held an important government function in the House of Lords.

Though William Cowper had all he could desire, all went wrong. William's and Theadora's parents were against the match and he funked taking examinations for a senior legal post at the House of Lords. At the same time a great conviction of sin came upon Cowper and he had a

---

[1] Ibid, p. 5.

nervous breakdown, becoming violently insane for several months during which time he tried to take his own life on numerous occasions. His younger brother John, a Cambridge Don, his cousin Martin Madan, Chaplain to the Countess of Huntingdon and Thomas Haweis, Madan's Evangelical assistant, obtained a place for Cowper at Nathaniel Cotton's Collegium Insanorum at St Albans. Here Cowper was locked in a cell, yet still he sought to take his own life.

Still there is mercy

The ex-lawyer and poet to be now suffered from evil and threatening hallucinations which tore at the roots of his nerves, but gradually the pictures he saw in his delirium took on a more positive shape. One evening when he was pacing backwards and forwards in his room he had a vision of such exquisite heavenly beauty that he could only cry out, 'Bless me; I see a glory all around me.' Gradually Cowper was allowed to go out of doors on his own and he found that the talks with Dr Cotton, were doing him good. Cotton was a fine Evangelical and also a poet. This news was sent to John Cowper in June 1764 so John immediately visited his brother. William noticed the look of disappointment on his face when they met. John had expected to see his brother fit and well. On asking William how he was, John received the answer, 'As much better as despair can make me.' John could not hold back his feelings and protested strongly at his brother's attitude, telling him that it was all a delusion. This touched William greatly who said, 'If it be a delusion then am I the happiest of beings.' After that William became more cheerful, constantly occupying his thoughts with the words 'Still there is mercy.' That night Cowper slept well and had the loveliest of dreams. He awoke more refreshed than he had been for many months. Before breakfast he went for a walk in the garden and found a Bible on a bench. He started to read and found he was reading the story of the raising of Lazarus from the dead. 'I saw so much benevolence and mercy,' wrote Cowper, 'so much goodness and sympathy with miserable mankind in our Saviour's conduct as melted my heart.' Then he adds, 'Little did I know that it was an exact type of the mercy which Jesus was upon the point of extending towards myself. I sighed and said, "Oh that I had not rejected so good a Redeemer! that I had not forfeited all His favour!"' Cowper went to breakfast and felt a change coming over him. He felt lighter and was almost happy. After breakfast he continued to muse on the change he was experiencing yet he was frightened to hope too much as he knew that he was capable of extremes of feeling. The dark clouds were, however, departing and soon Cowper would see the sunshine of God's smiling face.

What happened next is best told in Cowper's own words:

> The happy period that was to strike off my fetters and to
> afford me a clear opening into the free mercy of the Blessed
> God in Jesus was now arrived. I flung myself into a chair near
> the window seat and, seeing a Bible there, ventured once more
> to apply to it for comfort and instruction. The first verse I saw
> was the twenty-fifth of the third chapter to the Romans where
> Jesus is set forth as the propitiation for our sins. Immediately
> I received strength to believe it. Immediately the full beams of
> the sun of righteousness shone upon me. I saw the suffi-
> ciency of the atonement He had made, my pardon sealed in
> His blood, and all the fullness and completeness of my justifi-
> cation. In a moment I believed and received the Gospel. What-
> soever my friend Madan had said to me so long before re-
> curred to me with the clearest evidence of its truth, 'with dem-
> onstration of the Spirit and with power.' Unless the Almighty
> Arm had been under me I think I should have died with grati-
> tude and joy. My eyes filled with tears and my voice was
> choked with transport. I could only look up to Heaven in si-
> lence, overwhelmed with love and wonder! But the work of
> the Holy Ghost is best described in His own words. It was 'joy
> unspeakable and full of glory.' Thus was my Heavenly Father
> in Christ Jesus pleased to give me the full assurance of faith at
> once, and out of a stony and unbelieving heart to raise up a
> child unto Abraham.

All things made new

After this great experience Cowper spent many weeks in praise and prayer,
his heart overflowing. Dr Cotton did not know what to believe, at first, and
examined Cowper intensively concerning what had happened. Soon, however, he became convinced that a great work of God had occurred in his
patient's life and that Cowper was not only now converted but also cured
of his insanity. Such was the friendship of the two men that neither wanted
to become separated from the other so Cowper stayed on at St Albans
another year.

During this time Cowper studied the Scriptures diligently, read a
large number of Biblical studies by men such as Walter Marshall and
poured out his praise to God in verse. The following hymn is Cowper's
very first testimony of the change that the Lord had wrought in him.

BEHOLD I MAKE ALL THINGS NEW

How blest thy creature is, O God!
When with a single Eye,
He views the lustre of thy Word,
The day spring from on high.

Thro' all the storms that vail the skies
And frown on earthly things;
The Sun of Righteousness he Eyes
With healing on his wings.

Struck by that light, the Human heart,
A barren soil no more,
Sends the sweet smell of Grace abroad,
Where Serpents lurk'd before.

The soul a dreary province once,
Of Satan's dark domain;
Feels a new empire form'd within,
And owns an heav'nly reign.

The glorious orb whose golden beams,
The fruitful year control;
Since first obedient to thy word,
He started from the Goal;

Has chear'd the nations with the joys
His orient rays impart,
But Jesus, 'tis thy light alone,
Can shine upon the heart.

The Olney Lace-makers

The story of Cowper's calling to be a poet and an appreciation of his work in that field can be found in my book *William Cowper: Poet of Paradise*. My task now is to show how Cowper was also a great Christian campaigner. Though shy and retreating by nature, Cowper, who had settled down in the small town of Olney, Buckinghamshire, felt social injustice sharply. He was a Whig of the old school, hating any form of tyranny, monopoly or unjust suppression. He therefore campaigned strongly in verse and prose for a better deal for the poor Olney lace-makers and represented them legally. He wrote to wealthy and influential friends asking for money to be given to his poor neighbours and even solicited the help of the Lord Chancellor. "I am an eye-witness of their poverty," he wrote, "and do know that hundreds in this little town are upon the point of starving, and that the most unremitting industry is but barely sufficient to keep them from it."

Cowper did not believe in distributing alms indiscriminately, but always distinguished between those who needed help and were worthy of it and those who may have been in need yet had only themselves to blame for their situation. Writing in 1782 to an evangelical friend, the Rev. William Unwin, about how they should use an extra generous gift which Cowper had solicited, the poet says:

> We shall exercise our best direction in the disposal of the money, but in this town, where the Gospel has been preached so many years, where the people have been favoured so long with laborious and conscientious ministers, it is not an easy thing to find those who make no profession of religion at all, and are yet proper objects of charity. The profane are so profane, so drunken, so dissolute and in every respect worthless, that to make them partakers of his bounty would be to abuse it. We promise, however, that none shall touch it, but such as are miserably poor, yet at the same time industrious and honest—two characters frequently united here, where the most watchful and unremitting labour will hardly procure them bread, we make none but the cheapest laces, and the price of them is fallen almost to nothing.

Fighting cruelty to animals

Cowper loved animals and had a houseful of pets at one time, including rabbits, pigeons, a magpie, a jay, a starling, two goldfinches, two canaries, two dogs, a squirrel, a cat, several kittens and three hares. At least the latter had the free run of his house.

The poet was one of the first to take up his pen to campaign against blood sports and cruelty to animals. Cowper saw this cruelty as a direct result of the fall, believing that man and animals lived in harmony in pre-fall Eden. After the fall animals prey on one another but within measure whilst those in dependence on man (Cowper tells us in *The Task*):

> *... prove too often at how dear a rate*
> *He sells protection. Witness at his foot,*
> *The Spaniel dying for some venial fault,*
> *Under dissection at the knotted scourge.*
> *Witness, the patient ox, with stripes and yells*
> *Driv'n to the slaughter, goaded as he runs*
> *To madness, while the savage at his heels*
> *Laughs at the frantic suff'rer's fury spent*
> *Upon the guiltless passenger o'erthrown*

After denouncing men who beat and ride their horses to death Cowper proclaimed:

> *But many a crime deem'd innocent on earth,*
> *Is register'd in heaven. and these no doubt,*
> *Have each their record, with a curse annext.*

It is typical of Cowper that he uses biblical examples, such as the case of Balaam's ass, to show how God's word forbids cruelty to animals and how such offenders should be punished.

Condemning the East India Company

Cowper saw no Christian virtue in British efforts to colonise India. 'Whatever we are at home,' he told his cousin Lady Hesketh, "we certainly have been tyrants in the East."

In his mammoth poem *The Task*, Cowper tells how his ear was ever attuned to the 'twanging horn' of the 'herald of a noisy world', *alias* the postman bringing newspapers, letters and gossip. One of the poet's first questions was always:

> *Is India free? and does she wear her plumed*
> *And jewelled turban with a smile of peace,*
> *Or do we grind her still?*

Cowper detested the policies and politics of the East India Company, protesting that they had been given merely a charter to trade and yet believed that this gave them a royal prerogative to make war or peace at will. He wrote to William Unwin in January 1784, saying:

... they have possessed themselves of an immense territory, which they have ruled with a rod of iron, to which it is impossible they should ever have a right, unless such an one as it is a disgrace to plead, the right of conquest. The potentates of this country they dash in pieces like a potter's vessel as often as they please, making the happiness of 30 millions of mankind a consideration subordinate to that of their own emolument.

Cowper was, however, always balanced in his criticism. Soon the British government was sorting out the trouble and punishing the offenders. The poet saw at once that scapegoats were being sought out, in particular Governor General of Bengal, Warren Hastings—who was, if not spotless, the most innocent of the Company's officials. Hastings' trial dragged on for three years and, although he was finally acquitted, his enemies' tongues continued to wag. Cowper, who knew Hastings of old, wrote the following poem to a national newspaper:

To Warren Hastings Esq.
By an old schoolfellow of his at Westminster.

> *Hastings! I knew thee young, and of a mind,*
> *While young, humane, conversible and kind,*
> *Nor can I well believe thee, gentle **then**,*
> ***Now** grown a villain and the **worst** of men,*
> *But rather some suspect, who have oppressed*
> *And worried thee, as not themselves the best.*

History has subsequently shown that Cowper had hit the nail on the head. Those who slandered Hastings were found to be those who had abused the Indian people.

Criticising the Church

The Church, or rather its lazy ministers, often felt the whip of Cowper's poetical lash. In *The Task* he castigated ministers who preach, or rather read, other people's sermons, relying on 'theatrics' and joke-telling to win 'popular applause'. 'They mock their Maker,' he said, 'when I am hungry for the bread of life.' In his poem *Expostulations* Cowper was even more scathingly critical:

> *When nations are to perish in their sins,*
> *'Tis in the church the leprosy begins:*
> *The priest, whose office is with zeal sincere*
> *To watch the fountain, and preserve it clear,*
> *Carelessly nods and sleeps upon the brink,*
> *While others poison what the flock must drink:*
> *Or waking at the call of lust alone,*
> *Infuses lies and errors of his own:*
> *His unsuspecting sheep believe it pure,*
> *And, tainted by the very means of cure,*
> *Catch from each other a contagious spot;*
> *The foul forerunner of a gen'ral rot:*

In *Tirocinum*, itself a campaigning poem, Cowper criticised the practice of the Church in training unconverted men for the ministry. This produced church leaders who are 'Christian in name, and Infidel in heart', who are at best 'mere church-furniture'.

Cowper did not criticise here in a one-sided way, but showed his readers *the* true pastor in, for instance, the person of George Whitefield, of whom he wrote:

> *He lov'd the world that hated him: the tear*
> *That dropp'd upon his Bible was sincere*
> *Assailed by scandal and the tongue of strife,*
> *His only answer was, a blameless life.*

The Slave Trade

Much of Cowper's concern about India had to do with the poet's fight against slavery. He was very much afraid that Britain would misuse the Indians, as she was misusing the Africans in the West Indies. In his poem *Expostulations* Cowper reminded his readers of the time before the Reformation when Britain was enslaved under the yoke of Romanism from which the gospel freed her. He then wrote in reference to Britain's India policy.

> *Hast thou, suckled at fair freedom's breast,*
> *Exported slav'ry to the conquered East,*
> *Pull'd down the tyrants India serv'd with dread,*
> *And rais'd thyself a greater, in their stead, ...?*

Cowper, in fact, was writing against slavery a good decade before the matter was seriously taken up in Parliament. He had anti-slavery works published years before James Ramsey and Thomas Clarkson (who are credited with being the first in the field against slavery) had published anything on the subject.

Clarkson himself called Cowper a 'great coadjutor' in the fight for abolition. The poet, never guilty of exaggerating his own efforts—he usually played them down—wrote to Lady Hesketh, his cousin, in February 1788, expressing admiration for Hannah More's anti-slavery work and adding:

I have already borne my testimony in favour of our black brethren and I was one of the earliest, if not the first of those who have in the present day expressed their detestation of the diabolical traffic in question.

At first Cowper found the topic of slavery 'susceptible to poetical management' and brought into play all his expertise, coupled with a keen sense of humour and great proficiency in using satire. He poured scorn on the arguments of the planters who, for instance, in one poem said of their slaves:

> *I pity them greatly, but I must be mum,*
> *For how could we do without sugar or rum?*
> *Especially sugar, so needful we see?*
> *What? give up our desserts, our coffee and tea!*

Gentle Cowper could hardly believe that men could sink so low as to enslave their fellow-men for the sake of gaining more luxury. In 1781 he appealed to the slave traders in his poem *Charity*:

> *Canst thou, and honour'd with a Christian name,*
> *Buy what is woman-born, and feel no shame?*
> *Trade in the blood of innocence, and plead*
> *Expedience as a warrant for the deed?*

Cowper went on to argue that there is no 'discriminating hue' among God's creatures, but rather that all men are blemished because of the fall. He told his readers that Jesus' divine love goes out to all men 'irrespective of their skin'. He called slavery one of 'the foulest deeds' and, obviously having Proverbs 14.31 in mind, pronounced a solemn warning on the slave-traders:

> *Remember, Heaven has an avenging rod,*
> *To smite the poor is treason against God.*

In the late 1780s the newly founded Society for the Abolition of the Slave Trade approached Cowper through John Newton, an ex-slave trader, to write campaigning songs 'to be sung about the streets'. The poet was told that 'nobody could do it so well'. Cowper was not at all keen on the idea at first, as he found the subject far too horrible to sing about.

He eventually consented, however, and wrote several ballads, the two most popular being *The Negro's Complaint* (set to the then popular tune *Hosier's Ghost*) and *The Slave-traders in the Dumps*. The former is a sober description of the slave's tragic plight in which he says,

> *Forc'd from home and all its pleasures,*
> *Afric's coast I left forlorn;*
> *To increase a stranger's treasures,*
> *O'er the raging billows borne:*

As in almost all Cowper's campaigning poems, there is a sting in its tail for the offender. The slave, treated worse than an animal, says to the trader:

> *Prove that **you** have human feelings,*
> *Ere you proudly question ours.*

In *The Slave Trade in the Dumps* Cowper brought all his scathing satire to bear on the topic. The result was a gruesome, blood-curdling picture of the way slaves were tortured and maltreated on board the slavers. The following is an excerpt from the poem:

> *'Tis a curious assortment of dainty regales,*
> *To tickle the Negroes with when the ship sails.*
> *Fine chains for the neck, and a cat with nine tails.*
> *Here's padlocks and bolts, and screws for the thumbs,*

That squeeze them so lovingly till the blood comes,
They sweeten the temper like comfits or plums.
It would do your heart good to see 'em below,
Lie flat on their backs all the way' as we go.
Like sprats on a gridiron, scores in a row.

Cowper soon gave up writing anti-slavery ballads for two strong reasons. Readers will perhaps remember how depressed writing *The Screwtape Letters* made C. S. Lewis. He told us that, though he had never written anything more easily, he had never written with less enjoyment. Writing about the works of the devil gets the Christian down.

This was the case with Cowper, who was of a very sensitive nature. He had been a 'dabbler in rhyme' since his childhood. His fingers were always itching, he tells us, to write poetry. Yet the subject of slavery appalled him and made him ill. 'Slavery, and especially negro slavery, because the cruelest,' he wrote to his friend Mr Bagot, 'is an odious and disgusting subject ... I felt myself so much hurt in my spirits the moment I entered on the contemplation of it, that I have at last determined absolutely to have nothing more to do with it.'

The second reason why Cowper stopped writing ballads was, oddly enough, because of their popularity. At one time no less than five anti-slavery ballads, written by Cowper, were being sung in the streets and even in the taverns. Abolitionists wete distributing thousands of copies at their own expense.

The poet soon saw, however, that, though everybody was singing his songs, their hearts were not being pricked. People were only paying attention to the swinging tunes, to 'the fiddle of verse' and to the humour and satire in them. 'Verse', Cowper said, 'had stooped low'. Cowper had inadvertently become popular as an entertainer.

With this in mind the poet complained to his young lawyer friend, Samuel Rose, saying, "Woe be to us, if we refuse the poor captives the redress to which they have so clear a right, and prove ourselves in the sight of God and men indifferent to all considerations but those of gain."

Nevertheless, Cowper could not remain silent for long. Slavery continued and in 1792, though Cowper was very ill and at times felt himself as God's 'cast-away', and was plagued day and night by hallucinations and voices, he wrote the following verses which were published in the *Northampton Mercury*;

> *To purify their wine some people bleed A lamb*
> *into the barrel, and succeed:*
> *No nostrum, planters say, is half so good*
> *To make fine sugar, as a negro's blood.*
> *Now lambs and negroes both are harmless things,*
> *And thence perhaps this wond'rous virtue springs.*
> *'Tis in the blood of innocence alone -*
> *Good cause why planters never try their own.*

Cowper was greatly encouraged by the presence of young William Wilberforce in Parliament but had very mixed feelings about passing laws to curb slavery. 'What use are laws', he asked, 'when the people have scorned the voice that cried, "Repent"?' They would be at best 'stiff in the letter' but 'lax in design'.

Bishop J. C. Ryle, looking back on the great change which took place in the eighteenth century through the work of evangelicals, said with hindsight: 'The government of the country can lay no claim to the credit of the change. Morality cannot be called into being by penal enactments and statutes. People were never yet made religious by Acts of Parliament.'

Cowper was one of those eighteenth century evangelicals who campaigned for a change of heart rather than legislation. Writing to Newton, the poet said: 'Laws will, I suppose, be enacted for the more humane treatment of the negroes: but who will see as to the execution of them? The planters will not, and the negroes cannot . . . Where are the prosecutors? Where are the righteous judges? Where are the merciful masters?'

The poet maintained that there was a double blindness which prevented man from establishing the 'overflowing well of Charity' needed to promote true moral action. Man had no true picture of himself and no true picture of God. Only when God's enlightening grace came into a man's life was he able to perform true works of charity. Only that which squares with Scripture and springs from love to God and love to man will stand at the day of judgement. So argued the poet in his poems *Charity* and *Expostulations*.

Here is a difference, then, between the humanistic socialiser and the true Christian reformer. Only the latter has the true motives and wherewithal to effect true change. Cowper, because of these views, was called 'the father of moral criticism' by the nineteenth century. The twentieth century seems to have forgotten him—and his doctrines. May Cowper's example spur us on in this modern dark age to do more for our Master till 'the earth is full of the knowledge of the Lord, as the waters cover the sea.'

AUGUSTUS MONTAGUE TOPLADY (1740-1778)

26. Augustus Montague Toplady (1740-1778): A Debtor to Mercy Alone

Church morality deduced from nature and the fitness of things

Looking back in 1780 over the course of the Evangelical Revival, Erasmus Middleton said that forty years previously it had been hard to find an Evangelical in the Church of England and:

> ...our pupils sounded with morality, deduced from the principles of nature and the fitness of things, with no relation to Christ, or the Holy Spirit; all which the heathen philosophers have insisted upon and with perhaps more than modern ingenuity; and, in consequence, our streets have resounded with heathen morality. We had flowery language in the church, and loose language out of it.

God cleans up the city of London

Middleton goes on to say that ministers would read the Scriptural truths contained in the Anglican service and pray Biblical prayers from the pulpit, step down and discard their white garments and leave the church to joke in coarse language about the cant and nonsense of religion. The situation in London was the worst with ministers seen more often keeping bad company in the most evil places bringing dishonour to their calling. Then William Romaine, followed closely by Thomas Jones started reforming the city so that ecclesiastical no-goods such as Thomas Wilson complained to King George that his congregation was being completely drawn away by the new preachers. The King replied that if he made bishops of the Evangelicals, that would silence them. Soon Evangelicals such as

Hervey, Conyers, Grimshaw, Serle, Walker, Newton, Cecil, Scott, Thomson, Simeon, Venn, Hill, Haweis and Middleton himself were proclaiming Christ's righteousness from Anglican pulpits.

A sudden bright and brilliant comet

One of these great men of the Evangelical Revival was certainly Augustus Toplady, who was born on November 4, 1740 and died a mere 37 years later. Thomas Wright likens him to a bright and brilliant comet that adorns the skies for a moment and then fades away. The comparison is fitting but not adequate enough as the comet leaves a brief trail of light behind it during its short appearance in the sky but Toplady's illuminating witness to God's love manifested in Christ is as fresh today as it was over two hundred years ago and his hymns such as *Rock of Ages* are still loved dearly.

Toplady's family background and childhood

Major Richard Toplady, our subject's father, died of the yellow fever whilst campaigning in South America before his son's birth and left his wife Catherine in relative poverty. Toplady's mother was a sound Christian and a member of a family of clergymen and clergymen's wives who forgot that charity begins at home and even despised Catherine and Augustus for their humble station. Toplady received his first names from his godparents Augustus Middleton and Adolphus Montague and spent his early schooling at Farnham from where mother and child moved to London when Toplady was nine or ten years of age so that he could visit Westminster School. As Toplady wrote in his journal that he had no 'Sunday clothes' and was too poor to have a decent pair of stockings, it must have been a great sacrifice for Mrs Toplady to keep her son at Westminster amongst all the rich noblemen's sons. Major Toplady had been on friendly terms with the Vernons of Vernon House, Farnham and perhaps they assisted with school fees. The bond between Catherine and her son was very strong and we often find Toplady writing of her in his childhood diaries, comparing her to his aunts who were very hard on their children and saying, 'Oh, the difference there is between their mamma and mine!'

Toplady entered Westminster during William Cowper's last term and had the same teachers whom Cowper describes with so much sympathy in his poetry and letters. Like Cowper, Toplady found Nicholl, the Head, a man to love and respect but found 'Tappy' Lloyd and 'Vinney' Bourne too lax by far. Further peeps into Toplady's diaries show that he had already a love of the gospel and a strong desire to serve God, expressed by such entries as, 'I always love God, and endeavour to cast away all impurity and all sin whatever,' written when eleven years of age. Toplady's written prayers with places for free renderings have been preserved and we see how devoutly he prayed for his school masters and fellow pupils. On his birthday Toplady wrote, 'I am now arrived of the age of eleven years. I praise God I can remember no dreadful crime: and not to me but to the Lord be the glory. Amen. It is now past eight o'clock and now I think fit to withdraw, but yet my heart is so full of divine and holy raptures, that a sheet of paper could not contain my writings.'

Early attempts at sermon writing thwarted

During the following year, young Toplady began to write down sermons of his own making and showed them to his uncle Julius Bates, a leading Hutchinsonian, for approval. 'Uncle Jack' threatened to 'flay his nephew alive' for saying that he had composed them himself as he professed to know very well that children could not compose such sermons. It was, however, 'Aunty Betsy' i.e. Elizabeth Bates who dealt out the punishment, claiming that Toplady and his praying mother were 'liars'. This was used as an excuse for the Bates to sever contacts with their poor relations. Toplady dropped writing sermons for writing hymns, some of which have survived from those early years.

Conversion in Ireland leading to a reception of the doctrines of grace

Toplady left Westminster prematurely in 1755 as his mother had inherited an estate in Ireland and the two set up their new home in County Wexford. Though not yet fifteen years of age, Toplady was entered at Trinity College Dublin. This was the time of Toplady's first publication, a poem entitled 'To a Friend, asking what God was,' published in the *London Magazine*. The following summer, an unlearned but greatly gifted evangelist named James Morris preached at Cooladine on Ephesians 2:13, 'Ye who sometimes were far off are made nigh by the blood of Christ.' Toplady could now write, 'Under that sermon, I was, I trust, brought nigh by the blood of Christ, in August, 1756. Strange that I, who had so long sat under means of grace in England, should be brought nigh unto God in an obscure part of Ireland, amid a handful of God's people met together in a barn, and under the ministry of one who could hardly spell his name!'

Now a converted man, Toplady renewed his energies to finish his studies and be ordained in the Church of England but a shock awaited him. He was, to use his own words, 'a haughty and violent free-willer' and he found to his horror that the *Thirty-Nine Articles* of the Established Church were Calvinistic. Toplady turned to John Wesley for help but it was not the

Arminian leader who put Toplady right but an unknown old man who had
listened to Toplady speaking on universal grace and free-will. The old man
approached the young hot-head, took hold of a button of his jacket and
calmly said:

> My dear sir; there are some marks of spirituality in your con-
> versation; though tinged with an unhappy mixture of pride and
> self-righteousness. You have been speaking largely in favour of
> free-will; but from arguments let us come to experience. Do let me
> ask you one question, How was it with you when the Lord laid
> hold on you in effectual calling? Had you any hand in obtaining
> that grace? Nay, would you not have resisted and baffled it, if
> God's Spirit had left you in the hand of your own counsel?

Finding out the difference between sound and unsound literature
With the wise old man's words still in his ear, Toplady, now eighteen,
turned to read Manton which helped him see the follies of his Arminian
position. He now felt called anew to become a Church of England minister
according to the *Thirty-Nine Articles* but found no Anglican minister in
Dublin who believed them so he had fellowship with the Baptists, whom
he found were more Anglican than the Anglicans. A year later, Toplady
published his first volume of free-grace poetry and hymns. He read Calvin,
the Puritans, Witsius, Hervey and Zanchius with great profit, translating
the latter's *Absolute Predestination* into English. He also read Baxter's
Aphorisms Concerning Justification, of which he wrote, 'a cramp, dark
treatise, and in many respects directly contrary to the Word of God. It
ought to be burnt by the common hangman.'

Back with Whitefield, Gill and Romaine in London
Toplady took his Bachelor of Arts degree in 1760 and made plans with his
mother to return to London. An hour or so after reaching the city, Toplady
was seated in Whitefield's Tabernacle listening to the great preacher. During the following year and a half whilst awaiting ordination, Toplady heard
Romaine, Whitefield and Gill on numerous occasions, becoming close
friends with all three. His diaries shows how he would dash from an afternoon service with Gill to an evening service with Whitefield or listen to
Romaine giving a mid-week lecture. Toplady, who had learnt to love and
respect the Particular Baptists, was particularly drawn to Gill so that, according to Thomas Wright, Carter Lane became Toplady's true *alma mater*.
Toplady often visited Gill privately, prayed with him, attended his meet-

ings and corresponded with him when out of town. Gill looked through Toplady's unpublished manuscripts and urged him to send his works to the press. Toplady took extensive notes of Gill's sermons and lectures and quoted him extensively in his own works.

Discovering the Rock of Ages at his Blagdon curacy

In June, 1762, Toplady came of ordination age and was licensed to the curacy of Blagdon in Somerset. The congregation was not only small but also divided amongst itself because of an old quarrel. Toplady strove to unite and enlarge his congregation showing how he took no sides in the strife and felt equally committed to both sides. The young curate was obviously rather disappointed with his first church but served them faithfully. Near Blagdon there is a large cleft rock forming part of the Mendip Hills and the story goes that Toplady was caught in a storm one day and sheltered in the cleft. Whilst protected from the wind and rain, Toplady thought of 2 Samuel 2: 22 'The Lord is my rock, and my fortress, and my deliverer,'[1] and composed his famous Rock of ages cleft for me.

Two years later, we find Toplady preaching his farewell sermon at Blagdon, before receiving priest's orders, urging those who were grieved with their sin not to give up hope, saying:

> Let not such be afraid to meet Him: Let not such say, 'How shall I stand when He appears?' for such have a Foundation to stand upon, a Foundation that cannot fail, even Jesus, the Mediator and Surety of the covenant, Christ, the Rock of Ages. He died for such, their sins which lay like an unsurmountable impediment, or stood like a vast partition wall, and blocked up the passage to eternal life; I say He took the sins of his penitent people out of the way, nailing them to His cross.

Vicar of Harpford and Rector of Fenn Ottery

In 1766, after two short periods in London where Toplady renewed his fellowship with Romaine and Gill, and a brief stay in Farley Hungerford near Bath where Toplady harvested much fruit, he became Vicar of Harpford and Rector of Fen Ottery, two villages with a joint population of 300 souls. Here Toplady preached the doctrines of grace with success but was very ill for months with a numbness of the limbs, which greatly limited his work. Writing to a friend he says, 'Every affliction is a nail, intended to crucify us

---

[1] See Isaiah 26:4, margin.

to the world and hasten the death of the man of sin, that degenerate lust, which is so deeply entrenched in every human heart.' When Toplady took up regular preaching again in the villages, he was alarmed to find that Sandemanism was spreading so he began to preach on the nature of true faith. His reading at this time included Gill, Charnock, Polhill, Bunyan, Foxe, Ralf Erskine, Turretin and Sibbes, his favourite hymns being those of Joseph Hart.

Broad Hembury and Toplady's Vindication of the Church of England

Due to the complicated state of his patronage, Toplady found himself in difficulties of conscience alleviated by a call to Broad Hembury and Sheldon to where he moved early in 1768. The distance to London was not so very great for one so used to travelling as Toplady so he regularly took the stage coach to the Capital to hear Gill. It was during this period that Toplady wrote his *The Church of England Vindicated from the Charge of Arminianism*. The occasion was the 1768 expulsion of six students at Oxford, including Erasmus Middleton, for holding views held generally by Evangelicals (who were invariably Calvinists) and for holding a prayer meeting. Dr Nowell, Principle of St Mary Hall had argued in defence of the university's decision, claiming that the Church of England was Arminian. Toplady shows that no Arminian could subscribe with a good conscience to the Articles but true Calvinists could and did as they believed in accordance with the Articles in Original Sin, Election, Particular Redemption, Effectual Calling and Final Perseverance. Toplady also outlined the purpose and place of prayer in the life of a Christian and the doctrine of justification. Wright says that Toplady's arguments were never answered because they were unanswerably the truth.

Further friendships of Toplady

Toplady was now in close friendship with Anglicans John Berridge, Moses Brown (Hervey's former curate) and Martin Madan and also Baptists Andrew Gifford and John Ryland Sen.. Ryland increased his flock at Northampton seven-fold and Robert Hall, though not of his Calvinistic persuasion testified that after hearing one of Ryland's sermons it was as if one had experienced an earthquake.

Both Ryland and Toplady had an intense love and admiration for James Hervey, both editing and publishing his works. They did this without profit as the Arminians were spreading the rumour that they were publishing Hervey's best-selling works merely to enrich their own pockets. Both friends were lovingly critical of each other. Toplady told Ryland that if he had published less, he would have achieved more, referring to the careless way much of Ryland's work was hurriedly thrown together. Ryland told Toplady that his midnight studies would prove his early death. Both men's views were perfectly accurate.

John Wesley's remorseless persecution of Toplady

Now begins the dishonourable story of John Wesley's remorseless persecution of Toplady. Like Hervey, Toplady had been under Wesley's advisory care and Wesley could not bear to think that his protégés had become Calvinists. Wesley's quite extraordinary outbursts against Hervey came when the saint was on his death bed with Wesley claiming untruthfully that Hervey died cursing him. Toplady was to suffer such wild misrepresentation at Wesley's hand for eight years or so before his death and long after.

Strangely enough, Toplady, who suffered under Wesley the most, has been censored even by Evangelicals such as Bishop Ryle for the strong language he used in his defence. Yet, the same language used by Gill and Hervey in their analysis of Wesley's Hyper-Arminianism is, on the whole, excused. Wesley's ire was roused on hearing Toplady bless God for His electing love without which no one could be saved. He became more incensed when Toplady published his translation of Zanchius.

Wesley quickly forged a document entitled *The Doctrine of Absolute Predestination Stated and Asserted, by the Rev. A. T.* declaring, 'The sum of all this: one in twenty (suppose) of mankind are elected; nineteen in twenty are reprobated. The elect shall be saved, do what they will; the reprobate shall be damned, do what they can. Reader, believe this, or be damned. Witness my hand, A. T.' Not content with this, Wesley spread stories of Toplady using the smuttiest, most perverse sexual imagery to bring the clean-living saint into disrepute. It was thus no wonder that Toplady called Wesley a Lothario[1] for this and other indiscreet behaviour.

Toplady continued to preach election and justification by faith, though the Arminians ground their teeth when he asked them, 'Do you imagine that God could foresee any holiness in men which He Himself did not decree to give them?' It was the Arminians' criticism of God's mercy, imputed righteousness and final perseverance that prompted Toplady to write *A debtor to mercy alone* which outlines all the saving doctrines of grace.

---

[1] Immoral character, derived probably from Nicholas Davenant's *The Cruel Brother* (1630) and Nicholas Rowe's *The Fair Penitent* (1703).

In 1771 Thomas Olivers began to attack Toplady's faith, believing that such 'a man of yesterday', ought not to challenge such a 'gentleman of literary accomplishments' as Wesley. Knowing that Gill was terminally ill, Olivers taunted Toplady sarcastically with the disappointment he alleged dying Gill must feel to have his pupil remain an Anglican rather than a Baptist. On hearing of Gill's death, Toplady wrote a fine tribute to his life and works, showing his oneness with Gill in the faith. Gill's successor John Rippon added this short biography to his own highly positive work on Gill. Olivers thought it a great shame that on a cold rainy morning the crowds flocked to hear the 'Antinomian' Toplady, whereas he who preached 'the pure gospel' faced 18 or 20 pupils from the pulpit, all who came very late.

Meanwhile Toplady was being weaned from his village work. His health was waning and the London climate had always brought him relief from his particular ailment. Starting with Whitefield, most of his friends urged Toplady not to hide his light under his village bushel but come out into the world to be of greater Christian service.

Minister of the French Reformed Church, Orange Street

After several months of itinerant preaching at Lady Huntingdon's chapels and visiting his friend Ryland in Northampton, Toplady returned to London in December, 1775 to preach at St Botolph's before the Mayor and corporation and a large gathering. With his Bishop's permission, Toplady now preached constantly in London, welcomed by the clergy, who opened their pulpits to him, and their congregations. The French Calvinist Reformed Church in Orange Street, Leicester Square now called Toplady to become their minister and he realised at once that here was the church he was to pastor until death called him to his true home. Although only 35 years of age, the doctors had told Toplady that he was at his life's evening.

Before a fruit tree dies, it often bears its heaviest crop of fruit. This was the case with Toplady who preached to a vast congregation in the large church, drawing people from all over London with his elegant, spiritual prose which was indistinguishable from poetry. Those modern Philistines who dare call Toplady an Antinomian and a Hyper-Calvinist and one who did not preach repentance and faith should dip into his sermons from this period speaking of the joy in Heaven over one converted sinner as he goes into the highways and by-ways of his unconverted congregation's hearts compelling them by the Spirit to turn from their wickedness and live.

Editorship of the Gospel Magazine
Immediately on returning to London, Toplady took over the editorship of
the *Gospel Magazine* which still thrills the hearts of its readers by its
faithfulness to the doctrines of grace. John Hazelton, in his recently republished book *Hold-Fast!* shows how *Zion's Witness*, *The Gospel Advocate*, *The Gospel Standard*, the *Remembrancer* and a number of other free
grace magazines have been used of God to reap prodigious harvests.
Hazleton shows how gracious God has been to the *Gospel Magazine*,
providing it with editors such as Toplady, Row, Doudney and Cowell. One
could also mention Erasmus Middleton and James Ormiston. Since
Hazelton's days at the beginning of the century, the tradition of good
editors has continued. Toplady's *Gospel Magazine* articles on the practical life of the Christian ought certainly to be republished in a volume of
their own.

Dying in harness
As the year 1778 opened, Toplady realised that he was on the last lap of
his earthly journey and made his will and looked forward to the crowning
work of Christ in his life in his resurrection to glory. Friends marvelled at
the calm joy Toplady obviously experienced at the thought of his home-
call as he visited them one after another to say goodbye. Numerous friends
such as John Newton, William Bull and John Ryland travelled from near
and far to exchange a last word with the saint before their eternal reunion.
Toplady's last sermon on June 4 illustrated the fellowship he had with all
who hold to the doctrines of grace. He, the Anglican, preached in a French
Reformed Church, supported in his weakness on both sides by Andrew
Gifford and John Ryland, two Baptist men of grace. After the service,
Toplady continued to teach his flock the true nature of faith in his vestry.
Meanwhile, wicked Wesley, in keeping with his practice of attacking his
enemies most when they were being received into glory, was spreading
the rumour that Toplady had renounced his faith. Against his doctors
orders, Toplady prayed for strength to deny this evil rumour publicly and
was carried to Orange Street on June 14, saying that he wanted to die in
harness rather than in the stall. Toplady climbed slowly into the pulpit and
gave out 2 Peter 1:13-14, affirming that as long as he was in his earthly
tabernacle he would preach the doctrines the Lord had given him.
     Toplady's health deteriorated swiftly. When the doctor told him
that his heart was scarcely beating, he answered, 'Why, that is a good sign
that my death is fast approaching; and blessed be God, I can add that my

heart beats every day stronger and stronger for glory!' After saying, 'The sky is clear, there is no cloud. Come, Lord Jesus, come quickly,' he added 'I feel that I am dying: no mortal man could live after experiencing the glories which God has manifested to my soul.' May our gracious God grant the readers of this testimony not only the faith of this noble man of God, but also his death.

WILLIAM HUNTINGTON (1745-1813)

27. William Huntington (1745-1813): Pastor of Providence

A worthy successor of Gill and Whitefield

The gaze of the English-speaking world towards the end of the 18th century was caught by the great work of a humble-born man of no education who nevertheless proved to be a worthy successor of John Gill and George Whitefield and fore-runner of Spurgeon and Martin Lloyd Jones and a preacher to thousands. This man was William Huntington who was acclaimed by evangelicals and Reformed as the winnower whose work was to separate the chaff from the wheat of the Evangelical Revival. The bulk of the Christian press was most favourably inclined to Huntington's work and magazines such as *The Gospel Magazine, The Gospel Standard, The Gospel Advocate, Zion's Watchtower, The Spiritual Magazine, The Gospel Herald* and *The Earthen Vessel* published article after article from or about Huntington. These magazines represented all the major denominations, two of which, one Anglican and one Baptist, are still witnessing to the truths Huntington preached.

Those are the historical facts which are outlined in detail and documented at length in my book, *William Huntington: Pastor of Providence*. When this grand old soul-winner was called home, apart from an initial scurrilous attack in an anonymous book called the *Voice of Years*, another in an essay called *A Picture of an Antinomian*, which Andrew Fuller wrote, and a silly article by the Poet Laureate Robert Southey which a publisher named Murray paid him £50 to write in order to blacken Huntington's character, his memory was left honoured for 175 years.

A shameful attack on a man of solid worth and excellent testimony

In July 1988, however, an attack against Huntington was published by a 'Reformed' periodical named the *Banner of Truth Magazine* based on the above-mentioned articles under the auspices of another Murray, this time named Iain. Five points were added allegedly to prove that Huntington was an Antinomian but in reality, these five points were a general announcement that the Banner had radically changed its theology and was rejecting the Five Points of Calvinism. The Banner author declared that the new orthodoxy maintained 1. That justification is not a decree of God in eternity. Here the influence of a third Murray is shown, namely John Murray who denies that justification is a decree of God's. 2. The new man is not created in righteousness. Here Donald MacLeod's theory of the extinction of the old man but with the new man taking over the old man's sins has obviously given rise to this error. 3. A denial of the actuality of imputation. Here Iain Murray's own Fullerism is revealed. 4. Repentance and faith are human conditions for salvation. Here we see much of recent 'Leicester Conference' teaching. Added to this was the outlandish accusation that Huntington taught that sanctification hindered justification. Here, again, the Arminian-Fullerite doctrine of justification for believers only (as opposed to God justifying ungodly sinners) obviously coloured the unfounded criticism. Huntington would not have accepted this doctrinal U-turn provided by the Banner of Truth, therefore he had to be branded as an Antinomian and Hyper-Calvinist to prevent him from influencing the New Banner Evangelicalism.

I immediately sent in a defence of Huntington and the Five Points of Calvinism to the Editorial Manager of the *Banner of Truth Magazine* but this attempt at a correction, as a large number of others, were all ignored. Then the *Bible League Quarterly* kindly published my defence verbatim, telling me that they still maintained orthodox theology.

After claiming that Huntington was not worth writing about, the Banner then published another five or six anti-Huntington articles with Iain Murray enthusing over the 'important controversy' he had started. These articles showed a definite departure from the doctrines of the Reformation and a total denial of the facts of history. I sent Iain Murray very many pages of evidence in history for the sound teaching of Huntington and some thirty names of contemporary ministers of all denominations who supported him. Mr Murray, suppressed this information and had the audacity to publish, supported by Robert Oliver, that I denigrated all Huntington's contemporaries in all denominations and that Huntington was totally isolated and shunned by other evangelicals and other churches. There were cries of disbelief and some laughs at this scandalous way of standing history on its head and the obviously false, libel against me in his magazine. Had not Mr Murray formerly praised George Ella in print for the way he defended eighteenth century evangelicals and had he not himself published a number of works from Ella's pen in which he praises God for the teaching received from a bevy of such men?

Murray's historical revisionism disproved by orthodox magazines of the past

Britain's leading and oldest evangelical magazine clearly disproves Murray's historical re-write.—In 1850 *The Gospel Magazine* declared that Huntington was one of the very great in the history of the Church and said,

> Mr Huntington's great work was to manifest to the Church the various phases of experience that the soul passes through while here below. *No one since the apostolic age,*[1] I think, has so plainly instructed, and so clearly set forth to the Church, the manner in which the Lord carries out his work in the souls of his people.

The Gospel Magazine author regarded Huntington as emphasising true Christian experience even more than Whitefield. He declared that in days when 'the doctrines of Regeneration and Eternal Election were called the whines of enthusiasts and fools'. Huntington's testimony stood firm.

Who was this man of God now despised by renegades from the faith of our Reformers?

Who was this great man, once proclaimed as a greater man than Whitefield but now called an Antinomian fool? William Hunt, alias Huntington, was born on February 2, 1745, in a farm hand's cottage near Cranbrook in Kent.[2] He was the adulterous offspring of Elizabeth Hunt and her husband's employer Barnabas Russell. Elizabeth's husband William was a humble, God-fearing man, who was banned perpetually from his wife's bed, whilst she gave birth to nine children before William was born and at least one after.

    Barnabas Russell treated Hunt and his own bastard son as his personal slaves. They were kept on the border of starvation and young William was at times not even given trousers to cover his shame and a shirt to protect his back and had to hide himself from the scorn of his fellow

---

[1] My italics.

[2] Early details of Huntington's life are taken from *The Kingdom of Heaven Taken by Prayer*, *The Bank of Faith* and *The Naked Bow of God*.

children and especially from Barnabas Russell's other well-kept children. Huntington had no schooling to speak of. He spent a few months at a Dame's school when there was little work on the farm to be done. Huntington never forgot this school as its mistress taught him that God took notice of children's sins and they would be punished after death. Thus whenever a strange severe looking character was seen in the town, dashing in and out of shops carrying a mysterious stick covered in figures and an ink-pot suspended on a string from his button-hole, young William thought that he was God's accountant at work recording children's sins. Whenever William saw him, he would flee in panic knowing his own heart. Actually the energetic old man was an exciseman who entered shop after shop with his huge yardstick to work out the taxes the shopkeepers had to pay.

Elizabeth eventually persuaded her employer-lover to obtain a free school place for William at Cranbrook. He sat there for a further few months in rags and with an empty stomach, side by side with his well-clad, well fed half-brothers. Tuition was bad and Huntington tried to teach himself to read and write through copying passages in the New Testament. There were neither books nor food at home and late at night Huntington had to scavenge the fields on the look out for ripe apples or turnips or anything that would still his hunger. Huntington's mother was the only one fed at the farm house, but she taught and encouraged her son to steal for his own needs. Once William met a French boy strolling over a field, taking food to some enemy officers imprisoned at nearby Sissinghurst Castle. On seeing a loaf sticking out from under the boy's arm, William pounced on him and snatched a large piece of bread. Soon after William was confronted by the French prisoners but they took pity on him when they saw his poverty.

Just when William had learnt his alphabet and understood a few passages in the Bible, he had to return to farm work. Striving for something better, he gained a post as page to a yeoman and was so successful that he made the other servants envious because of the large tips he was receiving. His mistress therefore told William to share his tips with the others but William's mother interfered, demanding that her son should keep his tips. The result was that William lost not only his job but his uniform which was the only clothing he had and was forced to work once again for Russell.

Huntington remembers his Maker in the days of his youth

In spite of a life of poverty and misery, William, now eight years old, could not forget his Maker and prayed incessantly, soon receiving a number of jobs as a servant. Wherever he went, however, he was influenced by older servants who told him his trust in God was silly and encouraged him to be as wicked as themselves. Invariably, we find Huntington sacked from his job saying, '(I) went home as deeply stung with guilt for my folly as I had been before lifted up at the sight of God's mercy.'

A fourteen years of age, William almost died because of undernourishment. Barnabas Russell lay dying at the same time, nursed by his wife and his lover. William survived but his father died unrepentant in agony of soul. His last words to his poor wife and the woman who had usurped her place was a pathetic 'Do what you will to me, if you can but save my life.' He went to his Judge but left nothing in his will for his bastard son. William was left with a Scripture passage which haunted him: Deuteronomy 23:2. 'A bastard shall not enter into the congregation of the Lord; even to his tenth generation shall he not enter into the congregation of the Lord.' When such doubts assailed him, he would cry out concerning his adulterous parents, 'And is hell to be the reception of both progenitors and progeny? I see no way of escape. Oh wretched end! I shall hate them both to all eternity, for being instrumental in sending me into the world as the miserable issue of their lewd embraces; and to all eternity they will hate me as an aggravation of their heinous crimes, and as venom to their sting of guilt.'

A tragic romance

In 1762 Huntington entered the service of the Rev. Henry Friend, Rector of Frittenden, near Cranbrook and now begins the story that was to plague his life for decades to come. He befriended a local tailor named Fever who had made up clothes for him from time to time. Fever had an only child called Susan. William had never had any romantic thoughts towards Susan but once he had exchanged a few jocular words with her which made Mr Fever suspicious. He told William to keep away from his house. Some time later Mrs Fever visited William and confessed that she had not known that William and her daughter were in love and her daughter was waiting for him at home. William confessed that he knew of no such romance yet when he entered the Fevers' house he found Susan confessing her love with her parents' blessing. Soon William fell in love with Susan and marriage was planned.

Mr and Mrs Fever then made the acquaintance of a well-to-do cloth merchant and promised their daughter to him, forgetting their vows to Huntington. Huntington had now the offer of a good, steady job and the couple wished to marry before leaving for the new appointment. The Fevers showed Huntington the door for the second time but allowed their daughter to accompany Huntington for some way in order to say goodbye. Both lovers confessed that they would always be faithful to each other and united their bodies as a seal and token of this, also hoping that the knowledge of the act would force the Fevers to allow them to marry. They then parted, never to see each other again.

Huntington wrote countless letters which were confiscated by Susan's father who did not allow his daughter to write. He was in agony of mind for eleven months. He then received a visit from three parish officers who told Huntington that Susan was now a mother but the Fevers still planned to marry her off to another, yet Huntington should provide for the child. Huntington's insistence that he should marry Susan fell on deaf ears all round.

William went through months of turmoil suffering from a stricken conscience and helplessness. He tried for a time to forget his worries by dancing well into the night. This time and conscience-killer brought him into contact with the lowest of people and later Huntington was to criticise dancing severely, saying of it, '(Dancing) is just as serviceable a net to ruin souls as devils could invent, or frail mortals drop into'. Working hard long hours of the day and dancing through the night began to ravage William's weakened constitution and he again became seriously ill and the doctor gave him up for dead. After a period of intense repentance and prayer, William recovered determined to live a life closer to God and not to marry anyone else as long as Susan, his rightful bride, lived.

Now follows years of wandering for Huntington, blighted by severe illness and lack of work and wages. He could not pay the money demanded by the parish officers and became an outlaw on the run. His sense of remorse and shame made him almost lose his senses. Time after time, however, he experienced marvellous signs of the Lord's presence with him.

Huntington gives himself his own name

At this time Huntington made a major decision which was to trouble him as much as his wronging Susan. He hated been called Hunt as he had no birthright to the name. His true name was Russell, though he had never been called it and was first called Hunt some five years after his birth and this merely by church baptismal registration. He thought naively that a change of name would be legally impossible but it would be acceptable if he extended it. He thus adding the letters '-ington' to Hunt and Huntington was born. Years later Huntington used to explain that neither his birth name, assumed name nor baptism name were his true names, but because he was born again as Huntington and baptised of the Spirit in that name, he had no reason to change it. His conscience, however, did not agree with him.

With his shame concerning Susan and his changed name hanging like two great millstones around his neck Huntington struggled on now finding work, now losing it through illness, now sleeping under hedges and in barns and now going for days without food. In a matter of months he had wandered through fifteen different provinces to find work and avoid the law. At Danbury Park in Essex Huntington obtained work for a Squire Fitch. After only a few days at his new occupation, Huntington collapsed and was removed from the Squire's house without any ceremony whatsoever and literally dumped in the village inn though he had only two shillings in his pocket. God's hand was on Huntington even in the Bell Inn. The old widowed proprietor of the inn showed Huntington the same affection as she would have done her own child and nursed him back to health. A few years later when Huntington had a little money saved up, he went back to Essex to seek out the woman and reward her but was dismayed to find she had recently died.

Huntington marries Mary Short
Now Huntington heard that Susan had died and he felt free to look for another wife and found such a person in Mary Short of Dorsetshire whom he married some time in 1769 and settled down with her in Mortlake, Surrey. Huntington did not tell his wife his full story until some time after the marriage. Mary merely said it did not change anything at all. Huntington was burdened with more financial cares than ever, especially as a daughter was born. He had never learnt the basics of mathematics at school which always made it difficult for him to plan ahead financially. To make matters worse he became lame and was out of work again. Then early one winter morning the couple found their five months old baby lying cold, stiff and as black as coal. The young undernourished child had apparently frozen to death. Of this time Huntington writes, 'My lameness, poverty, distress of mind, the sufferings of my wife, loss of my child, and the sense of God's wrath, were the most complicated distresses I had ever felt.' He goes on to write, however, 'From this time spiritual convictions began to plough so deep in my heart as to make way for the word of eternal life; which at length brought me experimentally to know "the only true God and Jesus Christ whom he hath sent."'

Longing to find peace with God
Now Huntington confessed to his wife that he wanted to find peace with God and Mary told him that she had been put off by her husband's jocular worldliness and had secretly prayed for a change in her husband. This

change was now taking place. The couple now prayed, using set prayers, altered for their own use as they did not have the vocabulary for spontaneous prayer. But Mary had terrible nightmares which William interpreted as indicating that 'death, judgement and eternal damnation' were now his portion.

Huntington obtained employment as a nurseryman at Hampton Wick near Kingston having to walk the six miles from Mortlake to Kingston and back every day for many weeks before new lodgings were found. At Kingston Huntington determined to find friends only amongst professing Christians, keep up private prayer either alone or with his wife and go regularly to Church. William and Mary had a second child called Ruth who became very weak through lack of food. William felt that he must go back to his childhood habit of stealing turnips at night. He had been given a piece of bacon and felt that turnips would go nicely with it. Though the words, 'Thou shalt not steal' echoed in Huntington's ears, he pulled up a fine pair of turnips with tears in his eyes thinking of his dying daughter. Afterwards, he told his wife, 'Molly, I am undone for ever; I am lost and gone; there is no hope nor mercy for me; you know not what a sinner I am, nor what I feel!' He staggered to work the following morning looking at the horses and cows in envy telling them that they would never be punished for their sins and they would never have to stand trembling at the Judgement seat only to be cast into hell.

Huntington read his Bible earnestly, first finding he could only understand the passages that condemned him. Then, wherever he looked, he found passages telling him that only the elect would be saved, so, starting at Genesis, he made a list of all the references to man's hopelessness and God's sovereignty through the whole Bible. Such verses as 'No man can come to me, except the Father which hath sent me draw him', John 6:44 and 'I know whom I have chosen', John 13:18 fixed themselves so deeply in Huntington's memory that he never forgot them. He concluded 'the doctrines of predestination and election reflect the tremendous doctrine of reprobation in many passages of scripture.'

Huntington was in a worse dilemma than ever. What if he felt the damnation that was common to the non-elect What if his repentance and sorrow, however genuine, were in vain?

Huntington's conversion

One day whilst up a ladder pruning a pear tree, Huntington told himself that though he strove to be holy, he was as worldly as ever. 'If I am not one of the elect', he thought, 'I shall never be saved, do what I will.' His bitterness concerning his bastard birth came back to his mind and he thought of the horrible life and death of his true father. He thought also of his mother who took the Lord's Supper regularly but lived in open adultery. He thought of the Old Testament passages that damn bastards and cried out from the tree top. 'Is hell to be my reception? I see no way of escape. Oh wretched end!'

As Huntington was deep in self-pity and self-reproach a great light seemed to shine all around him and banned all his anxious thoughts. Huntington heard clearly the words of John 14:26 'But the Comforter, which is the Holy Ghost, whom the father will send in my name, he shall teach you all things, and bring to remembrance, whatsoever I have said unto you ... let not your heart be troubled, neither let it be afraid.' Two sets of Scripture passages poured into Huntington's now relaxed and receptive memory. All those which cursed the sinner and all those who spoke of the goodness and graciousness of God in salvation. Huntington climbed down the ladder wondering what was happening to him. The words then came to him clear as a bell. 'Lay by your forms of prayer, and go pray to Jesus Christ; do not you see how pitifully he speaks to sinners?'

Huntington dashed into the tool shed with his apron over his head and face for fear of what was happening. He knelt down and prayed, 'Oh Lord, I am a sinner, and thou knowest it. I have tried to make myself better, but I cannot. If there is any way left in which thou canst save me, do thou save me; if not, I must be damned, for I cannot try any more, nor won't.' The very moment that Huntington said these words, he felt a freedom to unburden his soul before the Throne of Grace and prayed with great fluency, repeating all the blessed promises of God to a repentant sinner and he bombarded the Heavens with all the Biblical claims on God's Grace he could muster. He then, with his mind's eye, saw Christ crucified for him and at that moment the full depth of his sin came upon him. He prayed loudly, 'I did not know till now that I had been sinning against thy wounds and blood! I did not know that thou hadst suffered thus for wretched me! I did not know till now that I had any concern in crucifying thee! I cannot beg mercy of my suffering Lord and Saviour. No: send me to hell for I deserve it.' The more Huntington denied his right to Christ's love the more Christ seemed to approach him in love. Slowly but very surely a conviction of God's forgiveness displaced Huntington's assurance that he was hellbound. Thoughts of Satan, death, destruction, horror and despair fled as a composure serene and full of new-born hope replaced them. Huntington had met his Lord at the one place where all must meet Him who are His— at the Cross. There the farm-labourer met the King of Kings. He went, to use his own words, into the tool shed in all the agonies of the damned, and came out with the Kingdom of God established in his heart. What a change!

Soon Huntington was asked around the churches to relate what God had done to his soul but this caused much opposition. When Huntington spoke on Romans 5 of the Lord's sovereign Grace in his life, they felt that such a babe in Christ could hardly have had such experiences and told him that he was suffering from a delusion and 'hardened under the deceitfulness of sin'. When Huntington was asked critically if his soul was not troubled by what they told him, Huntington replied that though his critics would preach hell and damnation against him for twenty years they could not rob him of the fact that Jesus Himself had delivered his soul.

Huntington starts to reap the fruits of his testimony

A young couple at Ewell asked Huntington to witness to them and friends who joined them speedily converted so that Huntington soon found himself pastoring a growing church. Soon opposition became acute and the High Church ministers employed the basest of thugs to tear Huntington from the pulpit. He was warned that he would be murdered if he preached at a certain place where a gang of thugs were waiting for him. The words came to Huntington, 'He that is ashamed of me and my words, of him will I be ashamed before the angels of God.' So he preached in the crowded place valiantly on the words, 'Upon this rock will I build my church, and the gates of hell shall not prevail against it.' Huntington's comment afterwards on the peaceful outcome of the service 'God stopped their mouths, and opened mine.'

One of Huntington's converts, John Pavey writes how when eating bread made of animal fodder with Huntington's family in their hovel of a home, 'the glory was fresh' in Huntington and the budding pastor said that he believed God was calling him to preach to thousands. Any stranger hearing such words would have laughed out loud as Huntington with his broad Kentish dialect was sitting in his one and only shirt with trousers cut from an old pair of someone's larger trousers and his feet were thrust into old multi-clouted shoes. At the time he was earning the grand sum of eight shillings a week.

Pastor at Woking

A tiny group of believers at Woking, fourteen miles from Ditton, had been hearing Huntington for about a year. They could by no means afford a pastor, yet felt moved of God to invite Huntington to be responsible for their spiritual oversight in 1776. The Rev. Torial Joss, who was the first man Huntington had heard preach the true Gospel, ordained Huntington and said in his exhortation, 'While I possess a Bible, I shall not be at a loss to prove that William Huntington has received from God a call to the ministry.' He then turned to Huntington and said, 'You may now take your axe and go to work.' Huntington took up that axe and used it so well that only a few years after he was able to fulfil his own heart's wish and calling and preach regularly to thousands in the Capital, a feat hardly any other minister performed at the time.

The Lord's help in times of acute need

One night Huntington and his wife were forced to put their children to bed on empty stomachs and wept for their loved ones and their own misery. In the middle of the night, whilst Huntington was weeping and praying, a man knocked at the window and said that there was a load of wooden hoops delivered to a near-by wharf and someone was urgently needed to unload it. Huntington set off at once and unloaded the goods. The owner of the hoops gave Huntington a meat pie and a flagon of cider. The preacher rushed home, knowing that his first child had died of hunger in the night, woke his children and fed them although they were too tired to know what was happening.

At times Mrs Huntington, too, discovered marvellous answers to prayer and showed great faith. Once, when Mrs Huntington was lying-in, the cupboard was bare. Huntington's first convert, Anne Webb, was looking after her and told her that there was no more tea in the caddy. Mrs Huntington said that she should nevertheless put the kettle on to boil. Before the water started to bubble a complete stranger came to the door and said that she had brought some tea for the preacher's wife.

King George comes to Huntington's assistance

Help was to come for Huntington from a very unexpected quarter. Whilst the riots against Huntington's flock were at full swing, His Majesty King George III drove by in his carriage. On hearing the jeers of the crowd, he stopped his coach and asked what the matter was. He received the answer that it was merely a clash between the town's people and the Methodists. This caused the King to leave his coach and in a very loud voice proclaim, 'The Methodists are a quiet, good kind of people, and will disturb nobody; and if I can learn that any persons in my employment disturb them, they shall be immediately dismissed.' This news travelled quickly around the area and the violence died down.

This incident may explain why Huntington had always a good word to say about the King. When he became a London pastor, the King's State Coachman, the Comptroller of the Household to Princess Charlotte, the Keeper of the Observatory in Kew Gardens and several servants from St James's Palace joined his church. Several princesses were regular hearers, especially the King's favourite daughter, Princess Amelia. King George regularly read the works of Evangelicals such as John Newton and William Romaine and there is an interesting story of how he became a reader of Huntington's works. One of his footmen was busy reading Huntington when he was called away to duties and left his book behind. The King passed by and picked up the book and took it with him to read, replacing it some days later. Hearing of this the footman carefully left Huntington's books around where he thought the King might pass. They disappeared one by one and were all replaced later. Once when he had forgotten to leave a volume for the King to pick up His Majesty came to him and said, 'Where is my book, Saunders?'

More than enough, now

Huntington tells us that his family at this time were no better off regards sleeping than the baby Jesus who slept in a manger as they, like Him, slept on straw. However, on a preaching visit to Richmond, Huntington was invited to a home and presented with a huge bundle, tied up so that no one could see what was inside. When Huntington asked he was told that he would find out when he got home.

On arriving back in Ditton the Huntingtons and their four children opened the bundle and found enough bedding for them all. Now Huntington, to use his own phrase, took 'Gospel courage' and asked the Lord for a bed. Soon after, four people visited the Huntingtons from London and each left a guinea before returning home. Huntington thus ordered his bed with a rug and a pair of good blankets to go with it. When he turned up to pay for the goods, he was told to hand the money over to the clerk who took it and gave Huntington a receipt. The gentleman who owned the shop then walked some way with Huntington deep in conversation but when the time came to depart, he gave Huntington the full amount back. More blessings followed. Now the Huntingtons rags were exchanged for decent clothing. Huntington was measured up for a new suit by a wealthy friend and Mrs Huntington was presented with new clothes and lengths of material to make up into clothing for herself and her children. 'We have more than enough clothing now,' Mary happily told her husband.

Preaching at Margaret Street Chapel

Huntington had started to preach in London through a friend's well-meaning deceit. This friend had invited Huntington to visit his London home and preach there and Huntington had accepted the invitation. After the house-meeting was over, however, the friend told Huntington that he had arranged for him to preach at the Margaret Street Chapel, a church made famous by its former pastor William Cudworth. Huntington was quite taken aback at this as he did not feel at all competent to preach before the more educated citizens of London. Not only had he no knowledge of Greek and Hebrew, he had little knowledge of standard English either. Huntington did not back away from the challenge and was rewarded by seeing a young man converted through his first sermon there. This young man became a minister himself some time after. The first of many of Huntington's converts who became preachers and pastors. The Londoners were so moved by Huntington's testimony that they begged him to preach weekly there.

Huntington's stance against Antinomianism

A great ignorance of spiritual things existed in the pastor-less chapel as ministers of different persuasions were asked to preach. A Deist would preach on the God that was far off, an Arminian would talk of God's supposed universal charity. Then an Arian would preach solely on the humanity of Christ and an Antinomian would set the Law aside and preach absolute freedom from its force. The Antinomians puzzled Huntington the most as, at first, he did not know 'what to do with such a strange beast, which seemed all tongue, but no heart.' He soon came to realise that Antinomians were not of the Saviour's fold and warned his hearers against them preaching on the status, function and scope of the Law and writing several books against Antinomianism.

Arminianism opens the doors to Arianism and Antinomianism

Huntington saw that the great hindrance to the spread of the Gospel was from Christians who either turned the eyes of the newly converted to Sinai rather than the Cross or trusted in their own personal holiness rather than Christ's imputed righteousness. He thus saw Arminianism as a great danger to the Christian faith as it included most other heresies. It contained the germs of Arianism as Christ's once-and-for-all-time perfect sacrifice was rejected. Christ, for them, had died in vain for the majority of those atoned for, thus diminishing His power, sovereignty and Godhead. Jesus, to the Arminian was a failure. Arminianism harboured Antinomianism, too, as it limited the laws of God to the Ten Commandments and preached that every man was free to seek Christ by his own effort, irrespective of the electing, sovereign will of God. They set aside the Biblical teachings of Grace and became a rule unto themselves. Traces of Deism could also be seen in Arminianism as its followers did not believe in the inner working of the Spirit in the heart of the elect keeping him from becoming a castaway. Huntington battled hard to find Biblical teaching against these heresies and as he was taught himself by the Scriptures he wrote down his findings for general publication.

After preaching for some weeks at Margaret Street, things changed radically. The Deist turned outright pagan and stopped preaching. The Arian failed in business and left the area. The Antinomian returned to Scotland and the Arminian was put in jail! Huntington testified, 'I am a greater wonder to myself than to any other, considering myself as a person of neither parts, abilities, nor learning: nothing but a mere "bruised reed" and yet supported by the omnipotent hand of a most gracious God!'

Providence Chapel
Soon influential friends sought out a site in the Metropolis for a large chapel where Huntington could look after his growing hearers. On being asked what name he wanted to give his chapel, he answered, 'Providence Chapel', realising that it was God's providence that had brought him thus far. Money material and practical assistance came in at break-neck speed. The person who showed the most energy in fund raising, was, however, Huntington himself. He went from friend to friend explaining what the costs of the chapel would be and later he was to confess that not one single person whom he approached refused to support the project. Only a year after Huntington left tiny Thames Ditton to preach to his thousands in the Metropolis his wish and calling came true. The chapel 'shot up', in the words of Thomas Wright, 'as if by enchantment' at a time when Huntington's fame as a preacher was spreading like wild-fire. Not a penny was funded outside of Huntington's circle of friends. Providence Chapel had seats for a congregation of well over a thousand but proved too small and was soon enlarged to hold almost two thousand. After completion, Huntington prayed:

> And now, O Lord, whom the heavens, nor the heaven of heavens, cannot contain, much less the little house which we have built, let it please thee to hear thy servant's prayer, and bless the house and let thine eyes and thy heart be there perpetually, and make it a Bethel to thousands. Direct the steps of sabbath-break-

ers, blasphemers, and the basest of mortals to tread its floors; let sovereign grace and dying love be displayed in their greatest power, and in their fullest latitude; and grant that when thou writest up the people, it may be said, of millions, that this and that man was born of God there. O Lord, make the pulpit like Aaron's golden bell; and let every tried and faithful preacher's tongue be like a golden clapper; so that Joy and gladness may be found therein, thanksgiving and the voice of melody. Let no dry formality ever be established in it. Let no ecclesiastical craftsman ever be heard there. Let no priestcraft ever prosper therein. Let no carnal inventions, however pleasing to flesh and blood, no human traditions, however ancient or highly esteemed; nor any doctrines of devils, however deep, or of whatsoever date, be ever heard in it. But let thy truth be credited by that faith which is thy own gift. Be thou ever addressed and supplicated in the language of thy own most holy word, ever adored by thy servants in the happy enjoyment of thy own eternal love, ever admired in thy own illustrious and most glorious light: and be thou ever worshipped in thy own spirit. O Lord of all lords, be thou our ALL IN ALL; and grant that all preachers of every denomination, that preach thee as the sinner's only, present, and everlasting portion may be blessed with thy internal testimony, thy supporting hand, the unutterable comforts of thy Eternal Spirit, and crown their honest labours with ten thousand-fold success.

Amen and Amen.

Huntington the preacher

Huntington aimed his ministry at the un-converted so as not to be accused of poaching. When the other denominations saw the crowds which came out of Providence, they quickly built churches in the area to tap off Huntington's flock. In spite of this, however, Huntington's preaching grew more powerful as the years went by so that even in the last six months of his life when a doddering old man, there were numerous conversions each service and Huntington was known as the old tree that bore much fruit.

Hundreds of hearers assembled outside Providence Chapel long before the doors opened. They took their seats in hushed, disciplined silence, either praying or reading their Bibles, Hart's hymns or a book written by their pastor. One clergyman described the scene as 'a people prepared for the Lord'. Huntington, called 'The Walking Bible' by his friends, recited his text off by-heart because of his acute short-sightedness. His prayers, too, were couched in the words of Scripture. He did not preach from a manuscript but used outline notes or spoke extempore. One sermon outline, on Romans 8:9, 'Now if any man has not the Spirit of Christ he is none of his.' has been preserved which, when preached, resulted in four conversions. First Huntington shows 'the insufficiency of a form of godliness without the power'. Secondly, 'the necessity of regeneration'. Thirdly, 'the operation of the Holy Spirit from the Word of God'. Fourthly, 'that God seeketh spiritual worshippers', and finally that 'the Holy Ghost is sufficient to work faith, to sanctify the soul, and prepare it for the reception of Christ; and sufficient also to lead the believer on in a course of spiritual devotion, as the spirit of grace and of supplication'.

Huntington was tall and, in the early years of his ministry, very slim. In the pulpit, he dressed in black but without clerical robes. Anglican and Dissenting ministers wore long flowing wigs with two to five rows of dangling curls, but Huntington thought this was too showy. He shaved his head for hygienic reasons and wore a small black wig which fitted his head closely. He would stand almost still for most of the sermon simply talking to his hearers. He rarely raised his voice nor did he use theatrical gestures but his clearly spoken words were carried easily to all parts of his chapel. The only movement noticed was when Huntington held a white handkerchief in his hand and occasionally passed it from one hand to the other, whilst preaching, and occasionally wiped his mouth with it. The only time that Huntington was known to thump the pulpit was when he preached his last sermon after being in the ministry forty years! One Anglican minister whose father had been excommunicated from a Baptist church for hosting Huntington, wrote of Huntington's preaching:

> Only those who heard him preach can have any idea of the greatness of his mind in spiritual things, or can ever feel what those felt who heard the glorious truths of the Gospel from his own lips, for 'his doctrine dropped as the rain and distilled as the dew.' I shall never forget the impression I received under the first sermon I heard from him, I could only weep and pray, for at that time I knew nothing of the Lord Jesus Christ, but I felt an inexpressible awe, as if on hallowed ground, as if the Lord was there, and that it was 'the House of God and the Gate of Heaven.' His valuable and extensive writings give a faint idea of this truly wonderful and holy man, but his power as a Preacher was seldom equalled, if ever surpassed; he spoke evidently not his own words and thoughts, but as taught by the Holy Spirit.

Huntington the teacher

As Huntington is now criticised for his attitude to heresy and his teaching on the law and gospel in conversion, I shall deal with these aspects alone for want of space.

In his Preface to the *Arminian Skeleton* Huntington says:

> Every essential truth that we part with is an infinite loss; and we daily see an awful departure from the doctrines of the gospel. Errors gain ground; and champions for the truth are but few in number when compared to the other host. If thou art a child of God by Faith, see to the ground-work of it. Hast thou the faith of God's elect? let election be its basis. Hast thou a justifying faith? let imputed righteousness be its basis. Hast thou a victorious faith? thy victory lies in a Saviour's arms. Hast thou a purifying faith? then faith fetches its purifying efficacy from a Saviour's blood. Give up none of these truths; for, if we think truth is not worth contending for, we may expect the Spirit to clap his wings, and take flight from us.

Huntington, thinking of John Wesley's comments against the doctrines of grace, called upon his readers to protect their faith so that, 'God's decree shall not always be called horrible, nor an everlasting righteousness be called imputed nonsense.' He goes on to say:

> If God of his infinite mercy keep you from Arminianism, Arianism, and Antinomianism, I shall think you are Christians indeed. I rank the errors of Arminianism at the front, because the others are not so well masked. While the Arminian is robbing you of the doctrines of sovereign grace, he puts the fable of sinless perfection into your hand, as a rattle to amuse you, while he robs and plunders your conscience; and, while he is teaching you to resist the sovereign will of God, he endeavours to charm your ears with free-agency. But the Arian is more open; he proclaims to everyone that goes by that he is a fool. However, they are all three agreed against Christ; the Arminian cries down his merit; the Arian cries down his divinity; and the Antinomian cries down the revelation of him to the heart. May God turn their hearts to the truth, and keep your souls from turning to their errors!

In the *Arminian Skeleton*, he tells us:

> The Arminian calls upon you to forsake the strong food, or
> every essential truth in the Bible; the Arian and Socinian want
> you to give up your God, and to bow your knee to a creature; the
> Antinomian calls upon you to give up the Spirit's quickening
> power, your daily cross, and a tender conscience.

Huntington on conversion

One of Huntington's first writings was on the doctrine of conversion as
Fullerism and Arminianism with their low view of both law and gospel were
challenging traditional orthodox teaching. First, he argued that a man must
be convinced of his sin. He must see that his life is a transgression against
God's laws. There are three witnesses to show a man that he is such a
sinner. His own thoughts, his own conscience and the voice of God in His
righteous law. The voice of God may come via the Scriptures directly or
from the preacher or from a Christian's witness. Huntington maintained
that conviction of sin does not necessarily mean that a man once convicted will confess his sin. The human heart is so wicked that even when
it knows it is sinful it will not go to God for healing. The Spirit must enter
the elect person's life and convince him of the goodness of God's law and
show him that he is weighed in the balance and found wanting. The Spirit
also shows the elect person that the balance can be regained by putting
ones trust in a Saviour who keeps the law and has arranged that His
keeping the law, His righteousness, will be acceptable to God on the sinner's behalf and what is more, imputed to the sinner as if he had not broken
the law. Huntington stressed time and time again that though the believer
was no longer under the condemnation of the Law on tablets of stone, that
same Law had become part (part—not all) of his new nature and was
written on his heart. This is why he argues that the Antinomian in rejecting
God's Law revealed to the Christian's heart, rejects that which distinguishes
the saved from the unsaved. In his work *The Kingdom of Heaven taken by
Prayer* Huntington makes it quite clear that the sinner is always the debtor,
God is always the creditor but Christ is always the elect sinner's security.

How this works out in practice

Huntington was always careful to show how this worked out in practice.
The Spirit's work in the heart of the elect is shown by the simple fact that
they look to God for help but the reprobate goes his own way. The elect
turn actively to God and confess their sins to Him. Not all the demons in
hell can stop this happening. A reprobate can confess that he has sinned

as Judas confessed that he had betrayed innocent blood, but he is not drawn to God by this but rather established in his turning away from God. Judas confessed his sin to those around him but went and hanged himself instead of bringing his sins to God. The conviction of those the Spirit leads, however, is mingled with hope while acknowledging their legal hopelessness. They count themselves as dung and realise that they have no righteousness whatsoever of their own. Most important, they submit themselves to the righteousness and justice of God and are prepared to do anything and be anything that God wishes. They come to Him to be different. They come to Him for a new holy life in Christ.

Huntington 'offers' Christ

We see then how utterly wrong the modern criticism is which presents Huntington as a preacher to the already saved only and one who would not dream of calling sinners to repentance. They are guilty of standing Huntington's theology of conversion on its head as they do with his teaching concerning Antinomianism. The idea has been spread by Huntington's traducers recently that the distinguishing feature of a gospel Christian is that he speaks in terms of offering Christ, whereas he who does not is a Hyper-Calvinist.[1] Thus these critics conclude that Huntington is a Hyper-Calvinist as he allegedly does not speak of an 'offer'.

This accusation is ridiculous on two counts. First: the use or non-use of the term 'offer' has nothing to do with an acceptance or rejection of the Great Commission. Great evangelists who stopped using the term 'offer', because of its misuse in Arminian-style preaching, such as Richard Davis and John Gill, were no less great for that. Secondly, Huntington never ceased to speak of the gospel offer. However, Huntington spoke of the gospel offer of Christ within His covenant. When preaching, he would use such words as 'Those that are weary and heavy laden are called; the lame, the halt, and maimed, are invited ... all that hunger and thirst are welcome; and those made willing to close with the gospel offer, and hold the truth as it is in Christ, have a right by divine invitation.'[2] Writing of a lady who had just died in the full assurance of faith, he wrote 'She closed in with the offer, and made a match with the heavenly Bridegroom, while I was publishing the bans.'[3]

---

[1] See Curt Daniel's *John Gill and Hyper-Calvinism* where this strange doctrine is taught.

[2] Works, 6, *Epistles of Faith*, p. 107.

[3] Ibid, p. 370. I am grateful to my friend Pastor Henry Sant for providing me with this information.

However, Huntington went even further in his gospel zeal. One would expect Huntington to have ruled out the possibility of Arminians and Roman Catholics being of the elect. This he did not do as his doctrine of God's sovereignty taught him otherwise. He continued in the *Arminian Skeleton*, 'Out of each host the elect of God will one day be called; and a light sufficient will be given them to discover the enemies of their liberties, to which, by a covenant of sovereign grace, they were predestinated.'

An old tree bearing much fruit

Huntington is one of very few pastors of whom one can say they were even more successful in old age than in their prime of life. This is certainly true of Huntington who, shortly before his death, was witnessing five to nine conversions a meeting so that his membership was continually growing. Few in the Metropolis were preaching to over three thousand per week in all.

When Huntington lay dying amongst people who can hardly be said to have wished for his best, he was not troubled. His thoughts were already in heaven and his words 'Why does the chariot tarry?' showed that he wanted to be with his Lord. The saint's last words were, 'Bless His precious name.' He then gave a deep peaceful sigh. God's chariot had come to fetch him.

HANNAH MORE (1745-1833)

28. Hannah More (1745-1833): The Woman who Stopped a Revolution

From Covent Garden to the Mendip Hills

Covent Garden Theatre was viewed by the eighteenth century evangelicals as the greatest corrupter of morals in the Kingdom. Playwrights spent their lives dreaming of putting on plays there as the crown of their life's work. One popular dramatist, Hannah More, though very young, succeeded in having her plays run for weeks on end at Covent Garden, featuring famous actors such as David Garrick. This blue-stockinged intellectual was regarded as one of the greatest national luminaries of the theatre. Great was thus the astonishment when she suddenly announced that she had been changed by the gospel and was renouncing entertaining idle rich adults so that she might write edifying school books for children and bring the Bible to the poor of the Mendip Hills.

Publishing plays, though still a schoolgirl

Miss More was born in Stapleton, Gloucestershire on February 2, 1745, receiving her first education at home given by her father, the Headmaster of the local Grammar School. She read fluently at four and soon mastered Latin. At eleven she entered her elder sisters' school in Bristol, working hard at literature, French and Italian and developing a keen interest in drama. She became so proficient at writing that her plays, such as *A Search for Happiness*, were published and dramatised whilst she was still a schoolgirl. Miss More was engaged early to a wealthy middle-aged man who kept postponing the marriage, so she broke off the engagement and worked out a settlement with him, receiving an endowment of £200 per annum. This left her an independent woman and she vowed never to marry. At the age of twenty, Miss More put on plays at Bath, the centre of the haute volée, and, by the time she was twenty-eight, she had moved to the Metropolis and become firmly established as a playwright and poet. Her Covent Garden play *Percy* outrivalled Sheridan's *School for Scandal* and drew crowds of 'fashionable' people. The 4,000 copies of the play printed were sold out in a fortnight and edition followed edition. At a time when even the best professional writers had difficulties making ends meet, Mistress More (as she was then styled) received over £30,000 for her plays and poems in a few years with apparently the greatest of ease. Only Goldsmith could rival, but not beat, her in bargaining with publishers for a good fee. It was no wonder that Garrick, Samuel Johnson, Edmund Burke, Joshua Reynolds, Mrs Montagu and Horace Walpole sought her company. Dr Johnson, the arch-critic, proclaimed that she was 'the most powerful versificatrix in the English language' and he was far from being alone in his estimate.

A slow but sure conversion

Miss More's conversion came slowly. Garrick's death in 1779 made her rethink her position as an entertainer. Bishop Beilby Porteus and John Newton turned her eyes to evangelical doctrines and she found deep instruction in Cowper's verse. She finally came to a knowledge of salvation through Newton's preaching. Just as Cowper had received his initial impetus to write to God's glory from Newton, the ex-slave master now showed Miss More how she could use her position in society to bring Divine truths to people who would never dream of going to church. This resulted in her *Sacred Dramas* of 1782 followed by *Thoughts on the Importance of the Manners of the Great to General Society.*

William Cowper and Hannah More

When Cowper read this book, which appeared anonymously, he thought its style and knowledge of upper-class society revealed Wilberforce as its author. Great was his surprise when he discovered that the work he had praised for its manly way of stating home truths was written by a woman. Cowper had recommended Hannah More for her poem against slavery. Now he wrote to his favourite cousin Lady Hesketh, a close friend of the Royal Family, saying:

> If anything could have raised Miss More to a higher rank in my opinion than she possessed before, it could only be your information that, after all, she, and not Mr Wilberforce, is the author of that volume. How comes it to pass, that she being a woman, writes so little like one? With a force and energy, and a

correctness hitherto arrogated by the men, and not very frequently displayed even by men themselves.

Miss More was equally pleased with Cowper's works, praising them for their 'genuine Christianity'. At last she had found a poet she could recommend to her well-to-do friends for Sunday reading instead of Sterne, Swift, Congreve or worse. George Colman the playwright, tells us that the reading of the rich was usually worse.

Keeping the Sabbath holy

Miss More, however, was determined to create a true Christian love for the Sabbath amongst her friends. She was thus shocked when wealthy evangelical patrons started to encourage 'sacred' Sunday concerts and oratorios in their churches to 'liven up' the worship. We read in her *Memoirs* the following words:

> I have just received a card invitation from a Countess, to a concert next Sunday, with a conditional postscript, 'if I ever do such things on a Sunday;' and I have sent for answer, that I never do such a thing. After such a public testimony as I have given, one would have thought I should have escaped such an invitation.

Soon Hannah More's Christian works were selling even better than her successful plays, running into an edition a week. This was an almost unheard of success. Several editions were bought up within hours of leaving the printers and two books, *Practical Piety* and *Christian Morals*, written later in life, were even sold out before they left the printers! Various foreign translations were made, including Cingalese, the latter sponsored by the Chief Justice of Ceylon himself. Even books Miss More wrote in extreme old age, such as *The Spirit of Prayer*, proved best-sellers. Miss More was thus able to donate thousands of pounds to charity. Sunday card-playing and the gambling attached to it began to disappear from the wealthy's homes.

Hannah More uses her talents to aid the under-privileged

Now Miss More turned her full attention to the poor, seeking to improve their lot socially and politically by presenting them with Christian virtues and aims and the gospel of salvation which alone could accomplish them. At first she did this by printing hundreds of thousands of tracts of her own composition. Next she started education work amongst poor women

and founded two-hundred schools, teaching children to read and write
with the Bible and her tracts as the main text books. Protests from all walks
of life poured in. She was told that her educated poor would soon be
telling their 'betters' what to do. Wealthy farmers argued that the poor
would always be ignorant and wicked and if they were educated they
would find more ingenious ways of being ignorant and wicked. Even the
poor protested. Children at school meant less workers at home and in the
fields and thus lower incomes for those already almost paupers. Parents
thus demanded compensation from the educators. It was even rumoured
that children were being educated to be sent as slaves to the colonies.
Some clergy campaigned against the schools arguing that men would
come home from a hard days work to find no dinner on the table but their
wives curled up in easy chairs reading *The Lady's Magazine*! In the notorious Blagdon controversy the magistrate-curate, Mr Bere, claimed that
the schools were 'seminaries of fanaticism, vice and sedition' and that the
pupils were taught to even pray for the French! He roused so much public
anger that a number of schools had to be closed. Dissenters complained
that Miss More was fostering anti-Dissenting sympathies as she equated
Christianity with the Monarchy and the Church of England.

Providing work for the unemployed and areas of service for Dissenters
To combat this negative image, wherever Miss More placed a school, she
provided work for the local crafts people, combining Bible studies with
instruction in household management, knitting and cookery. She even set
up adult schools welcoming the men and old people. Mr Bere's bishop
fought hard to be rid of his offensive curate and finally removed him from
his post in 1802. Immediately the closed schools were reopened. Miss
More began to work closer with leading Dissenters such as William Jay
and appointed Dissenters on a number of her committees and boards.

Hannah More defeats Thomas Paine
At this time anti-French feeling was strong in the Establishment yet Tho-
mas Paine's revolutionary ideas were spreading swiftly in the country.
There was enormous fear that England was on the brink of revolution.
Critics maintained that teaching the lower classes to read was bringing
Paine's pamphlets into lower class homes. Indeed, Paine's *The Rights of
Man*, was no learned treatise but a clever, though shallow, attempt to reach
such homes with simply put revolutionary ideas. There was only one
writer in England in the 1790s who could be sure of a gigantic readership
and combat these revolutionary arguments in the same easily understood,

forceful language. This was Hannah More. Miss More quickly produced a tract which she named *Village Politics*, teaching Biblical norms for honest citizenship. It spoke to the heart of England and this work, followed by a number of others under the general heading *Cheap Repository Tracts* reached a sale of two million within twelve months. For six years Miss More produced a regular supply of tracts, often on a weekly basis, which showed how God's revealed design for the world was worlds better than that which Paine's reason offered. When the Eclectic Society, founded by John Newton, met in February 1798 to discuss the subject, 'What can be done at the present moment to counteract the designs of infidels against Christianity?' they recorded the following words:

> Already had the powerful pen of Hannah More been most successfully employed in this important service, and her incomparable little tract, *Village Politics by Will Chip*, had, with astonishing rapidity, reached every corner of the kingdom: many hundred thousands were circulated in London alone: many thousands were sent by Government to Scotland and Ireland; and men of the soundest judgement went so far as to affirm, that it had been most essentially contributed, under Providence, to prevent a revolution.

Hannah More's place is with the greatest leaders of the Awakening
A major result of Miss More's action was that people began to flock to church. At Cheddar, for instance, there was formerly an average congregation of eight in the morning and twenty in the afternoon. Ten years later, because of the intense work done by Miss More in the area, there was a regular attendance of eight hundred per service, mostly composed of the enlightened poor. When Miss More started her work, she only knew of one Christian nobleman. She was able to lead another twenty-nine Peers and political leaders to cherish the crown of righteousness more than their earthy regalia. Thus, though much has been written about such great men of the Awakening as Whitefield and Wesley, Miss More's place in history as a great revival leader is just as secure and ought to be given more attention.

When Hannah More realised she was being relieved of her earthly duties and called home to God, she uttered just one word 'Joy' and then died. One cannot help thinking that there was a touch of extra joy, too, in the Lord's voice as He pronounced his 'Well done, my good and faithful servant' on greeting her in Glory.

ROBERT HAWKER (1753-1827)

29. Robert Hawker (1753-1827): Zion's Warrior

Expository gems

Great Christian writers are often remembered more by their commentaries than their other works. This is the case with Matthew Henry, John Gill and Thomas Scott and perhaps reveals the Christian's greater longing to have the Word of God explained to him directly, verse by verse, rather than in essay, biography or story form. Food for the soul which is cut and served for immediate digestion is a delight indeed. Robert Hawker's commentaries provide such a delight. Though Hawker authored numerous theological works, school text books, readers and primers, it is to his commentaries that Christians today still turn. His *Poor Man's Commentary* and *Poor Man's Morning and Evening Portions* are still considered gems of exposition. Indeed, modern booksellers have noticed that Hawker is increasing in popularity and second-hand prices are growing with the demand.

Robert studies with a view to becoming a surgeon for his mother's and aunts' sakes

Robert Hawker was born on April 13, 1753 in a house near Mary Steps Church, Exeter where his grandfather, an Alderman, had practised as a surgeon and where his father had now taken up that calling. In keeping with the covenant beliefs of his parents, he was baptised at Mary Steps on the following May 14. Hawker never knew his father who was carried off by a disease caught from a patient when his only surviving child was still a baby. This caused his mother and two aunts to take special care of little Robert and they made sure he grew up in the nurture and admonition of the Lord, teaching him to recite, read and write Scripture portions at a very early age.

Hawker attended the Free Grammar School, learning Greek, Latin and Hebrew. From his earliest years, he longed to become a clergyman, composed sermons and preached in secret but his mother, who had striven to keep up something of her husband's practice and worked as a midwife, begged Hawker to take up his father's profession. Hawker's aunts also felt that he could do the most good for his fellow creatures in the family profession. Having no heart to disappoint them, young Hawker was placed under the supervision of an Alderman White of Plymouth to be trained as a surgeon.

The surgeon's young apprentice developed into a most mischievous imp and did not leave his practical jokes outside of the church. One day, he smuggled himself into a service and set off a firework whilst Henry Tanner, the Evangelical minister, was preaching. Hawker never forgot this silly prank and when Tanner died, he supported his destitute widow and published Tanner's memoirs and works on her behalf.

A marriage made in Heaven

Though only nineteen years old, Hawker fell in love with Anne Rains, a girl of seventeen, whom he married at Charles Parish Church on January 6, 1772. Tongues wagged concerning their youth but the marriage proved of the Lord and the couple enjoyed over forty-five years of married life until Anne died in 1817, ten years before her husband. Robert and Anne had eight children, four boys and four girls. Three of the boys became ministers of the gospel and one a surgeon, three of the girls married well, Anna, the second eldest daughter, remained single, caring for her father until his death.

Hawker studied at St Thomas's before obtaining a three-year post as surgeon in the Royal Marines. Stories are told how Hawker later went abroad with the army and was converted but John Williams, one of Hawker's biographers and a convert of his, claims that most of these stories are quite untrue and that Hawker never joined the army. He did become an army chaplain when Vicar of Charles and wrote a book called *The Zion's Warrior, or Christian Soldier's Manual* in which army life was compared to the spiritual life. These facts may have given rise to the supposition. There are no records of Hawker's conversion and it is probable that he entered the ministry without a deep awareness of God's grace in his life.

Hawker studies for the ministry

Nevertheless, Hawker's longing to become a minister never left him and, in May, 1778, feeling he had done his duty to his mother and though he had a wife and family, he entered Magdalen Hall, Oxford with a view to be trained for the ministry. His proficiency in the subjects studied was so great that the Bishop of Exeter ordained him as deacon in September that year. A few weeks later, Hawker was called to take over the curacy of his home church in Charles where he stayed forty-nine years until his death in 1827. The first sermon Hawker preached at Charles was on November 22, 1778, his text being 2 Corinthians 5:20, 'Now then we are ambassadors for Christ, as though God did beseech you by us: we pray you in Christ's stead, be ye reconciled to God.'

Hawker kept up his matriculation and occasionally visited Magdalen for lectures and examinations. He received priest's orders in 1779. He now began to publish his sermons but complained later that they contained no more knowledge of the truth than the bats and the moles could have supplied.

Becoming the Vicar of Charles

Two years later, Hawker's vicar, John Bedford, died. By one of the strange historical quirks of the Church of England, the living did not rest in the hands of the congregation but was under the patronage of the Mayor and corporation and Hawker, backed by his church, found that a stranger had put in a claim for the living. Mr White, Hawker's former employer was now Mayor and he quickly took Hawker's side so that when it came to the vote, there was only one 'nay' to all the 'ayes' and Hawker received the Bishop's seal to the vicarage of Charles on May 20, 1784.

A new note now appears in Hawker's preaching. The fine eloquence and language is still there but it is more suited to the ears of the ordinary man and there is far more Scripture in it. Hawker began to teach the children and, instead of spending his evenings with musical entertainment and card-playing, he visited the sick, the aged, the spiritual needy and the poor. He also set hours aside for social prayer and testimony. His teaching shows that he had obtained a deep understanding of the covenant of works and the covenant of grace. We note, too, that Hawker began to invite such people as William Romaine to preach. At first, Hawker felt he had to correct Romaine's 'unguarded expressions' but gradually came to realise that Romaine's words were pure gospel.. In his work *Visits to and from Jesus*, we find Hawker looking back on his previous thoughts concerning free grace and God's sovereign, electing love with dismay, saying:

> How long and how daringly violent did I myself oppose this glorious truth, which now, through thy grace subduing my rebel-

lion, and teaching my soul its blessedness, is become my greatest
joy and delight. Lord! thou knowest well, with what bitterness of
a fallen nature, I contended against the sovereignty of thy grace,
in thy free-will election; while in the very moment audaciously
insisting upon my own power in a free-will ability of serving thee!
Oh, what mercy hath been shewn me on the recovery of my soul
from a delusion so awful!

Opposition from the Establishment and Dissent alike
Hawker was opposed by Presbyterians, Anglicans and Baptists alike. The
Presbyterian pastor in Charles was a man of ability who challenged Hawker's credentials as a man of God and his congregation as a true church. He,
himself, preached Socinian notions enthusiastically so that in 1790 Hawker
began to preach a series on Christ's divinity to protect and instruct his
own flock. Hawker discovered that his preaching on the divine nature of
Christ also angered many an Anglican minister so he decided to print his
sermons for general distribution. So skilled was his reasoning and so successful was the spread of true Trinitarianism through the sales of the book
that, two years later, the University of Edinburgh awarded Hawker a di-
ploma as Doctor of Divinity. It is a tribute to the understanding of the
university that a work that led to the conversion, edification and education of numerous souls received such formal acclamation. The Dissenting
church intensified their efforts to de-throne Christ and, under the leadership of a Mr Porter, declared themselves to be Arians and published a
Defence of Unitarianism complaining that the writers of the New Testament were not inspired by God and had misunderstood Christ. This caused
the *Evangelical Magazine* to write, 'While a *Porter* disseminates the per-
nicious dogmas of Socinianism and infidelity, a *Hawker* opposes to him,
and with success, the wholesome doctrines of grace and truth, which
came by Jesus Christ.'

Hawker takes on task after task
Next Hawker published a companion volume on the Holy Spirit and a
critique of rationalism. He founded several charitable works for the poor
and provided for the relief of the families of soldiers who had died in
service or from a fever which had spread through the Plymouth area. By
1798, he was busy building an orphanage and a school. He now preached
three times on Sundays besides holding numerous weekly teaching, prayer
and testimony, meetings. He also preached two or three times a week for
the soldiers and visited the military hospitals, never accepting a penny for

his services. As the military buildings were miles apart, this witness consumed much of Hawker's time and energy in all weathers. Hawker also started a work amongst destitute women who had chosen a life of sin as a means of income.

Sadly, such evangelistic work drew protests from within the Church of England and a Cornish minister by the name of Polwhele campaigned to discredit Hawker. He felt his chance had come when Hawker journeyed to Falmouth to fetch his daughter home after a visit and accepted preaching invitations from three churches on the return journey. Polwhele complained to the Bishop of Exeter that Hawker was carrying out a 'Quixotic expedition' in his area, teaching blasphemy. Hawker's theme had been the imputation of Christ's righteousness and Polwhele had protested that if what Hawker preached were true, in the eyes of God the believer stood as righteous as Christ Himself because he had been clothed with God's own righteousness! Hawker had expounded Romans 3:22, 'Even the righteousness of God which is by faith of Jesus Christ unto all and upon all them that believe,' so Polwhele had faithfully reproduced Hawker's teaching. Yet Polwhele's knowledge of Scripture was so poor that on hearing this truth, he thought it was blasphemy! Polwhele also accused Hawker of itinerancy and neglecting his own flock. Actually Hawker had been absent from his pulpit only three Sundays in twenty years, twice due to illness and once when he preached for a friend. He was the only minister in the whole diocese with such a record! The good Bishop, the army and marine authorities and their chaplains all took Hawker's side and ignored Polwhele's protests.

Hawker's literary pilgrimage to Zion

In 1798 Hawker started writing for the *Zion's Trumpet*, a periodical founded by himself and Evangelical friends with a keen mission to spread the Word, record the work of the Holy Spirit in the lives of Christians and defend the *Thirty-Nine Articles*. The word 'Zion' was to be attached to a number of Hawker's works, such as his *Zion's Warrior* and *Zion's Pilgrim*. In the latter, a pilgrimage of meditations along the paths taken by John Bunyan's hero, Hawker gives us insight into his own spiritual history, lamenting that he only became a true pilgrim after he had 'passed a very considerable portion of time in the life of man.' On viewing the whirlpool of time that draws many a sinner into its vortex and drags them doomed out of a life which ought to have been lived in repentance, Hawker says, 'Can I call to mind the past danger, and the present deliverance, unmoved with pity over the unthinking throng, and untouched with gratitude to thee the sole

Author of every mercy? I feel (blessed be the grace that inspires it!) the rising hymn of thankfulness in my heart, while the tear drops from my eye: "Lord, how is it that thou hast manifested thyself unto me, and not unto the world!'"

Hawker loved to muse on the pages of John Bunyan and John Milton. Like John Newton and Thomas Scott, he published notes on the *Pilgrim's Progress* and, like William Cowper, wrote a commentary on *Paradise Lost*. If we wish to find the heart of Hawker in his writings, it must be in *Zion's Warrior*, published in 1801. Here he defines the blessings of what it means to be a soldier of Christ, fighting the good fight with all his might, clothed in the armour of God. We also find him bemoaning the times spent as 'a deserter from the standard of Christ Jesus.' It is inspiring, when reading Hawker, to find him a man of flesh and blood as ourselves, yet one who was greatly used of Christ to proclaim His righteousness.

Hawker on missionary work

In 1802, we find Hawker distributing free Christian literature to the poor. He did this under the pompous title of *The Great Western Society for Dispersing Religious Tracts Among the Poor*, though he was the sum total of committee members, their chairman, treasurer, secretary and editor! During this year Hawker was invited to preach before the London Missionary Society and preached on *The Work of the Holy Ghost essential to give success to all missions for the Gospel* based on Romans 10:14-15. Hawker emphasised this need because the enormous fund-raising campaigns of the missionary societies were creating the impression that the more money raised, the more souls would be saved. He feared that the work of the Holy Spirit in the soul of a man, equipping him for the Great Commission was being reduced to a commercial enterprise that was doomed to waste money and neglect true soul-winning. Hawker also believed that true missionary work was church planting, each church having its own ministers and not to be ruled by an absentee committee thousands of miles away. Hawker withdrew his L.M.S. subscription but remained a praying and giving friend to a number of church-based missionary enterprises and supported missionaries such as W. B. Johnson at Sierra Leone, privately. Johnson's correspondence with Hawker reveals, contrary to the modern criticism that the doctrines of grace cripple evangelism, that preaching such doctrines is highly successful in converting sinners.

Hawker goes on his first preaching tour

In 1803, after twenty-five years at Charles, Hawker made his first preaching tour which lasted four weeks. Nowadays pastors seem happy to spend a month a year on holiday but Hawker never felt that such luxuries were necessary and preached twenty-five times on invitation during his month's leave of absence. The London ministers were glad to have Hawker at first as he filled all their pews and also the aisles. When, however, the doors were broken down by the sheer weight of the hundreds trying to get in and the masses outside caused a traffic chaos they began to fear Hawker was too much of a crowd-drawer for them. Notwithstanding, this Five-Point man whom many were calling an Antinomian and a Hyper-Calvinist received invitation after invitation to evangelise so that he had to plan a similar tour each year for the rest of his life. Yet modern critics of Hawker's doctrines invariably argue that such doctrines destroy evangelism! This is proof enough that such criticism is merely judgemental, and has no basis in true Christian experience. One tires nowadays of hearing the new, doctrinally wishy-washy, Reformed Establishment tell us that great preachers such as Tobias Crisp, Richard Davis, John Gill, John Ryland, James Hervey, William Romaine, Augustus Toplady, William Huntington, William Gadsby and, of course, Robert Hawker, believed doctrines that drive away the crowds, when history tells us that they were the very doctrines and the very people which drew them in their thousands.

Dealing with the 'righteous over-much'
Now Hawker worked hard on his penny commentaries for the poor. Dr Williams says concerning their teaching, 'It was said of two celebrated commentators, Cocceius and Grotius, that the one found Christ everywhere, and the other nowhere. Dr. Hawker is of the former school.' One well-bred lawyer, heartily disagreed with Hawker's testimony and in 1808 published an anonymous pamphlet to show that evangelical preaching encourages sin as it makes a man rely fully on Christ so that he does not strive to mend his own unrighteousness. Christian authors should therefore preach man-centred moral reformation. Needless to say, Hawker was soon telling the nameless man that in finding Christ he had also been taught the lesson of 'denying ungodliness and worldly lusts, and living soberly, righteously, and godly in this present world.' Seeing a man after his own heart in the nameless barrister, Polwhele rejoined the opposition, particularly after he had read Hawker's *A Prop Against All Despair* which even brings hope to those who feel they have sinned beyond all chance of pardon. It soon became obvious that these men's fight was not against Hawker but Christ Himself as they gradually revealed their Unitarian tendencies. Again, the church authorities and the Christian press stood fully behind the Vicar of Charles and we can thank God for such enlightened times.

Christ, our sole perfection

Now aged sixty-five and a widower, Hawker sent his last volume of the *Poor Man's Commentary* to the press. He professed that he had written the work 'to hold up and hold forth the Lord Jesus Christ as God's Christ, and as the sole perfection of all his people.' This endeavour met with mixed feelings in the churches. The perfectionist doctrine of progressive holiness was rampant owing to false teaching concerning the law and gospel. The believer's gaze was taken away from the Christ who had clothed him with righteousness. It was an effort to change fallen Adam into the New Adam by works of holiness. The folly of the view that the old man can become purer as the days go by, is well illustrated by Paul's testimony after many years serving the Lord, 'I know that in me, that is, in my flesh, dwelleth no good thing' (Rom. 7:18). On the other hand, we read of the new man 'which after God is created in righteousness and true holiness'. The believer is created unto good works but even they do not sanctify him progressively, he is wholly such already by God's grace. Good works are the fruits of holiness and not their seed. If fruit occurs, then it is a sign that Christ has made the sinner whole. We are called to mortify the body but this is not progressive holiness but the testimony and effects of the sanctified new man in Christ.

The Biblical teaching of the sanctifying work of the Spirit in the soul of man revived

Hawker revived the Biblical teaching of the sanctifying work of the Spirit in the soul of man and spent much of his final years writing on the Person, Godhead and ministry of the Spirit. He wrote several works on the Spirit for the needs of the labouring class but did not neglect their physical needs. He bought bread in bulk and sold it to the poor at half price. The Vicar vainly thought that he could preach to the crowds as they came to buy bread but so great was the rush and commotion that even his powerful voice could not be heard. He thus hit on the idea of giving a tract of his composition with every loaf sold besides a short word of admonition.

Hawker's energies grew with his age as he published one work after another. The more he published, the more opposition grew alongside his great popularity. He had a penetrating effect on ministers who were orthodox on the outside but nurtured some secret error in their hearts. When debating with Hawker, their true selves invariably came out, displaying Socinianism, Sabellianism, Arianism or worse.

The Sonship controversy

The harshest criticism came from those who seemed doctrinally close to Hawker. He had, for instance, experienced sweet fellowship with the Old School Particular Baptists who were one with him on the doctrines of atonement, election, imputed righteousness, justification and sanctification. Unexpectedly, however, John Stevens of York Street Chapel, London, who had done tremendous work for the gospel, and was currently protecting his churches from the onslaught of Grotianism and New Divinity teaching, attacked Hawker furiously, not only for being a member of the Church of England but for not believing in the pre-existence of Christ before the incarnation. The accusation was ludicrous and the charge rebounded on Stevens who had to give a reason for his bizarre claim. It turned out, under scrutiny, that Stevens believed that Christ already possessed a human *soul* before His birth and merely took on Himself a human *body* at the incarnation. This hypothesis, of course, Hawker questioned and asked Stevens for Biblical proof. Stevens, arguing from Revelation 3:14, stepped full-scale into Arianism by stating that Christ was the first of God's creation, mistaking Christ's office as the origin and author of creation for his being a created person. Hawker had no difficulty in demonstrating that the idea that Christ was created as a soul before time and as a body in time was quite unscriptural.

Hastening with joy beyond the boundaries of time

Still writing and preaching powerfully at seventy-three, Hawker was obviously thinking more about leaving this world than the time spent in it. As two of his children and three of his grandchildren died shortly after one another, he longed for the Lord to speed on the chariot. The first signs that the chariot was ready came in 1826. On the first Sunday of the year, Hawker preached on Isaiah 3:10, 'Say ye to the righteous, it shall be well with him'. After the service, Hawker was stricken with inflammation of the lungs and spent twelve weeks as an invalid. He strove to preach on March 25 but realised that his strength was failing and was ill for a further eighteen weeks after which he stood before his congregation again to tell them that his last days were his best days. In his preface to a new work on the Holy Spirit, he confessed that he was 'fast hastening towards the boundary of time . . . with more joy than they who watch for the morning—"For I know whom I have believed, and am persuaded that he is able to keep that which I have committed unto him against that day." Like the church of old, I can

and do say, "make haste, my beloved, until the day break and the shadows
flee away.'" Hawker's condition deteriorated and he continually vomited
blood, so his daughter took him to Totness for a change of air. Though
very weak, Hawker testified, 'My soul is overfilled with joy; my spirit hath
not room for its enjoyment; I am full of glory.' As his condition worsened,
Hawker asked to be taken home to die. Immediately on reaching home, he
called his family together and gave them his departing blessing, expounding Ephesians 1:6-12. After this, Hawker laid his head on his eldest daughter's shoulder and his other children took his hands in theirs. He seemed to
drop soundly to sleep. There were no physical signs of any kind that
ushered in the silent hand of death. It took some time before the loving
children realised that their father had fallen asleep in Jesus. As John Kent
described the scene:

> Death was to him as harmless as a dove,
> While floods of glory overwhelm'd his soul.

A brief look at Hawker's works

Perhaps the reader will not be averse to reading a review I wrote shortly
after the publication of the above in *New Focus* under the title *Hawker's
Guidebooks to Zion: Genesis 33:12*. It was written as I was very conscious of the growing demand for Hawker's works and the fact that they
were now available in an inexpensive edition:

> Robert Hawker (1753-1827) combined sound Biblical doctrine
> with intense evangelistic fervour. Wherever he ministered, crowds
> longing to hear the Word of Life thronged to hear him. Hawker
> preached with great feeling and compassion because he knew
> that his labour was not in vain and God's Word never failed in its
> purpose. Some years ago, longing for more of Hawker's works, I
> approached an international 'Christian' bookseller who had a com-
> plete set for sale. His price would have rigged me out with a com-
> plete computer system so my fond idea was dropped. Then I
> heard from a friend who had actually been given a set. How envi-
> ous I was! But the circumstances of the gift made me wonder what
> the Christian world is coming to. A certain denominational library
> had once treasured their set of Hawker's works but now they felt
> the books were an embarrassment to them; indeed dangerous for
> their modern-minded readers so they gave the gospel-bearing

books away! The library's action is symptomatic of the present down-grading of sound gospel principles which once led thousands to Christ and were held in honour by eighteenth and nineteenth century Trinitarian denominations.

These thoughts led to my *New Focus* article on *Robert Hawker: Zion's Warrior*. When I received issue No. 05, I was overjoyed to see a Gospel Standard advertisement adjacent to my article listing Triangle Press reprints of Hawker at £2.75—£3.45 per volume. I immediately sent off my order and the books arrived speedily and what a blessing they proved to be!

This article is more a recommendation than a review as twelve volumes have now been published which hardly allows for a detailed analysis. First I delved into Hawker's *The Divinity of Christ* and the *Divinity and Operation of the Holy Ghost*, bearing in mind modern erroneous teaching featuring a Godhead halting between two opinions on salvation and the inane idea that the Spirit breathes contradiction and contention into the Scriptures.[1] In arguing for dissension within the Trinity concerning man's salvation and a breach in the logical harmony of Scripture in bringing this salvation home to the sinner, such writers are tearing the churches apart and actually boasting that such disunity fosters church growth! What has Hawker to say to these modern contenders for forked paths to heaven? His readers will find that his message is a God-given antidote to this modern plague.

Hawker was confronted with the very same heresy in his day. This prompted him to write on the Trinity. His opponents left the field with their tails between their legs, doing the only honest thing they could. They became Unitarians. This is why it is of the utmost importance that Hawker is read once more. As God's watchman and Zion's Warrior, he has proved his value in showing how gospel truths prevail. It will be sad to see modern tension and paradox preachers joining the Unitarians, but as their views of Christ and Scriptures are so low, they will feel more at home there and leave true religion to get on with its true work. Read Hawker on the unity of the Godhead as displayed in the salvation of His

---

[1] See especially David Gay's 'Preaching the Gospel to Sinners: 2', *Banner of Truth*, Issue 371-372 and his review of Iain Murray's *Spurgeon v. Hyper-Calvinism*, *ET*, August, 1996, p. 19. These articles laid bare the tendency to Socinianism in the British evangelical establishment and pioneered the negative re-evaluation of Spurgeon spreading through the churches which is doing nobody any good.

people. It will not only thrill your heart and soul but equip you for proclaiming the truth and combating error. If you are a child of God, it will certainly make a convinced Trinitarian of you.

Coefficient to the work of the triune Unity is the operation of the Holy Spirit in rendering the work of salvation effectual in the application of what the Father has wrought out in His Son, regenerating corrupt and fallen sinners. Indeed, Hawker argues that it is through the unity of the Spirit-breathed Word that the sinner sees the unity of God's nature in preparing salvation for him and the unity of the triune action in effectually redeeming him. Hawker argues that if such a work had been referred to in a Bible of irreconcilable, conflicting passages, and had not the unity of action been insisted on in every part of God's Word, then some apology might be made for the incredibility of mankind respecting it. However, as the Scriptures refer to the work of the Father, Son and Holy Ghost in their joint and uniting enterprise of saving sinners and as thousands can testify to being born of God through this work, we see how trustworthy is the entire testimony of the revealed Word and the folly of men striving to find disharmony in the word via a reasoning which is in disharmony with God.

Union and Communion with Christ was written to prepare believers for the communion service and deals with the believer's standing in Christ. Christ is the Vine and we are its branches, He is the Head and we the body. Together we form a holy Temple and are members of one with another as the Bride of Christ and the family of God. I have rarely experienced the mysterious union we have with our Lord from eternity to eternity so sublimely taught as in this gem of a book. Hawker's advice on how to be assured of the unity one enjoys in Christ is pastoral care at its very best.

Hawker lays great stress on prayer and in his *Prop Against All Despair*, the writer coaches the believer lovingly through the most difficult of Christian exercises but perhaps the most rewarding. Hawker shows how prayer in the Spirit opens Heaven's doors. Few books have blessed their readers as Hawker's *Zion's Pilgrim*, *The Sailor Pilgrim* and *Zion's Warrior*. To believe that one is a stranger and pilgrim on earth but marching onwards to Zion is not just the theme of a revival hymn but the teaching of Scripture and the experience of every believer. Hawker shows in these works how the path upwards is strewn with grace, mercy and love from beginning to end. There is much personal testimony given here and I was left with the assurance that God had strengthened my weak faith by my following Hawker's advice on how to keep on Zion's true track. Hawker's testimony is so strong that, whilst reading, I actually imagined myself going on the way arm in arm with this great saint, feeling all the better for his company. Few books have such an effect on me.

Hawker was not only a parish pastor but a chaplain to the forces stationed at Plymouth and his book *Compassion for the Sick and Sorrowing* is based on a harrowing experience he had. Ship after ship entered the port full of troops dying of the fever and Hawker and his church did all they could to relieve them, converting barns into hospitals, but a thousand men died during the three months of the epidemic. Though Hawker had a heavy schedule in his parish, he spent hours each day comforting the dying and burying the dead. Anyone terminally ill without knowing whether they are bound for Zion or anyone wishing to help the dying over the threshold of death should read this book as there is not a theoretical word in it but sheer practical experience and genuine comfort from cover to cover.

The above works show Hawker at his desk and in his pastoral work, his two volumes of *Village Sermons* and *Sermons on Important Subjects* reveal his faithfulness in the pulpit. The words contained in Hawker's memorial tablet sum up Hawker's prowess as a preacher: 'The elegancy yet simplicity of diction, the liveliness and brilliancy of imagination, the perspicuity and vigour of thought, the depth and compass of Christian knowledge and experience, with which he was talented and blest, are still extant in his sermons.'

Hawker was a didactically gifted man and improved the quality of Christian education greatly. As a school text-book author and curriculum writer, I approached Hawker's *Catechism for Children* with what we might call 'professional interest'. Though the *Heidelberg Catechism* is prescribed in our schools (North-Rhine Westphalia), it is little used because of its ancient language. Hawker's language should be no problem for modern English-speaking children over the age of eleven or so and the book would still make an excellent addition to Scripture lessons and family worship. Some Christians object to 'putting words into children's mouths' in catechetical work but have no objection to their children learning parts in plays and singing songs and hymns learnt off by heart. Hawker's questions and answers are Scriptural throughout and as Scripture is the language that tunes the heart to God, Christians should surely not cavil at this means of evangelising their children. Furthermore, Hawker's catechism provides pupils with a thorough knowledge of the history of the Jews as also a detailed knowledge of the two Testaments and the way of salvation. The Great Commission compels us to make this way known to all mankind, especially to children.

I cannot recommend these soul-saving and edifying works enough. The modern equivalent of a widow's mite is sufficient to purchase a single volume, but the spiritual value of each book is so enormous that it stretches from here to Heaven.

HANS NIELSEN HAUGE (1771-1824)

30. Hans Nielsen Hauge (1771-1824): God's Tramp

The humble origins of one of Norway's greatest men

Hans Nielsen Hauge was born in Thune, Norway, the son of a small-scale farmer. He had no education to boast of but throughout his childhood was filled with a spiritual longing to be right with God. He learnt early to read his Bible, assisted by Luther's *Smaller Catechism* and Arndt's *True Christianity*. On April 5, 1796, at the age of twenty-five, he was working in the fields, singing a hymn when the Lord spoke to him through the words of Isaiah 6 revealing His glory which immediately made Hauge conscious of his sin and unworthiness before God. Almost simultaneously, however, Hauge received a conviction of forgiveness and a strong calling to shepherd in God's lost sheep. Hauge's own words describing his conversion experience have been preserved in a poem he wrote on the very same day. It is full of absolute surrender and joy in receiving the indwelling Christ who becomes our All in All.

Hauge's amazing preaching industry

Once Hauge's election and calling had become sure to him, he remained on the farm, helping his father, for another year when the urge to preach the gospel so overcame him that without any theological training or even church call he left home, setting out on foot to preach conversion to the lost and revival of heart to the saved amongst the highways and by-ways of rural Norway. Preaching on an average of between two and four times a day from the coast of the Barent Sea to the North down to the Skagerrak to the South, chiefly along the 2,740 kilometre long coastline of Norway, it is reckoned that Hauge covered a distance of fifteen thousand Scandinavian miles[1] within seven years, becoming widely known as 'God's tramp'. He was not only industrious in preaching but also composed many a pamphlet, book and homily (*postilla*) which extended his ministry even further. Soon Hans Nielsen Hauge could count converts in all parts of the country and all walks of life, including the Norwegian government.

Old conventicle laws revived to stop Hauge's gospel activities

Opposition was inevitable. In Norway at this time there was a Danish anti-conventicle law which had hardly been noticed for over sixty years. A number of rationalistic clergy now insisted that Hauge, as a wandering preacher, poached on the territories of the ordained ministers and therefore he ought to be restricted. Many of these ministers were Danes who were scarcely understood by the populace and behaved with the arrogance of an occupying, foreign power. By this time, however, a large number of Hauge's converts were preaching up and down the large country of Norway in the various local dialects and thousands were benefiting from their ministry. As the opposition of the clergy became stronger and stronger and Hauge's followers were being imprisoned one by one, Hauge urged his converts and fellow preachers not to become peripatetic but to settle down in societies attached to the local Lutheran churches. Where there was a believing pastor, they should put themselves under his authority and where such was sadly lacking, they should still meet together as a church but not break away from the Lutheran Church. Through the assistance of godly Lutheran ministers and people of influence, Hauge's preachers were called to serve at different societies or form new ones so that the work continued to grow.

Hauge introduces measures to protect the Norwegians from British oppression

This was the time of Britain's quarrels with France and their blockade of all her supposed allies. Norway had to import salt and the British warships patrolled the coastlines of Norway, preventing any cargo ships from coming through. To ease the situation, Hauge and his followers, called 'Haugians' or 'Readers', set up salt works all along the coast. A great percentage of the Norwegians were occupied in shipping but now the shipping industry in Norway was waning because of British interference.

---

[1] A Scandinavian mile is 10 kilometres. Other modern sources give 1,500 kilometres but as the mile was the common unit of the day, the figure of 1,500 Scandinavian miles is to be preferred.

Hauge thus successfully urged the Norwegians to take up agriculture and encouraged them to invest in the paper industry, using the vast natural resources of the Norwegian forests. He also helped build up a coastal fishing fleet in Bergen. It was now very difficult for Hauge's opponents to attack his work and his organisation, especially as the influential Bishop of Bergen, Nordahl Brun, perhaps the most famous of all Norwegian hymn-writers, kept his protecting hand over him.

The Danes set a trap for Hauge

Now Hauge's enemies concentrated their efforts on discrediting his person and bringing him into ill-repute, believing that if he were removed from his leadership, the whole movement would collapse. Their plotting intensified when they heard that Hauge was on a preaching tour of their native Denmark. Their opportunity came in 1804 when Hauge preached in Christiana without a license, far from Bishop Brun's influence.[1] He was immediately arrested and imprisoned for illicit preaching. Though the national protest was great, Hauge had to stay in a cell, chained to the wall, with one excuse after another been given for his detention. It was not until 1811 that court charges were brought against Hauge and his trial could begin. During this time, the sheer evil of his antagonists became evident. One example to illustrate this perversity is that the prison authorities arranged for the youth of the neighbourhood to organise a dance one Sunday accompanied by drinking revelries in front of Hauge's cell and planned to force their prisoner to join in. Man proposes, God disposes. As soon as the youngsters entered the prison, already the worse for their liquid intake, Hauge began to preach. Though in physical chains, he preached as a free man in Christ to those who were enchained by their sins. He told them how that day was the Day of the Lord and they were receiving the chance of their lifetime to become free from their sins. He also told them that there would come another day—the Day of Judgement—when no repentance would be possible and no forgiveness given. Soon all the dancing visitors left the prison. Most of them had gone home to pray that their sins might be forgiven.

The Danes lose Norway and Hauge's terrible sufferings end

The 1811 trial ended with Hauge's release, but the antagonism of a section of the clergy was so strong that they watched Hauge's every footstep and

---

[1] Other sources, such as Bernt Gustafsson in his *Svensk Kyrkohistoria* say that Hauge was arrested in Bergen which is difficult to accept given Bishop Brun's interest in Hauge.

when he was caught preaching again in 1814,[1] he was sentenced to two years hard labour for 'criticising the clergy'. This was a terribly un-Christian act by these pseudo-shepherds as they knew Hauge's health had suffered greatly from his imprisonment, especially during the severe Norwegian winters and the only reason they campaigned for two years hard labour and not more was because they were certain that Hauge would be dead before the end of the period. So great, however, was the national protest against this cruel sentence that the clergy feared to have Hauge imprisoned again because of the loss to their own reputation. It was thus decided that Hauge should pay a fine of a considerable amount and would then be given his freedom. This amount was quickly collected by his friends. Another factor which, by the grace of God, assisted Hauge, was that Norway as a Danish vassal, had been Napoleon's ally. When Napoleon was defeated in that year, France's allies were punished with her and thus, at the Treaty of Kiel, Norway was handed over to Swedish rule whose State Church had gone through a true reformation and was tolerant of 'mission' work. Sweden also allowed Norway, after something of a Norwegian rebellion, to be semi-autonomous.

Broken in body but strong in the Lord
From now on, till his early death, Hauge lived on his farm in Bredtvedt, broken in body. Unable to go on preaching tours, people from all over Norway flocked to him to hear the Word of God so that in his confinement and frailty he was able to reach almost as many as in the days of his freedom and bodily power. The joint King of Sweden and Norway personally intervened in the case of Hauge, granting him full pardon and lifting the ban on all his books and tracts. Hauge's societies with their lay-shepherds now grew even stronger and became so influential in the work of the churches that the Lutheran authorities had no option but to accept them as an integral part of their church organisation and ministry. In this way an 'inner mission' was formed which allowed for the calling and sending out of so-called lay-preachers.

Hauge's work spreads throughout northern Scandinavia
Hans Nielsen Hauge died at the early age of fifty-three on March 29, 1824, esteemed by the entire nation. He had become an old man before the normal time but had lived to see the work God had given him to do spread and prosper. After his death, his strong influence remained, spreading

---

[1] Other sources claim that Hauge was imprisoned until 1814.

twenty-five years later into Sweden where many fellowships of 'Readers' were formed in Värmland, Småland and Östergötland. The conventicle act was abolished in 1842 and colporteurs were free to travel throughout northern Scandinavia carrying the Bibles and books that the Readers were issuing through a number of printing houses they had set up. It was not long before most towns and villages in Norway, Sweden and Swedish-speaking Finland had their prayer-houses or chapels (bönhus) where the Readers met. Very many of these are still in existence, and still used, today.

A time of true awakening ensues

The latter half of the nineteenth century brought with it a true revival of experimental religion in the Haugean communities and the work of evangelism was intensified both at home and abroad. It is during this period that the Lutherstiftelsen (1868) was founded followed by Det norske lutherske indremisjonsselskap, Norsk lutherk misjonssamband and Kina (China) misjonsforbund in 1891 and Det vestlandske indremisjonsforbund in 1898. This work also spread to Sweden and was taken up by such as Carl Olof Rosenius[1] (born 1815) who founded similar inner and foreign missionary societies which are still in existence. Happily, such mighty written works as those of Rosenius which guided me through my early years as a Christian are now being translated into English.

Though the movement had started amongst the poorest of the poor, it was not long before even members of the Royal family were personally treading in Hauge's footsteps.[2] The Norwegian Storting (Parliament) organised a Hauge Society amongst their Members of Parliament and intensive prayer and Bible-study have gone hand in hand with political debate in Oslo ever since. These parliamentarians have taken Hauge's words as their motto, 'I have sworn allegiance to God's Holy Spirit and He has enabled me to keep to my resolution.'

The Nazi's endeavour to quench the Haugean spirit in Norway

When the German Nazis overran Norway during the Second World War, the peace-loving country was put under the governership of Terboven from the large industrial town of Essen who was credited with having the most evil mouth of any German and the most perverted ideas of religion of

---

[1] Rosenius' works are now being translated for North American readers.

[2] The author had the privilege of working with a countess member of the Bernadotte family in the middle sixties who had a great passion for evangelism, especially amongst the Lapps. She told him of similar work done by earlier members of her family.

any human being. Terboven with devilish intelligence soon realised that it was the high percentage of evangelical Christians in Norway, the great-great-grand children of the Hauge awakening, that gave the Norwegians their spirit of opposition to Fascist propaganda. He therefore resolved to have Bishop Eivind Berggraf, a man highly influenced by Hauge's works, executed so that Christian opposition to Hitler's pagan religion named Deutsche Christen with its Volkstestament (a Bible with all reference to Israel and the Jews removed) would be broken. Again man proposed but God disposed. S. S. leader Heinrich Himmler, a more evil man than even Terboven, realised that the Governor's fanaticism had blinded his common sense. If Berggraf were murdered, the Germans would lose all chance of ever being respected in Norway. The German Governor of Norway thus was not able to have his way and the Norwegian resistance increased so that it was he who feared for his life. Smarting under this rebuff from his Jesuit superior, Terboven heard that the Germans were on the retreat from Russia. He realised that his Nazi Millennium was coming to an end after only ten years of life. Terboven called the people under his evil rule to assemble themselves below his balcony. He presented himself in his best uniform before the crowds, lit a cigarette and appeared to be waiting. Suddenly there was a disintegrating roar and the great mansion house collapsed from beneath the Governor's feet. Terboven had capitulated before a people who put Christ before Hitler. He had blown himself into smithereens.

A sequel
When Wilhelm Busch of Weigle Haus, Essen, a German evangelist who started a great and continuing work amongst Germany's youth, visited old Bishop Berggraf many years after the war, he saw Gronland's portrait of Hauge hanging in the bishop's study, a copy of which was his own treasured possession. Knowing Berggraf's history and the fact that Terboven came from his own town and was well-known to him, post-war Busch, a member of a new Germany, could only say with a thankful heart and voice, 'When all the bishops in the church have a picture of the revivalist and lay-preacher Hans Nielsen Hauge hanging above their writing desks, then we can hope the best for our church.' If all church leaders and members of any denomination served their Lord with the same assurance and fervour as Hans Nielsen Hauge, how we might look forward to great revival blessings from on high!

HENRY MARTYN (1781-1812)

31. Henry Martyn (1781-1812): Pioneer Missionary

The poet John Greenleaf Whittier interests America for the life of Martyn
During the 1830s a great poet emerged in America who was speedily acclaimed as 'The Cowper of the West', because of his deeply experimental religious verse. His name was John Greenleaf Whittier and he, like Cowper, had the spread of the gospel at heart. Cowper's verses praised the work of the Moravians who had planted the Rose of Sharon on Greenland's icy mountains and Whittier strove to show how God was working out His purpose in the land of the Mogul. One of Henry Martyn's letters had given him the impetus. When Martyn arrived in India, he realised what a sacrifice it was to leave all and follow Christ, and wrote home:

> It is an awful, an arduous thing to root out every affection for earthly things, so as to live only for another world. I am now far, very far, from you all; and as often as I look around and see the Indian scenery, I sigh to think of the distance which separates us.

These heart-stirring words moved Whittier to write Martyn's biography in verse. It was read in almost every school in America and placed in almost every public library and awoke in America an awareness that the earth was being covered with the knowledge of the Lord as the waters cover the sea.

A good father, good books and good friends help Martyn on the way to Heaven
Born in 1781 at Truro, Cornwall, known for its revival under Samuel Walker's preaching, Martyn was the son of a miner who had worked himself up

in society. His mother died whilst he was but a child. Martyn studied at Cambridge where his brilliance was rewarded with prizes. He became senior wrangler and was elected fellow of St John's College whilst only twenty-one. Martyn, however, felt he was grasping at shadows. Then his father, a believer, suddenly died, and the shadow-grasper now felt that he had lost his anchor in life. He turned to his neglected Bible and read the Acts of the Apostles which forced him on his knees in prayer to thank God for sending his Son into the world to save him from his sins. Martyn now grew in grace through reading Doddridge's *Rise and Progress of Religion in the Soul* and sharing sweet fellowship and counsel with Charles Simeon the Cambridge Evangelical.

David Brainerd influences Martyn for the mission field

God called Martyn to his missionary task through the writings of David Brainerd. He was gripped by young Brainerd's testimony to the hardships of living amongst the Indians and times when God hid His face. Martyn saw how, after humbling Brainerd, the Lord suddenly smiled upon him and used him as an instrument of revival. He was also deeply struck by the fact that Brainerd had died, worn out for the gospel's sake, whilst only thirty-two. Soon Martyn had laid all ambitions of scholarly fame aside so that he might become a messenger of hope to foreign lands. He was ordained as an Anglican minister and applied to various missionary societies. Through the agencies of the Clapham Sect and Christian Board members of the East India Company, Martyn was offered a post as Chaplain to the troops and civil servants in India. As this included freedom to preach to the Sepoys and the native population, Martyn eagerly accepted the offer. He swiftly prepared himself to leave England, weeping tears of joy at being counted worthy to serve the Lord and tears of grief at leaving his friends. In great sorrow, he said farewell to a young lady whose heart he had hoped against hope would be united to his in marriage. Whittier says:

> He went forth
> To bind the broken spirit, to pluck back
> The heathen from the wheel of Juggernaut;
> To place the spiritual image of a God
> Holy and just and true, before the eye
> Of the dark-minded Brahmin, and unseal
> The holy pages of the Book of Life,
> Fraught with sublimer mysteries than all

The sacred tomes of Vedas, to unbind
The widow from her sacrifices, and save
The perishing infant from the worshipped river!

Hugh Martyn the Anglican fellowships with William Carey the Baptist
On April 21, 1806 Martyn reached India and his immediate impression was
one of horror at the bondage of the people to their idols. William Carey, the
Baptist missionary, was overjoyed to meet him and the Serampore trio
found such proofs of the young Anglican's calling and abilities that he
was accepted as one of their very own missionaries. Martyn swiftly proved
his prowess as a linguist and was soon preaching in Hindustani, drawing
450-800 hearers. He opened schools, providing good, well-paid staff to
teach the children. So obvious was the presence of the Divine hand on
Martyn's work that the authorities invariably backed him and his fellow-
missionaries in other denominations gave him their full support. Within
two years Martyn had translated the entire New Testament, a Bible commentary and a good part of the Prayer Book into Hindustani, had prepared
works in Hindi and had almost completed the Persian New Testament in
spite of failing health. He had caught tuberculosis. Instead of returning to
England for medical attention, Martyn made the hazardous journey to
Persia to complete his translation and witness to the Mohammedans there.
His constant prayer was, 'Oh, have pity on my wretched state and revive
Thy work, increase my faith. Thou art the resurrection and the life—let me
rest on this Scripture.' Though often threatened with death from without
for exalting Christ more than 'the Prophet' and wracked with death-bring-
ing fever and pain from within, Martyn entered public debate with the
most learned Mullahs and Mujahidins and the Shah himself received a
copy of his Persian New Testament.

**The gracious attitude of the Shah to Martyn contrasted with that of the
Pope**
How times have changed in that country is witnessed by the gracious way
in which the Shah accepted the Word of God. Commenting on the 'high,
dignified, learned, and enlightened Society of Christians, united for the
purpose of spreading abroad the Holy Books of the religion of Jesus (on
whom, and upon all prophets, be peace and blessing),' His Majesty said
how acceptable the book had proved to him and continued:

In truth, through the learned and unremitted exertions of the
Rev. Henry Martyn, it has been translated in a style most befitting

sacred books, that is, in an easy and simple diction. . . . We therefore, have been particularly delighted with this copious and complete translation. If it please the most merciful God, we shall command the Select Servants, who are admitted to our presence, to
read to us the above-mentioned book from the beginning to the
end, that we may, in the most minute manner, hear and comprehend its contents.

Fateh Ali Shah Kayar then authorised Martyn's New Testament to
be distributed in Persia with the blessing and full approval of His Majesty.

Papal opposition
The enlightenment of this gracious Muslim Monarch stands in stark contrast to the blind reaction of Pope Pius VIII to the news of Martyn's *Opus
magnum*. The Pontiff immediately produced two Bulls claiming that
Martyn's work was 'a crafty device, by which the very foundations of
religion are undermined.' 'It is evident from experience', he said, 'that from
the Holy Scriptures which are published in the vulgar tongue, more injury
than good has risen.' Such facts must be born in mind today as Rome
woos evangelicals by telling them that Tindale and the AV translators
jumped the gun as Rome was already preparing superior vernacular ver-
sions—based on their Latin texts—for the common man.

The hazardous homeward journey begins
Assured by his supporters that his translation would soon be printed,
Martyn turned his weary head homewards. His plan was to travel the 1,300
miles to Constantinople on horseback via Erivan, Kars, Etchmiatzin and
Erzroom, fording the strong currents of the great Araxes river made famous by Xenophon and skirting Mount Ararat where Noah's Ark landed.
Then somehow, he had no idea how, he would make for Britain via Malta.
It was all in God's hands. Sir Gore Ousely, the British Resident in Tabriz,
prepared Martyn's route and gave him letters of introduction to the various Persian and Turkish office-bearers on the way. The journey Martyn
undertook from Tabriz to Tokat reminds one of Carl May's multi-volumed
adventures of Old Shatter-Hand and his trusty servant Hadji Alef Omar in
Wild Kurdistan. Their hardships, however, were works of fiction and wherever they went, they left bloodshed and the cry of 'Curse the Infidels!'
behind them. Henry Martyn and his trusty, though less capable, servant
Sergius had no heavy guns to protect them, though once they had to carry
swords as the wilds were swarming with bandits. Their hardships were

excruciatingly real but Martyn never forgot that he was an ambassador for Christ. Though many a Turk treated him with harsh contempt, he caused more to believe that they had met a messenger from God. When Martyn reached Mount Ararat, he marvelled how the whole Church of God had once come to rest on its summit. Thinking of Noah, he wrote in his diary, miraculously preserved, 'Here the blessed saint landed in a new world; so may I, safe in Christ, outride the storms of life and land at last on one of the everlasting hills.' As Martyn approached Tokat, he was met by fleeing inhabitants who warned him that the plague had struck in Constantinople and had even caught Tokat in its grip. 'O lord, Thy will be done! Living, dying, remember me,' Martyn prayed and pressed on. He knew he was dying. Martyn reached Tokat on October 1, 1812 and penned his last words:

> No horse being to be had, I had an unexpected repose. I sat in the orchard, and thought with sweet comfort and peace of my God, in solitude, my company, my Friend and Comforter. Oh, when shall time give place to Eternity? When shall appear that new Heaven and new Earth wherein dwelleth righteousness! There, there shall nowise enter in anything that defileth; none of that wickedness which has made men worse than beasts—none of those corruptions which add still more to the miseries of mortality, shall be seen or heard of any more.

Death at thirty-one

Being thus at peace with God Henry Martyn experienced no more mortal miseries. He entered into his rest that day aged thirty-one, a year younger than Brainerd at his death. It is recorded that Martyn died alone. Whittier claims it was otherwise:

> God forbid
> That he should die alone!' Nay, not alone
> His God was with him in that last dread hour;
> His great arm underneath him, and His smile
> Melting into a spirit full of peace.
> And one kind friend, a human friend, was near -
> One whom his teachings and his earnest prayers
> Had snatch'd as from the burning. He alone
> Felt the last pressure of his failing hand,

> Caught the last glimpse of his closing eye,
> And laid the green turf over him with tears,
> And left him with his God.

In his work amongst Mohammedans, Henry Martyn has been likened to John the Baptist, preparing the way of the Lord. The work he pioneered was not followed up as it should have been by subsequent Christians and now, in many lands, the crescent has encompassed the cross. Martyn's life and death challenges us with the question, 'Who will follow in his train?'

ISAAC McCOY (1784-1846)

32. Isaac McCoy (1784-1846): Apostle of the Western Trail

The significance of McCoy's enormous work

The story of Isaac McCoy is of unique significance in the history of North America and in the history of the Christian Church. It is the tale of a man who was used by God to preserve the Indian Nations from certain extinction. It is the account of the founding and colonising of Arkansas,[1] Kansas[2] and Oklahoma[3] which were to become bright luminaries in the star-spangled banner of the nation which has become the envy of the world. Above all, it is the history of how the West was won; not by the efforts of countless politicians, honourable as many such efforts were, nor through the adventures of pistol-packing white pioneers who came much later. It is the history of a bunch of Baptist missionaries and their Indian friends who saw the writing on the wall in the northern, eastern and southern states and received the call to find a new Canaan in the west where righteousness and peace could live side by side and where politics and social fair-play could be built on the Christian gospel.

McCoy's boyhood on the Western frontier

This great American pioneer was born near Union Town, Pennsylvania on June 15, 1784. His grandfather, James McCoy had come to North America around 1700 as a ten-year-old orphan from Scotland. Calvin McCormick, a distant relative of Isaac McCoy's, tells how the young boy, tempted by tales from the New World, boarded a merchant ship which was to set sail for Baltimore and worked his way across the Atlantic as a cabin boy. After

---

[1] Statehood 15 July, 1836.

[2] Statehood 29 January, 1861.

[3] Statehood 16 November, 1907.

a time, James moved to Kentucky with a party of friends but settled down in Uniontown on his marriage to a Scot's girl of the Bruce family. The McCoys had six children. The third, William, Isaac's father, who married Elizabeth Rice, became a Baptist pastor.

In 1790, when Isaac was six years old, the McCoys moved from Pennsylvania to Kentucky where William evangelised amongst the settlers from the east. Kentucky was emerging as a separate State to Virginia (1792) and had recently been 'freed' from the hands of the Indians. The McCoys settled on the Ohio River in Jefferson County some seventeen miles from Louisville, moving a short time later to Shelby County where William became pastor of Buck Creek Church. An Indiana church by the name of Fourteen Mile Creek asked Buck Creek to provide them with ministers and McCoy was sent there with George Waller to preach alternately. This church is thought to be the oldest Protestant church in Indiana as it was founded in 1798 and became a member church of the Salem Association in 1799. In 1803 the Fourteen Mile Church decided to move to Silver Creek, Clark County, Indiana, where most of the members lived. William became its pastor and stayed there for the rest of his life.

We know little about Isaac's early life on the western frontier, except that he loved the studious rather than the outdoor life and became an avid reader of good books. We know nothing about how he came to profess faith in Christ apart from the fact that his mother was the chief instrument to this end. Isaac's father had him taught the trade of a wheelwright which he practised for a number of years and which remained a continuous source of income for him when he needed funds to fit him out for his preaching journeys. Isaac was converted at sixteen and baptised a year later by Joshua Morris on March 6, 1801 and became a member of Buck Creek. Two years later, on October 6, 1803, McCoy was married to sixteen-year-old Christiana Polke, known to her dear ones as 'Kittie'. The young Mrs McCoy's mother and three other members of her family had been held prisoners by the Ottawa Indians for several years. This had filled her with a longing to take the gospel to those people, which, by God's grace, she and her husband were now called to do.

Isaac's call to the ministry

The couple moved with Isaac's parents to the Silver Creek Church and Isaac now felt that he should start out on his ministry and be ordained as a Baptist preacher. His church told him that he was too young and advised him to carry out his trade as a wheelwright until official approval could be given. On July 11, 1807, McCoy preached a 'discourse' at the Silver Creek

Church before the elders and was put on a year's probation, after which, he received his preaching accreditation in 1808. He was ordained to the ministry by George Waller and his father on October 12, 1810, and put in charge of Maria Creek, a church formed by his converts. The McCoys spent eight years in the pastorate, working on the land for their daily bread according to the Baptists' practice in those frontier days. McCoy preached throughout Indiana, Kentucky and Illinois and established at least five churches and two evangelistic societies amongst his converts within a few years.

McCoy accepted as a missionary to the Indians
McCoy now realised that he was called to work among Indians rather than whites so he sent his ideas to the Wabash Association for approval. They contacted the Silver Creek and Long Run Associations for advice which proved favourable to McCoy's endeavours. McCoy, now thirty-four years of age, was accepted as a missionary for a trial period of a year. These associations were Calvinistic, holding to Elias Keach's *Declaration of Faith* based on the *London Baptist Confession*, though they rejected Supralapsarian or ritualistic interpretations. Sadly the New Light movement, a split-off from the Presbyterians, Campbellism and Dualistic Gnostic elements infiltrated local politics and the Baptist associations so that McCoy's contract was not renewed. He and his growing churches were dismissed from the association on the bizarre grounds that they supported evangelistic work. On June 19, 1812, President Madison declared war on Britain and as the Indians, led by Tecumseh the Shawnee, supported the British, Indian missions were now considered 'anti-American'. McCoy sympathised much with Tecumseh and his longing for Indian independence. He therefore campaigned that the Indians should be allowed to live self-administratively in white-free areas, represented by their own people in Congress. He also campaigned for Indian literacy and a Bible in the Indian languages, lobbying the government to provide schools to this end. None of these views were entirely original but they had either faded from view or had not spread because of the political situation.

The founding of the Baptist Board of Foreign Missions
In 1814-17 Baptists from eleven states and bordering territories founded the American Baptist Board of Foreign Missions. McCoy wrote to the Board on March 26, 1817 sending in his plans for Indian[1] missions and requesting them to place him under their patronage. The Board agreed to

---

[1] Indians were non-US citizens, therefore 'foreigners'.

send McCoy to the Indians for an initial period of a year. Thus he became one of the American Baptist Board's first missionaries alongside Adoniram Judson. McCoy laid the matter before his church and received their valedictory blessing. McCoy immediately opened contacts with the Weas, Miamies and Kickapoos, and distributed printed information leaflets regarding his plans. Soon after starting his work amongst the Indians, the McCoys eldest daughter, a thirteen-year old girl, was struck down by typhus fever. Little did the McCoys realise that they were to loose eleven of their fourteen children through the hazards of life in the Indian wilderness.

The most successful but most neglected missionary of the Baptist Board
By the time McCoy's first mission station and school at Racoon Creek were up and running, his probation time had run out but there had been no replies from the Board to his many reports and pleas for help. The financial support promised did not materialise and McCoy and his family were soon on the verge of starvation besides being struck down with measles and fever. Meanwhile, the Board were using McCoy's 'foreboding and apparently insurmountable difficulties' as also his 'pain and hardships' as public relations work for their own cause, saying, 'And, should we have the happiness to see the fruit of his labours, it will be his joy to say, not unto us, not unto us, but unto thy name, O! Lord, be all the glory.'[1] Never was a truer word spoken as McCoy remained their most successful but most neglected missionary so that his success was obviously the Lord's doing and not their's. On hearing of McCoy's enormous success, the Board put his contract with them on a permanent basis, still making unkept financial promises. Nothing daunted, McCoy laid plans for further mission stations at Fort Wayne, Carey (now Niles) and Thomas (now Michigan), along both sides of the Kansas River, on the banks of the Ohio River and throughout the Indian Territory east of the Mississippi and Missouri. The latter was purchased from Napoleon in 1803 and was equal in size to the nineteen states of the Union. Indeed, apart from work amongst the Cherokees, McCoy played a major part in evangelising all the North American tribes and educating their children. In fact, the pupils taught at schools McCoy and his son-in-law Dr Johnston Lykins founded equalled the sum total of all the pupils taught by other denominations including the Presbyterians and Roman Catholics. This accounts for the massive growth in the spread of Baptist churches in the area west of the Mississippi and why still today

---

[1] Vol. i, May, 1818, article dated March, 3, 1818, pp. 90-91.

many Indian Christians are Baptists. This also accounts to a great extent for the presence of Protestant religion in the north and west of the United States as McCoy worked chiefly in areas which had belonged to the French and Spanish and were formerly Roman Catholic.

Some of the 'firsts' of McCoy and his missionary family

Though called to evangelise the Indians, McCoy also left his mark on the anti-racist movement in the New World. The first church founded in present day Oklahoma at Three Forks near Fort Gibson in 1832 was inaugurated by McCoy and composed equally of Indians, Africans and Europeans. Great towns, such as Michigan and Kansas City, look to the McCoys as their founders, their towns being built on his former Indian Mission property. Johnston Lykins, McCoy's fellow-missionary and son-in-law, became Kansas City's first Lord Mayor.

We are also dependent on McCoy for the first detailed information on the flora, fauna and geology of the territory west of the Mississippi. Former expensive, well equipped expeditions to the Indian Territory by such as Meriwether Lewis and William Clark (1806) and Major Stephen H. Long (1820) had brought back little information and highly negative, reports of the new country but Isaac McCoy spent literally years riding and walking over thousands of square miles, making maps and surveying land so that he could find homes for the twenty-two tribes whom McCoy rescued from the bootlegging, land-grabbing lynch mobs of white civilisation. Major Long had proclaimed that the land between the Mississippi and Rocky Mountains was unfit for cultivation and uninhabitable. McCoy, who had experienced it in all seasons, found it fertile and inhabitable. It is also thanks to McCoy that we know so much about the traditions and ceremonies of the Indians as he gives us numerous detailed eye-witness accounts of such ancient practices.

The Indian Mission's Family Rules

On February 15, 1822, McCoy, acting on principles practised by William Carey at Serampore, felt he ought to establish the mission on a firm basis of co-operation and unity of spirit. He and Johnston Lykins had put together twelve rules for general missionary conduct to be accepted and signed by the missionaries and this was now forwarded to the Board for approval under the heading *General Rules for the Fort Wayne Mission Family*, which became known simply as the *Family Rules*.

On March 14, 1822 passed the following minute and resolution:

The Family Rules (forwarded by Mr. McCoy) of the mission
having being twice carefully read, Resolved, That the said rules
meet the full and decided approbation of the board.

The full text reads:

We, whose names follow, being appointed missionaries to the
Indians by the General Convention of the Baptist denomination
for missions, deem it expedient for our comfort and usefulness to
adopt, in the fear of the Lord, the following general rules for the
regulation of the mission family, viz:

1st. We agree that our object in becoming missionaries is to melio-
rate the condition of the Indians, and not to serve ourselves.
Therefore,
2^{d}. We agree that our whole time, talents, and labours, shall be
dedicated to the obtaining of this object, and shall all be bestowed
gratis, so that the mission cannot become indebted to any missionary for his or her services.
3^{d}. We agree that all remittances from the board of missions, amid
all money and property accruing to any of us, by salaries from
Government, by smith shops, by schools, by donations, or from
whatever quarter it may arise, shall be thrown into the common
missionary fund, and be sacredly applied to the cause of *this*
mission; and that no part of the property held by us at our stations is ours, or belongs to any of us, but it belongs to the General
Convention which we serve, and is held in trust by us, so long as
said society shall continue us in their employment: provided that
nothing herein contained shall affect the right of any to private
inheritance, &c.[1]
4th. We agree to obey the instructions of our patrons, and that the
superintendent shall render to them, from time to time, accounts
of our plans, proceedings, prospects, receipts, and expenditures;
and that the accounts of the mission, together with the mission
records, shall at all times be open for the inspection of any of the
missionaries.

---

[1] This had been a moot point with Sears and a matter of dispute with several new
missionaries who knew of this general agreement before they applied for a missionary
post in the missions founded by McCoy and Lykins.

5th. We agree that all members of the mission family have equal claims upon the mission for equal support in similar circumstances; the claims of widows and orphans not to be in the least affected by the death of the head of the family.

6th. We agree that when any missionary shall not find employment in his particular branch of business, it shall be his duty to engage in some other branch of business, as circumstances shall dictate.[1]

7th. We agree that, agreeably to their strength and ability, all the female missionaries should bear an equal part of the burden of domestic labours and cares, lest some should sink under the weight of severe and unremitted exertions; making the necessary allowances for the school mistress.[2]

8th. We agree to be industrious, frugal, and economical, at all times, to the utmost extent of our abilities.

9th. We agree that missionaries labouring at the different stations belonging to this mission are under the same obligations to each other, as though resident in the same establishment.

10th. We agree that it is the duty of missionaries to meet statedly at their respective stations, for time purposes of preserving peace and harmony among themselves, of cherishing kindness and love for each other, love to God, and zeal in the cause of missions.

11th. We agree to feel one general concern for the success of every department of the mission, for the happiness of every member of the mission family, and to feed at one common table, except in cases of bad health, &c., in which cases the persons thus indisposed shall receive special attention, and shall be made as comfortable as our situation will admit.[3]

---

[1] No better example was shown here than that of McCoy who was Superintendent, blacksmith, gardener and farmer.

[2] This was an important item as one of the chief causes of unrest amongst a number of would-be missionaries was that they thought their status forbade them to do menial chores. McCoy had no such inhibitions and often worked in the kitchen for his wider family and tilled the soil. Mrs McCoy never shunned bearing the major burden of domestic work. One of the chief weakness of the Board's missionaries (Evan Jones excluded) to the southern tribes were tantrums caused by class-consciousness amongst the various missionaries. Some of Jones' co-workers despised him, for instance, because he married a woman thought to be a mere domestic help. Eliza McCoy, Isaac's niece, came into a relatively large fortune and had enjoyed a first-class education but she always remained a humble co-worker with those from other, less affluent or learned backgrounds.

[3] As the family became too large to eat all together in one room, meals were taken in groups.

12th. We agree to cherish a spirit of kindness and forbearance for each other, and, as the success of our labours depends on the good providence of God, it is our duty to live near to him in public and private devotion, and to walk before him with fear, and in the integrity of our hearts, conscious that he ever sees us, and that by him actions are weighed; realising that we are, at best, only instruments in his hand, and hoping that when we shall have finished the work given us to do, we shall dwell together in heaven, in company with fellow-labourers from other parts of the vineyard, and with those for whom we are now strangers and sufferers in this wilderness, and, to crown our happiness, shall gaze eternally on Him whose religion we are now endeavouring to propagate, to whom shall be ascribed *all* the glory of the accomplishment of our present undertaking.

McCoy was to experience a number of disappointments regarding the *Family Rules* as a number of would-be missionaries who arrived at the station, refused to live by the rules. At first the Board was in wholehearted agreement with McCoy but when the Board eventually came under a new leadership and was transferred from Philadelphia to Boston, their views changed. Personally, however, McCoy lived by the *Family Rules* all his life, as did the majority of the missionaries connected with McCoy and those in other areas lived similarly.

The Fort Wayne Declaration of Faith
During the same year, the church founded at Fort Wayne drew up its *Declaration of Faith* which is surely one of the finest ever drawn up by an American Baptist church and reveals elements that have quite disappeared from modern Baptist witness. It will be quoted here in full as an incentive to ponder over. Perhaps it will serve to remind the one or the other what positive doctrines we have lost in today's churches.

We, whose names follow, being convinced of the propriety and utility of a church state, and having due knowledge of each other in respect to experimental and practical religion, by consent and with the assistance of Elder Benjamin Sears, of Meredith, New York, and Elder Corbly Martin, of Staunton, Ohio, do agree to unite in a church compact, upon the firm basis of the Scriptures of the Old and New Testament, as being of divine authority, and the only infallible rule of faith and practice. And whereas there are different opinions among professed Christians in relation to the true meaning of Scripture, therefore, in order to prevent unpleasant disputation, and to cherish harmony of sentiment, we deem it indispensable to subjoin the following expression of the leading features of those doctrines of the Gospel most liable to be disputed, which shall always be considered as the sentiments of this church.

ART. i. We believe in one only true and living God, who is infinite and unchangeable in all his divine perfections or attributes, such as wisdom, power, justice, love, &c., the Creator and Preserver of all things; and that he cannot be brought under the least obligations to any of his creatures.

ART. ii. We believe that in Deity there is a Trinity, of Father, Son, and Holy Ghost, in all respects equal, and unlike the subordination between father and son among men.

ART. iii. We believe that God is not liable to the least disappointment, but that eternity is at all times fully comprehended by him, so that neither the malice of hell, nor the wickedness of men on earth, can any way frustrate his eternal purposes.

ART. iv. We believe that God made man upright, but he has voluntarily fallen from his uprightness; that in his fall he lost all traces of virtue, (moral goodness,) and became wholly averse to godliness; yet he is, on that account, under no less obligations to his God.

ART. v. We believe that as there is nothing new with God, it is his eternal purpose to save those who ultimately will be received into heaven, not upon the supposition of any condition to be performed by them, but wholly in consequence of what Jesus Christ has done in their behalf.

ART. vi. We believe the Son of God united himself to humanity, and in that state fulfilled in his life the law of God, which was binding on man, and suffered in his death the penal requisitions of the same.

ART. vii. We believe, agreeably to the inevitable consequences of articles first, third, and fifth, that Christ's life, death, resurrection, and intercession, were, and are, in behalf of those, and those only, who shall enjoy the benefits thereof.

ART. viii. We believe that regeneration is effected by the operations of the Spirit of God only, and is an essential preparation for the enjoyment of God in heaven, and an assurance of title thereto.

ART. ix. We believe that, through grace, all who are regenerated will be preserved in a gracious state, and will certainly go to heaven.

ART. x. We believe it to be perfectly congenial to the Scriptures, and to the spirit of the foregoing articles, for ministers of the Gospel to command all men indiscriminately to repent, and to exhort them to believe the Gospel.

ART. xi. We believe that God hath appointed a day in which he will judge all men by Jesus Christ.

ART. xii. We believe that the joys of the righteous will be eternal, and that the sufferings of the wicked will be of endless duration

ART. xiii We believe that the suffering of the wicked is the spontaneous consequence of their own wickedness, and not the effect of any thing in or done by Deity, hostile to their happiness.

ART. xiv. We believe that none but believers in Christ ought to be baptized, and that immersion is the only scriptural mode of baptism.

ART. xv. We believe that none but baptized believers in Christ, united in Gospel order, have a right to communion at the Lord's table.

ART. xvi. We believe that God hath set apart one day in seven, for rest and religious worship, and that the first day of the week ought to be observed as such, in resting from our temporal concerns, excepting works of necessity.

And being united together upon the foregoing plan, we deem it our duty to walk in all the commandments and ordinances of the Lord blameless, which, that God may enable us to do, let every member, at all times, fervently pray.

Lobbying Congress

McCoy soon realised that there must be a political as well as an evangelistic solution to the Indian question and from 1817 onwards he lobbied the Government, arguing that humanitarian aid and preaching the Gospel should go hand in hand. By 1821, McCoy had become well-known in Congress and often quoted with favour in debates. At the Chicago Treaty, McCoy, backed by the Pottawatomies and Ottawas, was given land for missionary stations and put in charge of the Government's plans for what they called Indian Improvement to the chagrin of the Roman Catholics who had demanded the post. All the contracts McCoy entered into with the Government, however, were carried out under the authority and approval of the Board to whom he committed all ownership of lands and sole custodians of grants. McCoy even gave the entire proceeds of his own property and farm to the Board. The more McCoy saw how the Indians were being driven out of their ancestral homes and lands, the more he campaigned for the Indians to be allowed to colonise the territories west of the Mississippi. McCoy was eventually authorised to survey the Indian territory and supervise the move of the Indian tribes there. Finally, Congress approved of McCoy's plans for Indian resettlement and the great trails westward began. Most tribes moved gladly but the Cherokees who had the greatest amount of whites and part whites in their bands became greatly divided over the issue and the Baptist missionary Evan Jones allied with the Presbyterians and took the side of those who wished to remain in the east. Jones was to find himself an enemy of the Government, fighting a lost cause and his Indians were forced west by the military. McCoy sympathised with Jones in his attitude and always argued that the case of the Cherokees was different from all the other poorer tribes. He had always campaigned for a voluntary move from a worse position to a better and was totally against enforced removal.

The Indian Territory to belong to the Indians 'as long as grass shall grow and water shall run'
The initial boundaries of the country which was now designed as a permanent home for the Indians 'as long as grass shall grow'. McCoy describes in 1836 as:

> The country which we denominate the *Indian Territory,* is bounded as follows: Beginning at the source of a small river called Puncah, after a small tribe of Indians of that name, and running down the same eastwardly to Missouri river: thence down Missouri still eastwardly, about one hundred, and fifty miles: thence down Missouri southwardly, about two hundred miles, to the western line of the State of Missouri: thence south along said western line, to the N. W. corner of the State of Arkansas: thence southwardly on the western line of Arkansas, about seventy-eight miles to Arkansas river: thence south on the line of Arkansas to Red River: thence up Red River westwardly, to a meridian two hundred miles west: thence northwardly to the beginning. The whole about equal to a tract of six hundred miles long, and two hundred miles wide.
> It is proposed to limit the Territory to the distance of two hundred miles west of Arkansas and Missouri because the country farther west, for the distance of several hundred miles, is uninhabitable on account of the absence of wood.

Upon the propriety of establishing an Indian Territory, the southern boundary of which shall be Red River, and the eastern the States of Arkansas. and Missouri and Missouri river, there appears to be great unanimity of sentiment among government men. A Bill to this effect, and similar in its provisions to that before the Senate has been before the House of Representatives for the last three sessions of Congress. The condition of the tribes within the Territory, and their relation to one another, and to the U. States, are such as daily increase the necessity of civil organization.

The outlines of the plan of organization, are briefly the following, viz: Delegates are to be chosen by the several tribes, to represent them in a general council, once a year, or oftener if necessary. The character of this council will be similar to that of the legislative council of one of our Territories. It will be competent to enact laws of a general nature for the Territory. These laws will take effect after they have been approved by the President of the U. States. Each tribe will enact laws which relate merely to its own internal concerns: similar to the action of townships, or of city corporations. The tribes thus confederated, will choose a delegate, who must be an Indian, to represent them at the seat of government of the U. States, during each session of Congress; and who will act as agent for his constituents. He will be paid by the U. States and his compensation will be equal to that of a member of Congress. All civil offices, excepting two, which shall be created in the Territory by this organisation, will be filled by Indians, if such be found competent to discharge the duties.

In addition to the security given the tribes of their possessions by treaty stipulations, they may hold their lands by patents from the government of the U. States.'[1]

McCoy pooled back all his wages and income into the Mission

It must be repeated again and again in face of modern Roman Catholic and Mormon criticism that McCoy made himself rich through his Indian ministry that McCoy ploughed all his earnings back into the mission and refused to take any reward whatsoever from the Indians. Edward and Wallace

---

[1] See *Periodical Account of Baptist Missions within the Indian Territory for the Year Ending December 31,* 1836, pp. 6-7. and also *Remarks on the Practicability of Indian Reform, Embracing their Colonialization,* 1829.

Cone have well said of their father's best friend:[1]

> What men of the world would think a foolish honesty pre-
> vented Mr. McCoy from being a very rich man. At almost every
> cession of their lands to the United States by the Indian tribes,
> they insisted upon making it one of the conditions of the cession
> that he should receive a part of the land conveyed, and the ex-
> pression of their desire would have ensured the prompt acquies-
> cence of the government. But he invariably and peremptorily for-
> bade it. His desire was for the soul of the Indian, not for his lands;
> and his knowledge of human nature taught him that the least
> appearance even of a selfish care of his own interests would de-
> stroy his usefulness amongst them as a missionary.[2]

A sad tale

The part the American Baptist Foreign Missions Board played in the evangelising of the Indians is one of the saddest tales in the history of missions
and the American nation. From the very start, the Board failed to keep their
promises of support to McCoy, yet they fed the nation's Baptists with
glowing reports of McCoy's successes, decorated with their own lavish
stories of how funds were being sent to them. The truth was that the Board
saw in the monies that were coming in for Indian improvement a means of
financing their own commercial projects and work overseas. They demanded of all supporting churches and societies, a minimum membership
fee of $100 per annum and told the churches that they must not ear-mark
donations for Indian missions but trust in the Board's discretion. Soon the
Board members stopped regarding themselves as church, association and
society representatives and stewards of their evangelistic funds and took
on the role of a para-church business enterprise. Luther Rice, who had left
the mission field to head the Board, was said to have embezzled $1,300
Indian mission funding to pay off private debts, but the records show that
he was largely used as a scapegoat by the other members of the Board. To
cover up the scandal, Rice was merely deprived of his office without legal
steps being taken. Further Board members invested mission funds in a
newspaper and a publishing company which went bankrupt. The largest
fund-eater was the Columbian College, an educational project that also

---

[1] Spencer Cone, their father, was a founder member of the American Baptist Home
Mission.

[2] *Some Account of the Life of Spencer Houghton Cone, A Baptist Preacher in America,*
New York, 1856.

proved a flop. It was also a strongly racist organisation as McCoy found to his dismay. He sent seven Christian Indian students to the college who had shown great progress and wished to become missionaries to their own people. The Board refused to accept them, even though the Government promised to finance them. It was simply against their principles to grant the Indians higher education. McCoy was the means of gaining grants of thousands of dollars yearly for the Board and so improved the land on which his mission stations stood, that when they were sold because of the move to the west, the Board made tremendous gains, $5,721.50 on Carey alone. The Government maintained that these monies must be used to support the Indian missions in the New Territories. When Johnston Lykins opened the first mission station and school in the Indian Territory, the Board refused to give him a penny and he had to raise $1,500 himself, which he never recovered from the Board. By 1837, the Board had begun to dismantle the Indian mission piece by piece. When McCoy and Lykins protested that they had ample evidence that the Board were leaving their missionaries to starve and yet were using enormous funds earmarked for the Indians for other ends, McCoy was dismissed and Lykins was forced to resign. From then on, the Board did not send out any more missionaries to the Indians.

The founding of the American Indian Mission Association
This was too much for the staunch Kentucky and western frontier Baptists. With their troubles during the Campbellite infiltration mainly over, they rallied around McCoy and founded the American Indian Mission Association. This organisation was to be entirely church centred, each member church supporting its own missionary to the Indians. This work was so blessed that it gradually absorbed the work of the Baptist Board of Foreign Missions. McCoy became the A.I.M.A's Corresponding Secretary and many of the Board's missionaries joined the new work, which for them, was only a continuation of the old.

McCoy's last dying thoughts were with the Indians
Isaac McCoy had withstood many hardships as a missionary and won many battles but the wounds occurred were manifold as a result of his sufferings: his chest was crushed, his spine was twisted and a thigh-joint out of place. Though McCoy was always a very handsome man, as a result of his injuries, he could not walk upright and limped badly, often in great pain. He was given up for dead at least half a dozen times because of high fevers and his extremities had suffered frost-bite on numerous occasions

whilst embarking on journeys of a thousand miles and more on behalf of the Indians. Sleeping on wet or frozen ground in the same soaking clothing for weeks on end is hardly designed to make a man fit and healthy. McCoy travelled to Jeffersonville to preach on June 1, 1846 and on returning to his home in Louisville caught a cold which brought on the old complaint which he called 'putrid fever'. After an illness of three weeks, McCoy died at the age of sixty three, his work being done. His last words were, 'Tell the brethren to never let the Indian mission decline.' He was spared the further pain of seeing the Union, and with it the Baptist churches, split down the middle by the slavery question and the Civil War. His work was gradually absorbed into the domestic mission of the Southern Baptist Convention. He was buried in Louisville's Western Cemetery in a very humble grave and nobody seems to have noticed until long afterwards that the dates on the tomb stone were wrong by ten years. The inscription, however, was fitting and this reads:

Rev. Isaac McCoy,

Born June 13, 1784.
Died June 21, 1836.

For near thirty years his entire time and energies were devoted to the civil and religious improvement of the aboriginal tribes of this country. He projected and founded the plan of their colonisation, their only hope, and the imperishable monument of his wisdom and benevolence.

The Indians' friend—for them he toiled through life;
For them in death he breathed his final prayer.
Now from his toil he rests—the care, the strife.
He waits in heaven, his work to follow there.

In conclusion

I consider Isaac McCoy one of God's greatest 'Mountain Movers' and a man who has left a lasting imprint on my own life. All these godly people recorded in these pages have influenced me more than I can tell and have been a constant cloud of witnesses, used of God to guide me along His paths throughout my Christian life. One of the great charms of becoming elderly and gradually reaching life's journey's end, is the knowledge that all these mighty mentors will be there in Glory to bid me welcome one fine day when the Lord comes quickly to take me home. Even so, come, Lord Jesus.

Bibliography

Biographies other than those included in editions of collected works

Alexander, J.H., *More Than Notion*, Zoar Publications, 1976.

Andrews, J. R., *George Whitefield, A Light Rising in Obscurity*, Sovereign Grace Union, 1930.

Anonymous, *Life and Times of Selina Countess of Huntingdon* (2 vols), London, 1839.

Anonymous, *Life of the Rev. Augustus Montague Toplady, Vicar of Broad-Hembury*, Christian Biography Series, Religious Tract Society, undated.

Anonymous, *The Voice of Years*, A. Maxwell, 1814, Reprinted by John Crowter, Coventry.

Bailey, G. S., *The Carey Indian Mission at Niles, Michigan and Rev. Isaac McCoy, Its Founder*, St. Joseph River Baptist Association, Christian Herald Print, 1880.

Barker, William, *Puritan Profiles*, Mentor, 1996.

Beall, O.T. and Schryock, R.H., *Cotton Mather: First Significant Figure in American Medicine*, Baltimore, 1954.

Boas, Ralf and Louise, *Cotton Mather Keeper of the Puritan Conscience*, Harper & Brothers, 1928.

Bremer, Francis J., *The Puritan Experiment: New England Society from Bradford to Edwards*, London, 1977.

Brook, Benjamin, *The Lives of the Puritans*, 3 vols, Soli Deo Gloria, 1994.

Broome, John R., *Dr. John Gill*, Gospel Standard Publications, 1991.

Brown, John, *Memoirs of the Life and Character of the Late Rev. James Hervey, A. M.*, London, 1822.

Brown, John, *The Pilgrim Fathers of New England*, RTS, 1897.

Bull, Josiah, *John Newton: An Autobiography and Narrative*, The Religious Tract Society, London, 1868. (Contains Cowper's commentary on John's Gospel).

Bull, Josiah, *Memorials of the Rev. William Bull*, James Nisbet, London, 1864.

Busch, Wilhelm, *Plaudereien in Meinem Studierzimmer*, Schriftenmissionsverlag, 1965.

Cecil, Lord David, *The Stricken Deer / The Life of Cowper*, London, 1944.

Chalmers, A., *Life of Toplady*, Biographical Dictionary.

Cheever, George Barrell, *Lectures on the Life, Genius and Insanity of Cowper*, New York, 1856.

Christoffersen Svein Aage, (ed.), *Hans Nielsen Hauge og det moderne Norge*. Norges Forskningsråd. KULTs skriftserie nr 48, 1996.

Coleman, Thomas, *The Two Thousand Confessors of Sixteen Hundred and Sixty-Two*, John Snow, London, 1860.

Colstrup, Preben (ed.), *Hans Nielsen Hauge—Helt på jordet*. Norsk kristent Barneblad 1996.

Conant, H. C., *The Earnest Man: A Memoir of Adoniram Judson, D.D.*, London, 1861.

Cone, Edward and Cone, Wallace, *Some Account of the Life of Spencer Houghton Cone, A Baptist Preacher in America*, New York, 1856.

Coxon, Francis, *Christian Worthies* (2 vols), Zoar Publications, 1980.

Cragg, George G., *Grimshaw of Haworth*, London, 1947.

Craner, Thomas, *A Grain of Gratitude. A Sermon Occasioned by the Death of that Venerable, Learned, Pious and Judicious Divine The Revd John Gill D. D.*, London, 1771.

Culross, Dr James, *The Three Rylands* (Introduction by W. Ryland) Dent Adkins, London 1897.

Dallimore, Arnold, *George Whitefield* (2 vols.), Banner of Truth, 1979.

Dallimore, Arnold, *Spurgeon*, Banner of Truth, 1985.

Deacon, Malcolm, *Philip Doddridge of Northampton (1702-51)*, Northamptonshire Libraries, 1980.

Dictionary of National Biography, OUP.

Drake, Samuel G, M. A., *Memoir of Cotton Mather, D.D., F.R.S.*, reprinted in BTT edition, otherwise in 1853 Hartford edition.

Edwards, Jonathan, *The Life of the Rev. David Brainerd*, Christian Biography, Religious Tract Society, undated.

Ella, G. M., *James Hervey: Preacher of Righteousness*, Go Publications, 1997.

Ella, G. M., *John Gill and the Cause of God and Truth*, Go Publications, 1995.

Ella, G. M., *William Cowper: Poet of Paradise*, Evangelical Press, 1993.

Ella, G. M., *William Huntington: Paster of Providence*, Evangelical Press, 1994.

Farncombe, F. J., ed., *William Huntington, S.S.*, London, 1923.

Fausset, Hugh I' Anson, *William Cowper*, New York, 1968.

Fellows, John, *An Elegy on the Death of the Revd John Gill, D. D.*, London, 1771.

Free, William N., *William Cowper*, New York, 1970.

Fuller, Morris, *The Life, Letters & Writings of John Davenant, D. D., 1572-1641*, Methuen, 1897.

Fullerton, W. Y., *C. H. Spurgeon*, 1920.

Gadsby, J., *Memoirs of Hymn-Writers and Compilers*, Primitive Baptist Library, 1978.

Gaskin, J. M., *Baptist Women in Oklahoma*, Messenger Press, undated.

George, Timothy and Dockery, David, *Baptist Theologians*, Broadman Press, 1990.

Gillies, John, *Memoirs of the Life of the Reverend George Whitefield, M. A.*, T. Johnston, Falkirk, 1798.

Haddcock, Louise and Gaskin, J.M., *Baptist Heroes in Oklahoma*, Messenger Press, 1976.

Halvorsen, Jan, *Hans Nielsen Hauge og Åndens kraft*. Hermon forlag 1996.

Harper, James, *Memoir of the Rev. Ebenezer Erskine, A. M., Father of the Secession Church*, United Presbyterian Fathers, Fullarton & Co., 1849.

Harrison, Graham, *Dr. John Gill and His Teaching*, Evangelical Library, 1971.

Hartley, Lodwick C., *William Cowper: Humanitarian*, North Caroliana University Press,1938.

Hauss, Friedrich, *Väter der Christenheit* (3 vols), Wuppertal, 1959.

Hayward, Elizabeth, *John M'Coy: His Life and His Diaries*, The American Historical Company, Inc. New York, 1848.

Hazelrigg, Grey, (Ed.), *Footsteps of Mercy*, Coventry, 1993.

Hazelton, John E., *'Hold-Fast!' A Sketch of Covenant Truth and Its Witnesses*, Truth for Today, 1997.

Hooper, Ebenezer, *Huntington: Facts and Letters*, Collingridge, 1872, Reprinted by John Crowter, Coventry, 1993.

Hooper, Ebenezer, *The Celebrated Coalheaver*, Gadsby, 1871, Reprinted by John Crowter, Coventry, 1993.

Houghton, Elsie, *Christian Hymn-writers*, Evangelical Press of Wales, 1984,

Houghton, S. M. (ed.), *Five Pioneer Missionaries*, Banner of Truth, 1987.

Huntley, Frank L., *Bishop Joseph Hall 1574-1656*, Cambridge, 1979.

J. H. O., *Hervey, James (1714-1758)*, Dictionary of National Biography, vol. ix, OUP, pp. 733-735.

Janeway, James, *Invisibles, Realities, Demonstrated in the Holy Life and Truiumphant Death of John Janeway*, London, 1885.

Jay, William, *The Autobiography of William Jay*, Banner of Truth, 1974.

Ker, John and Watson, Jean, *Ralph and Ebenezer Erskine*, Edinburgh, 1880.

King, James, *William Cowper*, Duke University Press, 1986.

Krajewski, Ekkehard, *Leben und Sterben des Züricher Täuferführers Felix Manz*, Oncken, 1962.

Kullerud, Dag, *Hans Nielsen Hauge.—Mannen som vekket Norge*.Aschehoug 1996.

Kunitz & Haycroft, *American Authors 1600-1900: A Bibliographical Dictionary*, New York, 1968, pp. 514-518.

Lawton, G *Within the Rock of Ages*, James Clarke & Co. 1983.

Lewis, Peter, *The Genius of Puritanism*, Carey Publications, 1979.

Lloyd-Jones, D. M., *The Puritans: Their Origins and Successors*, Banner of Truth, 1987.

Lovelace, Richard F., *The American Pietism of Cotton Mather: Origins of American Evangelicalism*, Christian University Press, 1968.

Lyons, Emory J., *Isaac McCoy: His Plan of and Work For Indian Colonization*, History Series No. 1., ed. F. B. Streeter, Fort Hays Kansas State College Studies, 1945.

Magnus, Alv Johan, *Veirydder med gnagsår. Hans Nielsen Hauge og vekkelsen som forandret Norge*. Prokla Media, 1996.

Malone, Dumas ed., *Isaac McCoy*, (signed E. E. D.), Dictionary of American Biography, vol. vi, Charles Scribneis & Sons, N. Y., 1933.

Marvin, Abijah P., *The Life and Times of Cotton Mather, D.D., F.R.S. or A Boston Minister of Two Centuries Ago 1663-1728*, reprint of 1892 edition, Haskell House, 1973.

May, G. Lacey, *Some Eighteenth Century Churchmen; Glimpses of English Church Life in the Eighteenth Century*, Society for Promoting Christian Knowledge, London, 1920.

McCormick, Calvin, *The Memoir of Miss Eliza McCoy*, Dallas, 1892.

McLoughlin, William G., *Champions of the Cherokees: Evan and John B. Jones*, Princeton University Press, 1989.

McMurtrie, Douglas C. and Allen, Albert H., *Jotham Meeker: Pioneer Printer of Kansas*, Chicago, 1930.

Michaud, L., *Biographie Universelle Ancienne et Moderne*, Nouvelle Edition, Tome Dix Neuvième.

Middlekauff, Robert, *The Mathers: Three Generations of Puritan Intellectuals 1596-1728*, OUP, 1976.

Middleton, Erasmus, *Biographia Evangelica* (4 vols) Gill in vol. 4, Subscription, 1784.

Miller, Graham, *The Huntingtonians*, Huntingtonian Press, 1995.

Murdock, Kenneth B., *Increase Mather: The Foremost American Puritan*, Cambridge, Harvard University Press, 1925.

Murray, Iain (ed.), *C. H. Spurgeon: Autobiography* (2 vols), Banner of Truth, 1973.

Murray, Iain, *The Forgotten Spurgeon*, Banner of Truth, 1986.

Neal, Daniel N., *The History of the Puritans* (3 vols), Klock & Klock reprint, 1979.

Newman, William, *Rylandia: Reminiscences*, London, 1835.

Nicholson, Norman, *William Cowper*, London, 1951.

Norborg, Sverre, *Hans Nielsen Hauge, biografi*. Cappelen 1966 og 1970.

Nuttall, Geoffrey F., ed., *Philip Doddridge 1702-51: His Contribution to English Religion*.

O'Beirne, H. F., *Leaders and Leading Men of the Indian Territory*, American Publishers' Association, 1891.

Padwick Constance, *Henry Martyn: The Pioneer Translator Who Opened the Scriptures to the Muslim and Hindu Worlds*, Moody Press, 1980.

Padwick, Constance, *Henry Martyn: Confessor of the Faith*, IVF, 1953.

Page, Jesse, *David Brainerd: The Apostle to the North American Indians*, S. W. Partridge, undated.

Page, Jesse, *Henry Martyn of India and Persia*, Pickering and Inglis, undated.

Peabody, W. B. O., *Life of Cotton Mather*, J. Spark's The Library of American Biography, vi, p 163 ff.

Pennington, Donald and Thomas, Keith, *Puritans and Revolutionaries*, Clarendon Press, 1978.

Pike, G. Holden, *The Life and Work of Charles Haddon Spurgeon*, Banner of Truth, 1991.

Pond, E., *The Lives of Increase Mather and Sir William Phipps*, Boston, 1870.

Poole, W. F., *Cotton Mather and Witchcraft, Two notices of Mr. Upham. His Reply*, Boston, 1870.

Quinlan, Maurice J., *William Cowper: A Critical Life*, University of Minnesota Press, 1953.

Ramsbottom, B. A., *Stranger Than Fiction: The Life of William Kiffin*, Gospel Standard Trust Publications, 1989.

Reid, James, *Memoirs of the Westminster Divines*, Banner of Truth, 1982.

Reynolds, J. S., *The Evangelicals at Oxford 1735-1871*, Blackwell, Oxford, 1953.

Rippon, John, *Life and Writings of the Rev. John Gill. D.D.*, Gano Books, 1992.

Roberts, William. ed, *Memoirs of the Life and Correspondence of Mrs Hannah More*, New York, 1838.

Row, Walter, *Memoirs of Augustus Toplady, A. B.*, London, 1813, vol. v, Works.

Ryland, John, *The Character of the Rev. James Hervey, A. M. (including a collection of Hervey's letters to Ryland)*, London, 1791.

Ryle, J. C., *Christian Leaders of the Eighteenth Century*, Banner of Truth, 1978.

Sant, Henry and Ella, George M., *William Huntington: The Sinner Saved*, Focus Christian Ministries Trust, undated, (Essays published courtesy of the Bible League Quarterly).

Sant, Henry, *A Vindication of William Huntington*, private publication.

Sant, Henry, *The Life and Labours of William Huntington: A paper given to mark the 250th anniversary of Huntington's birth*, Huntingtonian Press, undated.

Sargent, John, *The Life and Letters of Henry Martyn*, Banner of Truth, 1985.

Schulz, George A., *An Indian Canaan: Isaac McCoy and the Vision of an Indian State*, University of Oklahoma Press, 1972.

Shea Jr., Daniel B., *Spiritual Autobiography in Early America*, Princeton, 1968.

Smith, George, *Henry Martyn: Saint and Scholar*, Religious Tract Society, 1892.

Spurgeon, C. H., *The Metropolitan Tabernacle: Its History and Work*, Passmore & Alabaster, 1876.

Stanford, Dr Charles, *Men Worth Remembering: Philip Doddridge*, Hodder & Stoughton, 1880.

Stevens, John, *Help for the True Disciples of Immanuel: Being an Answer to a Book, Published by the Late Rev. Andrew Fuller, entitled The Gospel Worthy of All Acceptation or, the Duty of Sinners to believe in Christ*, 3rd edit., Simpkin and Marshall, 1841.

Stevens, John, *The Pleasure of God in the Salvation of His People*, Simkin and Marshall, 3rd edit., 1844.

Stevens, William, *Recollections of the Late William Huntington*, Gadsby, 1868, Reprinted by John Crowter, 1993.

Stewart, W. S., *Early Baptist Missionaries and Pioneers, Isaac McCoy*, VIII, pp 189-228.

Stokes, Henry Paine, *Cowper Memorials*, Oliver Ratcliff at the Cowper Press, 1904.

Symington, Andrew J., *The Poet of Home Life: Centenary Memorials of William Cowper*, 'Home Words' Office, London, 1900.

Taylor, Thomas, *The Life of William Cowper*, R.B. Seeley and W. Burnside, 1835, 4th ed..

Thomas, Gilbert, *William Cowper and the Eighteenth Century*, London, Allen & Unwin, 1948.

Thorvaldsen, Steinar, *Visjonen Bak Plogspissen: Om Hans Nielsen Hauge ved hans 200-års jubileum*, Høgskolen i Tromsø, 1996, college web-site also steinar@hitos.no .

Tyerman, Luke, *The Life of the Reverend George Whitefield* (2 vols), Need of the Times Publishers, Hodder and Stoughton reprint, 1995.

Tyerman, Luke, *The Oxford Methodists: Memoirs of the Rev. Messers. Clayton, Ingham, Gambold, Hervey, and Broughton*, New York, 1873.

Valen, L. J. van, *Van kolendrager tot predikant: Het leven van William Huntington (1745-1813)*, Den Hertog-Houten, 1996.

Watkins, J. *Essay on the Character and Writings of Mr Toplady*, 1832.

Wedgwood, C. V., *The Trial of Charles I*, Reprint Society London, 1864.

Welsby, Paul, *George Abbot: The Unwanted Archbishop 1562-1633*, SPCK, 1962.

Wendell, Barrett, *Cotton Mather*, N.Y., 1891, also Barnes & Noble, 1992.

Whyte, Alexander, *Thomas Shepard, Pilgrim Father and Founder of Harvard, His Spiritual Experience and Experimental Preaching*, Oliphant Anderson and Ferrier, 1909.

Williams, John, *Memoirs of the Life and Writings of the Rev Robert Hawker DD*, Ebenezer Palmer, 1831.

Willison, George F., *Saints and Strangers: Being the Lives of the Pilgrim Fathers etc.*, New York, 1954.

Winters, W., *Memoirs of the Life and Writings of the Rev. A. M. Toplady, B. A.*, London, 1872.

Wolever, Terry, *The Life and Ministry of John Gano* (Vol 1), The Philadelphia Association Series, Particular Baptist Press, 1998.

Wright, Thomas, *The Life of Augustus M. Toplady*, Farncombe, 1911.

Wright, Thomas, *The Life of William Cowper*, London, 1892.

Wright, Thomas, *The Life of William Huntington*, Farncombe & Son, 1909.

Wyeth, Walter N., *Isaac McCoy: A Memorial*, Philadelphia, 1895.

Church Histories

Abbey/Overton, Charles/John H., *The English Church in the Eighteenth Century*, Longmans, Green & Co., 1887.

Adair, John, *Founding Fathers: The Puritans in England and America*, Baker Book House, 1986.

Armitage, Thomas, *A History of the Baptists* (2 vols), Baptist Heritage Press, 1988.

Balleine, G. R., *A History of the Evangelical Party in the Church of England*, Longmans, Green & Co., London, 1911.

Balleine, G. R., *A Layman's History of the Church of England*, Longman's, Green & Co., 1923.

Baptist Record Society, *The Records of a Church of Christ in Bristol 1640-1687*, 1974.

Bartlett, W. H., *The Pilgrim Fathers of New England*, Nelson & Sons, 1866.

Blackie and Son, 1862.Carlile, J. C., *The History of the English Baptists*, James Clarke, London, 1905.

Bready, J. Wesley, *England: Before and After Wesley*, Hodder and Stoughton, 1939

Bremer, Francis, *The Puritan Experiment*, St. James Press, 1977.

Brown, Raymond, *The English Baptists of the 18th Century*, Baptist Historical Society, 1986

Cady, John F., *The Origin and Development of the Missionary Baptist Church in Indiana*, Franklin College, 1942.

Campbell, Douglas, *The Puritan in Holland, England, and America: An Introduction to American History* (2 vols), Harper, 1893.

Carpenter, S. C., *Church and People 1789-1889* (3 vols), SPCK, London, 1933.

Carter, C. Sydney, *The English Church in the Eighteenth Century*, Church Bookroom Press, 1948.

Christian, John T., *A History of the Baptists* (2 vols), Bogard Press, Texas, undated.

Clifford, John, *The English Baptists: Who They Are and What They Have Done*, London, 1881.

Cockshott, Winnifred, *The Pilgrim Fathers*, Methuen & Co, 1909.

Cornish, Warre F., *A History of the English Church in the Nineteenth Century* (2 vols), Macmillan, 1933

Cragg, G. R., *The Church and the Age of Reason*, Penguin Books, 1960.

Cramp, J. M., *Baptist History*, Elliot Stock, London, 1871.

Crosby, Thomas, *The History of the English Baptists* (4 vols), Church History Research, 1978.

Davis, Horton, *The Worship of the American Puritans, 1629-1730*, Pewter Lang, 1990.

Donat, Rudolf, *Das wachsende Werk*, Oncken, 1960.

Fiske, John, *The Beginnings of New England Or the Puritan Theocracy in Its Relation to Civil and Religious Liberty*, Macmillan, 1889.

Frere, W. H., *The English Church in the Reigns of Elizabeth and James I*, London, 1904.

Gammell, William, *A History of American Baptist Missions in Asia, Africa, Europe and North America*, Boston, 1849.

Gardner, James, *The English Church in the Sixteenth Century*, London, 1902.

Gaustad, Edwin S., *Liberty of Conscience: Roger William in America*, Eerdmans, 1991.

Goadby, J. J., *Bye-Paths in Baptist History*, Elliot Stock, London, 1871.

Gustafsson, Berndt, *Svensk kyrkohistoria*, Verbum, 1957.

Hamilton, Robert, *The Gospel Among the Red Men: The History of Southern Baptist Indian Missions*, Nashville, 1930.

Harrison, Archibald, W., *The Evangelical Revival and Christian Reunion*, Epworth, Press, 1942.

Hart, A. Tindal, *The Curate's Lot*, John Baker, London, 1970.

Hart, A. Tyndal, *The Eighteenth Century Country Parson*, Wilding & Son Ltd, 1955.

Hayden, Eric W., *A History of Spurgeon's Tabernacle*, Pilgrim Publications, 1971.

Hayden, Roger, *English Baptist History & Heritage*, BU, 1990.

Hoad, Jack, *The Baptist*, Grace Publications, 1986.

Hutton, W. H., *The English Church from the Accession of Charles I. to the Death of Anne 1625-1714*, London, 1903.

Ivimey, Joseph, *A History of the Baptists* (4 vols), London, 1814.

Light, Alfred W., *Bunhill Fields*, Farncombe, London, 1915.

Littel, F. H., *Das Selbstverständnis der Täufer*, Oncken, 1966.

Lloyd-Jones, D.M., *The Puritans: Their Origins and Successors*, Banner of Truth, 1987.

Loane, Marcus, *Oxford and the Evangelical Succession*, Lutterworth Press, London, 1950.

Lowance, Jr., Mason I., *The Language of Canaan*, Harvard University Press, 1980.

Macaulay, Thomas B., *The History of England From the Accession of James II*, Everyman, 1917.

McLoughlin, William G., *Cherokees & Missionaries, 1789-1837*, University of Oklahoma Press, 1994.

Miller, Perry, ed., *The American Puritans: Their Prose and Poetry*, Doubleday Anchor Books, 1956.

Moorman, J. R. H., *A History of the Church in England*, Black, 1958.

More, Martin, *Boston Revival, 1842. A Brief History of the Evangelical Churches of Boston Together With a More Particular Account of the Revival of 1842*, Richard Owen Roberts, 1980.

Murray, Iain, *Revival & Revivalism: The Making and Marring of American Evangelism, 1750-1858*, Banner of Truth, 1994.

Murray, Iain, *The Puritan Hope*, Banner of Truth, 1975.

Naylor, Peter, *Picking up a Pin for the Lord*, Grace Publications, 1992.

Nettles, Thomas J., *By His Grace and For His Glory*, Baker Book House, 1990.

Noll, Mark A., *A History of Christianity in the United States and Canada*, SPCK, 1992.

Ollard, S. L., *The Six Students of St. Edmund Hall: Expelled from the University of Oxford in 1768*, A. R. Mowbray, 1911.

Olsen, V. Norskov, *Johne Foxe and the Elizabethan Church*, University of California Press, 1973.

Overton, John H. / Relton, Frederic, *The English Church 1714-1800*, Macmillan, London, 1906.

Overton, John H., *The Church of England* (2 vols), London, 1897.

Paul, S. F., *Historical Sketch of the Gospel Standard Baptists*, Gospel Standard Publications, 1961.

Peck, Solomon (ed.) *History of the Missions of the Baptist General Convention, in History of American Missions to the Heathen*, Worster, 1840, Johnson Reprint Corporation, 1970.

Pennington, David and Thomas, eds., *Puritans and Revolutionaries: Essays in Seventeenth-Century History Presented to Christopher Hill*, Oxford, 1978.

Plummer, Alfred, *The Church of England in the 18ᵗʰ Century*, Methuen, London, 1910.

Poole-Connor, E. J., *Evangelicalism in England*, FIEC, London, 1951.

Ray, D. B., *Baptist Succession*, Church History Research, 1984.

Ringwald, Alfred, ed., *Menshen vor Gott* (4 vols), Stuttgart, 1957.

Rister, Carl Coke, *Baptist Missions among the American Indians, Home Mission Board*, Atlanta, 1944.

Robertson, Sir Charles Grant, *England under the Hanoverians*, Methuen, London, 1938.

Robinson, Charles Henry, *History of Christian Missions*, T. & T. Clark, 1915.

Routh, E. C., *The Story of Oklahoma Baptists*, Baptist General Convention, 1932.

Scot, Thomas, *Letters and Papers*, ed. John Scot A.M., Seeley and Sons, London, 1824.

Sharp, W. A. Seward, *History of Kansas Baptists*, The Kansas City Seminary Press, 1940.

Sheehan, R. J., *C. H. Spurgeon and the Modern Church*, Grace Publications, 1985.

Simon, John S., Robert Culley, *The Revival of Religion in England in the Eighteenth Century*, London, undated.

Spencer, J. H., *A History of the Kentucky Baptists (1886)* (2 vols), republished by Church History Research & Archives, Lafayette, Tennessee, 1976.

Spurgeon, Charles Haddon, *The Downgrade Controversy*, Pilgrim Publications, Texas, undated.

Stoughton, J., *Religion in England under Queen Anne and the Georges* (2 vols), Hodder and Stoughton, 1878.

Sweet, W. William, *The Story of Religion in America*, Baker Book House, 1979.

Tracy, Joseph, *The Great Awakening*, Banner of Truth, 1976.

Tyler, Bennet, *New England Revivals*, Richard Owen Roberts, 1980.

Underwood, A. C., *A History of the English Baptists*, Carey Kingsgate, London, 1961.

Valen, L. J. van, *Een Rijke Oogst: De opwekking in Schotland in 1742*, J. J. Groen en Zoon, 1993.

Vedder, H. C., *A Short History of the Baptists*, Baptist Tract and Book Society, 1898.

Wakeman, Henry Offley, *An Introduction to the History of the Church of England*, Rivington's, 1914.

Walker, Robert Sparks, *Torchlights to the Cherokees: The Brainerd Mission*, Macmillan, 1931.

Walker, Williston, *A History of the Christian Church*, (revised ed.), Clark, 1958.

Watts, Michael R., *The Dissenters*, Clarendon Press, 1978.

Westin, Gunnar, *I den svenska frikyrklighetens genombrottstid*, Westerbergs, 1963.

White, B. R., (ed.), *Association Records of the Particular Baptists of England, Wales and Ireland to 1660, (Index by Howard, K. W. H.) Parts 1-3*, Baptist Historical Society, 1971-1977.

White, B. R., *The English Baptists of the 17ᵗʰ Century*, Baptist Historical Society, 1983.

White, Charles, L. *A Century of Faith, The American Baptist Home Mission Society*, Judson Press, 1932.

White, Mary Emily, *The Missionary Work of the Southern Baptist Convention*, Philadelphia, 1902.

Whiteley, J. H., *Wesley's England*, Epworth Press, 1945.

Whitley, W. T., *A History of British Baptists*, Kingsgate, London, 1932.

Whitley, W. T., *Calvinism and Evangelism in England especially among Baptists*, London, the Kingsgate Press, 1933.

Willison, George F., *Saints and Strangers*, Reynal & Hitchcock, 1945.

Wood, A. Skevington, *The Inextinguishable Blaze*, Paternoster Press, London, 1960.

Yoder, John H., *Täufertum und Reformation im Gespräch*, EVZ-Verlag, Zürich, 1968.

Background Material and Secular History

Addison, William, *The English Country Parson*, Dent, London, 1948.

Allen, Rowland H., *The New England Tragedies in Prose*, Boston, 1869. See Longfellow (poems) below.

Barnes and Noble, *An Outline History of English Literature*, vol. 2, New York, 1961.

Baugh, Albert C., *A Literary History of England*, London, 1948.

Benson, Louis F., *The English Hymn: Its Development and Use in Worship*, Hodder & Stoughton, 1915.

Berkhofer, Robert F., *A New Introduction to Isaac McCoy's History of Baptist Indian Missions*, Johnson Reprint Corporation, New York and London, 1970.

Birrell, Augustine, *Res Judicatae*, London, 1892.

Brooke, Stopford Augustus, *Theology in the English Poets*, Everyman's Library, (Introduction dated 1874).

Brown, William Adams, *The Church in America*, Macmillan, 1922.

Burr, G. L., *Narratives of the Witchcraft Cases 1648-1706*, New York, 1914.

Catlin, George, *Letters and Notes on the North American Indians*, ed. Mooney, Michael MacDonald, Gramercy Books, 1995.

Clarkson, Thomas, *The History of the Abolition of the Slave Trade*, London, 1808.

Clifford, J.L., *Eighteenth Century English Literature*, New York, 1959.

Crofts. J.E.V., *Eighteenth Century Literature: An Oxford Miscellany*, 1909.

Curteis, George Herbert, *Dissent in Relation to the Church of England*, Macmillan, London, 1906.

Cutler, William G., *History of the State of Kansas*, A. T. Andreas, 1883, as reproduced in the Kansas Collection Douglas, James, New England and New France, Toronto, 1913.

Davis, Horton, *The Worship of the American Puritans 1629-1730*, Peter Lang, 1990.

Day, M.S., *English Literature, 1660-1837*, (2), New York, 1963.

Debo, Angie, *And Still Waters Run: The Betrayal of the Five Civilized Tribes*, University of Oklahoma Press, 1989.

Dewar, Canon M. W. (ed.), *An Exact Diary of the Late Expedition of His Illustrious Highness the Prince Orange*, 1689, Reprint Focus Christian Ministries Trust (undated).

Drake, S. G., *The Witchcraft Delusion in New England*, Roxbury, 1866.

Eaton, Rachel, *John Ross and the Cherokee Indians*, University of Chicago, 1921.

Edwards, William, *Notes on European History* (6 vols), Rivingtons, 1948.

Ehle, John, *Trail of Tears: The Rise and Fall of the Cherokee Nation*, Anchor Books, 1989.

Elton, Oliver, *A Survey of English Literature (1780-1830)*, (2 vols), London, 1933.

Fagan, Brian M., *Kingdoms of Gold, Kingdoms of Jade: The Americas Before Columbus*, Thames and Hudson, 1991.

Fairchild, Hoxie N., *Religious Trends in English Poetry*, (5 vols), New York, 1939-1962.

Feingold, Richard, *Nature and Society: Later Eighteenth-Century Uses of the Pastoral and Georgic*, 1978.

Foreman, Grant, *The Five Civilized Tribes*, University of Oklahoma Press, undated reprint of 1934 edn, vol. 8 The Civilization of the American Indian Series.

Garraty, John A., *American History*, HBJ, 1982.

Gibson, Arrell M., *Oklahoma: A History of Five Centuries*, Harlow Publishing Corporation and University of Oklahoma Press, 1965 and 1981 editions.

Gill, Frederick C., *The Romantic Movement and Methodism*, Haskell House, New York, 1966.

Goodall, Abner C., *Further Notes on the History of Witchcraft in Massachusetts*, Cambridge, 1884.

Graham, Walter, *English Literary Periodicals*, New York, 1930.

Hale, John, *A Modest Inquiry Into the Nature of Witchcraft*, Boston, 1698.

Hansen, Chadwick, *Witchcraft at Salem*, New York, 1969.

Heim, William J., *Critical Survey of Poetry*, ed. Magill, Frank, Salem Press, 1982, pp 610-619.

Henry Stuart C., *Puritan Character in the Witchcraft Episode of Salem, in A Miscellany of American Christianity, Essays in Honor of H. Shelton Smith*, ed. Stuart C. Henry, *Durham, N. C.*, 1963, pp. 142, 148, 165.

Hill, Christopher, *The Century of Revolution 1603-1714*, Abacus, 1975.

Hutchinson, F., *An Historical Essay concerning Witchcraft*, London, 1720.

Hutchinson, F., *Hutchinson Papers*, Albany, 1865.

Hutchinson, F., *The Witchcraft Delusion of 1692*, ed. W. F. Poole, Boston, 1870.

Josephy Jr., Alvin M., *The American West Year By Year*, Crescent Books, 1995.

Kansas State Historical Society, *Guide to the Microfilm Edition of the Isaac McCoy Papers 1808-1874*.

Kittredge, G. L., *Witchcraft in Old and New England*, Cambridge, Mass. Harvard University Press, 1929.

Lecky, William E. H., *A History of England in the Eighteenth Century* (7 vols), London, 1899.

Lecky, William E. H., *Rise and Influence of the Spirit of Rationalism*, Longmans, Green & Co., 1910.

Longfellow, Henry Wadsworth, *The New England Tragedies (Poems)*, Boston, 1868.

Lyons, Grant, *The Creek Indians*, New York, 1978.

Macaulay, Thomas B., *The History of England From the Accession of James II*, Everyman, 1917.

Morison, *The Oxford History of the American People*, New York, OUP, 1965.

Murray, M. A., *The Witch-Cult in Western Europe*, Oxford, 1921.

Nolestein,W., *A History of Witchcraft in England from 1588 to1718*,Washington, 1911.

Nowak, Maximillian, E., *Eighteenth-Century English Literature*, Macmillan History of Literature, 1983.

Quinlan, Maurice James, *Victorian Prelude: A History of English Manners (1700-1830)*, Columbia University, New York, 1951.

Reynolds, Myra, *The Treatment of Nature in English Poetry between Pope and Wordsworth*, Chicago, 1909.

Rowse, A. L.,*The Elizabethans and America*, Trevelyan Lecture, Macmillan, 1959.

Saintsbury, George, *A History of English Prosody*, vols 2-3, New York, 1923.

Saintsbury, George, *A History of Nineteenth-Century Literature, 1780-1895*, Macmillan, New York, 1927.

Sargeaunt, John, *Annals of Westminster School*, London, Methuen, 1898.

Schöffler Herbert, *Protestantismus und Literatur: Neue Wege zur englischen Literatur des 18. Jahrhunderts*, Göttongen, 1958.

Shepherd, T.B. *Methodism and the Literature of the Eighteenth Century*, Haskell House, New York, 1966.

Sherwood, Gilbert and Piper, *The Rural Walks of Cowper*, undated, Paternoster Row, London.

Slocum, Charles E, *History of the Maumee River Basin*, 1904.

Thomson, J. M., *Lectures on Foreign History, 1494-1789*, Blackwell, 1951.

Trevelyan, G. M., *England in the Age of Wycliffe*, Longmans, Green, and Co., 1899.

Trevelyan, G. M., *England Under the Stuarts*, Methuen, London, 1928.

Trevelyan, G. M., *English Social History*, Reprint Society, 1948.

Unrau, William E., *The Kansas Indians: A History of the Wind People, 1673-1873*, University of Oklahoma Press, 1971.

Upham, C. W., *Salem Witchcraft, with an Account of Salem Village and a History of Opinions on Witchcraft and Kindred Subjects*, Boston, 1867.

Wilde, H.O., *Der Gottesgedanke in der englischen Literatur: Das Problem der Entwicklung von Puritanischer zu Romantischer Literatur*, Breslau, 1930.

Wolf, John B., *The Emergence of the Great Powers 1685-1715*, Harper, 1950.

Wright, Muriel H., *A Guide to the Indian Tribes of Oklahoma*, University of Oklahoma Press, 1986.

Zierer, Otto, *Geschichte Amerikas: Asyl der Freiheit (1600-1800)*, Sebastian Lux Verlag, undated.

Primary Works and Documents

Benham, William, ed, *The Poetical Works of William Cowper*, Globe Edition, London, 1879.

Bettenson, Henry (ed.), *Documents of the Christian Church*, OUP, 1967.

Bihlmeyer, Karl, *Die Apostolischen Väter* (Original texts), J. C. B. Mohr, 1956.

Bruce, John, *The Poetical Works of William Cowper / With Notes and a Memoir*, Aldine Edition, London, (undated copy).

Edwards, Jonathan, (ed.), *The Life and Diary of David Brainerd*, Moody Press, 1949.

Featley, Daniel, *The Dippers dipt. Or, The Anabaptists Duck'd and Plunged Over Head and Eares, at a Disputation in Southwark*, London, 1645.

Gill, John, *Ancient Mode of Baptizing by Immersion, Plunging, or Dipping into Water; Maintained and Vindicated, The*, 1726.

Gill, John, *Answer to the Birmingham Dialogue Writer, An*, London, 1737.

Gill, John, *Body of Divinity* (3 vols), Subscription, 1769.

Gill, John, *Cause of God and Truth, The*, Baker Book House, 1980.

Gill, John, *Sermons and Tracts, The*, (3 vols), Primitive Baptist Library, 1981.

Gill, John, *Song of Solomon*, Sovereign Grace Publications, 1971.

Gill, John, *Vindication of a Book Entitled The Cause of God and Truth, A*, London, 1740.

Hauges, Hans N., *skrifter, bind I-VIII* ved H. Ording. Andaktbokselskapet 1948-54.

Hawker, Robert, *Zion's Warrior; Zion's Pilgrim; Union and Communion with Christ; The Divinity of Christ; The Divinity and Operation of the Holy Spirit; Village Sermons* (2 vols); *Compassion for the Sick and Sorrowing; Sermons and Important Subjects and Particular Occasions; The Sailor Pilgrim; Chatechism for Children;* and *A Prop Against All Despair*, Triangle Press, 1996.

Hawker, Robert, *The Poor Man's Morning Portion*, Collingridge, 1854.

Hervey, James, *A Collection of the Letters of the late Reverend James Hervey* (2 vols with 'Life'), Thomson, Benson, Bland et al, 18th century, but undated.

Hervey, James, *A Series of Letters from the Late Rev. James Hervey, M. A. to the Rev. John Ryland, M. A. containing, Six Years' Correspondence before his Death which happened December 25, 1758.* Never before printed, (appended to John Ryland's *The Character of the Rev. James Hervey, A. M.*, London, 1791).

Hervey, James, *Letters to the Right Honourable Lady Francis Shirley*, 18th century, but undated.

Hervey, James, *The Works of the late Reverend James Hervey, A. M.* (6 vols with 'Life'), 1771.

Hervey, James, *The Works of the Rev. James Hervey, A. M.* (with 'Life'), Thomas Nelson, Edinburgh, 1837.

Huntington, William, *Works*, Bensley (20 vols), 1811 and Collingridge (6 vols), 1856, editions with dates of first publication. Collingridge was reprinted in 1989 by J.R. Broome and distributed by Gospel Standard Publications.

Huntington, William, *Farewell Sermon*, T. Bensley, 1813, Reprinted by John Crowter, 1993.

Huntington, William, *Further Gleanings of the Vintage*, Pickles, H.M. (Ed), Coventry, undated.

Huntington, William, *Popish Controversy: Letters to and from Miss Morton*, C. Verral, 1787, Reprinted under the confusing title of '*Epistles of Faith*' (See *Works* for 1785 and 1797 of that name), Focus Christian Ministries, 1990.

Huntington, William, *Posthumous Letters* (4 vols), 592 letters, T. Bensley, 1814-1822.

Huntington, William, *The Doctrine of Garrett Refuted*, E. Huntington, 1808.

Huntington, William, *The Glory of the Second House*, E. Huntington, 1811, Reprinted by John Crowter, Coventry, 1993.

Huntington, William, *The Lord Our Righteousness*, S. Huntington, 1811, Reprinted by John Crowter, Coventry, 1993.

Janeway, James and Mather, Cotton, *A Token for Children*, Soli Deo Gloria, 1994.

Kidd, B. J., ed., *Documents Illustrative of the History of the Church* (2 vols), SPCK, 1920.

King, James and Ryskamp, Charles, *The Letters and Prose Writings of William Cowper* (5 vols), Clarendon Press, Oxford, 1979-1986.

Mather, Cotton, D. D., *The Wonders of the Invisible World*, London, 1862.

Mather, Cotton, *Diary of Cotton Mather* (2 vols), ed. Worthington C. Ford, 1911-12.

Mather, Cotton, *Magnalia Christi Americana: The Great Works of Christ in America* (2 vols), Banner of Truth, 1979.

Mather, Cotton, *Triparadisus, The Threefold Paradise of Cotton Mather*, ed. Reiner Smolinski, University of Georgia Press, 1995.

Mather, Cotton, *Vital Christianity: A Brief Essay on the Life of God in the Soul of Man*, Rogers and Fowle, Boston, 1741.

Mather, Increase, D.D., *A Farther Account of the Tryals of the New-England Witches*, 1862, Amherst Press Reprint.

McCoy, Isaac, *A Periodical Account of Baptist Missions Within the Indian Territory For the Year Ending December 31, 1836*, private publication 1837.

McCoy, Isaac, *Annual Register of Indian Affairs, 1835-38*, ed. Terry Wolever, Particular Baptist Publishing, Enid, OK, 1998.

McCoy, Isaac, *History of Baptist Indian Missions*, Washington, 1840.

McCoy, Isaac, *Remarks on the Practicability of Indian Reform, Embracing their Colonization*, New York, 1829.

McCoy, William, *Notes on the McCoy Family*, (ed. Elizabeth Haywards), The Tuttle Publishing Company, Inc., 1939.

Richardson, Samuel, *Some brief Considerations On Doctor Featley his Book, intitled, The Dipper Dipt, Wherein In some measure is discovered his many great and false accusations of divers persons, commonly called Anabaptists, with an Answer to them, and some brief Reasons of their Practice*, London, 1645.

Richmond, Legh, ed., *Fathers of the English Church* (8 vols), London, 1807-1812 (with biographies and works).

Romaine, William, *The Whole Works of the Late William Romaine, A. M.* (with 'Life'), B. Blake, London, 1837.

Steadman, Thomas, Ed., *Letters to and from the Rev. Philip Doddridge, D. D.*, Shrewsbury, 1790.

Toplady, Augustus Montague, *Works* (6 vols, 8vo.), W. Row, London, 1794.

Toplady, Augustus Montague, *Works* (6 vols, 8vo.), W. Baynes, London and Edinburgh, 1825.

Toplady, Augustus Montague, *Works* (6 vols), W. Palmer, London, 1828.

Toplady, Augustus Montague, *Works* (1 vol), J. Chidley, London, 1837.

Toplady, Augustus Montague, *Works* (1 vol), J.Cornish, London, 1861.

Toplady, Augustus Montague, *The Works of Augustus Toplady* (1 vol), Sprinkle Publications, 1987, reprint of 1794 First Edition.

Toplady, Augustus Montague, *The Works of Augustus Toplady* (6 vols), Third Edition, 1813.

Wake, Archbishop, *The Apostolic Fathers*, Routledge, undated.

Wesley, John, *Works* (16 vols), London, 1812.

Whitefield, George, *George Whitefield's Journals*, Banner of Truth, Edinburgh 1960.

Whitefield, George, *Letters 1734-1742*, Banner of Truth, Edinburgh, 1976.

Whitefield, George, *Letters, A Select Collection of Letters* (3 vols), London, 1772.

Witsius, Herman, *The Economy of the Covenants Between God and Man*, Presbyterian and Reformed Publishing Company, 1990 reprint.

Zanchius, Jerome, *The Doctrine of Absolute Predestination*, trans. by Toplady with *Life of Zanchius* by Toplady and *Introduction* by Henry Atherton, Baker Book House, 1977.

Doctrinal Works and Creeds

Arbeitskreis Taufe und Gemeinde Rheinland, *ad hoc 2: z.B. Taufe: Ein Kapitel Kirchenreform*, Burckhardhaus-Verlag, 1970.

Barth, Karl, *Det Kristna Dopet*, Westerbergs, 1949.

Beasley-Murray, G. R., *Dopet idag och i Morgon*, Westerbergs, 1967.

Bicknell, E. J., *The Thirty Nine Articles*, Longmans, 1957.

Brine, John, *An Antidote Against a Spreading Antinomian Principle*, London, 1750.

Calvin, John, *Calvin's Calvinism*, SGU, trans. Henry Cole, D.D., 1927.

Calvin, John, *Institutes of Christian Religion* (2 vols.), Eerdmans, 1979.

Cullmann, Oscar, *Nya Testamentets Lära om Dopet: Vuxendop och Barndop*, Svenska Kyrkans Diakonistyrelses Bokförlag, 1952.

Ella, G. M., *John Gill and the Doctrine of Eternal Justification*, Go Publications, 1998.

Fisher, Edward, *The Marrow of Modern Divinity in Two Parts*, Philadelphia, undated.

Girardeau, John L., *Calvinism and Evangelical Arminianism*, Sprinkle Publications Reprint 1984.

Gosden, J. H., *What Gospel Standard Baptists Believe*, Gospel Standard , 1993.

Hardwick, Charles, *A History of the Articles of Religion*, Cambridge, 1859.

Hartman, Olov, *Dopets gåva förpliktar*, Svenska Kyrkans Diaonistyrelses Bokförlag, 1950.

Hendry, George S., *The Westminster Confession for Today*, SCM Press, 1960.

Hindson, Edward, ed., *Introduction to Puritan Theology*, Guardian Press, 1976.

Huehns, G., *Antinomianism in English History*, 1951.

Hussey, Joseph, *God's Operations of Grace: But No Offers of His Grace*, London 1707, reprint Primitive Publications, abridged, 1973.

Jeremias, Joachim, *Barndopet under de fyra första århundradena*, EFS-Bokförlag, 1959.

Lumpkin, William L., *Baptist Confessions of Faith*, Judson Press, 1959.

Murray, John, *Christian Baptism*, Presbyterian and Reformed, 1977.

Nichols, John Broadhurst, *Evangelical Belief*, Religious Tract Society, 1899.

Niesel, Wilhelm, *The Theology of Calvin*, Westminster Press, 1956.

Owen, John, *A Display of Arminianism*, Calvin Classics 2, 1989.

Sell, Alan, *The Great Debate: Calvinism, Arminianism and Salvation*, Walker, 1982.

Shedd, W.G.T., *Calvinism Pure & Mixed: A Defence of the Westminster Standards*, New York, 1893, reprint, 1986, Banner of Truth, Edinburgh.

Thomas, W. H. Griffith, *The Principles of Theology*, Church Room Book Press, 1945.

Toon, Peter, *Hyper-Calvinism*, The Olive Tree, 1967.

Warns, Johannes, *Baptism*, Paternoster Press, 1962.

Microfilms, Videos and CD-ROMs

American Baptist Foreign Mission Societies Records (Indian Mission), microfilm, Reels 99-101.

Bibliotheca Sacra, CD-ROM, 1995.

Christian Classics Foundation, CD-ROM, 1996,

Gjennomillustrert. Norsk film A/S (video): *Hans Nielsen Hauge*. Videokassett (VHS, 93 min), 1996.

Grolier's Academic American Encyclopedia (21 vols), CD-ROM, 1995.

Historical Commission, SBC, Pub. Nos 021, 025, British Baptist Materials

Isaac Mann Collection 1742-1831, National Library of Wales Reference N.L.W. 1207 D., micro film, Angus Library.

Isaac McCoy Papers (microfilm edition) manuscript division, Kansas State Historical Society, Topeka, (Reels 1-13), 1808-1874.

Microsoft Encarta, Funk and Wagnall (29 vols), CD-ROM, 1995.

Online Bible, CD-Rom, 1994.

The Multi-Bible by Innotech (with abstracts from numerous theological journals), CD-ROM, 1990.

The Sage Digital Library (vols 1-4), CD-ROM, 1996.

Handwritten Documents and Theses Unpublished and Published

Aarflot, Andreas, 'Tro og lydighet', doktorgrad om Hauge, Universitetsforlaget, 1969.

Black, Charles Herman, *One Hundred Years of Baptist Missionary Administration in Oklahoma, A Dissertation Presented to the Faculty of the Central Baptist Theological Seminary*, Kansas City, 1950.

Dane, John Preston, *A History of Baptist Missions Among the Plains Indians of Oklahoma, A Dissertation Presented to the Faculty of the Central Baptist Seminary*, Kansas City, 1955.

Daniel, Curt, *Hyper-Calvinism and John Gill*, Edin. Ph. D. 1884, (published privately, Dallas, 1984).

Ella, G. M., *Paradise and Poetry: An In-Depth Study of William Cowper's Poetic Mind*, Dr. phil., Duisburg, The Cowper and Newton Museum, Olney, 1989.

Goat Yard / Carter Lane Church Book 1719-1808, Metropolitan Tabernacle.

Hannay, Neilson Campbell, *The Religious Element in the Life and Character of William Cowper*, Harvard University, 1919.

Hantsche, Arthur, *William Cowper, sein Naturgefühl und seine Naturdichtung*, Leipzig University, 1901.

Hoffmann, Willy, *William Cowper's Belesenheit und literarische Kritik*, Berlin, 1908.

Huang, Roderick, Tsui En, *William Cowper: Nature Poet*, Oxford University Press, 1957. (As dissertation, *William Cowper's Conception and Description of Nature*, Northwestern University, 1955.)

Journal of the Affairs of ye Antipedobaptists beginning with ye Reign of King George whose Accession to the Throne was on the First of August, 1714, Benjamin Stinton and Thomas Crosby, Angus Library.

Journal of ye Proceedings of the Managers for Raising and Setting ye Funds, A, (2 vols) 1717 f., Angus Library.

Kirkby, A. H., *The Theology of Andrew Fuller and its relation to Calvinism*, Ph.D., Edin., 1956.

Lanham, Luise, *The Poetry of William Cowper in its Relation to the English Evangelical Movement*, University of North Carolina, 1936.

Lawton, Edith, *The Criticism of William Cowper*, Boston University, 1941.

Mack, Edward Clarence, *Public Schools and British Opinion 1780-1860*, Columbia University Press, 1938, reprint Connecticut, 1973.

Magnus Alv J., *Vekkelse og samfunn*, magistergrad Univ. i Oslo, 1978.

Possehl, Willi, *William Cowper's Stellung zur Religion*, Rostock, 1907.

Quinlan, Maurice James, *Victorian Prelude*, Columbia University Press, 1941.

Roustio, Edward, *A History of the Life of Isaac McCoy in Relationship to Early Indian Migrations and Missions as Revealed in His Unpublished Manuscripts, A Dissertation Presented to the Faculty of the Central Baptist Theological Seminary*, Kansas City, May 1954.

Ryskamp, Charles, *William Cowper of the Inner Temple*, New York, Cambridge University Press, 1959.

Schmidt, Kuno, *Das Verhalten der Romantiker zur Public School*, Bonn, 1935.

Seymour, R. E., *John Gill. Baptist Theologian, 1697-1771*, Ph. D., Edin., 1954.

Spears, W. E., *The Baptist Movement in England in the late Seventeenth Century as reflected in the work & thought of Benjamin Keach, 1640-1704*, Ph.D., Edin. 1953.

Thein, Adelaide Eve, *The Religion of William Cowper: An Attempt to Distinguish between His Obsession and His Creed*, University of Michigan, 1940. Dissertation Abstracts V. i., 1943, pp 24-25.

Tietje, Gustav, *Die poetische Personifikation unpersönliche Substantiva bei Cowper und Coleridge*, Kiel, 1914.

Lexica, Dictionaries and Miscellaneous

Bauer, W., eds Arndt, W. F. and Gingrich, F. W., *A Greek-English Lexicon of the New Testament*, Chicago University Press, 1957.

Benson, Louis F., *The English Hymn*, Hodder and Stoughton, 1915.

Douglas, J. D. (ed.), *Dictionary of the Christian Church*, Paternoster Press, 1974.

Ella, G. M., ed., *Weighed in the Balance*, The Huntingtonian Press, 1998.

Elwell, Walter, A. (ed.), *The Marshall Pickering Encyclopedia of the Bible* (2 vols), Marshall Pickering, 1990.

Engnell, Ivan, *Gammaltestamentlig Hebreiska*, Svenska Bokförlaget, 1960.

Gadsby, John, *Memoirs of Hymn Writers*, Gadsby, Bouverie Street, undated.

Gesenius, Wilhelm, *Hebräisches und Aramäisches Handwörterbuch über das Alte Testament*, Springer-Verlöag, 1962.

Hastings, James, *A Dictionary of the Bible* (5 vols), Clark, 1936.

Hastings, James, *Dictionary of Christ and the Gospels* (2 vols), Clark, 1906.

Hastings, James, *Dictionary of the Apostolic Church* (2 vols), Clark, 1915.

Hastings, James, *Encyclopedia of Religion and Ethics* (12 vols), Clark, 1908.

Liddell, Henry George and Scott, Robert, *A Greek- English Lexicon*, Clarendon Press, 1890.

Mills, Susan J., *Sources for the Study of Baptist History*, Baptist Historical Society, 1992.

Philpot, J. C., *Reviews by the Late Mr. J. C. Philpot, M. A.*, Frederick Kirby, 1901.

Schaff, Philip (ed.), *Schaff-Herzog Encyclopaedia of Religious Knowledge* (4 vols), Funk & Wagnalls, 1894.

Smith, William and Cheetham, Samuel, *A Dictionary of Christian Antiquities* (2 vols), John Murray, 1908.

Smith, William and Wace, Henry (eds), *A Dictionary of Christian Biography* (4 vols), John Murray, 1900.

Spurgeon, Charles H., *Commenting and Commentaries*, Kregel Publications, 1992.

Thayer, Joseph Henry, *A Greek English Lexicon of the New Testament*, Clark, 1930.

Underdown, David, *Pride's Purge*, Oxford, 1971.

Würthwein, Ernst, *Der Text des Alten Testaments*, Deutsche Bibelgeselschaft, 1973.

Magazine, Bulletin, Journal and Historical Society Articles Including Reviews

Abbreviations of Magazine Titles

American Antiquarian Society Proceedings	AASP
American Baptist Magazine	ABM
American Historical Review	AHR
American Quarterly	AQ
Anglia	A
Archiv für das Studium der neueren Sprachen und Literatur	ASNSL
Arminian Magazine	A M
Banner of Truth Magazine	BOTM
Baptist History and Heritage	BHH
Baptist Quarterly	BQ
Bible League Quarterly	BLQ
Biblical Repertory and Princeton Review	BRPR
Canadian Magazine	C M
Chapel Society Newsletter	CSN
Christian History	CH
Church Quarterly Review	CQR
Colonial Society of Massachusetts Publications	CSMP
Earthen Vessel	EV
Edinburgh Review	ER
Eighteenth Century	EC
English Churchman	EC
English Studies	ES
Essays in Criticism	EC
Evangelical Quarterly	EQ
Evangelical Times	ET
Focus	Fo
Foundations	F
Gentleman's Magazine	GenM
Gospel Advocate	GA
Gospel Herald and Voice of Truth	GHVT
Gospel Magazine	GosM
Gospel Magazine and Theological Review	GMTR
Gospel Standard	GS
Granite Monthly	G M
Hibbert Journal	HJ
Hymn	H
Journal of Christian Reconstruction	JCR
Journal of Ecclesiastical History	JEH
Journal of Religion	JR
Journal of Theological Studies	JTS
Kansas Historical Quarterly	KHQ

Latter Day Luminary	LDL
London Quarterly and Holborn Review	LQHR
Massachusetts Historical Society	MHS
Massachusetts Historical Society Proceedings	MHSP
Missouri Historical Review	MHR
Modern Language Association of America	MLAA
Modern Language Notes	MLN
Modern Language Quarterly	MLQ
Nederlands Theologisch Tijdschrift	NTT
New England Quarterly	NEQ
New Focus	NF
New York Evening Post	NYEP
Nineteenth Century	NC
North American Review	NAR
Notes and Queries	N & Q
Panoplist and Missionary Magazine	PMM
Papers of the Hymn Society of America	PHSA
Proceedings of the American Antiquarian Society	PAAS
Review of English Studies	RES
Saturday Review	SR
Spectrum	S
Strict Baptist Historical Society Bulletin	SBHSB
Transactions of the Baptist Historical Society	TBHS
Weekly Review	WeR
Westminster Review	WR
William and Mary Quarterly	WMQ

A.B.C., To the Author of a Pamphlet called the Polyglott, On the Doctrine of Justification by Faith, GenM, 1761, vol. xxxi, p 204.

Altwater, L. H., The Children of the Covenant and their Part in the Lord, BRPR, vol. xxxv, 1863, pp 622-643.

Amey, Basil, Baptist Missionary Society Radicals, BQ, 26 (8), 1976, pp 363-376.

Anon. Recent Lives of Cowper, (Southey and Grimshawe), ER, July 1836, pp 177-195.

Anon. Review of Cowper's Memoir, PMM, vol. xiii, 1817, pp 65-77.

Anon. Reviews on Wright's Life of Cowper, Hartley's William Cowper: Humanitarian, Fausset's William Cowper and Cecil's Stricken Deer, EC, pp 157, 197, 280-281, 306.

Anon., An Account of the Life and Death of William Cowper, GMTR, V, 1800, pp 428-437.

Anonymous , The Voice of Years, BOTM, July 1988, 8-11.

Anonymous, A Visit to Broad-Hembury and Fen Ottery, the Scene of the Sainted Toplady's Labours, Gos. M., Nov., 1860, pp 498-501; Dec., 1780, pp 553-556.

Anonymous, Antinomianism, BOTM, 259, 1985, pp 23-28.

Anonymous, Further Anecdotes of the late Rev. Mr. Hervey, GenM, 1760, vol. xxx, pp 553-554.

Anonymous, Of Reconciliation with God (criticism of Hervey and Marshall), GenM, 1760, vol. xxx, pp 555-556.

Anonymous, Salem Witchcraft; with an Account of Salem Village, and a History of Opinions on Witchcraft and kindred subjects. By Charles W. Upham, 2 vols. Boston (US): 1867, ER, cclxi, July, 1868, pp 1-47.

Anonymous, Some Account of the Life of the late Rev. Mr. James Hervey, GenM, 1760, vol. xxx, pp 377-381.

Anonymous, The Celebrated Coalheaver, GA, 1872, Ebenezer Hooper, pp 25,49,95,128.

Anonymous, The Excellent of the Earth: James Hervey, GHVT, Jan. 1, 1869, pp 107-109.

Bahnsen, Greg L., Introduction to John Cotton's Abstract of the Law of New England, JCR, vol. v, Winter, 1978-79, no. 2, pp 75-81.

Baines, Arnold H. J., The Signatories of the Orthodox Confession of 1679, BQ, vol. xvii, 1957-8, pp 35-42, 74-86, 170-178.

Baird, John D., Cowper's Despair: An Allusion to Terence, N & Q, February, 1978, p 61.

Baker, Frank, James Hervey: Prose Poet, LQHR, pp 62-8 (copy undated).

Barnes, Lela, Isaac McCoy and the Treaty of 1821, KHQ, vol. v, 1936, The Kansas State Historical Society, pp 122-142.

Barratt, David, The Crucible Reconsidered, S, vol. 23:2, Summer 1991, pp 161-163.

Beckwith, Frank, Dan Taylor and Yorkshire Baptist Life, BQ, IX, pp 297-306.

Beyer, A., Studien zu William Cowpers Task, , Braunschweig, ASNSL, 1888, pp 115-140.

Bowditch, N. I., et al., The Witchcraft Papers, MHS, May 1860, pp 30-37.

Bowman, J. C. The Hated Puritan, WeR, N.Y. vol. 10.

Boyd, David, Satire and Pastoral in The Task, Papers on Language and Literature, 10, 1974, pp 363-377.

Brick, John, The Funeral of William Huntington S.S., CSN, No. 2., December 1989, (Letter written 12th July, 1813).

Broome, J.R., William Huntington: Sinner Saved, GS, March 1991, Henry Sant and George Ella, pp 76-78.

Burr, G. L. New England's Place in the History of Witchcraft, AASP, xxi, Oct. 1911, p 185 ff.

Cavit, T.E., A Plea for Cowper, GenM, vol. 296, 1904, pp 607-616.

Champion, L. G., Baptist Church Life in London, BQ, 18, 1960, pp 300-304.

Champion, L. G., The Letters of John Newton to John Ryland, BQ, 27(4), 1977, pp 157-63.

Champion, L. G., The Theology of John Ryland, BQ, 28(1), 1979, pp 17-29.

Champion, L.G. The Theology of John Ryland: Its Sources and Influences, BQ, 1979, 28 (1), pp 17-29.

Champion, L.G., Evangelical Calvinism and the Structures of Baptist Church Life, BQ, 1980, 28, pp 196-208.

Clark, H. H., A Study of Melancholy in Edward Young, MLN, XXXIX, pp 129-36, 193-202.

Clark, Sydney F., Nottingham Baptist Beginnings, BQ, XVII, 1957-58, pp 162-69.

Clipsham, E. F., Andrew Fuller and the Baptist Mission, F(Am), 10 (1), 1967, pp 4-8.

Clipsham, E. F., Andrew Fuller: Fullerism, BQ, XX, 1963.

Cotton, John, An Abstract of the Law of New England as they are Now Established. Printed in London in 1641, JCR, vol. v, Winter, 1978-79, no. 2, pp 82-94.

Crito, A Dialogue respecting the Works of the late Mr. Hervey, GenM, 1960, vol. xxx, pp 468-469.

Cudworth, William, Answer by the Author of the Polyglot to Crito's Remarks, GenM, 1761, vol. xxxi, pp 251-252.

Danchin, Pierre, William Cowper's Poetic Purpose: as seen in his Letters, ES, 46, 1965, pp 135-244.

Demos, John, Underlying Themes in the Witchcraft of 17th Cent. New England, AHR, LXXV, June, 1970, pp 1311-26.

Dewar, M. W., Paradise and Poetry, EC, p 6, January 26 & February 2 1990.

Drake, Frederick C., Witchcraft in the American Colonies, 1647-62, AQ, Winter, 1968, pp 694-725.

Drury, Robert M., Isaac McCoy and the Baptist Board of Missions, BHH, vol. ii, No. 1, Jan. 1967, pp 9-14.

Editor, Unpublished Anecdotes of Mr. Huntington, GS, May 1861, pp 144-145.

Edmunds, R. David, Potawatomis in the Platte Country: An Indian Removal Incomplete, MHR, LXVII:4, 1974, Columbia, Missouri, pp 375-392.

Ella, G. M, Cowper the Campaigner, ET, October 1984, pp 4-5.

Ella, G. M., A Gospel Unworthy of Any Acceptation, Fo, No. 8, Winter 1993/94.

Ella, G. M., Cotton Mather (1663-1728): Puritan Pietist, ET, vol. xxix No. 01, January, 1995, p 18.

Ella, G. M., James Hervey:The Prose Poet, ET, vol.xxviii, No.09 September, p 15.

Ella, G. M., John Gill and the Cause of God and Truth, ET, vol. xxviii, No.04, April, 1994.

Ella, G. M., Philip Doddridge's Rise and Progress of Religion in the Soul, ET, vol. xxix No. 02, February, 1995, p 15.

Ella, G. M., Response to David Barratt's The Crucible Reconsidered, S, vol. 23:2, Summer 1991, pp 163-165.

Ella, G. M., The Olney Hymns and Their Relevance for Today, BLQ, April-June, 1986, pp 420-425.

Ella, G. M., The Poor Man's Preacher (Risdon Darracott), ET, vol. xxviii No. 12, December 1994, p 16.

Ella, G. M., Whose Righteousness Saves Us? (Hervey's doctrine of righteousness examined), BLQ, No. 366, July-September, 1991, pp 436-442.

Ella, G. M., William Cowper: A Burning Bush which was not Consumed, BOTM, Issue 256, January 1985, pp 4-11.

Ella, G. M., William Cowper: A Review Article, BOTM, Issue 274, July 1986, pp 16-22 and 24.

Ella, G.M., John Newton's Friendship with William Cowper, BOTM, Issue 269, February 1986, pp 10-19.

Ella, George M., The Crucible in the Classroom: An Examination of Arthur Miller's Technique of Dealing with the Devil, S, Paternoster Press, vol. 23:1, Spring 1991, pp 51-70.

Ella, George M., Sequel to The Sinner Saved, BLQ, Jan.-March, 1990, pp 305-312.

Ertl, Heimo, The manner wherein God has dwelt with my soul: Methodistische Lives im 18. Jahrhundert, A, Band 104, Heft 1/2, 1986, pp 63-93.

Foreman, H., Baptist Provision for Ministerial Education, BQ, XXVII, pp 358-61.

Fradgley, Mrs., A Letter by the Late Mrs Fradgley, of America, GS, August 1860, pp 238-239.

Gaustad, Edwin S., Quest for Pure Christianity, Christian History, Issue 41 (vol. xiii, no. 1).

Goodall, Abner C., Rebuttal to Moore's Suplimentary Notes, MHSP, 2nd ser. I, 1884, pp 99-118.

Goodell, Abner C., The Trial of the Witches in Massachusetts, MHSP, xx, Sept. 1883, pp 27-33. See ibid, Dr Everett's comment on pp 332-333.

Goodell, Abner C., The Trial of the Witches in Massachusetts, MHSP, June 1883, pp 280-326.

Griffin, Dusty, Cowper, Milton and the Recovery of Paradise, EC, 31, 1981, pp 15-26.

Griswald, Whitney A., Three Puritans on Prosperity, NEQ, VII, 1934, 475-493.

Guelzo, Allen C., When the Sermon Reigned, CH, Issue 41 (vol. xiii, no. 1).

Hall, David, D., Witch Hunting in Salem, CH, Issue 41 (vol. xiii, no. 1).

Hall, M.G., ed. The Autobiography of Increase Mather, PAAS, April 19, 1961—October 18, 1961, Volume 71, Worcester, Massachusetts, 1962, pp 271-360.

Hambrick-Stowe, Charles E., Ordering Their Private World, CH, Issue 41 (vol. xiii, no. 1).

Harper, George, New England Dynasty, CH, Issue 41 (vol. xiii, no. 1).

Harris, W.S., Robert Calef Merchant of Boston, GN, n.s. XXXIX, May, 1907, pp 157-63.

Hartley, Lodwick, Cowper and Mme Guyon: Additional Notes, MLAA Publications, 56, 1941, pp 585-587.

Hartley, Lodwick, Cowper and the Evangelicals, EC, 65, 1950, pp 719-731.

Hayden, R., Particular Baptist Confession 16, BQ, XXXII, 1988, pp 403-17.

Hervey, James, Theron & Aspasio on the Bible, BLQ, No. 366, July-September, 1991, p 456.

Hervey, James, Letter from the late Rev. Mr. Hervey to his Father, not published in his works, GenM, 1760, vol. xxx, pp 75-76.

Hewes, Henry, Arthur Miller and How He Went to the Devil, SR, 33:24-6, Jan. 31, 1953, pp 24-25.

Historical Society Proceedings.

Holmes, Thomas J., Bibliography of Cotton Mather, Cambridge, 1940 (3 vols).

Holmes, Thomas J., Bibliography of Increase Mather, Cleveland, 1931.

Holmes, Thomas J., Cotton Mather and His Writings on Witchcraft, Papers Bibl. Soc. America, XVIII, 1925, pp 30-59.

Houghton, Sidney M., Olney Hymns, BLQ, October-December, 1979, pp 276-279.

House, Kirk, The Salem Witch Trials, JCR, vol. v, Winter, 1978-79, no. 2, pp 133-152.

Hudson, Winthrop S., Westin, Gunnar, Who were the Baptists, BQ, XVII, 1957-8, pp 53-60.

Hughes, G. W., Robert Hall of Arnesby 1728-91, BQ, X, 1940-41, pp 444-47.

Hunt, Carew R.N., John Newton and William Cowper, NC, August, 1941, pp 92-98.

Huntington, W., Extracts from Mr. Huntington's Letters, GosM, August, 1870, pp 444-445.

Huntington, William, A Correspondence between Mr H. and a Friend, GS, 1850, pp 166-172.

Huntington, William, A Letter by Mr. Huntington, GS, pp 17-19.

Huntington, William, A Short Discourse on Sanctification, GS, 1850, pp 228-232.

Huntington, William, An Unpublished letter of W. H. to John Rusk, GS, April 1861, pp 114.

Huntington, William, Extracts from Mr. Huntington's Letters, GosM, September 1870, p 462.

Huntington, William, Mr. Huntington's Dying Testimony to the Power, GS, March 1860, pp 77-78.

Huntington, William, Short Discourses by Mr. Huntington, GS, 1850, pp 369-373.

Huntington, William, The Wedding Garment (Sermon), GS, March 1861, pp 77-81.

Huntington, William, Unpublished Letter from Mr. H. to Mr Brook, GS, January 1860, pp 21-22.

Huntington, William, Unpublished Letters by Mr. Huntington, GS, November 1861, p 337.

Jennings, Warren A. Isaac McCoy and the Mormons, MHR, vol. lxi, Oct. 1966, No. 1, pp 62-82.

Jewson, C. B., Norwich Baptists and the French Revolution, BQ, XXIV, 1963-66, pp 209-215.

Johansen, John Henry, The Olney Hymns, PHSA, XX, 1956, The Hymn Society of America, pp 1-25.

Jones, J. A., A Sketch of the Rise & Progress of Fullerism, or Duty-Faith; that Gangrene now Rapidly Spreading in Many Churches, EV, Sept. 2, 1861.

King, James, Cowper's Adelphi Restored: The Excisions to Cowper's Narrative, RES, 30, 1979, pp 291-305.

Kirkby, A. H., Andrew Fuller: Evangelical Calvinist, BQ, XV, 1954, pp 195-202.

Kittredge, G. L., Cotton Mather's Election into the Royal Society, CSMP, XIV, 1913, pp 81-114.

Kittredge, G. L., Cotton Mather's Scientific Communications to the Royal Society, PAAS, n.s. XXVI, 1916, pp 18-57.

Kittredge, G. L., Further Notes on Cotton Mather and the Royal Society, CSMP, XIV, 1913, pp 281-292.

Kittredge, G. L., Notes on Witchcraft, AASP, xviii, 1907, pp 148-212.

Kittredge, G. L., Some Lost Works of Cotton Mather. PMHS, XLV (1912), pp 418-479.

Knight, George Litch, William Cowper as a Hymn Writer, H, 1950, pp 5-12 &20.

Kuiper, E. J., Hugo de Groot en de Remonstranten, NTT, 38 (2), 1984, pp 111-125.

Legg, John, Paradise and Poetry, ET, p 17, April, 1990.

Levin, David, Salem Witchcraft in Recent Fiction and Drama, New England Quarterly, Dec. 1955.

Levin, David, The Hazing of Cotton Mather, NEQ, June 1963, pp 147-171.

Loomis, Grant C., An Unnoted German Reference to Increase Mather, NEQ, XIV, 1941, pp 374-376.

MacGregor, James, The Free Offer in the Westminster Confession, BOTM, 82-83, 1970, pp 51-58.

Maclean, George, Paradise and Poetry, BOTM, p 62, issue 323-324, August / September, 1990.

Manley, K. B., John Rippon and Baptist Histography, BQ, 28 (3), 1979, pp 109-208.

Martin, Bernard, Fresh Light on William Cowper, MLQ, XIII, Sept., 1952, pp 253-255.

Martin, H., The Baptist Contribution to Early English Hymnody, BQ, XIX, 1961-62, pp 199-207.

Martin, T.D., Paradise and Poetry: A Review Article and Reflection upon Cowper's Work, pp 321-327, BLQ, April-June 1990.

Mather Family, The Mather Papers, Massachusetts Historical Society Collections, VIII, 1868.

Mather, Cotton, The Deplorable State of New-England, Collections of the Massachusetts Historical Society, 5th Series, vi, p 118 ff.

McCoy, Isaac, Fort Wayne Indian Mission, LDL, vol. ii, May, 1821. p 386-387.

McCoy, Isaac, Fort Wayne Mission, Extracts from the Journal of the Reverend Mr. McCoy, LDL, vol. ii, October, 1822, 313-343.

McCoy, Isaac, Fort Wayne Mission, LDL, vol. ii, May, 1821, p 401, 478-488.

McCoy, Isaac, From Mr. McCoy, near Vincennes, LDL, vol. i, July,1818, pp 182-185.

McCoy, Isaac, From Mr. McCoy, nr. Vincennes, LDL, vol. i, May, 1818, p. 90-91.

McCoy, Isaac, From Mr. McCoy to the Corresponding Secretary, LDL, vol. i, March, 1818, pp 43-44.

McCoy, Isaac, From the Same to the Agent of the Board, LDL, vol. i, March, 1818, p 44.

McCoy, Isaac, Indians of Illinois, LDL, vol. i, August, 1819, pp 450-452.

McCoy, Isaac, Indians of Illinois, LDL, vol. i, October, 1819, pp 503-505.

McCoy, Isaac, Isaac McCoy's Second Exploring Trip in 1826, ed. John Francis McDermont, KHQ, Vol. XIII, 1944-1945, The Kansas State Historical Society, pp 400-462.

McCoy, Isaac, Letter from, Arkansas,— Creek Nation, ABM, vol. 12, Dec. 1832, No. 12, pp 496-397.

McCoy, Isaac, Miami and Other Indians, LDL, vol. i, May, 1819, p 412.

McCoy, Isaac, Station at Fort Wayne, LDL, vol. ii, August, 1820, pp 189-190.

McCoy, Isaac, Station at Fort Wayne, LDL, vol. ii, February, 1821, p 298.

McGiffert, Michael, The Problem of the Covenant in Puritan Thought. Peter Bulkeley's Gospel-Covenant, The New England Historical and Geneological Register, vol. cxxx, April 1976, pp 107-129.

Moore, George H., Bibliographical Notes on Witchcraft in Massachusetts, AASP, v, 1888, pp 245-73.

Moore, George H., Supplementary Notes on Witchcraft in Massachusetts: A Critical Examination of the Alleged Law of 1711 for Reversing the Attainder of the Witches of 1692, Massachusetts Historical Society Proceedings, 2nd ser. I, 1884, pp 77-98.

Morison, Samuel E., Harvard College in the Seventeenth Century, Cambridge, 1936.

Murray, Iain, William Cowper and his Affliction, BOTM, 96, Sept. 1971, pp 12-32.

Nicholson, J. F. V., The Office of Messenger amongst British Baptists in the Seventeenth and Eighteenth Centuries, BQ, xvii, 1957-8, pp 206-225.

Nicolson, Marjorie, The New England Mind: The Seventeenth Century by Perry Miller, NEQ, XIV, 1941, pp 377-381.

Noble, John, Some Documentary Fragments touching the Witchcraft Episode of 1692, Colonial Society of Massachussetts, Publications, x, Dec. 1904, pp 12-26.

Nordell, Philip G., Cotton Mather in Love, Harper's Magazine, CLIII, 1926, pp 566-572.

Norman, Hubert J., The Melancholy of Cowper, WR, CLXXV, 1911, pp 638-647.

Nuttall, G. F., Baptists and Independents in Olney, BQ, XXX, 1983, pp 26-37.

Nuttall, G. F., Calvinism in Free Church History, BQ, XXII (8), 1968, pp 418-428.

Nuttall, G. F., Northamptonshire and the Modern Question, JTS, NS, XVI, 1965, pp 101-23.

Oliver, R. W., By His Grace and For His Glory (Review) Nettles, BOTM, 284, 1987, pp 30-32.

Oliver, R. W., Historical Survey of English Hyper-Calvinism, Foundations (England), 7, 1981, pp 8-18.

Oliver, R. W., John Collet Ryland, Daniel Turner, BQ, XXIX, 1981, pp 77-79.

Oliver, R. W., Significance of Strict Baptists Attitudes to Duty-Faith, SBHSB, 20, 1993, pp 3-26.

Packer, J.I., Theology on Fire, Christian History, Issue 41 (vol. xiii, no. 1).

Parker, T. H. L., Calvin's Doctrine of Justification, EQ, XXIV, 1952.

Payne, E. A., Baptists and the Laying on of Hands, BQ, XV, 1954, pp 203-215.

Payne, E.A., More about Sabatarian Baptists, BQ, XIV, pp 161-66.

Payne, E.A., The Appointment of Deacons, BQ, xvii, 1957-8, pp 87-91.

Payne, Earnest, Abraham Booth, BQ, 26 (1), 1975, pp 28-42.

Payne, Earnest, Carey and his Biographers, BQ, 19, 1961, pp 4-12.

Payne, Earnest, The Downgrade Controversy, BQ, 28 (4), 1979, pp 146-158.

Peski, A. M. van, Waarom Grotius als Oecumenisch Theoloog Mislukken Moest, NTT, 38 (4), 1984, pp 290-297.

Philpot, J.C., Recollections of the Late William Huntington, GS, February 1869, William Stevens.

Philpot, J.C., William Huntington, God the Guardian of the Poor and the Bank of Faith, GS, March, 1867.

Philpot, J.C., William Huntington, Epistles of Faith, GS, September 1853, pp 285, 318.

Philpot, J.C., William Huntington, The Posthumous Letters of the Late William Huntington, GS, August 1856, pp 250-260.

Pollard, Arthur, Five Poets on Religion: Cowper and Blake, CQR, Oct., CLX. 1957-58.

Poole, W. F., Cotton Mather and Salem Witchcraft, Boston, 1869. NAR, cviii, pp 337-397. Reviews of The Mather Papers, Upham, Longfellow and Allen on Salem Witchcraft, Edinburgh Review on Salem Witchcraft all listed in this Bibliography.

Porter, Katherine Anne, Cotton Mather: Keeper of the Puritan Conscience by Ralf and Louise Boas, NYEP, Nov. 3, 1928.

Porter, Laurence E., James Hervey (1714-1758) A Bicentenary Appreciation, EQ, 31, 1959, pp 4-20.

Potts, E. Daniel, I Throw Away the Gun to Preserve the Ship: A Note on the Serampore Trio, BQ, XX, 1963-64.

Price, Lucien, Cotton Mather: Keeper of the Puritan Conscience by Ralf and Louise Boas, NEQ, April, 1929, II, pp 327-331.

Price, S. J., Reparing a Baptist meeting House, BQ, V, 1930-31, p 28.

Price, S. J., Sidelights from an Old Minute Book, BQ, V, 1930-31, pp 86-96.

Price, Seymour, Dr. John Gill and the Confession of 1729, BQ, IV, 1928, pp 366-371.

Quinlan, Maurice J., William Cowper and the Unpardonable Sin, JR, XXIII, 1943, pp 110-116.

Richards, Thomas, Some Disregarded Sources of Baptist History, BQ, NS 17, pp 362-379.

Ridley, H. M., Great Friendships: William Cowper and Mrs Unwin, CM, LIX, 1922, pp 438-442.

Robbins, John W., The Political Philosophy of the Founding Fathers, JCR, vol. iii, Summer, 1976, no. 1, pp 52-68.

Robinson, O. C., The Legacy of John Gill, BQ, XXVI, 1971, pp 111-125.

Rupp, Gordon, Salter's Hall 1719 and the Baptists, TBHS, V, 1916-17, pp 172-89.

Russel, Pamela, Mr. Russel of White Street and His relatives, BQ, XXVIII, 1980, pp 373-383.

Rutman, Darrett B., God's Bridge Falling Down, WMQ, xix, July 1962, pp 408-421.

Ryle, Bishop J. C., James Hervey's End, BLQ, No. 366, July-September, 1991, pp 442-443.

Sant, Henry, The Sinner Saved, BLQ, Jan-March, 1989, p 205-201.

Sellers, I., The Old General Baptists, BQ, XXIV, 1971, pp 30-38, 74-85.

Sheehan, R. J., The Presentation of the Gospel Amongst Hyper-Calvinists, F (England), 8, 1982, pp 28-39.

Sheehan, Robert J., The Presentation of the Gospel amongst Hyper-Calvinists: A Critique, F (England), 9, 1982, pp 42-46.

Shoup, Earl Leon, Indian Missions in Kansas, Kansas State Historical Society Collections, XII, Topeka, 1912, pp 65-69.

Skipton, Clifford, New England Clergy of the Glacial Age. Colonial Society of Massachusetts Publications, XXXII, Dec. 1933, pp 24-54.

Sparkes, D. C., The Portsmouth Disputation of 1699, BQ, pp 59-75.

Sparkes, D. C., The Test Act of 1673 and its Aftermath, BQ, XXV, 1973, pp 74-85.

Stanley, Brian C. H., C. H. Spurgeon and the Baptist Missionary Society, BQ, 29 (7), 1982, pp 319-328.

Starkey, Marion L., The Devil in Massachussetts, New York, Alfred A. Knopf, 1949, also Garden City, 1961.

Stout, Harry S. (interview), The Puritans behind the Myths, Christian History, Issue 41 (vol. xiii, no. 1).

Tayler, E.L. Hebden, The Rock from which America was Hewn, JCR, vol. iii, Summer, 1976, no. 1, pp 178-184.

Taylor Bowie, W., The Hollis Family and Pinner's Hall, BQ, I, 1922-23, pp 78-81.

Taylor Bowie, W., William Carey, BQ, VII, 1934-35, pp 167-74.

The Old Pilgrim, Personal Recollections of Mr. W. Huntington, GosM, October, 1870, pp 533-538.

Thomas, Roger, The Non-Subscription Controversy Amongst Dissenters in 1719: the Salters' Hall Debate, JEH, IV, 1953, pp 162-86.

Thompson, Evelyn, Isaac McCoy and His Work Amongst the Great Lake Indians, BHH, vol. ii, No. 1, Jan. 1967, pp 3-8.

Toon, Peter, The Growth of a Supralapsarian Christology, EQ, XXIX, 1967.

Toon, Peter, English Strict Baptists, BQ, XXI, 1965, pp 30-36.

Upham, C. W., Salem Witchcraft and Cotton Mather, Historical Magazine, vol. vi, 2nd series, Sept., 1869, pp 29-219.

W.S., An Anecdote of Mr. Lock, the Assistant of WH, GS, November 1859, pp 338-340.

Walker, W. The Services of the Mathers in the New England Religious Development, Papers of the American Society of Church History, vol. v, pp 61-85.

Ward, Nathaniel, Capital Crimes in the Massachusetts Body of Liberties (1641), JCR, vol. v, Winter, 1978-79, no. 2, pp 95-96.

Weeler Robinson, H,. A Baptist Student: J. C. Ryland, BQ, III, 1926-27, pp 25-33.

Wesley, John, Letter to Mr. Hervey, AM, 1778, p 136.

White, A.D., A History of the Doctrine of Comets, Papers of the American Historical Association, vol. ii, no. 2. date lost.

White, B. R., How Did William Kiffin Join the Baptists?, BQ, XXIII, 1969-70, pp 201-7.

White, B. R., John Gill in London 1719-1729, BQ, XXII, 1967, pp 72-91.

Whitely, W. T., The Influence of Whitefield on Baptists, BQ, V, 1930-31, pp 30-36.

Whiting, Mary Bedford, A Burning Bush: New Light on the Relations Between Cowper and Newton, The HJ, XXIV, 1926, pp 303-313.

Wilmeth, Roscoe, Kansa Village Locations in the Light of McCoy's 1828 Journal, KHQ, XXVI, 2, 1960, Topeka, Kansas, pp 152-157.

Windsor, Justin, The Literature of Witchcraft in New England, AASP, n.s. x, Oct, pp 371-73.

Indices

Index of Names

Abbot, Archbishop George, 53, 80, 82, 84, 102, 113, 115, 125, 137,
Ambrose, 49,
Amyraut, Moses, 89,
Anaxagoras, 174,
Andrewes, Lancelot, 60, 106, 137,
Andros, Governor Sir Edmund, 194-195, 211,
Aquinas, Thomas, 90,
Armitage, Thomas, 138,
Arndt, Johann, 363,
Ascol, Thomas, 157,
Aspinwal (family), 144,
Atkinson, Prof. James, 35-36,
Augustine (Hippo), 49, 77, 88, 91, 93, 111,
Baden-Powell, Lord Robert, 269,
Bagot, Walter, 304,
Balcanqual, Walter, 81, 108, 136,
Bancroft, Bishop Richard, 63-64, 69, 71-73, 137,
Barnard, Leslie, 34-35,
Bates, Elizabeth, 309,
Bates, Julius, 309,
Bauman, John, 229,
Baxter, Richard, 116, 173-174, 176, 184, 310,
Beauchamp. Dr, 58,
Beaumont, alias Rockwood, 117,
Beck, William, 267,
Beddome, Benjamin, 275,
Bedford, John, 349,
Bellamy, Joseph, 278,
Bellarmine, Robert, F. R., 68,
Berggraf, Eivind, 368,
Bernadotte family, 367,
Berridge, John, 312,
Beveridge, Bishop, 88,
Beza, Theodore, 59, 63,

Bodley, Sir Thomas, 113,
Bogaerdtius (Bogaert), J. van den, 156,
Bogerman, John, 82,
Bolton, Mr, 174,
Boone, Daniel, 287,
Borchorn, Aletta van, 156,
Boston, Thomas, 171, 199-200, 202,
Boswell, James, 294,
Bourne, Vincent, 308,
Bradford, John, 57,
Bradford, Mr, 22,
Brainerd, David, 261-265, 372,
Brainerd, Dorothy, 262,
Brainerd, Heziekiah, 262,
Bridges, Charles, 78,
Brine, John, 275, 279,
Bronte, Emily, 236,
Bronte, Patrick, 236,
Brook, Benjamin, 170,
Brook, Benjamin, 71, 173,
Brooks, Thomas, 236-237,
Brown, John (of Whitburn), 171,
Brown, Moses, 312,
Brun, Nordahl, 365,
Bucer (Butzer, Baucer), Martin, 59, 87-88, 129,
Bull, William, 240, 315,
Bullinger, Heinrich, 50-51, 59,
Bunyan, John, 312, 352,
Burgess, Cornelius, 107,
Burke, Edmund, 342,
Burroughs, Pastor, 212-213,
Busch, Wilhelm, 368,
Cadogan, W. B., 256, 259,
Caecilian, Bishop, 139-140,
Calamy, Edmund, 103-104,
Calf, Robert, 214-215,
Calvin, John, 51, 59, 232, 310,
Cameron, John, 89-91, 93-94,

Campian, Edmund, 68,
Capon, John, 48,
Carey, William, 37, 240, 373, 383,
Carleton, Bishop George, 51, 81-83, 87, 105-106, 116, 137,
Cartwright, Thomas, 52-53, 59-61, 71-73,
Cecil, Richard, 178, 308,
Cecil, William, 58,
Cennick, John, 270,
Chaderton, Dr, 67,
Chaloner, Dr, Luke, 113,
Chaloner, Phoebe, 113,
Charles I, 94, 118, 126, 136, 146, 151, 200,
Charles II, 119, 136, 151, 157,
Charnock, Stephen, 312,
Chauncey, Charles, 217,
Cherokees, 382, 389,
Christian, John T., 138,
Cistertians, 116,
Clark Marjorie, 16,
Clark, Betty, 16.
Clark, Mr, 277,
Clark, Samuel, 230,
Clark, Vera, 16,
Clark, William, 383,
Clarkson, Thomas, 302,
Clinton, General, 285, 286,
Colman, George, 294, 343,
Comenius, Johannes Amos, 152,
Cone Wallace, 390,
Cone, Edward, 390,
Congreve, William, 343,
Conyers, Richard, 308,
Cooke, Elisa, 195,
Cooper, Bishop, 104,
Corbert, Bishop Robert, 144,
Cory, Giles, 212,
Cotton, Anne, 197,
Cotton, Elizabeth, 186,
Cotton, John, 43, 147, 149, 151-152, 184, 186, 206,
Cotton, Maria, 186,
Cotton, Nathaniel, 295, 296,
Coverdale, Bishop Miles, 46,
Cowell, G., 315,
Cowper, Anne, 291,

Cowper, Ashley, 294,
Cowper, Dr John (Sen.), 291, 293,
Cowper, John (Jun.), 295,
Cowper, Theadora, 294,
Cowper, William, 43. 78, 83, 240, 275, 291-305, 342, 352,
Cowper. Judith, 292,
Cox, Dr, 176,
Cramp, J. M., 133, 136,
Cranmer, Archbishop Thomas, 46, 104, 129,
Crisp, Tobias, 161-171, 353,
Cromwell, Oliver, 119-120, 151,
Crosby, Thomas, 131, 134,
Cudworth, William, 331,
Daniel, Curt, 337,
Darracott, Risdon, 43. 248, 250, 267-272,
Davenant, Bishop John, 52-53, 77-97, 102-104, 106, 114. 116, 137,
Davenant, Edward, 79,
Davenant, James, 79,
Davenant, Joan, 79,
Davenant, Judith, 79,
Davenant, Margaret (married R. Townson), 79, 85,
Davenant, Nicholas, 313,
Davenant, William, 79,
Davenport, John, 187, 188,
Davis, John, 223,
Davis, Richard, 337. 353,
Denne, Henry, 134,
Denny, Lord, 101,
Dewar, Dr Michael D., 45,
Dewar, Margaret, 200,
Doddridge, Daniel, 229,
Doddridge. John, 229,
Doddridge, Monica, 229,
Doddridge, Philip, 42, 229, 250, 267-268, 270, 271-272, 275, 372,
Donne, John, 292,
Doudney, D. A., 315,
Dudley, Joseph, 196, 197,
Dunster, Dr, 236,
Dunster, Henry, 152,
Edmondes, Sir Thomas, 124,
Edward IV, 79,
Edward VI, 47,

Edwards, Jonathan, 262, 265,
Edwards, Morgan, 284,
Eliot, John, 159,
Elizabeth I, 51-52, 69, 74, 104-105
Ella, Mavis, 16,
Elliot, John, 262,
Emerton, Ephrain, 79,
Erasmus, Desiderius, 79,
Erastus, Thomas, 126,
Erskine, Colonel John, 200,
Erskine, Dr., 277,
Erskine, Ebenezer, 171, 199-200,
Erskine, Henry, 199,
Erskine, Margaret (née Simson), 201,
Erskine, Margaret, (née Dewar), 200-201,
Erskine, Ralf, 171, 312, 199-203,
Fairclough, (Daniel Featley's family name), 124,
Fairclough, John, 124,
Fawcet, John, 239-240,
Fawcett, Benjamin, 270,
Featley, Daniel, 118, 123-140,
Fenner, Dudley, 60,
Fever, Mr and Mrs, 323,
Fever, Susan, 323-324,
Fischer (Piscator); Johannes, 93,
Fisher, Edward, 202,
Fitch, Squire, 325,
Fitz-Simmons, Henry, 112,
Flavel, John, 277,
Foskett, Bernard, 275, 276,
Foxe, John, 86, 312,
Franke, August, Hermann, 216,
Franklin, Benjamin, 213,
Frederick the Elector, 229,
Frederick the Wise, 86,
Friend, Henry, 323,
Frith, Elizabeth, 276
Fugentius, 91,
Fuller, Andrew, 278,
Fuller, John Mee, 140,
Fuller, Morris, 78, 82, 125,
Fuller, Thomas, 51, 61-62, 64-65, 69, 72-73, 79, 84, 97, 102,
Fullerton, James, 111,
Gadsby, William, 353,
Gano, John (J. G.'s eldest son), 285,
Gano, John, 281-289,

Gano, Sarah, 284,
Gano, William, 286, 288,
Gård, Rolf, 24, 25,
Gardiner, Bishop Stephen, 47,
Garrick, David, 341-342,
Garth, Gregory, 57,
Gay, David, 357,
George III, 329-330,
Gerhard, Peter, 156,
Gifford, Andrew, 312, 315,
Gilby, Anthony, 99,
Gilby, Nathaniel, 99,
Gill, John (of St Albans, nephew of John Gill of Carter Lane), 226,
Gill, John, 78, 96, 131, 138-139, 157, 167, 171, 221-227, 232, 240, 257, 275, 310, 312-314, 319, 337, 347, 353,
Gill, Mary, 226,
Gillies, John, 269,
Gilpin, Bernard, 256,
Goad, Dr Thomas, 81, 102,
Goadby, J. J., 127, 134-135,
Goldsmith, Oliver, 342,
Gomarus, Francis, 83,
Goodwin, John, 107,
Gorton, Samuel, 43,
Goßlau, Dr. Werner, 40-41,
Graham, Billy, 22,
Gratian, Emperor, 49,
Gresham College, 257,
Grimshaw, William, 235-244, 308,
Grindal, Archbishop Edmund, 47, 57-58, 62,
Grotius, Hugo, 155, 157, 259,
Gualter, Rodolph, 50, 59,
Gustafsson, Bernt, 365,
Hall, Bishop Joseph, 53, 74, 81, 99-108, 115, 136-137,
Hall, Robert Jun., 278,
Hall, Robert Sen., 278,
Hall, Winifride, 99,
Hamilton, James, 111, 112,
Harding, Mr, 48,
Hardwick, Charles, 129,
Harrison, Major General John, 136,
Harsenet, Archbishop, 94,
Hart, Joseph, 312,
Hartley, William, 239, 240,

Hastings, Warren, 300,
Hauge, Hans Nielsen, 363-368,
Haweis, Thomas, 295, 308,
Hawker, Robert, 347-360,
Hazleton, John, 315,
Heathcliff, 236,
Helmsley, Maurice, 16, 19,
Henry II, 118,
Henry IV, 79,
Henry VII, 80,
Henry VIII, 47,
Henry, Matthew, 20, 275, 347,
Herbert, George, 86,
Hervey, James, 78, 88, 96, 157-158,
167-168, 171, 199, 221-222, 232,
240, 247-252, 257, 268-269, 275-276,
308, 310, 312-313, 353,
Hesketh, Lady Harriot, 299, 302, 342,
Heskin, 236,
Heylin, Dr Peter, 84,
Hiawatha, 261,
Hicks, John, 16, 19-21, 30,
Hill, Joseph, 294,
Hill, Roland, 308,
Himmler, Heinrich, 368,
Hinson, John, 52,
Hitler, Adolf, 40, 368,
Hog, James, 202,
Hogarth, William, 294,
Holt, Edmund, 146,
Hooker, Thomas, 147, 151,
Hooper, Bishop John, 129,
Hoornbeck, J, 156,
Hopkins, Bishop, 88,
Horrocks, Mr, 143-144,
Huflel, Shiela, 209,
Humphrey, Lawrence, 124,
Hunt, Elizabeth, 321-322,
Hunt, William, 319, 321,
Huntington, Lord, 100,
Huntington, Mary, 330,
Huntington, William, 171, 319-338,
353,
Hussites, 229,
Hutchins, Richard, 247,
Hutton, Archbishop, 81,
Hutton, Matthew, 69,
Hutton, W. H., 125,

Ingham, Benjamin, 243,
Jackson, Sidney, 22,
James I (VI Scotland), 80, 85, 102,
105, 111, 113, 115-118,
James II, 136, 158, 195, 207,
Janeway, James, 173, 176-177, 178,
262,
Janeway, John, 43, 173-180,
Janeway, William, 175,
Jay, William, 344,
Jenks, Benjamin, 250,
Jennings, John, 230, 231,
Jerome, 49,
Jesuits, 116,
Jewel, Bishop John, 45-55, 86, 104,
John the Baptist, 376,
Johnson, John, 83,
Johnson, Samuel, 342,
Johnson, W. B., 352,
Jones, Evan, 385,
Jones, Thomas, 307,
Joss, Torial, 329,
Judson, Adoniram, 382,
Kayar, Fateh Ali Shah, 374,
Keach, Benjamin, 221,
Keach, Elias, 381,
Keating, Mary, 16, 30,
Keighley, Mr and Mrs, 16,
Kent, John, 356,
Kephart, Horace, 261,
Kidd, B. J., 128,
Kiffin, William, 131, 135-137, 139,
Kinghorn, Joseph, 281,
Lambert, Sir Daniel, 256,
Lancaster, Mr, 167,
Lapps, 367,
Laud, William, 77, 84, 91, 94, 103,
125, 146, 148, 152,
Lecky, W. H. E.,
Lee, Mr, 16,
Leighton, Archbishop Robert, 78,
Lewis, C. S., 304,
Lewis, Meriwether, 383,
Lindé, Franz-Oskar, 31,
Lloyd, Dr, Pierson, 308,
Lloyd-Jones, Martyn, 34, 52-53, 71,
219,
Lockwood, Sarah, 237,

Long, Major Stephen, 383,
Longfellow, Henry Wadsworth, 261-262,
Louis XII, 157,
Lumpkin, William, 135, 139,
Luther, Martin, 39, 51, 86-88, 363,
Lykins, Dr Johnston, 382-384, 392,
Macaulay, Mrs, 104,
MacLeod, Donald, 320,
Madan, Martin, 295, 312,
Madison, President James, 381,
Malone, William, 117,
Manton, Thomas, 310,
Marcellus II (pope), 68,
Marck, John, 158
Margaret of Anjou, 79,
Maris, Mercy, 231,
Marprelate, Martin, 63,
Marshall, Walter, 248, 250, 268, 296,
Martin, Corbly, 386,
Martyn, Henry, 42, 236, 371-376,
Marvin, A. P. , 207,
Mary II, 195, 207, 211,
Mary Queen of Scots, 62,
Mary the Bloody, 46-47, 107,
Mather, Cotton, 143, 145, 149, 152-153, 184, 186-188, 192, 196-197, 205-218,
Mather, Dr, Samuel, 264
Mather, Eleazer, 185,
Mather, Increase (Cotton Mather's son), 218,
Mather, Increase, 152-153, 183-197, 206, 208-209, 212-214, 216,
Mather, Katherine, 146, 183-184, 186,
Mather, Margaret, 143,
Mather, Maria, 187, 206,
Mather, Nathaniel, 185,
Mather, Richard, 43, 143-153, 183, 186-187, 196, 206,
Mather, Samuel (Richard Mather's son), 185,
Mather, Samuel, (Cotton Mather's son), 218,
Mather, Thomas, 143,
Maurice, Prince of Orange, 80,
Mayo, Daniel, 230,
McCormick, Calvin, 379,
McCoy, Eliza, 385,

McCoy, Isaac, 379-393,
McCoy, James, 379,
McCoy, William, 380,
McGinn, Donald, 60-61, 63,
McMillan, Mr, 199,
Middlekauff, Robert, 148, 153, 205,
Middleton, Augustus, 308,
Middleton, Erasmus, 47, 53-54, 61-62, 64, 126, 173, 202, 226, 307, 315,
Miller, Arthur, 205, 208-209, 213, 215,
Miller, Perry, 205,
Miller, Samuel, 51, 81,
Milton, John, 105, 352,
Montague, Adolphus, 308,
Montague, Mrs, 342,
Montague, Richard, 87-88, 103,
Mordaunt, Lord and Lady, 117, 119, 120,
More, Hannah, 302, 341-345,
Morris, James, 309,
Morris, Joshua, 380,
Morton, Bishop, 103, 145,
Moulin, Peter du, 106,
Moyes, David, 20-21, 30,
Murdock, Kenneth B., 187-188, 196,
Murray, Iain, 319, 357,
Murray, John, 320-321,
Napoleon, 382,
Nauhaught, 261,
Neal, Daniel, 45, 47, 58, 105, 134, 270,
Newton, John, 130, 239, 275, 303, 308, 315, 330, 342, 345, 352,
Nicholl, John, 308,
Nonsence Club, 294,
Norton, John, 184,
Nowell, Dr, 312,
Nurse, Rebecca, 216,
Oakes, Thomas, 195,
Oakes, Uriah, 192,
Oakley, Henry, 34,
Old Vicarage, 293, 294,
Oliver, Robert, 320,
Olivers, Thomas, 314,
Olson, Alvar and Mirjam, 32, 33,
Ormiston, James, 315,
Ottawas, 380, 388,
Ottley, Robert, 60,

Ousely, Sir Gore, 374,
Overal(l), Dr, 87,
Owen, J. B.,
Owen, John, 78, 236-237, 275,
Packer, James I., 52,157,
Paine, Thomas, 344-345,
Parker, Archbishop Matthew, 59,
Parkhurst, John, 45, 47-48,
Pavey, John, 328,
Pearsall, Richard, 271,
Pelagius, 91,
Perkins, William, 53, 111, 144,
Perne, Dr, 58,
Petilianus, 49,
Philip, King (Metacomet), 192,
Philpot, J. C., 139,
Phips, Governor Sir William, 195, 211, 216,
Pius VIII, 374,
Pole, Cardinal, 58,
Polhill, Mr, 312,
Polke, Christiana, 380,
Polwhele, Mr, 351,
Poole, Matthew, 194,
Pope, Alexander, 292,
Porter, Mr, 350,
Porteus, Bishop Beilby, 342,
Pottawatomies, 388,
Price, Charles, 294,
Prideaux, John, 125,
Princess Amelia, 330,
Princess Charlotte, 330,
Proctor, John, 212-213, 216,
Prosper, 91,
Putnam, G. P., 79,
Rains, Anne, 348,
Ramsbottom, B. A., 131,
Ramsey, James, 302,
Ramus, Peter (Pierre de Ramée), 145, 185,
Randolf, Edward, 194-196,
Reynolds (Reinolds or Rainolds), Dr John, 62,
Reynolds, Bishop, 88,
Reynolds, Joshua, 342,
Rice, Elizabeth, 380,
Rice, Luther, 391,
Richards, Judge John, 216,
Richardson, Samuel, 134, 138-140,

Riesenfeld, Prof., 37,
Ringgren, Prof. Helmer, 38,
Rippon, John, 221, 314,
Rogers, John, 192,
Romaine, William, 221, 240, 243, 255-259, 307, 310. 330, 349, 353,
Rosenius, Carl Olof, 367,
Row, W., 315,
Rowe, Nicholas, 313,
Russell, Barnabas, 321-323,
Rutherford, Samuel, 151,
Ryland, Elizabeth, 277,
Ryland, John Collett, 157, 171, 240, 247, 275-279, 312, 315, 353,
Ryle, J. C., 305, 313,
Same (Lapps), 31,
Sant, Henry, 337,
Saravia, Adrian, 63,
Saunders, Nicholas, 68,
Schaff, Philip, 255,
Schwenckfeld, Caspar, 129,
Scott, Mrs, 277,
Scott, Thomas (Engl.), 308, 347, 352,
Scott, Thomas, (Am.), 81, 84,
Searle, Ambrose, 308,
Sears, Benjamin, 386,
Sears, John, 384,
Selina, Countess of Huntingdon, 233, 271-272, 295,
Semple, Robert B., 281,
Sergius, 374,
Shawnee, 381,
Shawnees, 284,
Shepherd (Shepard, Sheppard), Thomas, 184, 192,
Sherfield, Henry, 86,
Sheridan, Richard Brinsley, 342,
Shirley, Lady Francis, 167-168,
Short, Mary, 325,
Sibbes, Richard, 312,
Simeon, Charles, 236, 308, 372,
Sleigh, Edmund, 100,
Smeaton, George, 93,
Smith, Hezekiah, 283,
Smith, Richard, 239,
Southey, Robert, 319,
Spalatin, George, 86,
Spurgeon, Charles H., 45, 52-53, 78, 221, 225, 319,

Stanihurst (married Usher), Margaret, 111,
Stanihurst, Richard, 112,
Staughton, Vice-Governor, 213,
Sterne, Laurence, 343,
Stevens, John, 355,
Stillman, Samuel, 284,
Stinton, Benjamin, 131, 221,
Stites, John, 283,
Stites, Sarah, 283,
Stonehouse, James, 252,
Sundkler, Prof. Benkt, 37-38,
Susquehannah, 264,
Sutcliff, John, 226,
Swedish, 23,
Swift, Jonathan, 343,
Syriac, 233,
Tamil, 233,
Tanner, Henry, 348,
Tate, Dr., 276,
Taylor, Abraham, 224,
Tecumseh, 381,
Tennent, Gilbert, 282,
Terboven, Governor, 367, 368,
Thatcher, Thomas, 192,
Thielicke, Prof. Helmut, 39,
Thornton, Bonnel, 294,
Throgmorton, Sir Nicholas, 47,
Tillotson, Archbishop John, 195, 259,
Tindal, Humphrey, 69,
Tindale, (Tyndale) William, 46, 374,
Toland, John, 259,
Tomline, Bishop, 84,
Toplady, Augustus M., 96, 161, 171, 222, 240, 275, 307-316, 353,
Toplady, Catherine, 308,
Toplady, Major Richard, 308,
Torrey, Samuel, 192,
Townson, Robert, 85,
Traill, Robert, 164, 171,
Tryer, John, 79,
Turretin, Francis, 312,
Twisse, Dr William, 167, 171,
Tyerman, Luke, 270,
Tyndall, Humphrey, 79,
Unwin, William, 298-299,
Upham, Charles W., 215-216,
Usher, Archbishop (James' uncle), 113,

Usher, Archbishop James, 70-71, 77, 96, 111-120, 136,
Usher, Arnold, 111,
Vane, Sir Henry, 187,
Vaughan, Richard, 69,
Venn, Henry, 237, 243, 308,
Vermigli, Peter Martyr, 46-47, 49, 59,
Vernon House, 308,
Voetius (Voet), Gisbertus (Gijbert), 156,
Vorstius, Conrad, 80,
Walker, Samuel (of Truro), 269, 308, 371,
Waller, George, 380-381,
Walpole, Horace, 342,
Walton, Isaac, 61,
Ward, Samuel, 53, 81-82, 84, 86, 88, 106, 108, 114, 136-137,
Washington, George, 285, 289,
Watts, Isaac, 217, 231-232,
Webb, Anne, 329,
Wesley, John, 223, 239, 269, 309, 313, 315, 335, 345,
Whiston, William, 217,
Whitaker, William, 53, 59, 61, 64, 67-74,
White, Alderman, 348-349,
Whitefield, George, 171, 202, 221, 232, 238-240, 250, 256, 268, 270-271, 283, 301, 310, 314, 319, 321, 345,
Whitefield's Tabernacle, 310,
Whitgift, Archbishop John, 51, 53, 57-65, 67, 69-71, 73-74, 81, 104,
Whitgift, Henry, 57,
Whitgift, John (uncle of Archbishop), 57,
Whitley, W. T., 136, 138,
Whittesley, Mr., 263,
Whittier, John Greenleaf, 42, 261-262, 371-372, 375,
Wilberforce, William, 291, 305, 342,
Wilkes, John, 294,
Willard, Samuel, 215,
William of Orange (William III), 157, 159, 191, 195, 207, 211,
Williams, Daniel, 170,
Williams, John, 348,
Williams, Roger, 43,

Wilson, Gabriel, 202,
Wilson, Mary, 161,
Wilson, Thomas, 307,
Winthrop, Governor, 152,
Witsius, Herman, 155-159, 310,
Wolever, Terry, 281, 289,
Wolfius, H., 50,
Womack, Bishop, 84,
Wood, Anthony, 140,

Woral, Dr, 145,
Wotton, Sir Henry, 61,
Wright, Thomas, 308, 310, 312, 332,
Xenophon, 374,
Zanchius (Zanchy), Jerome, 310,
Zeisberger, David, 262,
Ziegenbalg, Bartholomaeus, 217,
Zouch, Lord, 84,
Zwingli, Ulrich, 50, 51, 59,

Index of Places, Churches, Public Buildings, and Educational Establishments

Abbey Road Baptist Church, 34,
Acton, 125,
Amiens, 28,
Änge Nomadskola, 37,
Araxes River, 374,
Arkansas, 379, 389, 390,
Ashby-de-la-Zouch, 99,
Australia, 23,
Baltimore, 379,
Barbados, 147,
Barent Sea, 363,
Barkerend Primary School, 17,
Bath, 311, 341,
Bell Inn, 325,
Bergen, 365,
Berkhamsted, 291,
Berlin, 40,
Berne, 80,
Blackburn, 236,
Blackfriars, 258,
Blagdon, 311,
Bodleian Library, Oxford, 113, 277,
Bohemia, 51,
Bordeaux, 89,
Boston (Am.), 148-149, 184, 186,
189, 192-193, 206-207, 209, 386,
Bradford, Yorkshire, 14-15, 22, 237,
Brandenburg, 80,
Brasenose College, Oxford, 145,
Bredtvedt, 366,
Bremen, 80,
Brindle, 236,
Brinkworth, 161,
Bristol Academy, 275,

Bristol, 147,
Bristol, 270,
Bristow Park, 99,
Brixworth, 267,
Broad Hembury, 312,
Buck Creek, 380,
Buckinghamshire, 297,
Buden, 45,
Burton-on-the-Water, 275,
Bury, 146,
Cambridge (Am.), 197,
Cambridge, 100, 161, 176, 372,
Carey, 382, 392,
Carter Lane Church, 222, 310,
Cartwright Memorial Hall, Bradford,
22,
Castle Hill, 231,
Charles Parish Church, 348,
Charleston, 283,
Charleton-upon-Otmore, 124,
Cheddar, 345,
Chelsea College, 125, 140,
Christ's College, Cambridge, 236,
Clark County, 380,
Collegium Insanorum, 295,
Columbian College, 391,
Connecticut River, 185,
Connecticut, 149, 262,
Cooladine, 309,
Cornwall, 371,
Corpus Christi College, 46, 124,
County Wexford, 309,
Covent Garden, 341,
Cranbrook, 321, 323,

Danbury Park, 325,
Danvers, 209,
Darlarna, 37,
Darly, 100,
Delaware, 263
Denholm, 237,
Denmark, 364-365,
Devonshire, 45, 186,
Ditton (Thames), 328, 330, 332,
Doddridge's Academy, 268,
Dorchester (Am.), 149, 153, 183, 186,
Dorsetshire, 325,
Drayton, 117,
Dublin College, 112,
Dublin, 185, 186, 309-310,
Duisburg, 36,
Durham Cathedral, 35,
Edinburgh University, 199, 350,
Edinburgh, 201, 277,
Eichstädt, 86,
Ellis Island, 205,
Emden, 80,
Emmanuel College, Cambridge, 99-100,
Enfield, 277,
England, 156, 159,
Enkhuysen, 155,
Erivan, 374,
Erzroom, 374,
Essen, 36, 367-8,
Essex, 101, 325,
Etchmiatzin, 374,
Eton, 161, 173,
Ewell, 328,
Ewood Hall, 237,
Exeter, 271, 347,
Falmouth, 351,
Farley Hungerford, 311,
Farnham, 308,
Fen Ottery, 311,
Finland, 367,
First Church, Boston, 188,
Fort Gibson, 383,
Fort Wayne, 382, 386,
Fourteen Mile Creek, 380,
France, 26-29, 124, 156, 159, 364,
Franeker University, 157-158,
Frankfort, 288,
Frankfurt, 47,
French Reformed Church, Orange

Street, 314,
Friesland, 156,
Frittenden, 323,
Fulneck, Yorkshire, 152,
Geneva, 51, 63,
Geneva, 80,
Germany, 26-27, 39-41, 47, 159, 216,
Glasgow University, 216,
Gloucestershire, 341,
Gloucestor, 102,
Goat Yard Church, Horselydown, 221-222,
Gothenburg, 23, 28,
Great Britain, 80,
Great Eastcheap, 222,
Grimsby, 57,
Guernsey, 185-186,
Hållands Folkhögskola, 36,
Halsted, 100,
Hamburg University, 36,
Hamburg, 39,
Hampton Wick, 326,
Hanson Grammar School, Bradford, 22,
Hardingstone, 247,
Harpford, 311,
Hartlepool, 255,
Harvard College, 152, 183, 185, 191-192, 196, 206,
Haworth, 235, 237-238, 239,
Hertfordshire, 173, 180, 184,
Hessen, 80,
Holland, 104, 136, 156,
Holme, 67, Bournley, 67,
Hopewell, 283,
Houghton-le-Spring, 256,
House of Bambridge, 99,
House of Lords, 294,
Hull University, 35, 36,
Hull, 39,
Hungary, 51,
Hyton, 144,
Illinois, 381,
India, 217,
Indian Territory, 382, 389, 392,
Indiana, 380,
Ipswich (Am.), 184,
Ireland, 118, 309,
Jämtland, 31,
Jefferson County, 380,

Jeffersonville, 393,
Jerusalem Farm, 235,
Kansas City, 383,
Kansas River, 382,
Kansas, 379,
Kars, 374,
Kaunaumeck, 263,
Kelshall Church, 180,
Kent, 321,
Kentucky, 286-288, 380-381, 392,
Kettering, 221,
Kew gardens, 330,
Kibworth Dissenting College, Leicestershire, 230,
King's College, Cambridge, 173, 175-176,
Kingston-upon-Thames, 229, 326,
Kirkgate Market, Bradford, 20,
Lambeth, Surrey, 125-126,
Lancashire, 235-236,
Lancaster, 67,
Lapland, 24, 33,
Leake, 80,
Leicestershire, 99,
Leuwarden, 156,
Leyden, 80, 159,
Lincoln College, Oxford, 247, 250,
Lincolnshire, 57,
Lisbon, 233, 272,
Liverpool, 143,
London Bible College, 30, 34,
London, 38, 185,
Lorimers' Hall, 170,
Louisville, 380, 393,
Lowton, 143,
Lutterworth, 231,
Luxembourg, 26-27,
Lylly, 173,
Magdalen Hall, Oxford, 124, 349,
Malta, 374,
Marefair, 231,
Margaret Street, 331,
Maria Creek, 381,
Market Harborough, 231,
Mary Steps Church, 347,
Maryland, 288,
Massachusetts, 147, 149-151, 153, 183, 193, 195, 206-207, 210-211,
Mendip Hills, 311, 341,

Merchant Taylors' School, 79,
Meredith, 386,
Merton College, Oxford, 45, 291,
Metropolitan Tabernacle, 221,
Michigan, 382-383,
Middlesex, 125,
Mile Lane, 257,
Mississippi, 382, 389,
Missouri (State), 389-390,
Missouri River, 382, 389-390
Monilaws, 199,
Monkton Farleigh, 45,
Morristown, 283,
Mortlake, 325,
Mount Ararat, 374-375,
Netherlands, 157,
New Brunswick, 287,
New England, 147, 152, 183, 189-191, 194, 210, 212, 215, 265,
New Haven Church, 207,
New Jersey, 283,
New Territories, 392,
New York, 284-287, 386,
Niles, 382,
North Carolina, 283-284, 287, 289,
Northampton (Am.), 185, 264,
Northampton, (Brit.) 231, 247, 250, 276,
Northamptonshire, 117,
North-Rhine Westphalia, 39, 359,
Northumberland, 199,
Norway, 33, 363,
Nottinghamshire, 80,
Ohio River, 287, 380, 382,
Ohio, 386,
Oklahoma, 379, 383,
Old North Church, 186, 207,
Olney, 297,
Opocken, 283,
Orange Street, 315,
Örebro, 24,
Östergötland, 367,
Oxenhope, 237,
Oxford, 46-47, 51, 161, 249, 256-257, 312,
Palatine (Pfalz), 80,
Peel Park, Bradford, 14,
Pemberton Square, 187,
Pembroke College, 57,

Pembroke Hall, 58,
Pennsylvania, 379-380,
Persia, 373,
Peter House, 58,
Philadelphia, 256, 284, 288, 386,
Plymouth (Am.), 184,
Plymouth (Brit.), 348, 350, 359,
Poland, 159,
Portmoak, 199,
Preston, 236,
Privy Council, 62,
Providence Chapel, 332, 333,
Puncah River, 389,
Queen Margaret's College (Queen's),
Cambridge, 67-68,79-80,
Racoon Creek, 382,
Red River, 389-390,
Rhode Island, 43, 288,
Richmond, 330,
Rochdale, 236,
Rome, 59,
Rönnefors, 31,
Royal Academy, 187,
Rygate, 120,
Salem Village, 209,
Salem, 209,
Salisbury Cathedral, 86,
Salisbury, 45,
Saumur, 89,
Scandinavia, 23,
Schaffhausen, 80,
Serampore, 383,
Shelby County, 380,
Sheldon, 312,
Sierra Leone, 352,
Silver Creek, 380,
Sissinghurst Castle, 322,
Skagerrak, 363,
Småland, 367,
Somersetshire, 269, 311,
South Africa, 38,
Southwark (see also Goat Yard and
Horselydown), 130, 134, 222,
Spain, 59, 156,
St Albans, 295,
St Antony's School, London, 57,
St Bartholomew's, 258,
St Bodolph's, 314,
St Botolph's, Billingsgate, 256,

St Clement's Church, York, 22,
St Dunstan's, 243,
St George's, Botolph Lane, 256,
St George's, Hanover Square, 256,
St James' Palace, 330,
St John's College, 74, 372,
St Mary Hall, 312,
St Nicholas Parish, Dublin, 111,
St Olave's, Southwark, 257,
St Patrick's College, Dublin, 113,
St Paul's Cathedral, 67, 256,
St Paul's Churchyard, 57,
St Paul's School, London, 67, 173,
St Pauli, Hamburg, 39,
St Thomas Hospital, 348,
Stapleton, 341,
States General, 80, 105,
Staunton, 386,
Stortford, 184,
Straßburg, 47,
Suffolk, 100,
Surrey, 325,
Sweden, 28-29, 33, 152, 156, 209,
367,
Switzerland, 51, 159,
Tabriz, 374,
Taunton, 270, 271,
Teversham, 58,
Thames, 65,
The Carolinas, 284,
The Second Church, 186-187, 207,
Thomas, 382,
Three Forks, 383,
Thune, 363,
Todmordon, 236,
Tokat, 374, 375,
Torrington, 186,
Totness, 356,
Tower of London, 104,
Town Fork Baptist Church, 288,
Toxteth, 144, 185,
Trier, 26, 30,
Trinity College, Cambridge, 58, 68,
Trinity College, Dublin, 185, 309,
Truro, 371,
Union Town, 379,
United Dutch Provinces, 80, 105, 156-
157,
Uppsala, 37, 39, 184,

Utrecht University, 158,
Utrecht, 156,
Värmland, 367,
Virginia, 284, 288, 380,
Waltham, 101,
Wapping, Bradford, 15,
Warwick, 276,
Wattling Street, London, 79,
Weigle Haus, 368,
Wellington, 269, 271,
Wellow Monastery, 57,
West Friesland, 159,
West Ryding, 238,
West Wouden, 156,
Westminster Abbey, 120,

Westminster Chapel, 258,
Westminster School, 294, 300, 308-9,
Weston Favel, 268,
Wiltshire, 161,
Winick, 143,
Withens, 236,
Woking, 328,
Wormeren, 156,
Worth Valley, 235,
Wuthering Heights, 236,
Yadkin, 284,
Yale College, 197,
York Street Chapel, London, 355,
Yorkshire, 23, 235, 258,
Zürich, 47, 80,

Index of Topics, Denominations, Councils and Organisations

Absolute decree, 96,
Act of Uniformity, 229,
Actual imputation, 320,
Adoption, 88, 114,
American Baptist Board of Foreign
Missions, 381, 388-389, 391, 392,
American Baptist Home Mission, 391,
American Indian Mission Association,
132,
American pietism, 217,
Amyraldianism, 81, 85, 90-91, 94-95,
170,
Anabaptists, 124, 128-129, 131, 139,
Anglicans, Anglicanism, 60, 91, 106,
137, 194, 222, 233, 238, 350,
Antinomianism, 167-168, 170-171,
202, 314, 319-320, 331-332, 335,
353,
Appropriating God's mercies, 282,
Arianism, 124, 128, 139, 217, 331,
335, 338, 350, 354,
Arminianism, 53, 77, 81-86, 89, 95,
103, 105, 107, 157, 170, 217, 222-
224, 312, 331-332, 335-336,
Atonement, 83, 91, 165, 232,
Authorised Version of the English
Bible, 64,
Baptism, 41, 42, 388,

Baptismal debate, 187,
Baptist Union, 221, 224,
Baptists, 123, 128, 130, 132, 135,
137, 222, 232, 239, 282, 350,
Battle of White Plains, 285,
Baxterism, 202,
Blue laws, 205,
Bohemian Brethren, 152,
Bondage of the will, 217,
Bradford Home Mission, 16,
Calvinism, 54, 78, 83, 89, 108, 232,
353,
Calvinist Methodists, 270,
Cameronism, 90,
Campbellism, 381, 392,
Cherokee War, 284,
Chicago Treaty, 388,
Christian Alliance, 22,
Christian duty, 170.
Christian knowledge, 242,
Christian liberty, 165,
Christian perfection, 242,
Church of England, 48, 50, 58, 61, 70,
80-81, 84-85, 88, 96, 104, 128, 146,
193, 195, 211, 249, 255, 270, 309,
344, 351,
Church of Scotland, 81, 105,
Church of the Nazarenes, 15,

Civil War (Am.), 393,
Civil War, (Brit.), 125, 171,
Clapham Sect, 372,
Coffee House fraternal, 221-222,
Colossians, 88,
Conditional decree, 96,
Confirmation, 64, 137,
Congregationalism, 146, 153, 188, 193-195, 197,
Conversion, 83,
Council of Arles, 128,
Council of Chalcedon, 128,
Council of Constantinople, 128,
Council of Epesus, 128,
Council of Nicea, 128
Council of Trent, 51,
Council Table, 94,
Covenants, 41, 155, 170, 200, 268-269, 311,
Crown rule, 211,
Dalton's *Justice*, 212,
Dancing, 324,
Declaration of Breda, 186,
Deism, 215, 217,
Deists, 264,
Det norske lutherske indremisjonsselskap, 367,
Deutsche (German) Christen, 39, 368,
Dissenters, 42, 58, 101, 151, 202, 268-270, 344,
Doctrine of man, 240-241,
Donatism, 49, 128, 139, 140,
Dunfermline presbytery, 200,
East India Company, 299, 372,
Eclectic Society, 345,
Edict of Nantes, 255,
Effectual calling, 217,
Election, 83, 87-88, 91, 94, 96, 114, 217, 312, 321,
Episcopacy, 42, 62-64, 81, 100, 103-104, 119, 132-133, 137, 139, 146,
Episcopalian Dissenters, 202,
Erastianism, 126,
Eternal decrees, 114,
Eternal life, 94,
Eternal Sonship of Christ, 222,
Evangelical Awakening, 269, 307, 319,
Evangelical righteousness, 170,
Evangelicals, 258,

Fall, 387,
Fifth Monarchy, 86, 103, 107-108,
Final perseverance, 312,
Franciscans, 116,
Free grace, 165, 170.
Free Will Baptists, 283,
Free will, 83, 170,
Freedom in Christ, 166,
French and Indian War, 283,
French Reformed Church, 28, 80,
Fullerism, 336,
Gallican Church, 89, 91,
General Baptists, 135,
General Convention, 384,
German retreat from Russia, 368,
Glorious Revolution, 211,
Godhead, 387,
Good works, 114, 165, 168, 170, 224,
Gospel exhortations, 388,
Great Armada, 59,
Great Commission, 360,
Greek Testament, 67, 143, 251,
Greek, 183,
Grotainism, 157, 164-165, 170, 264, 355,
Half-Way Covenant, 153, 187, 188, 211,
Hampton Court Conference, 62,
Hardest thing in religion, 249,
Haugians, 364,
Hebrew Testament, 251,
Hebrew, 183, 247,
Hessian troops, 285,
High Calvinism, 53, 70, 232, 279, 320,
Holy Club, 248, 250,
Holy Spirit, 42, 233, 249, 350, 354, 367,
House of Representatives, 390,
Huguenots, 281,
Hyper-Calvinism, 314, 337, 353,
Imputed righteousness, 164, 166, 217, 222-224, 351,
Incarnation, 117, 129, 241, 387,
Independents, 222,
Indian War, 193,
Interdenominational fellowship, 233, 239, 240, 271,
Irresistible grace, 83, 217,
John's baptism, 130,

Justification, 88, 166, 202, 320,
Justifying faith, 69,
Kina misjonsforbund, 367,
Laity baptism abolished, 64,
Latitudinarianism, 256-257, 264,
Laudians, 186,
Law, 157, 224, 279,
London Missionary Society, 352,
Long Parliament, 86, 96, 103, 125,
Lord's Day, 162,
Lord's Prayer, 55, 158, 213,
Lord's Supper (Table), 42, 45, 137,
238, 276, 388,
Lutheran Church, 38, 364,
Lutherstiftelsen, 367,
Marian Papists, 46,
Marriage Supper of the Lamb, 42,
Marrow Men, 202,
Marxism, 291,
Massachusetts Historical Society, 212,
Methodists, 329,
Modern Question, 278,
Moravians, 371,
Mosaic Law, 155, 157,
Mystical union with Christ, 101,
Nazi Millennium, 368,
Neonomianism, 89, 170, 201-202,
New charter, 190-191, 196,
New Covenant, 241,
New Divinity, 355,
New England Unitarianism, 188,
New Light, 381,
New man, 354,
Non-Conformists, 62,
Norsk luthersk misjonssamband, 367,
Old Covenant, 241,
Old man, 242, 354,
Original sin, 312,
Oyer and Terminer court, 212,
Papacy, 102, 124,
Particular Baptists, 131, 171, 221,
281, 289, 310, 355,
Particular Redemption, 312,
Pelagianism, 86-87, 91-93, 102, 129,
Penal substitution, 164,
Perfectionism, 129, 242, 354,
Perseverance, 83, 87, 223-224, 242,
388,
Persian New Testament, 373,

Pia antiquitas, 157,
Pneumatology, 268,
Predestination, 69, 83, 87, 94-96, 114,
223, 338,
Presbyterians, 42, 50, 52, 58-60, 62-
64, 77, 81-82, 85, 100-103, 105-106,
119, 123, 127-128, 137, 188, 282,
350, 381, 389,
Progressive holiness, 354,
Puritans, 52-53, 58, 100, 119, 210,
255, 310,
Quakers, 195, 210,
Readers, 364,
Redemption, 83,
Regeneration, 88, 321, 387,
Remission of sins, 91,
Remonstrants, 103,
Repentance, 91, 223, 320, 337, 388,
Reprobation, 69, 88, 95-96,
Restoration, 255-256,
Righteousness of Christ, 88, 241,
Roman Catholicism, 81, 117-118, 128,
338,
Royal Academy, 216,
Sabbath observance, 388,
Sabellianism, 128, 354,
Salem witch trials, 196, 208, 211-213,
215,
Sanctification, 88, 170, 320, 354,
Sandemanism, 312,
Saving grace, 69,
Scottish Assembly, 199, 202,
Scottish Society for Promoting
Christian Knowledge, 263,
Secession, 202,
Second World War, 14, 367,
Semi-Palagianism, 86, 90, 91,
Separatists, 52-53, 59, 102-103, 127-
128,
Seven Year War, 286,
Society for the Abolition of the Slave
Trade, 303,
Society for the Propagation of the
Gospel in Foreign Parts, 217,
Socinianism, 128, 157, 217, 350, 354,
357,
Sola scriptura, 157,
Solemn League and Covenant, 118-
119, 199,

Southern Baptist Convention, 393,
Sovereign grace, 328, 338,
St Bartholomew's Massacre, 145,
Storting, 367,
Sublapsarianism, 83, 95,
Submission to God's righteousness, 169,
Supralapsarianism, 83,
Svenska Kyrkan, 37, 38,
Swedish rule over Norway, 366,
Synod (Council) of Dort, 51, 70, 80,
87, 89-90, 102, 105, 108,
Ten Commandments, 331,
The 'offer', 337,
The believer's true service, 169,
The Great Western Society for
Dispersing Religious Tracts among

the Poor, 352, ˎ
Total depravity, 83, 217,
Treaty of Kiel, 366,
Trinity, 128, 156, 167, 222, 350, 358,
387,
Triple Alliance, 156,
Unitarians, 138, 205, 215, 357,
Vicarious, penal atonement, 387,
Volkstestament, 368,
Wabash Association, 381,
War of Independence (Dutch), 157,
Western Association Conference, 170-
171,
Westminster Assembly, 70, 103-104,
108, 118, 126, 151, 167,
Word of God, 161, 358,

Index of Works Quoted, Including Sermons and Declarations of Faith

*A Brief History of the Warr With the
Indians in New England*, 192,
A Call to the Unconverted, 116,
A debtor to mercy alone, 313,
A Dictionary of Christian Biography,
140,
*A Discussion of that great Point in
Divinity, The Sufferings of Christ*, 184,
A History of Baptists (Christian), 138,
A History of British Baptists (Whitley),
136, 138,
A History of the Articles of Religion,
129,
*A History of the Rise and Progress of
the Baptists in Virginia*, 281,
*A Method for Preventing the Frequency
of Robberies and Murders*, 257,
A Picture of an Antinomian, 319,
A Platform of Church Discipline, 151,
A Prop Against all Despair, 353, 358,
A Search For Happiness, 341,
*A Sermon Wherein is shewed that the
Church of God is sometimes a Subject
of Great Persecution*, 193,
*A Survey or Table, declaring the Order
of the Causes of Salvation and*

Damnation, 144,
A Treatise on Justification, 95,
*A View of the Seditious Bull Sent into
England by Pius V*, 52,
*A Vindication of the Divine Authority of
Ruling Elders*, 196,
Absolute Predestination, 310,
Adelphi, 293,
American Antiquarian Society, 190,
*An Essay for the Recording of
Illustrious Providences*, 194,
Ancilla Pietatis, 125,
Animadversions, 95,
Antichrist Unmasked, 134,
Aphorisms Concerning Justification,
310,
Aphorisms of Justification, 184,
Apology (J. Newton's), 130,
Apology of the Church of England,
45, 48-49, 52, 55, 113,
Apostles Creed, 158,
Arminian Skeleton, 335-336, 338,
Arthur Miller: The Burning Glass, 209,
*Atonement According to Christ and His
Apostles*, 93,
Banner of Sovereign Grace Truth, 43,

Banner of Truth Magazine, 43, 319,
Baptist Confessions of Faith, 135, 139,
Baptist History (Cramps), 133,
Baptist Quarterly, 43,
Baptist Standard Bearer, 43,
Belgic Confession, 77,
Bible League Quarterly, 43, 320,
Biographia Evangelica, 53, 61, 70,
106, 126, 173,
Book of Common Prayer, 126,
Bye-Paths in Baptist History, 127,
Canons of Dort, 36, 51, 77, 83-84,
113,
Cases of Conscience, 214,
Catechism for Children, 359,
Charity, 302,
Cheap Repository Tracts, 345,
Christ Alone Exalted, 171,
*Christian Liberty No Licentious
Doctrine*, 165,
Christian Morals, 343,
Church History (Collier's), 82,
Church History of Britain (Fuller), 51,
61-62, 69, 72,
Clavis Mystica, 124,
Collected Poems of Joseph Hall, 74,
Commenting and Commentaries, 45,
52, 55, 78,
*Compassion for the Sick and Sorrow-
ing*, 359,
Congregational Quarterly, 188,
Connoisseur, 294,
Contemplations (Bishop Hall), 53,
Counter-poyson, 60,
De Praestantia Veritatis Evangelicae,
158,
De vero Theologo, 157,
Declaration of Faith (Fort Wayne),
386,
Defence of Evangelical Churches, 190,
Defence of Unitarianism, 350,
Desiderius Erasmus of Rotterdam, 79,
Dissertation on the Death of Christ, 92,
Disputationes de Christianæ Fidei, 68,
*Divinity and Operation of the Holy
Ghost*, 357,
*Documents Illustrative of the History of
the Church*, 128,
Dunciad, 292,

Economy of the Covenants, 157,
Epistles of Faith, 337,
Evangelical Magazine, 350,
Evangelical Times, 43,
*Expositio Epistolæ D. Pauli ad
Colossenses*, 88,
Exposition of Colossians, 78,
Expostulations, 300, 301,
Family Expositor, 231,
Family Rules, 383, 386,
*First London Particular Baptist
Declaration of Faith*, 132, 134, 139,
Focus, 43,
Fountains of Free Grace Opened, 135,
Free Grace the Teacher of Good Works,
165,
Go forth O ye daughter of Zion, 281,
Gospel Magazine, 126, 315,
Gospel Mystery of Sanctification, 250,
268,
Gospel Sonnets, 199,
Harmony of the Gospels, 53,
Hawker's Guide Books to Zion, 356,
Heaven's Alarm to the World, 190,
Heidelberg Catechism, 77, 359,
Hermae, 74,
*Historical Collections of Accounts of
Revival*, 269,
Historical Magazine, 216,
History of England (Macaulay), 104,
History of the Baptists (Armitage), 138,
History of the Baptists (Crosby), 131,
*History of the English Church from the
Accession of Charles I to the Death of
Anne*, 125,
History of the Puritans, 45, 47, 60,
105,
Hold-Fast, 315,
Homilies of the Church of England, 81,
Human Nature in its Fourfold State,
199,
Illustrious Providences, 196,
Immanuel, 117,
Increase Mather Bibliography, 192,
Institutes (Calvin's), 83, 157,
Introduction to Puritan Theology, 52,
*Invisibles, Realities, Demonstrated in
the Holy Life and Triumphant Death of
John Janeway*, 177,

Irish Articles of Religion, 71, 113-116,
John Gill and Hyper-Calvinism, 337,
John Gill and the Cause of God and Truth, 133,
John Penry and the Marprelate Controversy, 60-61,
Justice (Dalton's), 212,
Justification, 236,
Lambeth Articles, 36, 59, 64, 70-71, 77, 81, 92, 113, 131,
Lancelot Andrewes, 60, 106,
Life and Death of John Janeway, 174,
Life of Archbishop Laud, by a Roman Recusant, 103,
Life of Mr. Richard Hooker, 61,
Life of Whitefield, 270,
Life, Letters and Writings of Bishop Davenant, 78, 82, 88, 103, 125,
Life, Walk and Triumph of Faith, 258,
Lives (Walton), 61,
Lives of the Puritans, 71, 173,
London Magazine, 309,
Magnalia Christi Americana, 143, 184,
Marrow of Modern Divinity, 202,
Meditations (Hall), 100,
Meditations (Hervey), 251,
Memoirs (More), 343,
More Wonders of the Invisible World, 215,
New Focus, 43, 356, 357,
North American Review, 216,
Northampton Mercury, 233, 304,
Nunc Dimittis, 225
On the Controversy, among the French Divines of the Reformed Church, concerning the Gracious and Saving Will of God towards Sinful Men, 89,
On the Death of Christ, 93
On the receipt of my mother's picture, 292,
Origins of Bishops and Metropolitans, 116,
Papa est ille antichristus, 58,
Percy, 342,
Periodical Account of Baptist Missions within the Indian Territory for the Year ending December 31, 1836, 390,
Pilgrim's Progress, 352,
Poor Man's Commentary, 347, 354,

Poor Man's Morning and Evening Portions, 347,
Practical Piety, 343,
Practice of Extraordinary Devotion, 125,
Pray for the Rising Generation, 193,
Preaching the Gospel to Sinners, 357,
Precious Remedies Against Satan's Devices, 236, 237,
Reasons for the Confirmation of the Charter Belonging to the Massachusetts Colony in New England, 190,
Returning unto God, 193,
Rise and Progress of Religion in the Soul, 372,
Rock of Ages, 308,
Roma Ruens, 127,
Sacred Dramas, 342,
Saints' Everlasting Rest, 174
Schaff-Herzog Encyclopaedia of Religious Knowledge, 70,
School for Scandal, 342,
Scouting for Boys, 269,
Second Helvitic Confession, 51,
Second London Particular Baptist Declaration of Faith, 132,
Sermons on Important Subjects, 359,
Smaller Catechism, 363,
Some Account of the Life of Spencer Houghton Cone. A Baptist Preacher in America, 391,
Some Brief Considerations On Doctor Featley, his Book, intitled, The Dipper Dipt, 138,
Spurgeon v. Hyper-Calvinism, 357,
Stranger than Fiction, 131,
Submission to the Righteousness of God, 250,
Survey of Discipline, 64,
Suspira Vinctorum, 218,
Svensk Kyrkohistoria, 365,
The Articles of the Synod of Dort, 81,
The Bank of Faith, 321,
The Cause of God and Truth, 222, 224,
The Church of England Vindicated from the Charge of Arminianism, 312,
The Crucible, 208,
The Cruel Brother, 313,
The Dipper Dipt, 127, 131, 134, 136, 138,

The Dissenter's Reason for Separating from the Church of England, 132,
The Distracted Puritan, 145, 146,
The Divine Right of Infant Baptism Asserted and Proved from Scripture and Antiquity, 193,
The Divinity of Christ, 357,
The Doctrine of Absolute Predestination Stated and Asserted, 313,
The Dutch Annotations on the Whole Bible, 106,
The Earthen Vessel, 319,
The Excellency of a Publick Spirit, 190,
The Fair Penitent, 313,
The Fathers of the Church of England, 54, 55,
The First Principles of new England Concerning the Subject of Baptism & Communion of Churches, 188,
The Folly of Sinning, 190,
The Glorious Throne, 190,
The Gospel Advocate, 315, 319,
The Gospel Herald, 319,
The Gospel Magazine, 315, 319, 321,
The Gospel Standard, 315, 319, 357,
The Kingdom of Heaven Taken by Prayer, 321, 336,
The Lady's Magazine, 344,
The Life and Times of Cotton Mather, 207,
The Mathers, 148,
The Naked Bow of God, 321,
The Negro's Complaint, 303,
The Old Religion, 102,
The Percy Reliques, 145,
The Psalter, 84,
The Puritans, 52, 71,
The Remembrancer, 315,
The Righteous Man a Blessing, 190,
The Rights of Man, 344,
The Rise and Progress of Religion in the Soul, 231,
The Sailor Pilgrim, 358,

The Screwtape Letters, 304,
The Sermons of Tobias Crisp, 164, 167,
The Slave Trader, 303,
The Spirit of Prayer, 343,
The Spiritual Magazine, 319,
The Task, 298, 299, 300,
The Times of Men are in the Hands of God, 193,
The Use of the Law, 165,
The work of the Holy Ghost essential to give success to all missions for the Gospel, 352,
Theatre Essays, 208,
Theron and Aspasio, 89, 158, 251,
They Subdued Kingdoms, 45,
Thirty-Nine Articles, 36, 59, 70, 77, 79, 81, 92, 94, 128-131, 135, 137, 309-310, 351,
Thoughts on the Importance of the Manners of the Great to General Society, 342,
Tirocinium, 301,
Token for Children, 178, 262,
Token for Mourners, 277,
Triangle Press, 357,
True Christianity, 364,
Union and Communion with Christ, 358,
Village Politics, 345,
Village Sermons, 359
Visits to and from Jesus, 349,
Voice of Years, 319,
Westminster Confession, 132, 137,
Westminster Standards, 137,
Whole Duty of Man, 248, 348,
William Cowper: Poet of Paradise, 297,
William Huntington: Pastor of Providence, 319,
Wonders of the Invisible World, 215,
Zion's Pilgrim, 351, 358,
Zion's Trumpet, 351,
Zion's Warrior, 348, 351-352, 358,
Zion's Witness, 315,

Index of Scripture References
Old Testament

Genesis
18:19, p. 150
33:12, p. 356

Leviticus
Lev. 19:17, p. 151

Deuteronomy
6:7, p. 150
23:2, p. 323

1 Samuel
22:23, p. 285
25:1, p. 120

2 Samuel
2:22, p. 311

2 Chronicles
16:9, p. 223

Nehemiah
9:33, p. 150
10:29-31, p. 150

Job
17:9, p. 223

Psalms
4:4, p. 150
37:30, p. 151
55:17, p. 150
55:22, p. 150
56:12, p. 150
66:13-14, p. 150

71:16, p. 222
119:59, p. 150
119:106, p. 150
139:7-13, p. 25

Proverbs
3:5, p. 29
6:9-10, p. 150
10:21, p. 151
14:31, p. 303
15:17, p. 151
20:13, p. 150
22:6; p. 150
26:4, p. 215

Ecclesiastes
9:10; p. 150

Song of Solomon (Canticles)
3:11, p, 281

Isaiah
3:10, p. 355
24:16, p. 223
26:4 (margin), p. 311

Jeremiah
48:10, p. 150

Lamentations
3:40, p.150

Daniel
6:10, p. 150

Index of Scripture References

New Testament

Matthew
6:6, p. 150
6:25, p. 150
14:23, p. 150
16:2, p. 249
25:44, p. 169

Luke
14:23, p. 203

John
6:39-40, p. 92
6:44, p. 326
13:18, p. 326
14:2, p. 327

Acts
16:14, p. 150
24:14, p. 49
27:44, p. 287

Romans
1:16, p. 58
2:14 ff, p. 256
3:22, p. 351
3:25, p. 296
4:2, p. 163
5, p. 328
5:19, p. 94
7:18, p. 354

8:9, p. 334
8:28-29, p. 90
10:3-4, p. 165
10:14-15, p. 352
11:6, p. 165
12:1, p. 111

1 Corinthians
3:6, p. 150
10:24, p. 151
11:08, p. 150

2 Corinthians
5:20, p. 349

Ephesians
1:3-5, p. 90
1:6-12, p. 356
2:4-10, p. 162
2:13, p. 309
3:12, p. 163
3:17-19, p. 242
5:16, p. 150
6:4, p. 150

Philippians
1:21, p. 243
2:4, p. 151
2:7-8, p. 94
4:6, p. 150

2 Thessalonians
2:13, p. 53

1 Timothy
4:13,15, p. 150

2 Timothy
2:15, p. 21
3:14-17, p. 21
3:16, p. 49
4:6-8, p. 153

Hebrews
10:18-20, p. 163
12:1, p. 13, 14
13:16, p. 151
13:7, p. 14

1 Peter
5:7, p. 150

2 Peter
1:13-14, p. 315

Revelation
3:14, p. 355
22:17, p. 164